D1129982

WILMINGTON'S LIE

ALSO BY DAVID ZUCCHINO

Myth of the Welfare Queen

Thunder Run

WILMINGTON'S
LIE

THE MURDEROUS COUP
OF 1898 AND THE RISE OF
WHITE SUPREMACY

DAVID ZUCCHINO

Atlantic Monthly Press
New York

Photo credits are as follows: Photos 1.1 (fugitive slaves), 2.1 (Alfred Moore Waddell), 7.1 (rapid-fire gun crew), 7.2 (state militiamen), 12.2 (armed escort): Courtesy of the Cape Fear Museum of History and Science, Wilmington, NC. Photos 1.2 (Abraham Galloway), 5.2 (George Rountree), 9.2 (Donald MacRae), 10.2 (Fourth and Harnett): Courtesy of New Hanover County Public Library, North Carolina Room. Photos 2.2. (Alexander Manly), 3.1 (Furnifold Simmons), 3.2 (Democratic Hand Book), 4.1 (cartoon 1), 4.2 (cartoon 2), 4.3 (cartoon 3), 4.4 (cartoon 4), 5.1 ("Remember the 6"), 6.2 (John C. Dancy), 10.1 (committee response), 12.1 (Daniel Russell): Courtesy of the University of North Carolina at Chapel Hill, Wilson Special Collections Library. Photo 4.5 (Josephus Daniels): Courtesy of the Library of Congress, Prints and Photographs Division. Photo 6.1 (William Everett Henderson): Courtesy of Lisa Adams. Photos 8.1 (Charles Aycock), 8.2 (Red Shirts), 11.2 (burning *Record*): Courtesy of the State Archives of North Carolina. Photo 9.1 (Roger Moore): Courtesy of the Internet Archive/NC Government and Heritage Library, originally published in *Biographical History of North Carolina from Colonial Times to the Present*, ed. Samuel A'Court Ashe (Greensboro, N.C.: C.L. Van Noppen, 1905). Photo 11.1 (Alex and Frank Manly): Courtesy of East Carolina University, Joyner Library.

FIRST EDITION

Published simultaneously in Canada
Printed in the United States of America

This title is set in 13-pt. Centaur by Alpha Design & Composition of Pittsfield, NH.

First Grove Atlantic hardcover edition: January 2020

Library of Congress Cataloging-in-Publication data available for this title.

ISBN 978-0-8021-2838-6
eISBN 978-0-8021-4648-9

Atlantic Monthly Press
an imprint of Grove Atlantic
154 West 14th Street
New York, NY 10011

Distributed by Publishers Group West

groveatlantic.com

20 21 22 23   10 9 8 7 6 5 4 3 2 1

To the dead and banished, known and unknown

CONTENTS

Dramatis Personae   xi

Prologue   xv

Book One: Days of Hope

One: Cake and Wine   3

Two: Good Will of the White People   11

Three: Lying Out   17

Four: Marching to the Happy Land   22

Five: Ye Men of Unmixed Blood   31

Six: The Avenger Cometh   41

Seven: Destiny of the Negro   45

Eight: A Yaller Dog   52

Book Two: Reckoning

Nine: The Negro Problem   65

Ten: The Incubus   77

Eleven: I Say Lynch   83

Twelve: A Vile Slander   90

CONTENTS

THIRTEEN: An Excellent Race 96

FOURTEEN: A Dark Scheme 102

FIFTEEN: The Nation's Mission 107

SIXTEEN: Degenerate Sons of the White Race 114

SEVENTEEN: The Great White Man's Rally and Basket Picnic 121

EIGHTEEN: White-Capping 127

NINETEEN: Buckshot at Close Range 132

TWENTY: A Drunkard and a Gambler 139

TWENTY-ONE: Choke the Cape Fear with Carcasses 144

TWENTY-TWO: The Shepherds Will Have Nowhere to Flee 152

TWENTY-THREE: A Pitiful Condition 162

TWENTY-FOUR: Retribution in History 167

TWENTY-FIVE: The Forbearance of All White Men 174

BOOK THREE: LINE OF FIRE

TWENTY-SIX: What Have We Done? 189

TWENTY-SEVEN: Situation Serious 200

TWENTY-EIGHT: Strictly According to Law 220

TWENTY-NINE: Marching from Death 228

THIRTY: Not the Sort of Man We Want Here 235

THIRTY-ONE: Justice Is Satisfied, Vengeance Is Cruel 246

THIRTY-TWO: Persons Unknown 257

THIRTY-THREE: Better Get a Gun 265

THIRTY-FOUR: The Meanest Animals 273

THIRTY-FIVE: Old Scores 285

CONTENTS

THIRTY-SIX: The Grandfather Clause   301

THIRTY-SEVEN: Leave It to the Whites   309

THIRTY-EIGHT: I Cannot Live in North Carolina
    and Be Treated Like a Man   318

EPILOGUE   329

ACKNOWLEDGMENTS   353

NOTES   357

BIBLIOGRAPHY   399

Index   409

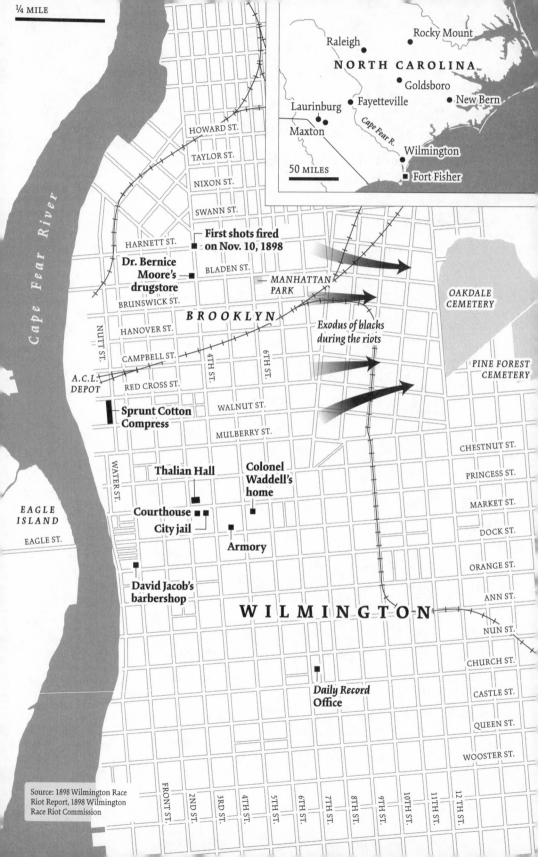

¼ MILE

Cape Fear River

HOWARD ST.

TAYLOR ST.

NIXON ST.

SWANN ST.

HARNETT ST.

First shots fired
on Nov. 10, 1898

Dr. Bernice
Moore's
drugstore

BLADEN ST.

MANHATTAN
PARK

BRUNSWICK ST.

B R O O K L Y N

HANOVER ST.

Exodus of blacks
during the riots

NUTT ST.

CAMPBELL ST.

4TH ST.

6TH ST.

A.C.L.
DEPOT

RED CROSS ST.

Sprunt Cotton
Compress

WALNUT ST.

MULBERRY ST.

WATER ST.

Thalian Hall

Colonel
Waddell's
home

Courthouse
City jail

Armory

EAGLE
ISLAND

EAGLE ST.

David Jacob's
barbershop

W I L M I N G T O N

Daily Record
Office

CHESTNUT ST.

PRINCESS ST.

MARKET ST.

DOCK ST.

ORANGE ST.

ANN ST.

NUN ST.

CHURCH ST.

CASTLE ST.

QUEEN ST.

WOOSTER ST.

OAKDALE
CEMETERY

PINE FOREST
CEMETERY

FRONT ST.
2ND ST.
3RD ST.
4TH ST.
5TH ST.
6TH ST.
7TH ST.
8TH ST.
9TH ST.
10TH ST.
11TH ST.
12TH ST.

NORTH CAROLINA

Raleigh

Rocky Mount

Goldsboro

Laurinburg

Fayetteville

New Bern

Maxton

Cape Fear R.

Wilmington

50 MILES

Fort Fisher

Source: 1898 Wilmington Race
Riot Report, 1898 Wilmington
Race Riot Commission

DRAMATIS PERSONAE

Charles Aycock—His speeches incited whites to attack blacks. Conspired to deny blacks the vote. Elected governor in 1900.

Claude M. Bernard—Republican US Attorney in Raleigh, failed to indict white supremacists for murders and coup

Robert H. Bunting—White Republican, US Commissioner in Wilmington, married to black woman

Thomas Clawson—White supremacist city editor of *Wilmington Messenger*, sold used press to Alex Manly

John C. Dancy—Black customs collector at Wilmington port, counseled appeasement of white supremacists

Josephus Daniels—Editor of *News and Observer*, militant voice of white supremacy campaign

Mike Dowling—Brawling leader of a Red Shirt brigade in Wilmington

George Z. "Gizzard" French—White Chief Deputy Sheriff in Wilmington, Republican targeted by coup leaders

Abraham Galloway—Escaped slave, Union spy, state senator, early leader of black defiance in Wilmington

William E. Henderson—Leading black lawyer and political figure in Wilmington

Captain Thomas C. James—Commander of a Wilmington Light Infantry company

Edward Kinsley—Massachusetts abolitionist, urged Abraham Galloway to raise black Union regiments in North Carolina

Reverend J. Allen Kirk—Outspoken black minister in Wilmington, wrote "A Statement of Facts"

Captain Donald MacRae—Commander of a Wilmington Light Infantry unit, brother of Hugh MacRae

Hugh MacRae—Wealthy president of Wilmington Cotton Mills Co., leader of Secret Nine conspiracy

Alexander Manly—Editor of black-readership *Daily Record*, confronted white power structure in Wilmington

Carrie Sadgwar Manly—Wife of Alex Manly and vocalist for Fisk University Jubilee Singers

John Melton—White Fusionist police chief of Wilmington, targeted by coup leaders

Thomas C. Miller—Entrepreneur, wealthiest black man in Wilmington, loaned money to whites and blacks

Colonel Roger Moore—Former Confederate officer, commander of Ku Klux Klan and Red Shirts in Wilmington

George Rountree—White lawyer in Wilmington, leading organizer of coup

Daniel Russell—Republican governor of North Carolina, member of Wilmington plantation gentry

Colonel William L. Saunders—Former Confederate officer from Wilmington, commander of Ku Klux Klan in North Carolina

Armond Scott—Young, ambitious black lawyer in Wilmington

Furnifold Simmons—State Democratic Party chairman, political organizer of white supremacy campaign

James Sprunt—Wealthy white owner of Sprunt Cotton Compress

J. Allan Taylor—Member of Secret Nine conspiracy, brother of Walker Taylor

Lieutenant Colonel Walker Taylor—Commander of Wilmington Light Infantry, member of Group Six conspiracy

"Pitchfork" Ben Tillman—US senator from South Carolina, led white supremacist attacks on the state's blacks

Colonel Alfred Moore Waddell—Former Confederate officer in Wilmington, leading orator of white supremacy campaign

George Henry White—US congressman from North Carolina, only black man in Congress in 1890s

Silas P. Wright—White Republican mayor of Wilmington, targeted by coup leaders

The white man's happiness cannot be purchased
by the black man's misery.

—Frederick Douglass

PROLOGUE

White Man's Country

Wilmington, North Carolina,
November 10, 1898

THE KILLERS came by streetcar. Their boots struck the packed clay earth like muffled drumbeats as they bounded from the cars and began to patrol the wide dirt roads. The men scanned the sidewalks and alleyways for targets. They wore red calico shirts or short red jackets over white butterfly collars. They were workingmen, with callused hands and sunburned faces beneath their wide-brimmed hats. Many of them had tucked their trousers into their boot tops and tied cartridge belts around their waists. A few wore neckties. Each one carried a gun.

Throughout that summer and autumn, white men had been buying shotguns, six-shot pistols, and repeating rifles at hardware stores in the port city of Wilmington, North Carolina, set in the low Cape Fear country along the state's jagged coast. It was 1898, a tumultuous midterm election year. White planters and business leaders had vowed to remove the city's multiracial government and black public officials by the ballot or the bullet—or both. Few white men intended to navigate election week that November without a firearm within easy reach.

There was concern among whites in Wilmington, where they were outnumbered by blacks, that stores would run dry on guns and that suppliers in the rest of the state and in nearby South Carolina would be unable to meet the demand.

Gun sales soared. J. W. Murchison, who operated a hardware store in downtown Wilmington, sold 125 rifles in October and early November alone. That was four or five times his normal sales. These were Colt and Winchester repeating rifles, capable of firing up to sixteen rounds in rapid succession. Murchison also sold more than two hundred pistols during that same period and nearly fifty shotguns. Owen F. Love, a smaller hardware dealer, sold fifty-nine guns of all types during October and early November. Murchison and Love were proper white men, which meant they sold firearms only to other white men and primarily to those who were supporters of the white supremacist Democratic Party. They did not sell to blacks. When pressed on the subject later, Owen Love responded, "I had no objection to selling to any respectable man, white or colored, but I would refuse to sell cartridges, pistols or guns to any disreputable Negro."

Years later, one of the city's leading white supremacists wrote, "It is doubtful if there ever was a community in the United States that had as many lethal weapons per capita as in Wilmington at that time." This was only a slight exaggeration. Among the city's whites, there were almost as many guns as men, women, and children. Wilmington, with a population of twenty thousand, was the largest city in North Carolina, but the demand for weapons had exhausted the supplies of all the gun merchants in town. They telegraphed emergency orders to dealers in Richmond and Baltimore, who loaded guns and bullets onto railroad cars headed south.

For months, whites had been railing against what they called "Negro rule," though black men held only a small fraction of elected and appointed positions in the city and the state. White politicians and newspapers warned that if blacks continued to vote and hold office, black men would feel empowered to seize white jobs, dominate the courts, and rape white women. "Nigger lawyers are sassing white men in courts; nigger root doctors are crowding white physicians out of business," complained Colonel Alfred Moore Waddell, a former Confederate officer who led the white gunmen as they raced through the streets on the morning of November 10.

In 1898, a field representative for the American Baptist Publication Society called Wilmington "the freest town for a negro in the country." Three of the city's ten aldermen were black, as were ten of twenty-six city policemen. There were black health inspectors, a black superintendent of streets, and far too many—for white sensitivities—black postmasters and magistrates. White men could be arrested by black policemen and, in some cases, were even obliged to appear before a black magistrate in court. Black merchants sold goods from stalls at the city's public market—a rarity for a Southern town at the time. Black men delivered mail to homes at times of day when white women were unattended. They sorted mail beside white female clerks.

A black barber served as county coroner. The county jailer was black, and the fact that he carried keys to the lockup infuriated whites. The county treasurer was a black man who distributed pay to county employees, forcing whites to accept money from black hands. In 1891, President Benjamin Harrison had appointed a black man, John C. Dancy, as federal customs collector for the port of Wilmington. Dancy had replaced a white supremacist Democrat, and he drew an astonishing federal salary—$4,000 a year, or $1,000 more than the governor earned. A white newspaper editor ridiculed Dancy as "Sambo of the Custom House."

Black businessmen pooled their money to form two small banks that loaned cash to blacks starting small businesses. Several black professionals ran small law firms and doctors' offices, serving clients and patients of their own race. A black alderman from Raleigh, the capital, noted with some surprise that certain black men in Wilmington had built finely appointed homes with lace curtains, plush carpets, pianos, and even, he claimed, servants. The city's thriving population of black professionals contradicted the white portrayal of Wilmington's blacks as poor, ignorant, and illiterate. In fact, Wilmington's blacks had higher literacy rates than virtually any other blacks in North Carolina, a state in which nearly a quarter of whites were illiterate.

For whites, this was an intolerable situation. The planters, lawyers, and merchants who had dominated Wilmington since its founding in 1739 had lost control of the city during the Civil War and Reconstruction. Through terror and intimidation by the night riders of the Ku Klux Klan, white supremacists had returned to power in the 1870s. They did not intend to surrender Wilmington again.

The armed men emerging from streetcars on the mild, sunny morning of November 10, 1898, had heard rumors that black men, in response to white gunmen coursing through the streets, were massing at the corner of North Fourth and Harnett Streets. The intersection lay at the heart of a predominantly black neighborhood known as Brooklyn. The white men were inflamed with excitement and eager to fire their weapons. Some had already shot rifles from a streetcar, sending rounds whistling past black homes and small businesses along nearby Castle Street. One of the men carried a .44-caliber US Navy–issue rifle, though he was not a member of the city's Naval Reserves. Others wielded army or police revolvers, belt revolvers, or small pocket revolvers. A few of the younger men still owned guns their fathers or uncles had fired during the Civil War. Some veterans called the weapons blueless guns because the dark blue finish had worn off to expose a dull gray color.

The men moved in columns with their weapons raised, in something approaching a military formation. They swept past clapboard houses and muddy yards in a mixed neighborhood of blacks and whites at the edge of Brooklyn. Wilmington was not yet a uniformly segregated city. In fact, some considered it the most integrated city in the South, with blacks and working-class whites living side by side in each of the city's five wards. But this was still the South. Some Wilmington neighborhoods were largely black, such as the First Ward and most of Brooklyn; or almost purely white, such as the tidy blocks of tree-lined streets near the Cape Fear River.

Around eleven o'clock on November 10, a group of whites from the mob arrived to find a crowd of black men gathered at North Fourth and Harnett Streets, outside a popular drinking spot called Brunjes' Saloon. Some of the men were known to whites as "Sprunt niggers." They worked as stevedores, laborers, and machine operators at the Sprunt Cotton Compress on the Cape Fear riverfront. They loaded boulder-size bales of cotton onto merchant ships bound for Europe. The compress was the largest cotton export firm in the country, providing jobs to nearly eight hundred black men.

Some of the Sprunt workers had abandoned their posts at the compress after hearing rumors that a white mob was burning black homes in Brooklyn and plotting to butcher blacks at Sprunt's. No homes had been burned, and no one had been killed. But the Sprunt workers were convinced that their lives—and the lives of their wives and children—were at risk. They made their way to Brunjes' Saloon, where they could see packs of white gunmen descending on the clay streets of their neighborhood. The white men were cursing blacks. The black men bristled and cursed them back.

The white men hollered for the blacks to disperse, which only offended and aroused them. A city newspaper reported that the black men were "in a bad temper." They stood their ground, anxiously eyeing the growing cluster of armed white men on the opposite corner. As the two sides exchanged more curses and taunts, one of the white men shouted out the mob's purpose: they were "going gunning for niggers," he said. The rising tensions pierced the tranquillity of a pleasant fall day, bright and cool, with a gentle river breeze.

A black man named Norman Lindsay tried to calm his neighbors. He told them that their families were in danger of being burned out and shot dead if they continued to antagonize the white men.

"For the sake of your lives, your families, your children, and your country, go home and stay there. I'm as brave as any of you, but we are powerless," Lindsay told them in a defeated tone.

The black men argued with him. They insisted that they had every right, as citizens and residents of their neighborhood, to gather where they pleased, particularly with their families under threat from a mob seemingly bent on murder.

Aaron Lockamy, a white police officer, decided to offer his services as a mediator. Lockamy did not look or act like a police officer. He was a middle-aged man, deliberative and tentative. Even at age fifty-eight, he was not an experienced cop. He had served only on occasional part-time duty before he was deputized earlier that month as a full-time officer in anticipation of trouble during the week of the election.

Lockamy wore his police badge prominently on his chest that morning. He had been stationed in Brooklyn to monitor the opening at eight o'clock of two saloons elsewhere on North Fourth Street. He had been instructed by the city's white police chief not to arrest anyone, black or white. He was simply to keep an eye on the saloons. Negotiation was not part of his job, but Lockamy believed he could appeal to the more reasonable men among the two camps in the showdown near the saloon.

When Lockamy appeared at the corner of Harnett and North Fourth Streets looking hesitant, he was summoned by several white men gathered there. They asked him—not very politely, considering that he was a fellow white man—to move the black men off the corner. Lockamy sighed. He walked over to the men. They seemed wary and defensive. They did not appear to be carrying weapons, at least not overtly.

Lockamy persuaded the black men to move a short distance to the opposite corner, by W. A. Walker's grocery store, a frame structure with a low, tilted roof that shaded a wooden slat walkway. This provided a slightly better opportunity for them to gauge the intentions of the white mob. The whites responded by moving to a more protected position just down the street from Brunjes' Saloon, near the white steeple of St. Matthew's Evangelical Lutheran Church.

The black men's new position did not satisfy all the white men. Several of them summoned Officer Lockamy again. They dispatched him once more to try to move the black men. Again, the blacks rebuffed him and continued to hold their ground. Lockamy trudged back to the white men. They demanded to know what the blacks had told him. "They told me that I might go to hell, or where I pleased," Lockamy said evenly. "They were not going anywhere. They did not need me over there, nohow."

The white men were through with Lockamy. They told him they would move those Negroes themselves. Lockamy gave up trying to negotiate. He decided to return to his original mission of monitoring the two saloons farther south on North Fourth Street. He had walked about a block from the crowded corner when he heard a sharp volley of gunfire.

Ten blocks away stood the Wilmington Light Infantry armory, a two-story Greek Revival building of pale white marble and pressed brick that towered over Market Street. Billeted inside were more than a hundred well-drilled soldiers who had recently returned from federal duty in the Spanish-American War. The Light Infantry was part of the state's militia system. It ostensibly reported to the state adjutant general and thus, ultimately, to North Carolina's governor in Raleigh. But the infantry effectively served as the private militia of Wilmington's white supremacists, many of them related by blood or marriage. An appointment to the Light Infantry was a symbol of achievement and social standing. Prospective members had to be approved by current members, ensuring that the Light Infantry remained a closed club for upper-class and middle-class whites wedded to white supremacy.

Earlier that summer, the city's white merchants worried that the Light Infantry lacked the firepower to properly intimidate and control Wilmington's black majority. They raised $1,200 to purchase a Colt rapid-fire gun for the unit. It was a relatively new weapon, developed just nine years earlier. Under optimum conditions, the air-cooled gun could fire up to 420 rounds in extended bursts without overheating the barrel.

A few blocks away, another militia, the Naval Reserves, was also ready and waiting on the morning of November 10. The Reserves, formally known as the North Carolina Naval Militia, was a more egalitarian unit than the Wilmington Light Infantry. While men from the gentry dominated the Naval Reserves' upper ranks, middle-class and working-class men were permitted to join. Most were from families active in the white supremacy campaign. Like the men of the Light Infantry, members of the Naval Reserves had served on federal duty during the Spanish-American War, aboard the USS *Nantucket* off South Carolina. They, too, returned to Wilmington late that summer. And they, too, were supposed to report to the governor but served instead as a local white supremacist militia.

The Naval Reserves had been supplied with its own rapid-fire gun—a Hotchkiss gun that could fire eighty to one hundred rounds a minute. The gun's bore was three-quarters of an inch. Its effective range was five miles. At three miles, the steel rounds were said to be able to penetrate a thick steel plate. One of Wilmington's white newspapers called it "a very destructive piece of ordnance."

Just before midday on November 10, reports of gunshots at North Fourth and Harnett Streets reached the militiamen of the Light Infantry and the Naval Reserves. The men began to muster. They readied their weapons. Their new rapid-fire guns had been mounted on horse-drawn wagons. The orders came to move out. The soldiers and sailors rushed to Brooklyn, the wagon wheels churning, the men holding on to their hats and clutching their rifles, the animals snorting and panting, the two big guns cocked and ready to fire.

BOOK ONE
DAYS OF HOPE

CHAPTER ONE

Cake and Wine

Wilmington, North Carolina, Winter 1865

T HE CLOSING WEEKS of the Civil War brought chaos and upheaval to Wilmington. In late February 1865, great fires rose up, belching oily black smoke across the city. Supplies of rosin, turpentine, and cotton bales were set alight—not by invading Union troops, but by fleeing Confederates. General Braxton Bragg and his army had managed to move most of their matériel out of Wilmington to use during their retreat, but Bragg ordered the remaining supplies put to the torch to keep them from the enemy.

Union troops were bearing down on the city a month after their capture of Fort Fisher, a Confederate fortress of earth-and-sand battlements twenty miles south of Wilmington, where the Cape Fear River flowed into the Atlantic. The US Navy had unleashed upon Fort Fisher the heaviest naval bombardment in history at the time. The fall of the fort in January 1865 had closed all access to the port of Wilmington, the Confederacy's last functioning seaport. For much of the war, Wilmington's sleek blockade-runners had skirted an armada of Union warships strung like beads off the Atlantic coast. After New

Orleans and Norfolk were captured by Union forces in the spring of 1862 and Vicksburg fell in July 1863—and with Charleston under Union siege for much of the war—Wilmington had become the main source of weapons, clothing, food, and supplies for the Confederacy. Among the Union units that overran Fort Fisher in January 1865 were colored brigades that included black soldiers from Wilmington.

As Union forces approached Wilmington that February, General Bragg destroyed several railroad lines leading out of the city and set fire to bridges, wharves, and shipyards. Portions of the main rail line—the Wilmington, Charlotte and Rutherford Railroad—remained intact, though some of the rails on the line would later be ripped up for use as scrap iron by Union troops. Before the Confederate soldiers retreated, some looted shops. When Union soldiers arrived, they looted, too. Food shortages broke out. Whole hams were briefly offered for sale at the preposterous price of $525. Corn sold for $40 a bushel and salt pork for $6 a pound. People begged for food on the streets.

By the time General Alfred Howe Terry led a column of Union soldiers on bay chargers to city hall to take command of Wilmington on February 22, the city had become a vast refugee camp. Many Union soldiers released from Confederate prisoner of war camps were afflicted with "jail fever"—typhus—a contagion characterized by rash, chills, and fever that killed two doctors who treated them. Carpenters struggled to build enough caskets for the estimated forty to fifty people who died daily—from jail fever but also battle wounds, sepsis, or other maladies. Every available house or outbuilding was crammed with people seeking shelter. One visitor claimed that rents in Wilmington were higher than in New York City. Thousands of people lived in camps, tents, or shanties, watched over warily by an occupying force of nearly fifteen thousand Union soldiers, among them blue-suited colored troops.

The *Wilmington Herald* reported that despite "a large force of darkies . . . cleaning the streets," the city was an open sewer. "There is not a private residence, a kitchen, a business house of any kind but has now filth enough about and around its doors to make every person in the city sick . . . no person can pass without holding their breaths . . . cows, pigs, cats, dogs and low negroes are together in this pen."

For blacks in Wilmington, the end of the war left their lives only slightly less constrained and miserable than before. Any civil liberties envisioned by the Emancipation Proclamation had not materialized by the summer and fall of 1865. The full remedies of Reconstruction had not yet taken hold in the city so soon after the end of the war. Just a few months earlier, a black woman; three black children aged one, five, and seven; a black girl; and four mules had been offered for sale in town. The same day, a railroad company offered a $50 reward for the return of a slave named Dick, who had escaped from his owner, the railroad's superintendent. Dick was considered guilty of insolence as well as escape; his master noted that the missing slave "carries himself with his shoulders considerably thrown back."

Even with Wilmington under federal military control, freedmen could expect no special protection. Union troops were spread thin, making it difficult to restore law and order in the face of Southern defiance. Barely six thousand federal troops were still stationed in North Carolina by late 1865, the smallest Union force in any Southern state. And by the fall of 1865, three-quarters of Union troops who had fought in the war had been mustered out nationwide. Union commanders, seeking the most efficient ways to get local government functioning again, turned to the men who knew how to run local affairs. Wilmington's former mayor, an ardent white supremacist, was restored to his post by the local Union command. The mayor quickly installed a former Confederate general as his chief of police, presiding over a new force composed mainly of former Confederate soldiers.

Just after the war ended, President Andrew Johnson sent Carl Schurz, a German immigrant, to tour North Carolina and report on conditions there. Schurz later told the president that whites resisted any attempt to grant equal rights to their former slaves.

"Wherever I go—the street, the shop, the house, the hotel, or the steamboat—I hear the people talk in such a way as to indicate that they are yet unable to conceive of the Negro as possessing any rights at all," Schurz wrote. "The people boast that when they get freedmen's affairs in their own hands, to use their own expression, 'the niggers will catch hell.'"

Cape Fear rice and cotton plantation owners, though under Union occupation and stripped of their slaves, still wielded considerable influence. Some plantations had been seized by the federal Military District of Wilmington and settled with freed slaves in April 1865. But General Joseph Hawley, a dedicated abolitionist who had settled slaves on the plantations, was replaced in June 1865 by General John Worthington Ames, an ardent conservative. In September, Ames evicted the former slaves and returned plantations to their white owners under a national policy instituted by President Johnson. Freedmen who worked on Cape Fear plantations were supposed to be paid for their labor. But the Freedmen's Bureau in Wilmington was inundated with complaints from black workers that white plantation owners had reneged on promises to pay them to bring in the harvests in the summer and fall of 1865.

General Ames made a show of imposing Union authority. A general order issued on July 10, 1865, for instance, prohibited former Confederates from wearing Confederate rank, "as required by good taste and a respect for the government of their country." But Ames was willing to be courted by the white supremacists who seethed under his command. One leading black man in the city attributed the tendency of Union officers to accommodate their former enemies to the "cake and wine" influence—the extravagant Cape Fear hospitality resurrected from antebellum society.

The white men accustomed to running Wilmington were bitter and resentful after the war. Under General Ames, Northern troops afforded white police officers wide latitude to violently counter any attempts by blacks to assert their limited rights. Most of the new police officers did not wear uniforms; they wore only a small yellow star that served as a police badge. They received no training as policemen, but they brought to the job their military skills and their contempt for blacks. They preyed on freed slaves, whipping the men in public and beating the women with boards. In the countryside, former Confederate soldiers banded with white residents to form county militia companies that rampaged through the area, terrorizing black families in their homes.

W. H. H. Beadle, a Union lieutenant colonel stationed in Wilmington, was appalled by the attacks. Colonel Beadle had been installed as a local officer of the Freedmen's Bureau, established by Congress in March 1865 to advance the rights and living conditions of freed slaves— although nearly 40 percent of food rations distributed by the bureau in the summer of 1865 went to white families. It was a thankless task, and it frustrated Beadle. He realized that the whites of Wilmington had not truly been defeated. He watched them return from the war unbowed, full of rage, and more committed than ever to white supremacy. He was convinced that whites would have reclaimed blacks as slaves if not for the Freedmen's Bureau. "They would endeavor to return them to a system of peonage immediately," Colonel Beadle reported.

Colonel Beadle once saw a frail black woman clubbed unconscious by a white officer because she had been drinking in public. In another incident, Beale watched a dog bite a white policeman as the officer was beating a black boy on the street; the boy's entire family, which owned the dog, was thrown into jail. "The policemen are the hardest and most brutal looking and acting set of civil or municipal officers I ever saw. All look bad and vicious," Beale reported.

The police whippings inspired other white men in the city, and physical abuse of blacks was perhaps more rampant than ever. White civilians often flogged blacks in public, typically unimpeded by police or, on many occasions, by Union soldiers. "A colored man sometimes does not know who attacks him, or why," Colonel Beadle reported. One day, he recalled, a white man pointed a revolver at a young black man, then "choked him, whipped him with a club, tied his hands, whipped him with a half a hoop, kept him tied six or seven hours, whipping him every few minutes with a doubled leather strap, hurting him so bad as to disable him for two days."

Police arrested blacks on trumped-up charges such as vagrancy or trespassing, then forced them, in some cases, to work without pay. During a visit to Wilmington in the summer of 1865, a reporter for the *Philadelphia Inquirer* took note of tense race relations in a city where blacks were nominally free and where whites had been defeated and occupied by their Northern enemy. The reporter wrote of whites: "They perceive insolence in a tone, a glance, a gesture, or failure to yield enough by two or three inches in meeting on the sidewalk."

Physical abuse of freed blacks by white police officers and citizens was rampant, on and off the plantations. Plantation squatters were evicted by force. Police seized guns owned by black men. They searched their homes and seized their belongings. In the summer of 1865, an officer in a Freedmen's Bureau office in Wilmington maintained a ledger of complaints of whippings and beatings filed by former slaves:

> By colored man, Dick: that J. W. whipped him severely, striking him seventy-two blows.
>
> By colored woman, Martha: That J. F. Parker overtook her while on her way to the Office of the Superintendent of Freedmen, put one end of rope around her neck, tied the other round the neck of his mule, and so dragged her more than two miles.
>
> By colored woman, Louisa: That J. T. is whipping her children continually, and when she asked him not to do it, ordered her off his place and told her not to come back.
>
> By colored man, Elias: That some citizens took his gun away from him and told him no nigger had the right to carry a gun.
>
> By colored man, Levi: That W. F. L. has whipped him severely with a buggy-trace. Shows his back all raw.

Wilmington's new police officers were not the only white men given free rein by some Union troops. County militias, formed to protect white interests, roamed the Cape Fear countryside. The militias were an outgrowth of the Confederate Home Guard, formed during the war to track down and punish Confederate deserters, among other duties. After the war, many Home Guards joined county militias, which raided black homes on the pretexts first of confiscating illegal firearms and later of recovering "stolen" property. Militiamen descended on black dwellings, confiscating cash, personal items, and farm equipment. The militias were especially proficient at appropriating horses and mules, many of them awarded to former slaves by the Union army.

Sometimes the militiamen brought their friends along on raids of black homes so that they might share in the spoils. "A tour of pretended duty is then turned into a spree. Houses of colored men have been broken open, beds torn apart and thrown about the floor, and even trunks opened and money taken," Colonel Beadle, the Union officer, reported.

Some Union soldiers shared white Southerners' contempt for blacks. Among them were soldiers from border states or former Confederate states, including men who had once owned slaves. In Charleston in July 1865, a squad of Union soldiers attacked blacks and destroyed their stalls at a city market, then bayoneted to death a black man who protested. In Mississippi that same year, federal soldiers who had received a complaint from a plantation owner about his troublesome former slaves responded by flogging the black men. Across the South, Union commanders complained about the casual use of the slur "nigger" by their troops.

And the discrimination extended to black soldiers' pay, which was supposed to be the same as for whites—$13 a month. But blacks were paid $10 a month, with $3 deducted for clothing.

In Wilmington, blacks seethed over abuse of freedmen by local whites under the noses of Union soldiers. The city's white authorities complained in a letter to the provisional governor that colored soldiers, motivated by "smothered revenge," were inciting local blacks to mount an insurrection against white authority. In February 1866, black soldiers marched to Wilmington's city jail to protest the whipping of black prisoners by white jailers. They stormed the lockup and freed the captives. Such incidents unnerved both local whites and white Union occupiers. Ultimately, federal military commanders replaced black troops with white soldiers along the Lower Cape Fear.

The *Wilmington Journal*, edited by William L. Saunders, the state's Ku Klux Klan leader, noted an emerging alliance of whites, Northern and Southern.

> *The true soldiers, whether they wore the gray or the blue, are now united in their opposition—call it conspiracy and resistance if you will—to negro government and NEGRO EQUALITY.*
>
> *Blood is thicker than water.*

CHAPTER TWO

Good Will of the White People

EVERYONE CALLED HIM "Colonel," even his wife, though Alfred Moore Waddell had never quite earned the rank. He had served as a Confederate lieutenant colonel for less than a year during the Civil War, and his brief command of North Carolina's Third Cavalry ended in shame. After serving "without any record worth mentioning," Waddell wrote years later, he abruptly resigned his command at the pinnacle of the war, in August 1864. "My health was completely wrecked," he wrote. He was, he confessed, "an invalid." He was twenty-nine years old. He went home to Wilmington a broken man.

Just a few months later, in the spring of 1865, Waddell had recovered his health and his reputation. With Wilmington's white leadership in disarray under Union occupation, he filled a political vacuum by positioning himself as the city's leading voice of enduring white supremacy. His mediocre performance as a Confederate officer did not impede his political rise. Waddell took charge of white resistance to the rising tide of freedmen flowing into Wilmington. Even with blacks evicted from plantations and harassed daily by white police officers, Waddell helped lead a campaign to crush any attempts by blacks in the Cape Fear country to assert their newly won rights.

He was a natural choice, given his upbringing and pedigree. Waddell was born into North Carolina's white planter aristocracy in 1834 in Hillsboro, a town in the rolling Piedmont landscape of central North Carolina. He was raised on a plantation built by his great-grandfather, Alfred Moore, a US Supreme Court justice. Two other great-grandfathers, General Hugh Waddell and General Francis Nash, had been Revolutionary War officers. Waddell studied law at the University of North Carolina in Chapel Hill, graduating in 1853. Five years later, his family's political connections helped earn him an appointment as a clerk of court in New Hanover County. He moved to Wilmington, the county seat, and began a long career as a lawyer, essayist, historian, and public speaker.

Even as a young man freshly admitted to the state bar, Waddell exhibited sharply calibrated political instincts. He sensed the prevailing winds and bent accordingly. In the late 1850s, when Unionist sentiment was strong in Wilmington, Waddell had aligned himself with Unionists opposed to secession. He bought the *Wilmington Herald* newspaper to promote his Unionist views.

In January 1861, just before the outbreak of the Civil War, North Carolina secessionists seized two small military forts, Fort Johnston and Fort Caswell, which guarded access to Wilmington at the mouth of the Cape Fear south of the city. In an editorial in the *Herald*, Waddell objected to the takeovers. He pointed out that North Carolina was still a loyal member of the Union and bound by United States law.

But the bold attacks on the forts inflamed secessionist sentiment in Wilmington, and soon Unionists were in retreat. Waddell adjusted accordingly. Just eighteen days after writing the editorial, he attended a secessionist rally in Wilmington, where he performed an abrupt about-face. He told the meeting that there was no longer any hope of North Carolina's remaining in the Union. He was now fully in favor of secession. He declared himself a loyal Confederate.

By June 1865, Waddell's days as a Unionist seemed forgotten, and he emerged as an unofficial spokesman for Wilmington's aggrieved white ruling class after the war. That month, he wrote an anguished letter to North Carolina's provisional postwar governor, William Woods Holden. He told the governor that black soldiers posted in Wilmington posed a mortal threat to the white population. He referred to "daily outrages" by colored troops. They "insult and curse the most respectable ladies in Wilmington," Waddell wrote. Other whites complained in letters to the governor that the city's black residents "still insist that they are entitled to all the social and political rights of white citizens."

Though Governor Holden was a Republican who would later instigate a war against the Ku Klux Klan, he had issued a proclamation in June 1865 advising blacks not to expect to be granted suffrage or other civil rights immediately. Those sentiments were consistent with Presidential Reconstruction, then in effect under President Johnson, a white supremacist Southerner born in Raleigh and raised in Tennessee. Johnson sought to bring the Southern states back into the Union, with slavery technically outlawed but with white supremacy largely unchallenged and blacks granted limited rights, which did not necessarily include the right to vote.

In July 1865, a group of freedmen invited Waddell to speak at the Wilmington Theatre. They acknowledged the colonel as the public face of white supremacy in the city. Through Waddell, they sought to gauge the depth of hostility toward freed slaves and their new place in the postwar era. Both blacks and whites were struggling to define just what it meant to be a freedman at a time when nearly 4 million former slaves were now liberated, among them 360,000 in North Carolina.

For whites in Wilmington, blacks had ceased to be slaves, but they had not ceased to be black. They were still considered unworthy, unequal, and inferior, still subservient to whites by any measure—social, political, or economic. For freed slaves, the defeat of the Confederacy and the end of slavery promised not just citizenship and the right of black men to vote but also the right to work for fair pay, and to live on something approaching an equal, if separate, status with the whites who had so recently enslaved them. They sought to be free citizens, not just free Negroes. And now they wanted to measure the gap between their vision and Colonel Waddell's.

Waddell accepted the speaking invitation. He was eager to publicly dictate the terms of postwar race relations in Wilmington. And for him, and the white aristocracy he represented, those terms were the same terms that had always circumscribed the daily lives of blacks under white domination: whites would continue to rule; blacks would continue to obey.

Waddell announced that he intended to speak "upon the proper condition of the freedmen under the present state of affairs." Though he had limited formal training, Waddell considered himself a learned historian. He had convinced himself that no other white man in Wilmington possessed his ability to draw lessons from the past and prescribe the future. One of Wilmington's white-owned newspapers called Waddell a "ripe scholar" and a "gentleman of culture and scholarly achievements."

Waddell titled his speech "An Address Delivered to the Colored People by Their Request." On a still July night, when the Cape Fear oozed humidity, the seats of the Wilmington Theatre were filled by the city's leading black men, fanning themselves in the oppressive heat. Some wore dark suits with high white collars, as proper in appearance as any white man. Others wore workmen's clothes. Seated on the stage behind Waddell was the city's white mayor, flanked by several white dignitaries.

Waddell strode across the stage like a military officer. The Colonel was not a big man, but he carried himself in a way that suggested command and authority. He stood five foot nine, with a large head, shaggy eyebrows, a long patrician nose, and calm gray eyes. On this evening, he was dressed in his customary dark wool suit, his wavy hair brushed back and his well-groomed beard forming a broad V at his chest.

As Waddell addressed the black men, he was characteristically condescending. He began with a bold lie, which his audience received in silence: he assured them that whites meant blacks no harm. His vision was of two races, one superior, one servile, but the two sides living in harmony. It would be a mistake, he said, "to suppose that the white people among who you were born and raised, with whom you played when you were children, and served as you grew up, have all at once turned to be your enemies." He was interrupted by a round of polite applause, for even the black men recognized the thin thread of humanity that had linked children of both races since slavery.

Waddell mentioned that "some ignorant and misguided colored people . . . are under the impression that they are not only free, but that the property of their former owners will be taken and given to them. Of course, this is a cruel mistake."

Then Waddell laid down the law as he saw it. He told the black men they were not likely to be granted the vote anytime soon. Perhaps some of them might vote someday, with certain provisions, he said. Personally, Waddell said, he favored a test of "intelligence or property, or both" for prospective voters of any race.

"I believe that there are some colored men in this hall who could vote now with quite as intelligent a conception of what they were doing as many white men. But I believe, also, that a large percentage of the colored people are not yet qualified to exercise this privilege . . . they would be mere tools in the hands of demagogues."

No one in the audience objected, at least not publicly. The black men seemed to obey the Southern rules of civility that obliged both races to extend simple courtesies under certain social conditions. According to a white reporter for the *Wilmington Herald,* "The most perfect order was maintained by every one." Nor was there more than a slight stir in the audience when Waddell instructed freedmen to establish their own segregated schools as a way to "do all you can to show the world that you deserve and can maintain the freedom and the privileges which have been bestowed upon you."

Waddell reminded the former slaves that they were indeed fortunate to share a city as fine as Wilmington with white men: "The great advantage which your race enjoys here is contact and daily association with the white race. Their influence upon you, as far as civilization is concerned, must be beneficial, and therefore you ought to cultivate the friendship and good will of the white people."

Waddell also advised blacks to stop moving to Wilmington in search of work. He and other whites feared they would soon be outnumbered by freed slaves and their families, who sought shelter and work in the state's largest city, with its busy port, its rice and cotton exports, and its artisan trades. Waddell instructed itinerant blacks to find work on farms, in timber swamps, in the tar and turpentine trade among the towering longleaf pine forests, or along the railroad lines outside town, and to leave Wilmington for the whites who owned it. There was polite applause.

The speech ended, and the white man and his black audience made their separate ways out of the theater and into the hot night. A few hours later, the body of a soldier from the United States Colored Troops was found floating in the Cape Fear River, his face flayed by buckshot.

CHAPTER THREE

Lying Out

IT WAS OFTEN PERMISSIBLE for a white man in Wilmington to side with Union soldiers against blacks, but it was unforgivable for him to join with Northerners in attacks on other Southern white men. Even as the Civil War drew to a close, Confederate Home Guards continued to roam the Cape Fear countryside much as they did during the war, enforcing a brutal form of righteous justice. Home Guard patrols made it their business not only to terrorize blacks but also to hunt down and punish white Southerners who had betrayed the Confederacy by secretly conspiring with invading Union troops. And should the Home Guards be arrested by Union soldiers, Wilmington's leading lawyer, Colonel Waddell, stood ready to defend them.

In the spring of 1865, Matthew Sykes, a notorious Yankee sympathizer, lived in the flat, humid, Piney Woods along the Cape Fear River, about forty miles northwest of Wilmington. Sykes and his family had been Unionists before the war, but he was pressured to join the Confederate army after hostilities began. To avoid a long conscription, Sykes reluctantly enlisted for a limited tour of duty. He completed his service in June 1864. Several months later, he began secretly serving the invading Union army as a spy and guide.

He participated in the rapid advance of Union troops from Fort Fisher through Wilmington and into the Piney Woods in early 1865.

Worried about the safety of his wife, Catherine, Sykes requested a week's leave to return home in the spring of 1865. But by the end of his leave, Union forces had already swept past his home region in the Piney Woods, clearing the way for surviving Home Guard squads to operate freely. The leader of the local Home Guard was Neill McGill, a Confederate officer whose family homestead was among the properties looted by Union troops in the nearby farming village of Elizabethtown, about fifty miles upriver from Wilmington. A fellow Confederate had told McGill that the "damn son of a bitch" Matt Sykes was a secret scout with the Yankee marauders. McGill vowed to hunt down and punish the white traitor.

There was a tactic among Unionists in North Carolina known as "lying out"—sleeping in the forest to avoid being attacked at home late at night by Home Guards and county militias. Matt and Catherine Sykes had been lying out for most of the week. But on April 10, 1865, Palm Sunday, a cool rainy day, they decided to spend the night at the double frame house of Catherine's father, Elias Edwards. Matt went to sleep, but Catherine stayed up late, sitting by the fire. Two hours before dawn, she heard noises outside. She looked out and saw that Neill McGill and two Home Guard companions had crept up to the house. Catherine ran to wake her husband. She hid Matt, still in his nightclothes, beneath a dense pile of raw cotton inside a storeroom.

McGill and his men, armed with pistols, knocked at the front door. Elias Edwards answered, and the men announced that they had come for Sykes. Edwards tried to stall them. He asked: "Which Sykes?" But McGill and the others pushed roughly past Edwards and searched the house by torchlight. One of the men kicked at the cotton pile and discovered Sykes.

"Don't kill him!" Catherine shouted.

McGill bound Sykes's hands with a strand of rope. The Home Guards began to haul Sykes toward the door and into the damp night in his nightgown. Catherine begged them to let her to fetch her husband's clothes.

As the men waited, they accused Sykes of having "piloted" Yankees, leading Union soldiers to their homes. One of the Home Guards, John McMillan, said he wanted to kill Sykes as badly as he wanted to kill "any goddamn Negro." He told Sykes he intended to hang him "without judge or jury."

Sykes, now fully dressed and with his hands still bound, was ordered to sit between McMillan and Elias Edwards. Edwards asked McMillan what they intended to do with his son-in-law. They would certainly do something with him, McMillan replied, but they would not need a jail.

McGill gestured toward Sykes and said, "He lives between two fires. The North, or the Yankees, ought to kill him for deserting their army—and the South *will* kill him." Then the men led Sykes away. McMillan told him to say good-bye to his family because he would never see them again.

McGill and his men, hauling their captive, made their way from the Edwards home to a spot known as the eight-mile post. They paused there to drink whiskey. The three Home Guards were on foot; Sykes, his hands bound, sat astride the men's horse. They offered him a drink. Sykes did not respond. His face was buried in his hands, and he was weeping. McMillan eyed Sykes and felt a stab of pity. He told the others: "Boys, he has not done enough to us—don't let us kill him."

McGill was unmoved. Suddenly he yanked Sykes from the horse and threw him to the ground. McGill and the others stomped, kicked, and beat Sykes until they thought he was dead. They then stabbed him in the ribs and hanged his body from a sapling.

It did not take the Edwards and Sykes clans long to mount a search party. Nearly three dozen relatives and neighbors assembled on horseback at Edwards's home after first light to begin the search for Matt.

Catherine Sykes and Unity Sykes, Matt's mother, were among them. Progress was slow. The woods and fields were thick with wire grass and longleaf pines and scrub oaks. The ground was carpeted with damp pine needles. Rain had washed out some tracks.

But soon the search party came across faint tracks of men and a horse. The depressions in the soft soil led down past the eight-mile post to Shady Grove, a corduroy track made of sand-covered logs. The group followed the track through a swampy bog known as Juniper Bay and on to spot called Piney Island. They crossed a field and came upon a sapling with a rope attached. At the end of the rope hung the body of Matt Sykes.

Matt's mother went over to him. She saw that her son's legs were splayed and did not touch the ground. There was enough space for Unity to place her foot between her son's foot and the damp soil. Someone cut Matt down. His chest and stomach bore wounds, and there were deep cuts on his chin, neck, and torso. One side of his face looked as though it had been skinned.

Not long afterward, McGill and McMillan were captured by Union military authorities and taken before a court-martial in Wilmington, in October 1865. The Home Guards' supporters hired one of the best-known lawyers in the Cape Fear country—and the only attorney in Wilmington at the time, the former Confederate officer, Alfred Moore Waddell.

The Colonel called his clients "highly respectable men" and their military trial "an absurdity." Waddell built his defense on denigrating the character of Matt Sykes and his family and, by extension, the reputation of all residents of the Piney Woods. Outsiders were sometimes taken aback by the rough ways of the Piney Woods people, and Waddell used this prejudice to his advantage. He persuaded one defense witness to say of a Piney Woods woman who had testified on behalf of the Sykes family: "She is a woman of loose virtue, very low."

In his summary to the court, Waddell administered what he considered the coup de grâce. Unity Sykes, he announced, was "the mother of a colored child!" He offered no evidence. But he went on to claim that the entire Sykes clan and their neighbors in the Piney Woods lived "together in one foul nest of vice and infamy."

Waddell described the defendants, on the other hand, as upstanding citizens and stout defenders of the South. He argued passionately for acquittal.

"Sykes was arrested by McGill and McMillan in the discharge of their duties as members of the home guard," Waddell told the court. "He was delivered by them to the cavalry, and was executed by the cavalry."

The military panel was not swayed. It pronounced the two Home Guards guilty of murder. They were sentenced to die.

McGill and McMillian were held in Wilmington's brick jail, guarded by a single Union sentry. One day the sentry was approached by a distinguished-looking white man who described himself as a supporter of the two condemned men. He offered a bribe. The sentry agreed, in return for a cash payment, to smuggle in a jackknife that would let McGill and McMillan carve a small escape hole and then to stand aside as they fled.

In the end, the Union sentry delivered more than he had promised. He used his military bayonet to carve a hole in a back wall, near the prison fireplace, where the bricks were only a foot thick. From inside the jail, McGill and McMillan chipped away with the smuggled jackknife. Just after 3:00 a.m. on February 23, 1866, the efforts of the three men hacked out an opening measuring sixteen by nineteen inches, large enough to accommodate a man's body. All three men disappeared, leaving behind only the Confederates' jackknife and a worn Union bayonet.

The man who negotiated the bribe that secured the escape never came forward. But there was little doubt among Wilmington's leading whites that the conspirator who paid $1,000 to buy the sentry's cooperation was the condemned men's lawyer, Alfred Moore Waddell.

CHAPTER FOUR

Marching to the Happy Land

O NE MONTH AFTER Colonel Waddell delivered his lecture to Wilmington's leading black residents in July 1865, an escaped slave named Abraham Galloway gave a speech of his own to a gathering of freed slaves in New Bern, ninety-five miles up the coast from Wilmington. It was the first time freed slaves had held a mass political meeting in North Carolina—"a great sensation," the *New York Times* reported. Galloway, just twenty-eight years old, was clearly in charge that day in New Bern, whose population was swollen by thousands of escaped former slaves. He was described by the *Times* as "a mulatto . . . an eloquent orator and a general favorite with those who know him . . . a leading spirit." Frederick Douglass's abolitionist newspaper described Galloway as "tall and rather portly, quadroon complexion, dark eyes, and with a handsome suit of jet black hair. His features partook strongly of the Comanche."

Though functionally illiterate, Galloway had taught himself to choose words that would resonate with his audiences. His speeches had a rhythmic quality, rising in pitch when he expressed outrage. On this sweltering August day on the damp coastal flats, he chose to open his address with a demand not just for citizenship but also for education: "We want to be an educated people and an intelligent people.

We want to read and write and acquire those accomplishments which will enable us to discharge the duties of life as citizens."

Galloway also demanded the right to vote—without educational requirements or other restrictions dictated by whites. If all voters were required to read and write, Galloway pointed out, perhaps half the whites in North Carolina would be ineligible. The crowd erupted in applause and knowing laughter. Galloway, energized, referred to colored Union regiments, trained and toughened, fresh from a war that had ended just a few months earlier: "If the Negro knows how to use the cartridge box, he knows how to use the ballot box."

Another roar emerged from the crowd, this one louder. Galloway responded by mocking whites for their sexual hypocrisy.

"The white man says he don't want to be placed on equality with the Negro," Galloway said. "Why, Sir, if you could only see him slipping around at night, trying to get into Negro women's houses, you would be astonished." There was a burst of applause. A voice rang out: "That's the truth, Galloway!"

When Galloway's speech ended, the gathering issued a formal resolution that demanded full citizens' rights for former slaves, including the vote, in order "to qualify for the higher stations of life." Copies of the resolution were distributed across southeastern North Carolina—a bold challenge at a time when whites were determined to crush black aspirations and many blacks lived in fear of white night riders.

The leaders of the New Bern meeting also announced a political convention of freedmen, the first of its kind in the South, to be held in the state capital, Raleigh, the following month, September 1865. On September 8, Galloway placed an ad in a Wilmington newspaper:

Freedmen of North Carolina, Arouse!! . . . shake off the bands, drop the chains, and rise up in the dignity of men. The time has arrived when we can strike one blow to secure those rights of Freemen that have been so long withheld from us.

*   *   *

Over a period of eleven years, beginning in 1863, Abraham Galloway would rise from slave to state senator. He was born just outside Wilmington, came of age as a slave in the city, and fled to freedom in the North. He went behind Confederate lines during the Civil War, working as a spy for the Union army. He returned to Wilmington after the war to help build a dynamic resistance movement against white supremacy.

The path Galloway took from New Bern to Wilmington helped clear the way for a fertile strain of black defiance in Wilmington and much of southeastern North Carolina. Perhaps more than any other single man, Galloway was responsible for the transformation of many blacks in Wilmington from oppressed slaves to free men who demanded the rights promised them by their government. And it was the boldness and fortitude of the black men of Wilmington who followed Galloway's example that ultimately provoked the deadly white backlash of 1898.

Galloway was born into slavery. His mother, Hester Hankins, was an illiterate black woman who was owned by the widow of a Methodist minister. Hankins was seventeen when she gave birth to Abraham in 1837 in the coastal settlement of Smithville, just below Wilmington at the mouth of the Cape Fear. Abraham's father, John Wesley Galloway, was a twenty-five-year-old descendant of Scottish sailors who made his living as a ship pilot working the Cape Fear River. Abraham later said that his white father "recognized me as his son, and protected me as far as he was allowed to do."

John Wesley Galloway did not own his son. Abraham was the property of Marsden Milton Hankins, the son of the widow who owned Abraham's mother. Galloway considered Hankins "a man of very good disposition . . . He always said he would sell before he would use a whip." Galloway never learned to competently read or write, but he was permitted to learn a trade as a brickmason. Because Wilmington's whites relied on blacks, both free and slave, for labor, many slaves were paid for such skilled artisan work as masons, blacksmiths, wagoners, and wheelwrights. To work his trade, Galloway was permitted to move to Wilmington, where he lived in a small cottage with Hankins, who was only seven years older. Hankins required Galloway to provide him $15 a month from his mason's wages, along with a $15-a-year "head tax"—about $280 today.

By the time he turned twenty, in 1857, Galloway had grown weary of working to pay his master. He also feared being sold at Wilmington's thriving slave market and sent to perform backbreaking labor in the sugarcane and cotton fields of the deep South—the fate of many North Carolina slaves. "Times were hard," he recalled later. "I thought I would try and do better."

Galloway and a fellow slave, Richard Eden, a barber, concocted a plan to escape to the North on one of the ships that transported naval stores extracted from the maritime pine forests along the Cape Fear. The two men had learned from friends that a ship captain from Wilmington, Delaware, had docked his schooner at the port in Wilmington, North Carolina. The ship was to be loaded with naval stores to be delivered to Philadelphia. The two slaves were told that the captain was sympathetic to the abolitionist struggle—"the right man in the right place," they said later. They arranged with the captain to be hidden in a hold belowdecks.

North Carolina's slave owners had passed a law requiring vessels bound for the North to be fumigated by burning turpentine dregs to smoke out stowaway slaves, while also killing mosquitoes. Typically, pots of burning turpentine were set belowdecks and the hatches shut tight. Galloway and Eden devised a defense. They cut oilcloth into shrouds and tied them at the waist with drawstrings, then pulled them tightly over their heads and shoulders as a sort of primitive gas mask. They also devised a makeshift bladder wrapped in wet towels to be held against their noses and mouths to ward off smoke.

The ship set sail with the two fugitives in the hold, wrapped in their shrouds. To their surprise and relief, no turpentine fires were lit. But

Galloway and Eden were sickened and weakened during the journey by turpentine fumes. They were ill and exhausted by the time the ship docked in Philadelphia. But they were free.

They made their way through Philadelphia's narrow streets to the office of the Vigilance Committee, a stop on the Underground Railroad. There, they were nursed back to health. "The invigorating northern air and the kind treatment of the Vigilance Committee acted like a charm upon them," one of the committee members reported. The committee asked Galloway for one of the oilcloth shrouds and for a photograph of himself that he carried with him. The photo showed a handsome, full-faced young man dressed in a dark suit coat and white collar fastened by a patterned ascot.

Even in Philadelphia, Galloway and Eden were at risk of capture by bounty hunters, who had the legal right to capture escaped slaves and return them South for a reward. The committee sent the two men farther north by train in late June. On July 20, 1857, Eden wrote to the Vigilance Committee from Kingston, Ontario, to report that he and Galloway had arrived safely in Canada; slavery across the British Empire had been abolished in 1833. Eden said he intended to open a shop. Galloway had found unspecified work paying $1.75 a day.

Galloway ultimately returned to the South, where he was recruited to spy on Confederates and report back to Union officers. Posing as a slave, he traveled from Maryland to Mississippi and collected intelligence. In Union territory, he moved among captured Confederates, persuading some to sign oaths of loyalty to the Union.

By 1863, Galloway had made his way to New Bern, headquarters for Union forces in the state. The city, once a Confederate coastal outpost, had fallen to Union troops the previous spring. Federal soldiers now lived in former Confederate homes and bivouacked in grimy camps illuminated by cooking fires. There were other camps nearby, these more squalid. Thousands of fugitive slaves had escaped plantations to seek refuge among the Union forces, settling in sprawling tent cities and shantytowns along the sluggish Trent River. Union officers called them contrabands and put them to work as laborers.

In New Bern, Galloway was drawn to Mary Ann Starkey, one of the most prominent freed slaves in the city. Starkey ran a boardinghouse and helped organize a relief society that provided money and supplies to fugitive slave families. She held regular Bible study and evening educational classes for black adults. Raised as the slave of a prosperous New Bern merchant, Starkey had a refined eye for home furnishings and often prepared gourmet meals for Union officers.

One of her table guests was Edward Kinsley, a flinty Massachusetts abolitionist. Kinsley was thirty-three years old, stout, with a broad face, a wide-set mouth, a high forehead, and untamed sideburns. He had helped raise money to form volunteer military units of free blacks in the North. But because there were only enough free blacks there to form two small regiments, Massachusetts governor John Albion Andrew had enlisted Kinsley, a lifelong friend, to travel to North Carolina to raise a larger black regiment composed of fugitive slaves. Both men sought to answer a question that would help shape the course of the war: how many former slaves in North Carolina would fight and die for the Union?

In May 1863, Kinsley arrived in New Bern aboard a Union steamship. He carried a military pass he had secured from President Lincoln during a White House meeting to discuss his journey to raise a colored regiment. The pass, addressed to officers of the Army of the Potomac and signed by Lincoln, read: "You will allow the bearer, Mr. Edward W. Kinsley, to pass inside our lines at whatever time he may choose and at any point he may desire, and officers will see that he has proper escort."

Kinsley was confident that fugitive slaves were eager to serve the Union. But as he approached them, they seemed to be awaiting permission. Kinsley soon discovered that they deferred to a separate authority, a fugitive slave who seemed to wield enormous influence among fellow contrabands in New Bern. "Among the blacks was a man of more

27

than ordinary ability, a coal black negro, named Abraham Galloway," a military historian wrote later.

The day after he arrived in New Bern, Kinsley called on Mary Ann Starkey at her boardinghouse. He believed that his path to Galloway lay through Starkey, whom he called "a very intelligent colored woman." The next day, Starkey said something that raised Kinsley's hopes: she was expecting "a couple of friends from rebel lines" that evening. She told him to meet her at her boardinghouse at midnight.

Kinsley appeared as instructed, and he soon heard footsteps. A black man appeared in the kitchen doorway just after midnight. Starkey introduced him as "Uncle Issac"—the Reverend Isaac K. Felton, a well-known black minister. A second black man appeared, addressed by Starkey as "Mr. Randolph"—John Randolph Jr., a freed slave and Methodist preacher.

Soon a third man emerged from the darkness. "Mr. Galloway," Starkey announced.

Starkey led the group to a cramped upstairs room. Kinsley took a seat at a small table that held a Bible and a candle which gave off a sickly yellow light. "It was dark and close," he wrote later. Galloway and Randolph told Kinsley that they had heard rumors of an attempt to raise a colored regiment in New Bern. Kinsley described his mission.

Galloway assured Kinsley that he could raise a full regiment in a matter of days. But he insisted that Kinsley first agree to several conditions. First, any colored regiment formed in New Bern would receive the same pay, uniforms, and rations as white troops. Second, the Union army must provide shelter, supplies, and jobs for the families of black soldiers. Third, colored schools must be reopened and education for blacks guaranteed. Kinsley had no authority to agree to any of the demands. And the final demand was impossible for him, or even Lincoln, to satisfy: Galloway wanted an assurance that any captured black soldier would be treated by the Confederacy as a prisoner of war, not as an escaped slave.

Galloway and other escaped slaves in New Bern had little faith in the Union's commitment to unfettered freedom for former slaves; the treatment of contrabands in New Bern hardly presaged a promising future. For instance, the Union army provided small relief packages of flour, beef, bacon, and bread to seventy-five hundred fugitive slaves and their families. But white citizens received sixteen times more rations. And while white military workers earned $12 a month, black workers, who helped build military fortifications, were paid $8. Escaped slaves were serving Union troops as scouts and spies, risking their lives. Yet some Union soldiers treated blacks with contempt, ordering them to perform menial chores and showering them with racial slurs. Some Union soldiers robbed blacks of cash, tools, and horses.

Two incidents in New Bern had especially incensed the fugitive slaves there. First, Edward Stanly, the military governor of Union-controlled areas of North Carolina, had closed several colored schools operated by a Northern missionary. Under existing North Carolina law, it was a crime to teach blacks to read and write.

The second incident involved a fugitive slave, "a young Miss of sixteen summers, nearly white and of very attractive appearance," who had escaped her master, reportedly with the help of Union soldiers. The young woman took refuge in Union-occupied New Bern but was tracked down by her owner, Nicholas Bray, who maintained that he had received permission from Governor Stanly "to hunt his darkies." Stanly, after first compelling Bray to swear allegiance to the Union, had granted him permission to retrieve his human property. Bray and his wife rode a horse-drawn cart from their farm two miles to New Bern, where Bray found the young woman and carted her triumphantly off to his farm.

It was little solace to blacks that a detachment of Union soldiers later rode to Bray's farm, put a gun to his head, burned one of his outbuildings, and returned the young woman to New Bern. For fugitive slaves seeking freedom in Union-occupied areas, the episode convinced them that their civil rights would not be given to them. They would have to demand them.

Inside Mary Ann Starkey's boardinghouse, the men in the attic talked until nearly 5:00 a.m. At last, Kinsley, determined to raise the regiment, agreed to Galloway's demands and promised to report details of their agreement to President Lincoln.

What followed was "one of the most curious experiences of my life," Kinsley wrote. Galloway insisted that he swear an oath. Two pistols were held to Kinsley's head as he took the Bible in his hand. Galloway recited an oath demanding that Kinsley honor his promises. Kinsley repeated Galloway's words. The deal was done. The black men retreated into the night.

The next day, hundreds of fugitive slaves began filing into the Union recruiting office in New Bern. The following week, a column of several thousand former slaves and their families left the river camps with torchlights and filed into a vacant lot in New Bern. Leading the column were the two preachers from the attic, Felton and Randolph. Marching beside them was Abraham Galloway. Kinsley described the scene: "[Four thousand] men women and children. It seemed to me the entire population of the South, from 'Old Uncle Ned' to the baby just born, to all the Aunt Dinahs, and with all the colored minstrel shows were marching to the happy land."

In all, nearly five thousand black men from the New Bern camps signed up for the Union army. They enlisted in the First North Carolina Colored Volunteers also known as the African Brigade. Galloway would soon help raise three units in New Bern, the Thirty-Fifth, Thirty-Sixth and Thirty-Seventh Regiments of United States Colored Troops, whose soldiers were among the 180,000 black men, most of them former slaves, who ultimately fought for the Union.

CHAPTER FIVE

Ye Men of Unmixed Blood

B Y THE AUTUMN OF 1863, halfway through the war, Abraham Galloway had turned his attention to events beyond New Bern. He embarked on a new venture as a national advocate for expanded rights for blacks and especially for soldiers in the new colored regiments. He built a reputation as a dynamic public speaker who demanded universal suffrage for black men, free of literacy tests or property requirements. He attracted national attention, largely through the reporting of Robert Hamilton, a free black man from New York who published the *Anglo-African*, the most widely read black-run publication in the country.

The following April, in 1864, Galloway and four other former slaves from North Carolina walked through the front door of the White House—rather than through a rear entrance, as required of blacks in the South. They were taken to meet President Lincoln, who greeted them cordially. Lincoln, who had met with black leaders from the North during the war, had agreed to listen to the concerns of Southern black men. Galloway's group thanked him for the Emancipation Proclamation, but also demanded the right to vote.

In a signed petition—Galloway's signature was the first of five names—the men asked the president to grant black men "the right of suffrage, which will greatly expand our sphere of usefulness, redound to your honor, and cause posterity." Lincoln assured the men that he understood their position, but he was equivocal. He made no promises.

In the autumn of 1865, Galloway moved to Wilmington, drawn to the city by its burgeoning population of freedmen, who lived in wretched encampments along the Cape Fear waiting to see if the Union victory would deliver true freedom or merely a different form of slavery. He plunged into local affairs, delivering ardent speeches that implored freed slaves to confront white domination and demand their rights.

Galloway was unlike any black man the whites of Wilmington had ever encountered. He was neither docile nor obedient—he had a reputation for carrying a pistol—and he defied racial customs. He did not step aside to let white men pass on the street, and he did not allow whites to make purchases ahead of him in shops. Even white supremacist newspapers acknowledged his oratorical skills. The *Wilmington Post* proclaimed Galloway "a fine speaker—uses grammatical language and has a clear musical voice that can be heard distinctly at a long distance." A Northern reporter wrote of Galloway: "His power of sarcasm and brutal invective, and the personal influence given him by his fearlessness and his audacity, always secured him a hearing."

In his speeches, Galloway taunted and ridiculed whites, eliciting guffaws from black audiences. Because freed slaves were routinely arrested on phony charges such as vagrancy, he suggested that it was "a crime to be a black." He referred to the New Hanover County white judiciary as "a bastard born in sin and secession" and later accused white judges in Wilmington of jailing black men at election time to prevent them from voting.

In July 1867, almost two years after moving to Wilmington, Galloway spoke for an hour during a mass meeting in downtown Wilmington, warning freedmen of a growing danger: a militant new white supremacist threat had emerged in parts of the South, including North Carolina, that was more menacing and more violent than the Home Guard. A secretive band of former Confederate soldiers and white supremacists called themselves, variously, the White Brotherhood, or the Constitutional Union Guards or, more commonly, the Invisible Empire of the Ku Klux Klan. In North Carolina, the leader of the Invisible Empire was a former Confederate officer from Wilmington, Colonel William L. Saunders.

In Wilmington, the Klan was led by a former Confederate colonel, Roger Moore, a wealthy member of the rice gentry. Moore was a descendant of a North Carolina governor, James Moore; and of an earlier Roger Moore, an eighteenth-century Indian fighter and wealthy landowner known as "King Roger." After the Civil War, Colonel Roger Moore was among those in North Carolina who considered the Klan a noble and necessary endeavor mounted "to protect the South from ravages and depredations of the spoilers who came South immediately after the war."

In 1868, Moore made a clandestine trip to Raleigh to swear a secret oath of allegiance as commander of the Ku Klux Klan in Wilmington. Moore's Klan camp in the city claimed to be "made up of the best blood of the South." Many of Wilmington's Klansmen had served under Moore in the Third North Carolina Cavalry after Moore had taken command of the Confederate unit from the ailing Lieutenant Colonel Waddell in 1864.

"He did yeoman's service for his section as Chief of the Division of the Ku-Klux-Klan in Wilmington," one of Moore's admirers said. Moore, just thirty years old in 1868, also happened to be a major in the all-white New Hanover County militia, a convenient source of well-trained gunmen for the night-riding Klan.

The Klan considered itself a highly secretive organization—"one of the closest hide-bound secret orders ever known," one Wilmington Klansman wrote. To operate in a Southern state under federal jurisdiction during Reconstruction, the group felt obliged to adopt a clandestine code of conduct. Some members went to comical lengths, concealing themselves in light-colored robes and caps with veils attached. The robes were made, often by Klansmen's wives, of bleached linen "starched and ironed, and in the night by moonlight it glitters and rattles."

The outfits were intended, in part, to terrorize blacks roused from sleep as their homes were besieged at night. The Klan attacked with brutal intimacy in North Carolina—whipping blacks with tree branches, beating them with ax handles, stripping them naked, burning their pubic hair, strangling them, shooting them in the face. Violence and terror were ingrained in the oath sworn by new Klansmen. The penalty for violating the oath was death; for some initiates, a noose was looped around their neck as they held a Bible and swore fealty to the oath:

You solemnly swear, in the presence of Almighty God, that you will never reveal the name of the person who initiated you: and you will never reveal what is about to come to your knowledge . . . you will oppose all radicals and negroes in all of their political designs; and that should any radical or negro impose on, abuse or injure any member of this brotherhood, you will assist in punishing him in any manner the camp may direct.

The Klan devised secret signals of recognition. Touching the head above the right ear was supposed to prompt a fellow Klansman to touch his own head above the left ear, signifying Klan membership. Another sign was thrusting the right hand into a trouser pocket with the thumb exposed. In response, a fellow Klansman was to jam his left hand into a pocket with only the thumb exposed. The nighttime password was: "I say." The response was: "Nothing." When challenged: "Who goes there?" The proper response was: "A friend." When asked: "A friend of who?" The correct reply was: "A friend to his country." Whether such parody was performed with any regularity is debatable, but the terror instilled by the Klan was not. One North Carolina Klansman distilled the essence of the organization: "To keep down the style of the niggers."

No black man antagonized Wilmington's whites more than Abraham Galloway, who went out of his way to defy them. Late one night in September 1867, a loud procession of blacks bearing torches and shouting, "Galloway! Galloway!" demanded a speech condemning white supremacy. Galloway responded by delivering an address from the roof of Wilmington's market house.

"My people stand here to-night fettered! Bound hand and foot by a Constitution that recognizes them as chattel!" he screamed to the crowd.

Galloway promised that within six months blacks would be entitled to vote on a new state constitution that would expand their rights. His demands were anathema to Wilmington's white supremacists, who continued to behave as though slaves had never been granted their freedom. In 1866, North Carolina's legislature, controlled by reactionary whites, refused, on a vote of 138–11, to ratify the proposed Fourteenth Amendment, which would grant citizenship to former slaves born in the United States and guarantee equal protection under the law.

That same year, the North Carolina legislature passed a Black Code, which restored blacks to near-slave status. In fact, the new law referred to blacks as "lately slaves." The code prohibited blacks from serving on most juries or testifying against whites. It severely restricted blacks' right to own firearms. Interracial marriage was outlawed. Black children could be "bound out" for work by whites without their parents' permission, and the working rights of black adults were severely restricted.

In 1865 and 1866, other former Confederate states passed similar Black Codes designed to restrict the rights of freedmen and to control their labor and movements. Mississippi was the first, followed by South Carolina. The codes relied on vagrancy laws, which granted whites broad authority to arrest blacks and farm them out as unpaid labor. Other Black Codes imposed onerous labor contracts or required written proof of employment.

In Wilmington, whites embraced North Carolina's Black Code and worked to stave off any move to grant suffrage or other civil rights to former slaves. The city's civic leaders formed "white men's clubs" to agitate against blacks. White-run newspapers derided Republicans for courting potential black votes and for treating blacks as citizens. SHALL NEGROES OR WHITE MEN RULE NORTH CAROLINA? the *Wilmington Daily Journal* asked. Even after North Carolina's Black Code was nullified by a new state constitution in 1868, Wilmington's whites behaved as if the code were still in effect, intimidating or beating any black man who resisted.

Former slaves continued to make their way to the Cape Fear country in the years after the Civil War, drawn by the promise of jobs, no matter how dirty, miserable, and poorly paid. They were drawn especially to Wilmington, where railroad lines cut razor straight through the longleaf pine forests to deliver the commodities of the countryside to the city's burgeoning port. Cotton, rice, tobacco, corn, peanuts, turpentine, tar, rosin, guano, hemp, and fruits and vegetables ranging from asparagus and potatoes to strawberries and blueberries—all of it had to be hauled to the port city, unloaded, and then much of it reloaded onto ships bound for the Caribbean and Europe. Black men took exhausting jobs as stevedores, loaders, draymen, haulers, and laborers. For a dollar a day, they hauled and loaded bulky, four-hundred-pound cotton bales onto ships along the Cape Fear.

In the pine forests outside Wilmington, there was an even more punishing form of labor available deep within pocosin swamps infested with snakes, ticks, and mosquitoes. There, a black man could work in the lumber and naval store trades. For a time, North Carolina produced two-thirds of the world's supply of naval stores—tar, pitch, rosin, and turpentine. It all came, sticky, dark, and smelling of rot, from pines that grew so straight and tall that they were later felled for use as telephone poles.

The longleaf pines had narrow but sturdy trunks above the low wire grass and scrub oak. Blacks were paid to cut "boxes" into the trunks about a foot aboveground. A skilled cutter could carve out a hundred boxes a day. The cutters sliced a V-shaped gash just above each box to encourage the flow of sticky pale sap into the square cavities below. "Dippers" ladled the sap from the boxes into barrels made from shaved and trimmed pine logs by skilled black coopers paid up to $2 a day. As each box and gash dried up, the trees were slashed again, higher and higher, until the trunk was scarred with several boxes that rose toward the green-tipped limbs.

The sap was processed into turpentine in crude ten-gallon copper stills often manned and fired by black workers. They poured the turpentine into barrels and loaded them onto wagons for the long trek to Wilmington. Other unskilled black men found work in the crude, turf-covered kilns that cooked tar out of the heart of longleaf pine logs. Others boiled concentrated tar to produce pitch.

The naval stores trade was a hot, sweaty, unpleasant business, but it paid a subsistence wage that could support a family. Shortly before the war, Frederick Law Olmsted had roamed the Cape Fear swamps and spoken with workers there. "The negroes employed in this branch of industry, seemed to me to be unusually intelligent and cheerful," he wrote. "Decidedly they are superior in every moral and intellectual respect to the great mass of the white people inhabiting the turpentine forest."

After the war, freedmen in Wilmington began carving paths to the working class through the naval stores trade or through other unskilled or semiskilled jobs created year after year, as the city steadily grew. Before the war, nearly six hundred free blacks had lived in the city, working as tradesmen and artisans. North Carolina's thirty thousand free blacks had once enjoyed limited rights; between 1776 and 1835, they had been permitted to vote. After the war, they were joined in Wilmington by former slaves who found work not only as servants, such as maids and butlers, but also as wheelwrights, draymen, barbers, grocers, butchers, tailors, and restaurateurs. Black craftsmen flourished—carpenters, blacksmiths, masons, and bakers. Within a few years after the war, a quarter of the skilled workers in Wilmington's building trades were black men; black crews helped build the city's ornate Thalian Hall and several white-owned mansions. By 1880, Wilmington would boast the highest proportion of black residents of any large Southern city—60 percent, compared with 44 percent in Atlanta, 27 percent in New Orleans, and 17 percent in Louisville.

Hard, rough jobs such as road gang work and the dockside labor of stevedores went to unskilled blacks who sought new lives in the city. Jobs were plentiful at the sprawling port, in the cotton and naval stores export markets, and in farming, logging, and railroad work in the flat, sandy pine country where the Cape Fear met the Atlantic. Five railroads set up their eastern terminals at Wilmington's port, providing unskilled and semiskilled jobs that typically paid blacks less than whites; the Carolina Central Railroad, for instance, paid white brakemen 96 cents a day but black brakemen just 75 cents.

But black men kept coming, and with them their families and their longing for the new lives and new freedoms promised by the triumph of the Union war effort.

The year 1868 was pivotal for all North Carolinians, white and black. Under the Reconstruction Acts, North Carolina and other Southern states were required to hold conventions to write new, postwar constitutions as a prerequisite for readmission to the Union. Congress denied the right to vote and hold office to any former Confederate who did not sign an oath of allegiance to the Union. Many refused and stayed away from the polls, diluting white conservative voting strength just as blacks were on their way to winning the right to vote.

In North Carolina, former slaves were permitted to vote on whether to hold a constitutional convention in 1868, the same year the Fourteenth Amendment was finally ratified, granting citizenship to former slaves born in the United States and guaranteeing equal protection under the law. It would be the first time former slaves had voted in the state—two years before ratification of the Fifteenth Amendment, which prohibited denying voting rights because of "race, color or previous condition of servitude." Black men in North Carolina were also permitted to run for election as delegates to the 1868 convention. With the help of nearly seventy-three thousand newly registered black voters, the constitutional convention won voter approval. Of the 120 delegate seats, Republicans took 107—13 of them won by black men.

Among the new delegates was Abraham Galloway, who became the star of the convention, which was held in the state capital, Raleigh, in early 1868. He advocated universal suffrage, with no property requirements. Galloway's prominent role at the convention outraged Wilmington's white newspapers. His hometown *Daily Journal* referred to him as a "claybank," a yellowish-brown horse, and published insulting headlines:

THE NIGGER CONVENTION

THE GORILLA CONSTITUTION

THE KANGAROO KONVENSHUN

In Raleigh, white women and children were kept indoors to avoid what white newspapers called the "motley horde" of blacks, scalawags, and carpetbaggers inside the state legislature building. One newspaper editor professed shock "that a set of apes and hybrids should be holding a brutal carnival in her halls of legislation." Galloway had the temerity to share a meal of oysters in a restaurant with a white man—the president of the convention—as reported with great indignation on the front pages of Wilmington's white newspapers.

One morning during the convention, Galloway held aloft a Raleigh newspaper that had referred to black delegates as "niggers." He told the delegates that if the insult was not publicly addressed at the convention, he would seek redress elsewhere. That prompted an acrimonious discussion of the proper address for a colored gentleman and whether, in fact, the term "nigger" was intended as an insult. A black delegate said the term meant "a low, dirty fellow." The white reporter who had published the slur said he indeed intended it as an insult. He also said he wouldn't object to being expelled from the convention. He was.

During another debate, Galloway listened patiently to diatribes by white delegates who insisted that blacks were too ignorant and gullible to vote. Finally, he stood up to respond. He mentioned his white father.

"The best blood in Brunswick County flows in my veins," he said. "If I could, in justice to the African race, I would lance myself and let it out."

In April 1868, the delegates voted to establish a constitution that would guarantee universal male suffrage, with no property qualifications for voting or holding public office. County and executive officers were to be elected by citizens rather than appointed by politicians. The proposed constitution was sent to the voters—black and white—for approval during statewide elections on April 21, 1868.

With former slaves now permitted to run for office, Galloway became the first black man in North Carolina to campaign in a statewide race. He was quick to respond to white taunts. After a white editor suggested that the new constitution would encourage black men to pursue white women, Galloway responded: "As I have never taken a *white* or *colored* woman from her husband, I think I can debate this matter pretty well."

Congress required the constitution to be ratified by popular vote, which would also select a new legislature. By now, nearly 80,000 black men in North Carolina had registered to vote, versus 117,000 white men. In Wilmington, the Klan was determined to keep blacks out of polling stations; there were not enough Conservative Party whites in the city to outweigh votes by the city's blacks, especially if those votes were bolstered by those of white Republicans. In 1868, blacks slightly outnumbered whites in New Hanover County: 11,096 to 10,619. But if enough black men could be frightened away from the polls, the measure would fail, at least in the state's biggest city. For whites and blacks alike, the election was the most decisive battle since Fort Fisher fell to Union guns three years earlier.

In the end, it all boiled down to race—specifically, the prospect of racial equality, which for whites meant interracial marriage and, ultimately, a "mongrel race."

"Shall MARRIAGE BETWEEN NEGROES and WHITES—*amalgamation*—be allowed?" the *Wilmington Journal* asked white readers. "Arise then, ye men of unmixed blood, the pure blood of the country, and put down this Radical platform."

CHAPTER SIX

The Avenger Cometh

THE KU KLUX KLAN'S election intimidation campaign in Wilmington began on Sunday, March 22, 1868. That morning, notices signed by the headquarters of the Ku Klux Klan suddenly appeared at prominent locations in the city. The placards, described by one white supremacist newspaper as "done up beautifully in carmine writing fluid," delivered warnings that were both ominous and baroque:

K. K. K.

Baker's Tomb, Eastern Division, Windy Month, Cloudy Day, Bloody Hour.

Ku Klux: The hour approacheth! Shake up, dry bones, and meet the Mysterious Circles of the Dry Sphere. From East to West, from North to South, they come. To measure justice for the traitor's doom. When darkness reigns, then is the hour to strike.

By order of the Great Grand Centaur.

Another placard contained what appeared to be a coded reference to Colonel Moore, the Klan's grand captain general: "The Shrouded Knight will come with pick and spade. The Grand Chaplain will come with the ritual of the dead."

One bright April day in 1868, Colonel Moore's Klansmen made their first public appearance in Wilmington: They hauled a cartload of bones through the streets. Then, on the night of April 16, a skeleton appeared propped in an alleyway, wrapped in a sheet. It was just five days before the election. The Klansmen seemed to believe that these crude stunts would so terrify black men that they would not dare leave their homes to vote. The *Journal* published a fanciful account under the headline: KU KLUX—THE AVENGER ABROAD:

> *Terrible was the phantom seen in the alley near the Postoffice Thursday night last. A skeleton, with a winding sheet drawn about his dry bones . . . the frightened darkies who chanced to be near the spot took to their heels. As they departed in their indecent haste, these words reached their ears as if borne upon the wind:*
>
> *THE KU KLUX ARE ABROAD! THE AVENGER COMETH WITH THE NIGHT WHEN MAN SLEEPETH! BEWARE! THE HOUR IS NEAR AT HAND!*

Like the Klan, Wilmington's black resistance operated in secrecy. Many members were former Union soldiers who were trained in firearms and secretly owned guns despite an election season order outlawing the carrying of deadly weapons. They were not intimidated by the Klan threats. Some black men flaunted their pistols in public. The *Journal* complained in April that "many negroes in the city . . . almost constantly go armed." A rowdy group of black men amused themselves by hollering and firing off several shots one evening that month.

In other Southern states, among them Tennessee and Arkansas, former Union colored troops and other freedmen were organized into militias chiefly to protect blacks threatened by the Klan and by other white vigilantes. These black militias were commanded by state governors but were not often mobilized, for fear of antagonizing whites. In North Carolina, the black militia was known as the North Carolina State Militia, or N.C.S.M. Whites called it the "Negro, Carpetbag, Scalawag Militia." In deference to whites, no black militiamen were sent to Wilmington. Instead, the city's blacks, with Galloway at the forefront, chose their own form of resistance—an informal militia of armed men, loosely organized, but well drilled and ready to mobilize in the face of the new Klan threat in the city.

By the spring of 1868, Roger Moore's Klansmen had accomplished little more than posting threatening notices and trying to frighten blacks with mysterious bones, skeletons, and skulls. But on the night of April 18, just three days before the election, Moore's Klansmen decided to carry out the threats issued in their placards. They laid a plan to terrorize blacks.

Wilmington's informal black militia, led by Galloway, was prepared for them. The militiamen had armed themselves, some with pistols and others with heavy fence rails carried over their shoulders like rifles. Over the next three nights, from April 18 through April 20, they patrolled the streets in search of Klansmen. They confronted white men on the sidewalks, alert for weapons or signs of Klan membership or sympathies. A white lawyer and a former Confederate officer publicly complained that they had been harassed late at night by blacks exhibiting "undisguised insolence."

But Moore's Klansmen failed to show themselves. On the rain-swept night of April 20, election eve, Galloway led a torchlight procession of several hundred black men "hooting and yelling and firing pistols and guns at imaginary representatives of the Ku Klux Klan," the *Wilmington Star* reported. Another newspaper complained, "The negroes are very disorderly to-night, shouting, firing pistols in the streets."

There is no record of whether the Klansmen stood and fought or whether they ever confronted Galloway's roving bands during those three nights in April. After weeks of threats and bluster, Moore's men seemed to have vaporized like the Ku Klux phantoms described in the white newspapers. They were gone. The Ku Klux Klan would not appear again on the streets of Wilmington until the twentieth century.

During three days of voting in April 1868, black men turned out en masse in Wilmington; one rode an ambulance to the polls a half hour after having a leg amputated. Statewide, the new constitution was approved by a comfortable margin: 93,086 to 74,086. The constitution guaranteed black men's voting rights with no literacy or property restrictions. New Hanover County also voted in favor of the constitution, 3,568 to 2,235, thanks in large part to a vigorous turnout of new black voters. Abraham Galloway was elected to the state senate by a nearly identical margin. "Galloway ought to be arrested at once," the *Journal* demanded.

White politicians claimed there had been massive voter fraud. They demanded that the election results be invalidated. They vowed to renew their fight against a "mongrel race" and black suffrage. They recommitted themselves to white solidarity and to vengeance against blacks and against the blacks' white allies. "Niggers, white and black, are badly scared at our unanimity and earnestness," one Wilmington newspaper warned.

As Galloway led the armed bands by torchlight, Roger Moore could be found sitting inside the city's Thalian Hall. The first full day of voting had passed, and Wilmington's white leadership had begun to sense that the election was turning decisively against them. Still, they held a boisterous political rally, with speeches from the city's white elite, delivered "manfully and with true dignity and eloquence," one newspaper reported.

Though Moore was a Conservative Party vice president, he did not address the gathering. He sat rigidly on the Opera House stage. He did not wear the robes or mask of the Klan. That was over for him. He had failed to suppress the black vote. But thirty years later, in 1898, Moore's men would dress in red shirts and again patrol the streets of Wilmington, this time fully armed and more remorseless than the Ku Klux Klan.

CHAPTER SEVEN

Destiny of the Negro

A T AGE THIRTY-THREE, Abraham Galloway was gone. He died in Wilmington on September 1, 1870, early in his second term as state senator. Newspapers speculated that the cause of death was fever and jaundice or perhaps rheumatism or a heart ailment. Six thousand people attended the funeral, among them a substantial number of whites and either "nine-tenths of the colored people" or "two-thirds of our colored population," depending on the newspaper's estimate. It was described as the largest funeral ever held in the city. Wilmington's courts were closed, for much of the city's population was either attending the funeral or hemmed in by the throngs of mourners who jammed the roadway and sidewalks along Market Street for half a mile.

Flags flew at half-mast. Former slaves attended, along with the colored fire brigades in their dress uniforms. Everyone was there: Twelve colored Freemason pallbearers. The colored fraternal societies. The Ancient Order and the Sons of Lavender, in full splendid regalia, and various dignitaries, riding on horseback at an easy canter. There were post office clerks and moneymen from the customhouse, and officers from city and county government dressed in dark suits. A hundred carriages, some conveying ministers of the gospel, rolled solemnly through the streets toward St. Paul's Episcopal Church, a black house of worship, where Galloway's metallic coffin lay on display with a simple inscription: name, date of birth, date of death. The church was filled to overflowing, and those who could not squeeze inside gathered shoulder to shoulder in the blocks around St. Paul's, paying their respects at a remove from the obsequies inside.

Galloway was nearly penniless at his death. "He died poor, very poor indeed," a journalist for Frederick Douglass's Washington-based *New National Era* reported from Wilmington. The newspaper's obituary called Galloway brave and bold, eminent and honorable: "He was full of charity—kind, benevolent, liberal, with a disposition to help the poor." The *New National Era* obituary was published as part of a collective front-page dispatch of news and notes from Wilmington that included a report on the election of Colonel Alfred Moore Waddell to Congress. Waddell had prevailed over an incumbent Republican who had antagonized black voters because he had failed to vote for the Fifteenth Amendment granting them suffrage. The newspaper displayed Waddell's victory more prominently than Galloway's funeral.

The rebellious spirit of Abraham Galloway soon emerged in another son of the Black Belt, also born with both black and white blood, who also chose to live in Wilmington as a black man, telling white men what they did not care to hear.

Alexander Lightfoot Manly was born on a rural outpost outside Raleigh in 1866, four years before Galloway's death. His paternal grandfather was North Carolina's white governor, Charles Manly, who served from 1849 to 1851. His grandmother, possibly named Lydia, was one of several slave women said to have given birth to children fathered by Charles Manly. Like many slaveholders, Charles Manly kept two families—one white, one black. Among the black Manly clan, family tradition held that Charles Manly granted manumission to his mulatto children, along with grants of farmland and farming equipment.

Alex Manly's father was Samuel Trimetitus Grimes Manly, nicknamed Trim, a mixed-race (a US Census Bureau form listed him as "mulatto") former slave and son of Charles Manly; by 1870 Trim was working as a farmer and railroad fireman. Alex's mother, Corrine or Corina, also of mixed race, was listed in an 1870 census report as a "housekeeper."

In 1880, the federal census listed Alex, then fourteen, as living in his father's household in Selma, North Carolina, a railroad town thirty miles southeast of Raleigh. By the standards of the time, the black Manlys built a successful working-class existence. The family sent Alex to Hampton Normal and Agricultural Institute in Virginia, a colored school established in 1868 by the American Missionary Association to educate freedmen. Alex's teachers were New Englanders who exposed him to current events and world affairs while also stressing proper Victorian manners and deportment.

Alex studied printing and painting at Hampton but lasted just one school year, from the fall of 1886 to the spring of 1887. He was fined five times—from 5 cents to 35 cents per infraction—for talking after taps, burning a light after taps, and seventeen absences from roll calls. At his father's request, Alex was permitted to leave school in the spring of 1887 because his mother was ill. He never graduated. After Alex moved back home to central North Carolina, he could not find work as a painter or printer. He struck out for Wilmington, which had a rapidly expanding black working class, and found a job as a housepainter.

Young and idealistic—and better educated than many freedmen raised in the rural Black Belt—Manly held higher aspirations than painting houses. He considered himself a spokesman for ambitious black men and sought a platform for his progressive ideals. With his brother Frank, who had also gravitated to Wilmington in search of work, Alex decided to publish a newspaper dedicated to black empowerment and advancement. It was a provocative act in a city where the white planter class had for years worked to beat back black gains at the voting booth and where all newspapers were published by white supremacists.

Alex and Frank bought a used Jonah Hoe press from Thomas Clawson, an editor at the *Wilmington Messenger*. Around 1893, the two light-skinned brothers ("nearly white," in Clawson's description) began publishing a weekly black newspaper, the *Record*, from an office above a saloon and directly across the street from a white newspaper, the *Wilmington Star*. The Manly brothers promised a "clean newspaper with good reading matter." It was a family affair. Alex was editor, and Frank was general manager. Two other Manly brothers—Lewin, a foreman; and Henry, a compositor—also joined the business.

In the early 1890s, Alex posed for a formal portrait that revealed a handsome, prosperous-looking young man dressed in a dark suit jacket and vest, a white shirt with a high starched collar, and a white cravat. His smooth, pale face was adorned with a handlebar mustache, the ends waxed and tapered. His straight brown hair was brushed back from his temples in a modest wave. Manly could easily have passed as white, the preferred option of many so-called mulattoes. "They all looked like whites," Alex's son, Milo Manly, said years later of his father and uncles. "My father's family looked so much like whites, sometimes I wondered myself." A reporter from Chicago was impressed by Alex Manly. "The young editor is prepossessing in appearance, smooth faced, bright-eyed and rapid talking, with scarcely a trace of the color of his race in his clear complexion," he wrote.

Alex refused to pass. He considered himself a proud black man who just happened to have white blood. He was the embodiment of the Talented Tenth, a term coined in 1896 by a northern white Baptist, Henry Lyman Morehouse. It referred to a black man of achievement and distinction—with "superior natural endowments, symmetrically trained and highly developed . . . an uncrowned king in his sphere." Men of the Talented Tenth considered themselves fully-formed citizens equipped to confront white bigotry. In Manly's case, his crusade for racial justice played out in the newspaper. Manley's early columns in the *Record* demanded better public services for Wilmington's black neighborhoods, where the roads were dirt and pocked with ruts, and where raw sewage was dumped in gutters or in alleyways. In the mid-1890s, Manly printed an exposé of deplorable conditions in the colored wards of the city hospital, forcing the white board of county commission to grudgingly order modest improvements.

In an editorial in early 1895, Manly openly challenged the white power structure by pointing out that black voters outnumbered white voters in the city. It was his first venture into the maelstrom of racial politics in Wilmington. It helped establish Manly, in the eyes of whites, as a nettlesome black man who did not acknowledge his proper place.

"The air is full of politics, the woods are full of politicians," he wrote. "Some clever traps are being made upon the political board. In North Carolina the Negro holds the balance of power which he can use to the advantage of the race, state, and nation if he has the manhood to stand on principles and contend for the rights of a man."

Manly concluded with a warning: "We will wait till the iron is hot, then grasp our sledge and strike at selfishness, corruption and every man who looks as if he wants to use the Negro vote to further personal ends."

White men grumbled at Manly's audacious talk of rebellion, and even some blacks expressed alarm. The Raleigh *Gazette*, a black-run weekly, warned that the young black editor in Wilmington was exhibiting an unsettling "aggressiveness in battling for race."

The *Record* struggled to turn a profit. In a front-page message on September 28, 1895, Manly reminded his readers that "the *Record* is of the Negro, for the Negro and *by* the Negro. We will continue to look after the interests of the Negro." The message was followed by a plea for readers to pay their subscription fees: "We have been sending the *Record* to a good number of persons who have never paid one cent for it."

At times, Manly played race relations for laughs. In the same September 28 issue, he published a story about W. C. Coleman, "the wealthiest colored man in the state," under the headline: COLEMAN'S

49

JOKE. The article described how Coleman, who was often mistaken for a white man, was escorted to the finest room in an expensive white hotel one evening. Coleman "humored the joke," Manly wrote, until finally informing the porter that "it was not customary for Negroes to be entertained at hotels in this state."

Despite its focus on black-themed news, the *Record* attracted white advertising. The paper carried a broad range of ads—for patent medicines, toy dealers, ladies' corsets, coal deliveries, wine merchants, and grocers. Clawson, the white *Messenger* reporter and editor, called the *Record* a "worthwhile publication, patronized by the leading white merchants of Wilmington." In an especially charitable moment, Clawson pronounced the *Record* "a very creditable colored paper."

By 1897, black readership was reliable enough for the Manly brothers to begin publishing the *Record* as a daily, sold for 2 cents a day or $3 a year, from a small building at the corner of Water and Princess Streets. The *Daily Record*'s front-page banner proclaimed, "The Only Negro Daily in the World!"

In August 1897, Manly rattled blacks and whites alike with a provocative *Record* column about sex, race, and lynchings. It was a critical response to an appeasement offered earlier that month by a group of black Baptist pastors outside Raleigh. The clergymen had announced that they were willing to cooperate with "all law-abiding citizens" in arresting and convicting black men accused of raping white women. The ministers seemed convinced that black complicity in apprehending black men who had sex with white women would somehow halt all the lynchings of black men.

"Outrages on defenseless women" by accused black rapists "threaten to perpetuate the greatest alienation of the two races," the pastors wrote in a resolution published in the *Raleigh Gazette*, under the headline: DESTINY OF THE NEGRO. Their resolution included a pro forma condemnation of lynching. But the pastors also accepted the entrenched white supremacist principle that no sexual union between a black man and a white woman could possibly be consensual. The only question was how to punish the black brute—with a lynch rope, or by a court-imposed execution?

The *Gazette* agreed. In a column in the same edition, under the headline THE NEGRO PROBLEM, the black-run paper concluded: "There is but one remedy for rape, and that is the death penalty, speedily executed."

Manly struck back quickly. In a *Daily Record* editorial headlined MISTAKEN POLICY, he accused the pastors of abandoning their race to curry favor with whites. He pointed out that they had failed to mention the white men who raped black women with impunity. If the pastors were so concerned about rape and punishment, Manly wrote, then the law should apply equally to blacks and whites, not just to unfortunate black paramours caught with white women.

The *Gazette* warned Manly that he was stirring up trouble: "Be careful, young man, ere you critcise the sages of your race." It would not be Manly's final word on race and sex.

CHAPTER EIGHT

A Yaller Dog

ALEX MANLY was hardly the only successful black man in Wilmington with middle-class aspirations and a position of prominence. He was merely the most outspoken.

Whites in Wilmington often complained that blacks behaved as if they owned the city. Every January, on Emancipation Day, blacks marched through the city to celebrate Lincoln's Emancipation Proclamation of 1863—a day that for the white planter class signaled the beginning of the end of an ingrained and cherished way of life. In 1895, blacks had held one of the largest annual Emancipation Day rallies in Wilmington's history. A musical group known as the Convivial Cornet Band led a loud procession that marched into the downtown Opera House, filling the hall from pit to dome. Poetry was read, and a forty-voice choir sang. A black newspaperman read Patrick Henry's speech on liberty and death. Alex Manly wrote a formal thank-you note to the progressive whites who had allowed blacks to gather in the sanctity of the Opera House.

Blacks and whites honored their war dead in separate public ceremonies. Every May, Wilmington's blacks made a point of commemorating Memorial Day, ignored by most whites as an oppressive federal holiday for fallen white and colored Union soldiers. Blacks decorated graves in the national cemetery on Market Street on Memorial Day, even as Wilmington's whites considered moving the street so that they would not have to pass by the cemetery. White citizens gathered later in May on Confederate Memorial Day to honor their dead.

Another public display of black culture that upset Wilmington's whites occurred every Christmas Day, when Wilmington blacks paraded through the streets dressed in African costumes, their faces painted in bold colors or obscured by wild masks. The parade celebrated Jonkonnu, a tradition passed down from West Africa via the West Indies. During slavery, black plantation workers had used the holiday to slyly mock the social pretensions of their white masters. These and other displays of black expression conveyed a strong spirit of community and belonging among free blacks and former slaves in the face of widespread white hostility. But they underscored the fragility of Wilmington's segregated black experience in a city where whites wrote the rules.

In 1896, the US Supreme Court upheld separate but equal public accommodations for blacks and whites in its landmark *Plessy v. Ferguson* decision. Homer Plessy, a Creole shoemaker in Louisiana, had been charged in 1892 with violating the state's segregation statute, which required blacks and whites to travel in separate railway coaches. Plessy challenged his arrest, arguing that it violated the equal protection clause of the Fourteenth Amendment. But the Supreme Court ruled that while the Fourteenth Amendment guaranteed equal treatment under the law, this guarantee applied only to political rights such as voting and not to social rights such as public accommodations. In the eyes of the nation's highest court, blacks had attained political equality but not social equality.

The court pointedly rejected Plessy's contention that the Louisiana law stamped blacks with "a badge of inferiority." The justices noted that blacks and whites not only were provided equal facilities but were also punished equally for violating the separate but equal law. Their decision endorsed state-mandated racial segregation. Separate but equal was now the law of the land.

For Wilmington, *Plessy v. Ferguson* merely confirmed public accommodation practices that had been in place for generations. Many jobs were apportioned by race as well. By 1897, Wilmington's city directory listed forty-two separate labor categories open to blacks—from cooks and porters to draymen and coopers. Literate blacks, many of them women, found work teaching black children in the segregated school system. In 1898, black teachers were paid an average of $32 a month, versus $34 a month for whites in a city school district that spent $858 a year per school to educate white children and $523 to educate blacks. Black children typically were permitted to study only through the sixth grade, whites through the twelfth grade.

A common accusation from whites in Wilmington, particularly the working classes dominated by Irish immigrants, was that blacks did not pay taxes or did not pay enough. But the city's 1895 tax rolls listed 2,238 blacks who paid their taxes in full. In 1897, at least 13 blacks, one of them a woman, owned at least $2,000 in property and paid taxes on every parcel. Tax revenues paid for street improvements, electric lights, sanitation, and other city services—but primarily for white neighborhoods. Predominately black neighborhoods were denied most public conveniences, including reliable police and fire services. Black homeowners often paid twice as much as whites for fire insurance.

Wilmington in 1898 was inching slowly toward the twentieth century. The first telephones had been installed in 1879. Electric streetlights had arrived in 1886. Horsecar lines began converting to electric trolleys in 1892. But many of the city's residents, black and white, had recently moved from the countryside and clung to their agrarian ways. They visited relatives on farms, returning to the city with cows, chickens, pigs, and crops that they grew in the dirt behind their homes. Livestock roamed the streets, grazing contentedly. Chickens and hogs were kept in backyards, perfectly legally under local ordinances. After complaints about the stench of hog manure downtown between Market and Dock Streets in April 1898, the city board of health warned the animals' owners to keep the pens cleaned out or risk losing their livestock.

As the city modernized, enterprising black men rode a rising economic tide to prosperous lives. The richest black man in Wilmington—and one of the wealthiest men of any race—was Thomas C. Miller, a pawnbroker and auctioneer who built a small real estate empire. Miller was light skinned and charming and was thus considered a nonthreatening "good Negro" by some whites, at least for a time. As early as 1880, Miller was a respected deputy sheriff. By 1889, he owned a combination saloon and restaurant on Dock Street—the only such establishment in Wilmington operated by a black man at the time. Though not well educated, Miller was a savvy negotiator and an astute businessman. He accumulated property, buying and selling lots as he built a small cash fortune. His estate was valued at $10,000 at his death—about $280,000 today. He loaned money and charged interest to men of both races. It was a hardened belief in the black community that many whites, including some of the city's most prominent businessmen, owed Tom Miller money.

At the pinnacle of black economic and social life in Wilmington stood professionals educated at black universities—doctors, lawyers, pastors, and funeral directors. It was a small but proud class of some sixty-five men. Most of them dressed in the same style as prosperous white citizens. They wore dark wool suits, starched white collars with cravats, and long snug overcoats in the winter. Their well-barbered heads were topped year-round with the distinctive, narrow-brimmed hats in style among the elite.

The city's most prominent black lawyer was William Everett Henderson, a tall, striking, fair-skinned man with chiseled features. His hair was dark and wavy and swept back from his forehead. He had hazel eyes, a strong jaw, and an imposing mustache. It would have shocked whites, and many blacks, in Wilmington to learn that William Henderson was not a Negro at all. His father was a white man in Salisbury, North Carolina, known as "Colonel Henderson." His mother was a Cherokee. Born in Salisbury in 1858, Henderson was pronounced colored at birth and was sent to a Presbyterian mission school for coloreds. He lived the rest of his life as a black man.

At about age twenty, Henderson traveled to California, where he earned a law degree at Hastings College of the Law. Back in North Carolina, he was active in Republican politics, securing a position as an alternate delegate to the Republican National Convention in Chicago in 1888. The next year, the incoming Benjamin Harrison administration rewarded Henderson by appointing him deputy tax collector in the town of Statesville, North Carolina. He lost the job three years later, when Democrat Grover Cleveland won the 1892 presidential election.

By the mid-1890s, Henderson was practicing law in Salisbury. In one case, he defended a black man accused of killing a white man at a corn shucking. After white residents threatened mob justice, Henderson sent for a white lawyer from a nearby town to help with the case. It made no difference. Whites threatened to kill Henderson as well as his client. He fled with his wife and children to Wilmington, hoping that a black majority city with a thriving black middle class would provide both safety and opportunity.

In 1897, Henderson opened a law practice in downtown Wilmington. By the following year, he spent $400 in cash on a comfortable house with a yard and parlor, where he lived with his wife, Sally Bettie, the granddaughter of a slave; and their four young children. The children attended colored schools, Henderson represented black clients, and the family settled into Wilmington, surrounded by black neighbors, with a white family living on the next block. "Wilmington was a fine city," Sally Bettie wrote in her dairy.

Henderson plunged into Republican politics. He became an unofficial spokesman for black professionals in their wary dealings with white Republicans. He was pleasant and conciliatory but still insisted on a role for blacks in political party affairs. He became the most successful black lawyer in the city, the man whites went to see when they needed to deal with Wilmington's black professionals.

Over time, Henderson became a friend and confidant of Alex Manly. And that friendship would soon mark Henderson as a target of white resentment and rage.

Not all of Wilmington's black professionals were advocates for their race. John C. Dancy, the highly paid federal customs collector, was a careful, conservative man—and no friend of Alex Manly. The son of a free black man, Dancy dressed well, was polite and deferential toward whites, and jealously protected his elevated status as a political appointee. The customs sinecure was the pinnacle of a political career built from the ground up. Dancy began in a low-level job at the US Treasury Department in Washington after graduating from Howard University in Washington, DC. Back in his hometown, Tarboro, in eastern North Carolina's Black Belt, Dancy ran for county registrar of deeds and won two terms. His prominence in the state Republican Party brought him to the attention of President Harrison, who appointed him to his first stint as federal customs collector in 1889.

In Wilmington, Dancy represented the accommodationist faction of the city's black population. These men were grateful to whites for providing jobs. They lived in fear that their comfortable lives would be upended if blacks offended white men. They kept their heads down—literally—and did not look whites in the eye. They avoided conflict, acquiesced to white wishes, and, in the view of whites, knew their place. Dancy was especially sensitive to white resentments because he had replaced a white supremacist Democrat, Captain William Rand Kenan Sr., as customs inspector in 1897. He chose to lie low. "The colored man looks on the situation with equanimity and satisfaction, since he hopes to cease to be the bone of political contention much longer," Dancy wrote in a church newsletter.

Dancy was a deeply religious man. He required his children to recite a verse from the Bible before sitting down to their meals. He attended the local African Methodist Episcopal Church and was appointed editor of the AME Zion Church's two publications, the *Star of Zion* and the *Quarterly Review*. From those platforms, he espoused a philosophy of restraint, rectitude, hard work, and common sense. He often lectured his children, "If I had the money, I would establish a school of common sense, because this is something that so few people have."

Dancy was a friend and supporter of Booker T. Washington, who rejected open confrontation with whites in favor of education and entrepreneurship—the fundamental building blocks of black progress. On Dancy's block in Wilmington, only the neighbors next door were black. All other residents of the block were white. That was fine with Dancy.

Dancy moved easily among blacks and whites alike, and he adopted upper-middle-class ways. His rented home on North Eighth Street had a fine parlor. He visited the white officers of schooners and cutters that docked at the Wilmington port and took his family to the beach. He sent his son, John Jr., to an elite prep school.

But even as cautious a man as John Dancy could not always anticipate how his words might be interpreted by whites. He once gave a speech extolling the achievements of Booker T. Washington, a seemingly innocuous tribute. But Washington's second wife happened to be white, and this detail did not escape the attention of Wilmington's whites. They accused Dancy of endorsing interracial marriage or sex, commonly referred to by Southern whites as "amalgamation." Dancy had unwittingly touched on the single most incendiary taboo among whites and now struggled to explain himself. "I had never advocated mixed marriages because I am content always to marry in my own race," he wrote to the *News and Observer* in Raleigh.

Dancy's brand of accommodation was welcomed by many whites and some blacks, but he was not universally admired. His habit of deferring to whites repulsed Henderson, who called Dancy "a large souled sycophant." The two men would take divergent paths—and meet different fates—during the heat of the white supremacy campaign, but Henderson expressed no regrets. Afterward, the stubborn lawyer said of the deferential customs collector: "I'd rather be a yaller dog and bay at the moon than such as he."

Wilmington's poisonous racial history had taught cautious black men like John Dancy to avoid antagonizing whites, for such behavior could prove fatal. At the same time, the city's violent past had also instilled in Wilmington's white men an abiding fear that their deferential black neighbors might one day rise up and slit their throats. For all their dominance over blacks in the city, whites had never extinguished the malignant dread of black rebellion—"a nightmare constantly haunting the American imagination," Alexis de Tocqueville wrote in *Democracy in America*. By 1898, white memories of a momentous black rebellion half a century earlier still had not faded.

In August 1831, the slave preacher Nat Turner mounted a slave uprising in Southampton County, Virginia, near the North Carolina border. He and his disciples murdered at least fifty-five (some accounts said fifty-seven) white men, women, and children before Turner was captured and executed on November 11. His body was flayed and quartered. Scraps of his skin were later fashioned into a purse. His bones were handed out as souvenirs. His head was hacked off and put on public display.

But while Turner and his band of fugitive slaves were still at large, rumors of a statewide slave uprising spread throughout North Carolina. White newspapers published sensational stories of slave armies marching south toward Wilmington, butchering white families and recruiting and arming local slaves along the way. Terrified whites in one town telegraphed an urgent request for assistance to the governor, warning of a slave "invasion and slaughter."

In fact, not a single white citizen of North Carolina was killed by a slave that summer and autumn. But alarmed whites, primed to believe any tale that described savagery by black men, rounded up and killed scores of slaves throughout eastern North Carolina. Whether the murdered black men were even aware of Turner's Virginia uprising was of little consequence to whites. They killed indiscriminately.

In Wilmington, whites read newspaper accounts of a slave named Dave, who lived in the farming town of Kenansville, sixty miles north. After he was tortured for hours inside the county jailhouse—"whipped without mercy," one newspaper reported—Dave confessed to a plot. He said he and several other slaves planned to murder Kenansville's white families, steal their guns and horses, and then free and arm other slaves. The men would ride in military formation to Wilmington, where two thousand slaves and free blacks were waiting to provide more guns and ammunition, to be seized from their murdered white masters. The conspirators would kill Wilmington's whites, break into banks, then ride through North Carolina to free more slaves and expand the rebellion across the South. DISTURBANCES AMONG THE SLAVES! a newspaper headline warned.

Kenansville's whites had heard enough. One accused slave was burned at the stake on the courthouse lawn. Dave and a slave named Jim, who had been implicated by Dave's confession, were dragged from the county jail and shot dead. Their heads were hacked off and mounted on posts.

As panic spread south and east toward the coast during late August and early September 1831, the white citizens of Wilmington braced for an attack by an army of slaves. Men were instructed to bring out their guns. An artillery piece was rolled into place. Plans were made for white women and children to hide inside homes and churches, protected by sentries armed with muskets.

On September 12, Moses Ashley Curtis, a twenty-three-year-old graduate of Williams College who was tutoring the children of a prominent Wilmington family, stumbled across 120 white women who had fled, "half dead with fear" and carrying jewelry and mattresses, to a makeshift garrison at the edge of a swamp outside town.

"One was stretched out on a mattress . . . in hysterics, a number fainted, & one was jabbering nonsense, in a fit of derangement," Curtis wrote in his dairy. "A few men too I noticed with tremulous voices, & solemn visages, pacing back & forth in fearful anxiety."

When Curtis returned to his home in Wilmington, he found the house overrun with frightened women. They handed Curtis a loaded rifle and insisted that he take it to bed with him. The next day, he wrote: "We did not awake this morning & find our throats cut."

That evening, September 13, the citizens of Wilmington met to muster a militia to defend the city from the impending slave invasion. Weapons and ammunition were distributed. Curtis was assigned a musket and balls, and then returned home.

Late that night, several newly minted militiamen towed a field artillery piece into the woods just north of Wilmington. They fired the cannon several times. The booms of the big gun echoed through the forest and swamps and into Wilmington, where citizens were roused from sleep.

"Here folly shines out," Curtis wrote later. Mistaking the explosions as gunfire from black invaders, women and children ran from their homes and took refuge at prearranged safe sites. The city's white militiamen cowered behind them—"quite in the rear of the women," Curtis wrote.

There was no invasion of slaves, no uprising, no mass murder of whites. Nonetheless, on September 17, a dozen black men were brought before a white magistrate in Wilmington. After a round of savage beatings and torture, each accused prisoner confessed to his role in "a diabolical plot" to set fire to Methodist and Baptist churches on opposite ends of town, then to murder white men, women, and children while townspeople fought the fires. "The guilt of these monsters in human shape, is established beyond a doubt," the *Cape-Fear Recorder* concluded. The men were sentenced to death.

Wilmington's whites were relieved. "A deep conviction settled in every bosom—that the measure was indispensable to the safety of the community," the *Cape-Fear Recorder*'s editors wrote. "If ever stern necessity required a prompt and vigorous course, in making public examples, this *necessity now exists* in our country."

Four of the condemned men were accused as ringleaders. They were hauled from the county jail and decapitated. Their severed heads were mounted on poles along a public roadway. From that day on, throughout the 1890s and well into the 1950s, the roadway's name served as an enduring warning to any rebellious black man in Wilmington who might dare challenge white supremacy: Niggerhead Road.

BOOK TWO

RECKONING

CHAPTER NINE

The Negro Problem

New Bern, North Carolina, March 1898

I N MARCH 1898, two of the most powerful white men in North Carolina met at the elegant Chatawka Hotel in New Bern, ninety-five miles up the jutting Carolina coast from Wilmington. Josephus Daniels and Furnifold Simmons wanted to discuss what they called "the Negro problem" and, more significantly, what do to about it.

Daniels was the editor and publisher of the *News and Observer* in Raleigh, the state's most influential daily. The newspaper was the strident mouthpiece of Democratic politicians alarmed by the reemergence of black men as a political force in North Carolina in the 1890s. Simmons was the state chairman of the Democratic Party, the party of white supremacy. With white dominance challenged by blacks at the ballot box, Simmons was the man most directly responsible for leading the white fight to eliminate the threat. "The Negro shall know his place," he assured his followers.

The power base for both Simmons and Daniels was in Raleigh, the state capital, but Simmons's hometown, New Bern, was the logical place to plot strategy. The port city on the Neuse River lay in the heart of what Daniels and Simmons called "the Negroized East" of North

Carolina. Blacks were a majority in sixteen eastern counties, including New Hanover County and its biggest city, Wilmington. The Black Belt region was set in the hard clay soil and sandy lowlands of the coastal plain that stretched eastward from Raleigh to the Atlantic. In 1868, universal male suffrage provided under the new state constitution had represented the culmination of generations of struggle for Black Belt blacks led by Abraham Galloway. But for whites, it had unleashed a terrifying new menace in the eastern counties—the majority black vote.

Blacks in eastern North Carolina voted overwhelmingly for the party of Lincoln, briefly helping Republicans take control of the state legislature from 1868 to 1870. The Conservative Party, dominated by white supremacists, reclaimed the legislature in the 1870 election. In 1876, Democrats (the Conservative Party was renamed that year) refined the race-baiting tactics of the 1868 constitutional convention campaign, rallying white voters by demonizing black men. Democrats returned to power statewide in 1876, taking over the legislature, the governor's mansion, and county governments. It was a pivotal election, coming just a year before the last federal troops were withdrawn and Reconstruction lurched to an end.

Once in power, Democrats maneuvered to undermine the newly won black vote by eliminating the popular election of county commissioners. Instead, commissioners were to be chosen by justices of the peace, who were in turn selected by the state legislature. The change guaranteed that for as long as Democrats controlled the legislature, even Black Belt counties were powerless to elect black county officials. Democrats also controlled local election officials, who relied on procedural ruses to disqualify black voters. In 1876, Democrats congratulated themselves on redeeming the state in the name of white supremacy. Well before the close of Reconstruction in 1877, the vengeance of the Redeemers had essentially suspended the Thirteenth, Fourteenth, and Fifteenth Amendments in North Carolina. White supremacy was triumphant. For the next seventeen years, the Redeemers ruled North Carolina.

But by the early 1890s, during a punishing economic recession, Democrats had alienated white farmers and laborers of the Populist Party by supporting railroads, banks, and other powerful interests at the expense of jobs, workers' wages, and schools. White farmers in the Populist Party, also known as the People's Party, were driven to ruin during the devastating recession. Cotton prices collapsed—from 25 cents a pound in 1868 to 12 cents by the 1890s. Banks refused to loan money to most farmers, forcing them to borrow at usurious rates from the merchants who bought their crops. They turned against the bankers and railroad men who dominated the state's white supremacist Democratic Party.

It was a grassroots rebellion against Democratic plutocrats. Populists demanded electoral and economic reforms and better education opportunities for the children of farmers and laborers. Many poor whites were as virulently racist as any Democrat, but Populists aligned themselves with Republicans against moneyed interests, even at the risk of aligning themselves with blacks, at least politically. They teamed with Republicans, white and black, in an uneasy political and racial alliance known as Fusion. Many black voters did not fully trust their new partners. They had given the Fusionists their votes, but not their hearts.

It was a bold and virtually unprecedented experiment. Nowhere else in the South during post-Reconstruction did whites and blacks so successfully unite in a multiracial political partnership. Fusionists managed to win the statewide election in 1894 and seize control of the North Carolina legislature.

The victory sent shock waves across the South. White men willing to join blacks in voting against white supremacist interests in a leading Redeemer state like North Carolina represented an existential threat to white supremacy everywhere—from Virginia to Louisiana. Daniels was dumbfounded. "Men who a few years before had been the most bitter in denunciation of the Republican party and its Negro cohorts, actually joined hands and defended the nomination of Negroes for office," he wrote of Populist whites. The next year, the Fusion-dominated

legislature restored the popular vote for county officials, reestablish-
ing local black voting majorities in the Black Belt, the sixteen eastern
North Carolina counties with black majorities.

Black politicians began to demand and receive a share of the political
spoils from the Fusionist takeover. Scores of black men were appointed
to political posts across the Black Belt. Black men were also elected to
the state legislature, reclaiming positions they had held during Reconstruction. A black politician represented New Hanover County, which
included Wilmington, in the state house of representatives. Another
black man, George Henry White, was elected to the United States
House of Representatives—the only black man in Congress. White
served North Carolina's heavily black Second District in the eastern
part of the state, known as the Black Second. He was ridiculed by a
white Wilmington newspaper as "a saucy, bitter nigger with the strange
name of White, as if a nigger was ever white."

It was only a matter of time before Democrats in the state's largest
city were deposed by ascendant Fusionists and Wilmington emerged
as the leading majority-black city in the South. By 1897, Wilmington
had a Fusionist mayor and police chief, and Fusionists dominated city
and county government. Wilmington was now 56 percent black. In a
city of some twenty thousand people, there were three thousand more
blacks than whites.

Democratic leaders like Daniels and Simmons were appalled when
black men took over positions previously held by whites in Wilmington
—as aldermen, magistrates, deputy sheriffs, police officers, and regis-
ters of deeds. Blacks were still a distinct minority among Republican
politicians in Wilmington and in the Black Belt, but a single black
face in public office was more than either Daniels or Simmons could
bear. The two men believed that careful planning and execution by the
Democratic Party and its capital city newspaper could end what they
called Negro rule and restore Democrats in the November 1898 elections. They knew, too, that violence might be required.

But first Daniels and Simmons focused on the well-refined strategy of racist demagoguery perfected by white supremacists of previous generations. For years, those white men had used a crude phrase for the time-tested tactic of frightening white voters by warning of the twin menace of black suffrage and black beast rapists: "Crying nigger." And that was precisely what Daniels and Simmons intended to do.

A close friend called Daniels "the most cock-sure" man he had ever met, a pragmatist who set clear goals and "flashed like an arrow to the mark." Just under six feet tall and solidly built, Daniels could dominate a room. His straight hairline sprouted a shock of dark brown hair that flopped over his right eye, and his forehead bore a scar from an accidental blow from an ax wielded by a childhood playmate. He had deep-set eyes, a prominent nose, and pursed lips.

Daniels studied to be a lawyer and briefly practiced law. But he was at heart a newspaperman. He recognized that publishing was politics. He loved power and influence and knew how to apply both to great effect. With friends and family, Daniels was "a very gentle man," his son Jonathan once said, but "he was also a very violent man . . . editorially."

Daniels was born during the second year of the Civil War, in May 1862, in the tiny town of Washington, North Carolina, often called Little Washington, a shipbuilding center on the north bank of the Pamlico River. Daniels's mother, Mary Cleaves, was the daughter of slave owners. His father, Josephus, nicknamed Jody, was a shipwright.

Before the war, Jody Daniels was among many North Carolinian Unionists who opposed secession. Even as he served the Confederacy by helping to build and maintain expensive blockade-runners in Wilmington—at a cost of $150,000 each—he secretly approached Union officers during one home visit to Little Washington. He received written permission from Union commanders to transport food and other supplies from Union-held territory to besieged Little Washington, then still in Confederate hands. In return, he was to provide badly needed cotton to Union troops. But there was a steep cost: Jody had to swear allegiance to the Union.

In early 1865, as Union troops attacked Fort Fisher before seizing Wilmington, Jody left his shipwright post in Wilmington for Union-held New Bern. Residents of Little Washington, thirty-eight miles north, petitioned the Union commander in New Bern for supplies. The general permitted a steamer carrying food and other goods to leave New Bern for Washington in exchange for cotton to be supplied by Washington's farmers. On January 21, 1864, Jody Daniels boarded the ship. On the return trip, Confederate troops on the banks of the Pamlico River opened fire on the steamer. Daniels was grievously wounded and died a week later.

Such an ignominious war record might have ruined the career prospects of Jody Daniels's son. For any young man raised in North Carolina during the Civil War, a father who conspired with Yankee troops was a source of deep shame. But the episode seems to have been buried by the time young Josephus reached manhood. He was able to win the confidence of former Confederate officers as he slowly worked his way into the inner circles of Democratic politics.

In 1885, Daniels learned of the death of a former Confederate soldier who had published a pair of ailing weekly newspapers in Raleigh. Most stock in the State Chronicle Company, which published the *State Chronicle* and another weekly, was held by another former Confederate soldier, Julian Shakespeare Carr, known as "General Carr." He was a wealthy industrialist and tobacco baron in Durham, North Carolina, and a partner in a company that sold the popular Bull Durham tobacco. The State Chronicle Company published a merged edition of the two weeklies. Daniels visited Carr and asked about his plans for the newspaper.

"What paper?" Carr replied. "I am not in the newspaper business."

Carr had forgotten that the late publisher had repaid a debt to him by granting him stock in the State Chronicle Company. Carr was intrigued by Daniels's earnest description of his lifelong dream—publishing a paper in the state capital. He gave young Daniels the Chronicle stock, saying that Daniels could later repay what he thought it was worth.

In October 1885, on the same day that he earned his law license, Daniels spent his first evening as a publisher of the *State Chronicle*. It was published the next morning on rag paper. Daniels later claimed he had only $20 in his pocket at the time. (He often joked that after all his years in publishing, he wished he had his $20 back.) Five years later, in 1890, Daniels converted the *Chronicle* into a daily to compete with the larger capital daily, the *News and Observer*.

Even as he published his newspaper, Daniels plunged into state politics. He had married into a prominent family, which provided an entrée into Democratic society. With his genial personality and easy charm, he was well received.

By 1887, with Democrats in control of the state legislature, Daniels used his political contacts to secure the lucrative patronage position of public printer. That earned him $2,500 to $3,000 a year, far more than the $1,200 he cleared from the *Chronicle*. The arrangement drew the ire of the rival *News and Observer*, which accused Daniels of "persistent, cold-blooded, calculating defamation."

Daniels quickly devised a plan to silence the *News and Observer*: he would buy it. For advice, he turned to Colonel William Saunders, the former state Klan leader and now North Carolina's secretary of state. Saunders urged Daniels to buy the paper no matter the cost. When the *News and Observer* came up for public sale in 1894, Daniels bought it, relying on another generous loan from General Carr.

Daniels brought a deeply partisan tone to the capital's dominant daily, burnishing the reputations of his political allies and attacking his enemies. He made no pretense of journalistic impartiality. He met almost daily with Democratic politicians in his newspaper office or at party headquarters and served on the party's executive committee. In time, Daniels became one of the most powerful men in North Carolina—a politician who published his own newspaper. Daniels owned the loudest megaphone in the eastern half of the state. And his most venomous attacks were launched against what Daniels considered mortal threats to Anglo-Saxon domination: Negroes, Republicans, and Fusionists.

After meeting with Simmons in New Bern in 1898, Daniels concluded that the Democratic campaign to end "Negro domination" would require three types of men—men who could speak, men who could write, and men who could ride. The men who could speak were orators like Colonel Waddell and Charles Aycock, a white supremacist lawyer who was now a polished orator and rising Democratic star. Daniels and other Democratic editors did the writing. And the men who could ride were the armed white men known as Red Shirts, the vigilante militia of the Democratic Party. According to local legend, their red shirts and jackets represented the bloody shirts waved by widows of Scottish Highlanders killed in battle. Many of the early settlers of the Cape Fear countryside were Scottish and Irish immigrants. The Red Shirts were most active in southeastern North Carolina along the South Carolina border in the summer of 1898. Only later, in the weeks before the November election, would Red Shirt brigades begin forming in Wilmington.

A man with strong organizational skills was needed to coordinate the new collection of writers and speakers and night riders—to conduct the orchestra of militant white supremacy. That man, Daniels decided, was Furnifold Simmons. At first glance, Simmons was not an impressive man. He was small and homely, with downcast, slanted eyes, a weak chin, and prominent ears. He wore his hair parted down the middle, and his round face was sliced by a bristly mustache. "He might be any bookkeeper, any village banker, or sexton . . . One gains the impression of a small boy about to cry," wrote the acerbic North Carolina author W. J. Cash.

But Simmons was politically nimble, tactically resolute, and a genius at organizing—"a compact dynamo of a man" one colleague called him. Even one of his fiercest critics conceded that he possessed "an extraordinarily shrewd mind." Simmons could be ruthlessly effective and utterly humorless, but even those who disliked him personally were eager to accept the patronage jobs he doled out, particularly coveted positions such as postal clerk and rural letter carrier. To his constituents, Simmons was an attentive benefactor. He sent them flowering shrubs for their homes, fish to stock their ponds, and seeds for their gardens. This was the fuel that propelled what came to be known as the Simmons machine.

Simmons was born in 1853 on a hundred-slave plantation outside Pollocksville, North Carolina, just down the Trent River from New Bern. He came of age during Reconstruction, which shaped and hardened his dyspeptic views of Yankees, scalawags, and Negroes. He considered the Emancipation Proclamation a tragic miscalculation and the escape of slaves from plantations like the one his family owned the ruination of the South. He grew up with the same reductive view of race as Daniels.

"The present generation will never fully realize the terrible conditions which followed the [Civil] war, the horrors and debauchery that resulted from Negro domination and the drunkenness encouraged by the many open saloons," Simmons wrote in his memoir. "The Negro was ignorant, brutal and violent. Occasionally whole families of whites were wiped out during the night. No white person went to bed without a gun in reach."

Simmons's father, a planter, sent his son to private academies and then to Wake Forest College and Trinity College. Simmons did not earn a law degree but instead studied law books on his own after graduation and passed the state bar exam two weeks shy of his twenty-first birthday. He began representing clients the same week.

Like Daniels, Simmons was able to pivot seamlessly from his chosen profession to state politics. In 1886, at age thirty-three, he launched his first campaign for Congress, against two black Republicans—a "yellow Negro" (meaning of mixed race) and a "black Negro," as Simmons described them. Simmons was backed by his wealthy and politically connected father-in-law, Colonel L. W. Humphrey. The colonel also secretly paid the campaign expenses of the two competing black candidates, a scandalous act if it had become public. Humphrey wanted to keep both black men in the race to split the black vote. Simmons campaigned almost exclusively on racial fears, tropes, and animosities. He easily won the race.

When Simmons ran for reelection in 1888, he was again opposed by a black Republican— "a mulatto type," Simmons called him. As a first-term congressman, Simmons had taken care to hand out patronage jobs to constituents of both races. He arranged for a post office to be established for blacks in the town of James City, and he pushed for construction and road projects that provided jobs to black laborers. But it wasn't enough. He lost the election. "I did not obtain a vote from James City, not even that of the Negro postmaster," he complained.

Four years later, Simmons won an internal Democratic Party election that launched him on a path to statewide power and influence. He was installed as the state party chairman, charged with keeping Democrats in power in the face of mass defections by Populist whites. Simmons was a sophisticated behind-the-scenes operator skilled in the dull details of retail politicking. He sent party workers out to canvass voters. He dispatched poll watchers to make sure Democratic supporters voted properly—and to hector opposition voters. He set up a speakers' bureau that arranged speeches by party loyalists statewide. The Democrats coasted to victory.

Simmons's reward was a federal patronage position—collector of internal revenue for the Eastern District of North Carolina. The assignment required him to resign as party chairman, but he remained active in Democratic politics. But without Simmons in charge of the party apparatus, Democrats lost the next two elections, and it became clear to party leaders that something had to be done about the black vote. Simmons, a master of race-baiting, was brought back as party chairman for the 1898 election. He had a plan. "Simmons made the Nigger his major theme," the writer W. J. Cash observed.

After meeting with Daniels in New Bern in the spring of 1898, Simmons began to craft the party's white supremacy message. The effort soon acquired a formal name proudly embraced by Democrats: the White Supremacy Campaign. Its ultimate goal was to evict blacks from office and intimidate black voters from going to the polls. But first, it was necessary not only to terrify black families but also to convince white men everywhere that merely voting in November was not enough. Whites had to be persuaded that free blacks posed an imminent threat to their privileged way of life. And they were told, every day, in newspapers and at campaign rallies next to cotton farms and tobacco fields, that the only way to eliminate that threat forever was for the good white men of Carolina to bring out their guns. A popular song, belted out at bonfire rallies by white men bearing Winchesters, contained the affirming verse: "Rise, ye sons of Carolina! Proud Caucasians, one and all."

To launch the campaign, Simmons produced a two-hundred-page screed, the *Democratic Party Hand Book*. The booklet reflected Simmons's ingrained belief that blacks were genetically doomed at birth as members of an inherently ignorant and incompetent race. It was distributed to thousands of white voters, with instructions to vote "the white man's ticket." Within its pages, Simmons distilled the Southern white man's burden:

> *It is no fault of the negro that he is here, and he is not to be punished for being here; but this is a white man's country and white men must control and govern it . . .*
>
> *Under the benign rule of the Democratic Party during the long period it held unbroken power in North Carolina, the negro race enjoyed peace and quiet, and had the full protection of the laws . . . But there is one thing the Democrat Party has never done and never will do—and that is to set the negro up* TO RULE OVER WHITE MEN . . .
>
> *Republican rule in the East means negro rule; and negro rule is a curse to both races . . .*
>
> *It is useless to tell the people of Wilmington that there is no danger of negro domination, when they see the negro policemen every day parading the streets in uniform and swinging the "billy" . . . . where you see the negro policemen and negro officers as thick as blackbirds.*

The handbook was distributed statewide, intended for literate white men. But that left out nearly a quarter of the state's white population, who could not read or write. Daniels found a solution in the artistic hand of a country boy from North Carolina's Sampson County, Norman E. Jennett, known as "Sampson Huckleberry" for his small-town ways and the juicy berries grown in his native county.

As a child, Jennett had drawn pictures on chunks of wood and engraved them with a pocket knife. He first came to the attention of Daniels after winning a $10 prize in a newspaper cartoon contest. Shortly afterward, in 1895, Daniels hired Jennett at the *News and Observer* for $6 a week to serve as a mail clerk and part-time political cartoonist. During a statewide election campaign the following year, Daniels instructed Jennett to use his cartoons to lampoon his political rivals— Republicans, blacks, and wayward Populists. Jennett learned quickly and was soon promoted to full-time cartoonist. During the 1896 election, Daniels recalled: "We would decide together what particular Republican or Populist deserved to be hit over the head that day."

After the election, Jennett went to New York, with Daniels's help, to enroll in a cartoonist course at an art school. But in July 1898, Daniels urgently summoned Jennett back to Raleigh for the white supremacy campaign—with his salary paid by the Democratic Party, according to party chairman Simmons. With his skills sharpened, Jennett helped Democrats fan white outrage toward blacks and Republicans during the 1898 election. Blacks were particularly ripe for cartoon ridicule, given the antebellum tradition of minstrel shows, where whites performed as buffoonish Negro characters with thick lips, bulging eyes, and wild nappy hair. Jennett adopted the same caricatures but added a new element—the looming black beast rapist.

Daniels assured his young cartoonist that all he had to provide would be the drawings. Daniels would supply the content.

CHAPTER TEN

The Incubus

THE SHERIFF in Pamlico County, not far from New Bern, was the type of white man Josephus Daniels considered a disgrace to his race. For one thing, Sheriff John Aldridge was a Populist who had become a Fusionist. But worse, in Daniels's view, the sheriff was so eager to court black votes in the 1898 election that he permitted a black politician to live in his house and share his meals.

The sheriff had a young daughter, Bessie, described by Daniels's *News and Observer* reporters as combining "the freshness and bloom of girlhood with the charm and grace of womanhood." Bessie soon began to look upon her father's black guest as "her protector," according to the *News and Observer*.

But just as Daniels might have predicted, Bessie soon became pregnant —with the black politician's child. Daniels did not blame the girl. He blamed her father, who, by placing a black man on equal social terms with whites, "was sealing even then his daughter's doom—a doom worse than death, more disgraceful than the deepest disgrace," the *News and Observer* wrote.

The scandal in Pamlico was first unearthed by a small local newspaper, but Daniels made certain that the lurid details were known to white voters across eastern North Carolina. In early 1898, the *News and*

Observer published a series of accounts detailing the affair, presenting it as a cautionary tale. The articles warned of the risks of allowing black men to hold office and thus instilling in them the mistaken impression that they were equal to whites. Daniels concluded that this could only lead to the twin scourges of rape and race mixing, as poor Bessie had discovered.

POLITICAL MIXING WITH NEGROES MEANS MISCEGENATION; THE AWFUL PRICE PAMLICO'S SHERIFF PAID FOR THE POLITICAL SUPPORT OF THE NEGRO VOTERS; A WARNING THAT WHITE FATHERS SHOULD HEED, a headline in the *News and Observer* read. Daniels's reporters underscored the point by reporting, without evidence, that Bessie had attempted to abort her bastard child but died from a "concentrated lye given her by her negro destroyer."

Bessie's tragic tale was a godsend for Daniels in his campaign to frighten whites into voting Democratic. The Bessie articles were among the early salvos he fired in a political propaganda campaign that gained momentum during the spring and summer of 1898. More than a century before sophisticated fake news attacks targeted social media websites, Daniels's manipulation of white readers through phony or misleading newspaper stories was perhaps the most daring and effective disinformation campaign of the era. It reached a climax that fall in Wilmington—a special target for Daniels because of its majority black population. "A reign of terror was on" in the city, he warned.

Daniels sent his best reporters to Wilmington "to detail the result of Negro control in the city." He was particularly pleased with an August story about Wilmington that in his words "described the unbridled lawlessness and rule of incompetent officials and the failure of an ignorant and worthless police force to protect the people." What he did not say was that much of the story was based on exaggerations or outright fabrications.

"We were never very careful about winnowing out the stories or running them down . . . ," Daniels wrote in a memoir years later. "In fact, the people on every side were at such a key of fighting and hate that the Democrats would believe almost any piece of rascality." As a result, he noted, "The propaganda was having good effect and winning Populists."

Daniels arranged for a hundred thousand free copies of the Wilmington article, reprinted in his weekly paper, the *North Carolinian*, to be distributed to voters whose names and addresses were supplied by the Democratic Party. He and Simmons continued the practice for other racially incendiary articles in the *News and Observer*. Daniels sold copies of his *North Carolinian* at cost to the Democratic Party. Simmons raised the money to pay for them, then made sure they were distributed to white voters.

The most sensational stories focused on what Daniels and other Democrats claimed was the black beast rapist. As a native of the South, Daniels understood implicitly the sexual insecurities of white Southern males. Already emasculated by Union troops who had occupied their towns, they risked further shame if black men were elevated to something approaching equality. A black man who could vote or hold public office was a man who might, by their logic, become a rival for the affections of white women.

Daniels worked to portray black men as sexually insatiable and, at the same time, weak willed and easily duped. Even in situations where a white woman was merely in the presence of a black man, the *News and Observer* found cause for alarm. In May, it published an article about a white woman who spotted a black man crossing her yard while she was using her outhouse. The woman screamed. The man fled. That was all. But the *News and Observer* headline suggested a narrow escape for the terrified woman: NO RAPE COMMITTED; BUT A LADY BADLY FRIGHTENED BY A WORTHLESS NEGRO.

Daniels escalated trivial incidents into front-page outrages. All that was required was incidental contact between a white woman and a black man. Daniels noticed an item in the *Wilmington Star* about a fifteen-year-old white girl, the daughter of "an honest and respectable farmer"; she was purportedly approached by two black teenagers on her way home from Sunday school. The boys did not so much as "place their unholy hands on her person," Daniels reported—but only because the girl screamed. That was the extent of the incident. But Daniels made sure the account dominated the front page of the *News and Observer*, under the headline MORE NEGRO SCOUNDRELISM. The article urged white men to "assert your manhood, go to the polls and help stamp out the last vestiges of Republican-Populist-Negro Fusion."

In Daniels's view, placing any black man in public office served only to further arouse his carnal desires. "One of the best known traits of the negro is his tendency to become 'puffed up with a little, brief authority,'" Daniels added. It was a very short leap, he suggested, from authority to rape.

In a separate story about "incompetent negroes" holding public office, Daniels reported that "the prevalence of rape by brutal negroes upon helpless white women has brought about a reign of terror in rural districts." He spread fears of an incubus, a winged demon who rapes sleeping women. AN INCUBUS MUST BE REMOVED, a newspaper in Furnifold Simmons's hometown, New Bern, demanded.

In fact, there was nothing approaching a rape epidemic in eastern North Carolina; crime statistics from 1897 and 1898 show no increase in rapes or sexual assaults in the region. In New Hanover County, home to Wilmington, just one rape and one "seduction" were reported between July 1896 and July 1898. Years later, Daniels acknowledged that rapes of white women by black men were "few in number."

To help pay for the white supremacy campaign, Simmons raised money from banks, railroads, lawyers, and manufacturers. The plan hatched by Daniels and Simmons in New Bern was carried out during frequent Democratic Party meetings in Daniels's *News and Observer* office. Daniels presided, taking notes while fielding complaints from some politicians that they couldn't read his handwriting. The main topic was, as Daniels explained, "the issue that unless the ignorant Negro could be eliminated from politics good government could not be attained."

Daniels worked until 2:00 or 3:00 a.m. most nights, filling the news columns with the latest fabricated outrages and writing blistering editorials designed to arouse white voters to "fever heat," he said. He boasted that his newspaper was "the militant voice of White Supremacy."

Other white newspapers joined in. In Wilmington, the *Messenger* reported that an elderly white man was knocked off his feet by two young black men. It was difficult for white victims of these and other outrages to identify the perpetrators, the *Wilmington Morning Star* complained, because "all coons look alike."

The *Charlotte Observer* dispatched a reporter to Wilmington in the summer of 1898 to take the measure of local blacks. "The Negroes about the street of the town are saucy and overbearing," he wrote. The *Atlanta Constitution* reported that blacks were plotting "a thoroughly Negro sovereign state" in North Carolina—"the refuge of their people in America."

In Raleigh, Daniels used his newspaper to humiliate Daniel Russell, the Republican governor from Wilmington. Daniels considered Russell a fraud who courted black voters publicly but privately held them in contempt. He was certain that the governor believed, as Daniels himself did, that blacks were genetically inferior. In fact, in a letter written in 1888, Russell had described Southern blacks as "largely savages." They were no more qualified to govern white men "than are their brethren in African swamps," he wrote.

Russell was an obese man with a double chin and sagging jowls, and Daniels delighted in exaggerating his features. One Norman Jennett cartoon of the governor, whom Daniels called "big-jowled Russell," implied that Russell had paid for black votes. In the drawing, Russell's suit was decorated with images of what Daniels called "a repulsive, very black, kinky-headed Negro."

"It was horrible-looking, and Russell raved every time he saw it," Daniels wrote in triumph.

With each cartoon and with each provocative article, Daniels pitted blacks against whites. For Democrats, winning the election was only the first step toward removing black officeholders and political appointees. It provided momentum for the next step: denying the black man the right to vote. The day was coming, Daniels wrote in the *News and Observer*, when white men "will take the law in their own hands and by organized force make the negroes behave themselves." A race war was inevitable. "A clash is surely coming between the races," Daniels assured his readers. "And in such clashes the white race is always victorious."

CHAPTER ELEVEN

I Say Lynch

IN AUGUST 1897, newspapers in Georgia reported an outbreak of lynchings—five in a single week. Rebecca Latimer Felton, a chronic author of scathing letters to the state's editors, was distressed—not by the lynchings of black men but by the purported rapes that precipitated them. She suggested that Georgia's white men lacked "manhood enough" to protect their women from predatory black men. She suggested that they summon the courage to lynch any black man caught with a white woman. In a letter to the *Atlanta Constitution*, she wrote, "The black fiend who lays unholy and lustful hands on a white woman in the state of Georgia shall surely die!"

Felton was a rarity in the post-Reconstruction South: a woman who spoke her mind. Her hectoring newspaper letters were widely read. She delivered blustery small-town speeches attended by farmers and their wives. She demanded that white women be permitted to vote and to enroll at the University of Georgia. She first rose to state prominence as the outspoken wife of a US congressman from Georgia, W. H. Felton, but she soon became a compelling figure in her own right. She managed her husband's campaigns and, it was rumored, wrote many of his speeches.

Like the white supremacists of North Carolina, Felton could not envision a consensual sexual relationship between a black man and a white woman. In her view, any black man who approached a white woman had rape on his mind. She blamed black men's right to vote; it led them to believe they stood on an equal footing with white men—not only politically, but socially.

One hazy summer day, Felton delivered a speech titled "The Needs of Farmers' Wives" to several hundred white men at the Georgia State Agricultural Society inside the stately South Bend Hotel in Tybee, Georgia. She spoke of "poor white girls on the secluded farms," unprotected from predatory black farmhands. Those women, she said, would prefer to die rather than subject themselves to sex with a Negro and the subsequent "suffering of innocence and modesty."

The solution, Felton said, was the lynch rope. "If it needs lynching to protect women's dearest possession from the ravening human beasts—then I say lynch; a thousand times a week if necessary," she shouted. The men's shouts and cheers reverberated off the hall's rafters. "They cheered me to the echo," Felton said later.

Felton's "sensational speech," as the *Atlanta Journal* called it, was warmly received by the leaders of the white supremacy campaign in North Carolina. In Wilmington, the *Morning Star* displayed the speech prominently in its August 18, 1898, editions, under the headline: MRS. FELTON SPEAKS. The *Morning Star's* republication of the *Atlanta Journal's* original dispatch carried a dateline of August 12. The editors did not mention that Mrs. Felton had delivered the speech a year earlier, on August 12, *1897*. It had received little attention in North Carolina at that time because there was no election and no white supremacy campaign. But now, in August 1898, Felton's declarations on race and rape were useful to Democrats. The inconvenient discrepancy in dates was never addressed by the *Morning Star*. The timing was not important. The message was.

Alex Manly got the message. He read the account of Felton's remarks in the *Morning Star* the morning of the eighteenth in his upstairs office at the *Daily Record*. All that summer, Manly had seethed under the withering assault against black men in the white press, but he had remained silent. He had kept the *Record* focused on black empowerment and self-improvement. He published articles for an aspiring black middle class—on fashions and society, on home furnishings and household upkeep, on the latest advances in science and technology. His editorials helped deliver paved roads and bicycle paths to some black neighborhoods, and miserable conditions in the colored wards of the city hospital were improving, thanks to an earlier Manly exposé.

Just a year after expanding from a weekly to a daily, the *Record* was now the leading voice of black aspirations in North Carolina and parts of South Carolina. Even Josephus Daniels conceded that the *Record* "had a good local circulation." Manly maintained cordial if cool relations with white advertisers, describing his interactions as of "the usual friendly nature." Even during the heat of the white supremacy campaign, white merchants continued to advertise in the *Record*.

Manly recognized that even a mild response to Felton's speech was fraught with risk. His newspaper had barely survived the uproar, from blacks and whites alike, that greeted his August 1897 editorial pointing out that persistent rapes of black women by white men went unpunished. By August 1898, Manly had achieved something approaching a bourgeois existence. He had been appointed deputy registrar of deeds. He taught Sunday school. He was a member in good standing of the Chestnut Street Presbyterian Church, the first black Presbyterian church in North Carolina. Its pews were populated on Sundays by members of the city's striving black middle class.

Manly had also fallen in love. He was engaged to Carrie Sadgwar, a slender, refined young woman who attended the Gregory Normal School, the first legal school for blacks in Wilmington. Manly had first spotted Carrie before he began publishing the *Record*. He was working as a painter for Carrie's father, Frederick Sadgwar Jr., the light-skinned grandson of a French sea captain. He was one of Wilmington's most prominent carpenters and builders. Carrie walked past one day. She saw her father, who was supervising Manly, and waved. Manly thought she was waving at him, so he smiled and waved back. Carrie was flustered. She assumed Manly was a white man, and no proper black girl would dare smile and wave at a strange white man. She put her head down and walked away.

Manly asked Frederick Sadgwar if he had noticed the pretty girl who had just walked by. Sadgwar nodded but didn't mention that Carrie was his daughter. Manly said he'd like to meet her. Sadgwar told him to focus on painting rather than "gazing at every little petticoat going down the street."

For the next three months, Manly attended services at every black church in the city, hoping to spot Carrie. Finally, he stopped by the Friday Night Literary Evening at the Gregory Normal School. Carrie was onstage, singing a solo of "Gaily I Wander." Manly asked a friend sitting with him to arrange an introduction. The friend refused, saying Carrie was Frederick Sadgwar's daughter. Sadgwar, he said, would have Manly "smoked" if he approached his daughter. Manly left the school "like a little dog with his tail cut," the friend said.

Later, Manly arranged for a letter of introduction, signed by a minister at his Presbyterian church. The letter opened the door to the Sadgwar home, and Manly began a formal courtship of his boss's daughter. They attended parties and picnics and took leisurely trips to segregated beaches outside Wilmington. The relationship continued after Carrie left Wilmington to attend Fisk University in Nashville. She studied music, graduated, and returned home to Wilmington.

Frederick Sadgwar suggested that his daughter, who was spending idle hours at home, help Manly and other young black men publish the newspaper that spoke for Wilmington's black community. Carrie took a job "slinging type," as she put it, which put her into daily contact with her young suitor. Manly charmed her, and soon she and Alex were engaged.

✳   ✳   ✳

When Manly read the Felton speech in August 1898, he was torn. He risked losing his paper—if not his life—if he were to challenge Felton in print at a time of simmering white rage. Losing his white advertisers would be the least of his worries. Even so, Manly felt compelled to say publicly what he and every other black man in Wilmington knew intuitively: the leading whites of the city were hypocrites, especially in matters of race, sex, and violence. Manly decided that he had no choice but to defend what he called "defamed colored men."

On the morning of August 18, he picked up his pen. He wrote passionately. As his anger rose, his editorial took on a bitter, almost vengeful tone. Manly was not only deeply offended but also outraged. He finished quickly and had the editorial set in type.

Late in the afternoon on the eighteenth, just hours after the *Morning Star*'s article had appeared, the *Record* published an editorial titled "Mrs. Felton's Speech." A black writer from Wilmington later called Manly's reply "the retort which shook the state from the mountains to the sea."

A Mrs. Felton from Georgia, made a speech before the Agricultural Society at Tybee Ga., in which she advocates lynching as an extreme measure. This woman makes a strong plea for womanhood and if the alleged crimes of rape were half so frequent as is oft times reported, her plea would be worthy of consideration . . .

The papers are filled often with reports of rapes of white women, and the subsequent lynching of the alleged rapist. The editors pour forth volumes of aspersions against all Negroes because of the few who may be guilty. If the papers and speakers of the other race would condemn the commission of crime because it is crime and not try to make it appear that the Negroes were the only criminals, they would find their strongest allies in the intelligent Negroes themselves . . .

We suggest that the whites guard their women more closely, as Mrs. Felton says, thus giving no opportunity for the human fiend be he white or black. You leave your goods out of doors and then complain because they are taken away. Poor white men are careless in the matter of protecting their women, especially on the farms . . . our experience among poor white people in the country teaches us that the women of that race are not any more particular in the matter of clandestine meetings with colored men than the white men with colored women. Meetings of this kind go on for some time until the womans infatuation or the mans boldness bring attention to them and the man is lynched for rape.

Every Negro lynched is called a "big, burly, black brute," when in fact many of those who have thus been dealt with had white men for their fathers, and were not only "black" and "burly" but were sufficiently attractive for white girls of culture and refinement to fall in love with them as is very well known to all.

Mrs. Felton must begin at the fountain head if she wishes to purify the stream. Teach your men purity. Let virtue be something more than an excuse for them to intimidate and torture a helpless people. Tell your men that it is no worse for a black man to be intimate with a white woman, than for a white man to be intimate with a colored woman.

You set yourselves down as a lot of carping hypocrites in that you cry aloud for the virtue of your women while you seek to destroy the morality of ours.

Don't think ever that your women will remain pure while you are debauching ours. You sow the seed—the harvest will come in due time.

The whites of Wilmington had never read anything like it. A black man had mocked the myths that had sustained whites for generations, piercing the buried insecurities of Southern white men. Manly had placed the blame for sex between black men and white women on white men—for failing to properly protect their supposedly cherished and virtuous women, reduced in Manly's view to mere "property." He upended the core white conviction that any sex act between a black man and a white woman could only be rape. In fact, he wrote—and this was the primal fear that gnawed at white men—some white women lusted for or even loved black men. Manly exposed white men as hypocrites for demanding sex with women of a race they considered servile, stupid, and inferior. And he taunted whites with their own weakness and carelessness, warning them that they, not blacks, would ultimately pay the price for race mixing.

Inside the cramped *Record* newsroom and office, and in the small frame home they shared on a lot between Ninth and Tenth Streets, Manly and his brother Frank braced for a storm. There was nothing. For several days, Wilmington remained hot, drowsy, and calm.

CHAPTER TWELVE

A Vile Slander

WHEN FURNIFOLD SIMMONS READ Manly's editorial, he was incensed. But he was also pragmatic. He believed Manly had handed whites a perfectly valid pretext to lynch him and torch his newspaper. But Simmons recognized the value of timing white outrage for maximum political impact. August was too early. Simmons advised the city's white elite—planters, politicians, lawyers, and merchants—to suppress the explosion of white rage until closer to Election Day in November.

Simmons happened to be in Wilmington the week after Manly's editorial was published. He was supervising efforts to denigrate blacks and Fusionists while seeking new ways to intimidate black men who insisted on registering to vote. In urging a restrained response, he argued that Manly's words would ultimately ensure an Election Day victory. But their impact would dissipate before then if whites were permitted to unleash their fury too soon. Lieutenant Colonel Walker Taylor, a Democrat who commanded the Wilmington Light Infantry, recalled seven years later that "when that article appeared, it required the best efforts we could put forth that we could prevent the people from lynching him." According to Taylor, Simmons "told us that the article would make an easy victory for us and urged us to try to prevent any riot until after the election."

After a brief interlude, the *Record* office was inundated with threat-ening letters: "Leave [Wilmington] on the pain of death," one man wrote. Another told Manly to "apologize for that slander" or face a lynching. One unsigned letter read: "You are the sorriest scoundrel in North Carolina . . . if you are the sample of the nigger of Wilmington, you are all dirty rascals . . . I would advise you to go to Africa where you belong."

Several white men threatened to storm the newspaper office and lynch Manly. On the evening of August 24, knots of black men began surging toward the *Record* office on Princess Street. Some carried clubs or broken pieces of lumber. Several men climbed the wooden outdoor stairway that led to the newspaper's second-floor office. Others took up posts inside the tiny newsroom. Still oth-ers surrounded the two-story wooden building, vowing to protect Manly and his press.

Two white police officers and a police captain were dispatched to disperse the crowd. But soon the captain reported to Police Chief John Melton at city hall that the black men refused to leave.

Melton said he would go confront the men himself. He did not regard them as citizens rallying behind a wronged leader of their race or even as defenders of a free press. He considered them troublemakers and petty criminals. When Melton arrived, he recognized some of "the darkies," as he called them. He had released one man from jail earlier that day. Some of the others, Melton said later, were "crap shooters and reckless kind of Negro boys." He and his officers tried, with little success, to usher them off the premises.

The boldness of the black men placed Melton in an uncomfort-able position. He was a white Populist who supported the Republican Party. A butcher by trade, he owed his appointed police position at least in part to the black votes that had helped Republicans win control of local government. Melton had been vilified by Democratic politi-cians and newspapers for permitting ten black men to serve on his twenty-one-man police force. To mollify whites, he had assigned black officers to black neighborhoods and instructed them never to arrest a white man. "Let the white men arrest the white men," he told them.

The confrontation also created difficulties for the mayor, Silas P. Wright. As a white Republican politician, Wright was perhaps even more indebted to black voters than Melton was. Black votes had helped usher in the Republican-dominated board of aldermen, appointed by Republican governor Russell, that had selected Wright as mayor following a bitterly contested election in 1897. And Wright, from Massachusetts, was a carpetbagger ridiculed in the local press as a petty, overmatched outsider.

Wright was aware that failing to control the gathering of agitated blacks would only subject him to more abuse from Democrats. He decided to go to Princess Street himself. Wright chatted casually with the black men, hoping to persuade them that neither Manly nor his newspaper was in any real danger. There were no white mobs, no torches, no lynch ropes. With the help of Chief Melton, the mayor persuaded the black men to leave.

In Raleigh, Josephus Daniels did not heed Simmons's advice to tamp down white emotions. He reprinted Manly's editorial under the headline: VILE AND VILLAINOUS. Manly had "inflamed the white people of the State" and "aroused the people to white heat," the editorial said.

Daniels's relentless coverage of Manly's editorial intensified pressure on Governor Russell to condemn it. Russell was reluctant to offend the black voters who had helped put him in office. But as the son of a plantation master who had owned two hundred slaves, and as a lifelong member of Wilmington's rice gentry, he shared the attitudes of Southern whites regarding sex and race. Manly's editorial offended him. And while Russell courted black votes out of political expediency, he certainly did not consider blacks equal to whites. While serving as a judge, he had once remarked that "all Negroes are natural born thieves; they will steal six days in the week and go to church Sundays."

On August 24, Russell arranged for the *Raleigh Morning Post* to publish a statement on his behalf: "The negro who edits the Wilmington paper, and who wrote the vile calumny upon the wives of poor white farmers and young white ladies of culture, is not his friend and supporter, but has been his enemy throughout, and that the Governor denounces the scoundrel as severely as any can."

White merchants began pulling their ads from the *Record*. As Manly had feared, the white owner of the building housing the *Record* responded to his editorial by ordering him to vacate the premises. Manly and his staff gathered up everything in the office and hauled it several blocks to a two-story frame building on South Seventh Street, between Nun and Church Streets. The structure, called Love and Charity Hall, was owned by a black fraternal organization.

The *Record*'s future was decidedly uncertain, even as it continued to publish from the new location. Because of Manly's editorial, the paper had suddenly become one of the best-known publications in the state. For a brief interval, the *Record* attracted a level of reader interest it had never enjoyed when Manly was writing about street improvements and the colored hospital ward. Both blacks and whites clamored for copies of the *Record*'s August 18 issue. A bidding war erupted. The issue was sold and resold for up to five times the 2-cent cover price. The *Wilmington Star* offered to pay 25 cents a copy. The *Wilmington Messenger* received so many requests for the *Record* issue that it reprinted the editorial in full.

Desperate to keep the *Record* afloat, Manly appealed for support from the most respected cadre of blacks in the city—the clergy. He asked the Ministerial Union, composed of Wilmington's leading black ministers, for a public statement of support. After considerable debate, the ministers published a formal resolution that tepidly backed Manly:

Resolved, That the Ministerial Union is in hearty sympathy with the efforts of the Daily Record in defending the rights of the race, and that each minister inform his congregation of the present situation and endeavor to sustain the paper by swelling its subscription list and urging prompt payment.

Another black religious group, the Wilmington District Conference and Sunday School Convention of Methodists, vowed to stand with Manly "in the protection of the ladies of our race," even at the risk of "hazarding our lives." But fearing white repercussions, the group tried to hedge. It stipulated that its support of the *Record* came "without any thoughts of endorsing the much talked about article."

Other black leaders preached accommodation. John C. Dancy, the Republican customs collector, gathered several prominent black men and demanded a meeting with Manly. Dancy was resented by some blacks as a "trimmer," a man with elastic convictions who sought expediency at the cost of fortitude. But Dancy considered himself a practical man with a long-term view of race relations. He enjoyed support among the city's more prosperous blacks, and he feared that Manly had jeopardized his lucrative customs posting as well as the livelihoods of other black officeholders and appointees. Moreover, Dancy warned that Manly had upset the "most cordial and amicable" relations between Wilmington's whites and blacks. "The white men of the South will not tolerate any reflection upon their women," he warned.

With what Dancy called "the leading colored men of Wilmington" in tow, he confronted Manly. At first, Dancy adopted a fatherly tone, trying to soothe the editor and persuade him that he had acted rashly, like some hotheaded schoolboy. He suggested that Manly suspend the *Record* until white tempers cooled. Manly refused. Dancy then asked Manly to at least retract the editorial to atone for the "folly of his course." Manly again refused, saying he had intended not to insult white women but only to defend the integrity of his race.

Finally, Dancy presented Manly with what he considered a reasoned apology, written by Dancy himself. Would Manly publish it? Manly, insulted, brusquely declined the offer. Dancy and his entourage walked out of the meeting. "Manly is responsible for the whole unfortunate condition of things," Dancy said later.

But he was not through with the stubborn young editor. Dancy began agitating for Wilmington's black leadership to publicly disavow Manly's editorial and to recommend his removal as the *Record*'s editor. "The intelligent colored people of the State did not indorse the utterances of Manly," Dancy wrote in a church newsletter.

With circulation plummeting and death threats in the air, Manly and his brother Frank continued to publish the *Record*, even after receiving a letter from a man who threatened to burn down their office. Alex stood by his editorial, patiently explaining to anyone who confronted him that he did not intend to insult white women. He published the truth, he said, and for the white men who sought to rule Wilmington, the truth was explosive.

CHAPTER THIRTEEN

An Excellent Race

F URNIFOLD SIMMONS was a creature of organization. His Democratic Party was systematized down to the ward and block level across the state, including—and especially—in Wilmington. He had established a chain of command that allowed him to direct political maneuvers in hundreds of cities and towns.

By the summer of 1898, among Simmons's most useful tools to suppress black voting under the white supremacy campaign were White Government Unions, also known as white supremacy clubs. Simmons had begun setting up the unions earlier that year, intending them as counterweights to black voting majorities in his "Negroized east." But they proved so popular with white supremacists that there were soon eight hundred White Government Unions around the state, most of them in the east. They held regular meetings in homes, businesses, and town halls.

In Wilmington, home to the largest and most aggressive White Government Unions, the groups served as the intelligence and tactical arms of the local Democratic Party. Their aim, according to one member, was "to announce on all occasions that they would succeed if they had to shoot every negro in the city."

In 1898, the chairman of Wilmington's Democratic Party was George Rountree, a Harvard-educated lawyer. Unlike most members of Wilmington's white leadership, Rountree was not a native of the city. He was from Kinston, a Black Belt town ninety miles north of Wilmington. He had married a woman from a prominent Wilmington family and, after practicing law in New York City and Richmond, moved to Wilmington in 1890. Ambitious and cunning, Rountree soon vaulted to the top of the city's Democratic machine, challenging Simmons's attempts to control the local party from Raleigh. With his bald pate, droopy mustache, and tall frame, Rountree was a ubiquitous figure on Wilmington's dirt streets, buttonholing townsfolk on the sidewalks and stopping at shops and offices to troll for the latest political gossip.

Rountree had concluded that Wilmington's Democratic Party committeemen, and even some White Government Union members, were complacent and poorly motivated. "It soon became apparent to me that we did not have a ghost of a chance to win the election with the organization constituted as it was," he wrote.

Rountree and three other white men appointed themselves as the new directors of the white supremacy campaign in the city. They took charge of a committee of twenty prominent Democratic businessmen and political figures.

Colonel Waddell was conspicuously left off the committee. Although Waddell had been recruited to deliver searing speeches on behalf of Democratic candidates, he was considered a has-been by Rountree and several other white power brokers. With his imperious ways and posture of moral superiority, Waddell had offended and alienated several members of the city's white political elite. He carried on running feuds with politicians over slights and insults that were by now decades old. He quietly nursed a sense of grievance. Lonely and adrift, he brooded about being blackballed from the leadership of the supremacy campaign.

To friends and family, he vowed to find a way in. His moment would come, he assured them.

But Rountree, no friend of Waddell, took over the effort to raise money to finance the twenty-man committee. He and several other Democrats visited every white businessman in the city and assessed each one a required cash contribution. Only five men refused to pay up. Two later gave Rountree money; one "sneaked up to my office and gave me $50," Rountree wrote. In all, the committee collected $3,000, a significant sum.

Even with the money in hand, Rountree still feared that the white establishment was not sufficiently alarmed or energized. He delivered a fiery speech at a White Government Union meeting. The reaction startled him; he had badly underestimated white rage. "I started to endeavor to inflame the white men's sentiment, and discovered that they were already willing to kill all of the office holders and all the negroes," he wrote. He now began to worry that whites were *too* energized.

Word of Rountree's speech reached Raleigh, where Simmons feared that Wilmington's White Government Unions would provoke violence too soon. He dispatched an acolyte to the city to order Rountree to consult with Simmons before taking any further action. Rountree agreed that prudence was required. But he was pleased that his machinations in Wilmington had managed to "astonish and annoy" the state party chairman. He later wrote that he told Simmons's emissary: "Simmons might go to H----, as we were going to run the campaign to suit ourselves down here."

But Rountree could not control every white man in Wilmington. The campaign was fracturing into secret cells with grandiloquent titles, each composed of prominent white business and political leaders from the same social stratum. One group of nine white men called the Secret Nine held clandestine meetings at the home of Hugh MacRae, an M.I.T.-educated mining engineer and president of the Wilmington Cotton Mills Co. Some Democrats were not even aware the group existed. At the same time, six other white men met independently at another home, calling themselves the Group Six.

Whatever their titles, the white cabals had a goal in common: to prevent blacks from voting, while also ensuring that every eligible white man went to the polls on Election Day. But their efforts could not stop there: even if white supremacists prevailed on November 8, black men and their white Republican patrons would remain in municipal positions. The November election included only federal, state, and county offices. Posts such as mayor and city alderman were not up for reelection in Wilmington until March 1899. Thus, it was tacitly understood among white supremacists, at both the state and the local level, that violence might well be required to overthrow city government regardless of the election outcome in November.

Thomas Clawson, the white editor who earlier bragged that he had "unloaded" his used Hoe press on the Manly brothers, fanned white rage in his *Wilmington Messenger* while also observing firsthand the plans being laid for violence.

"For a period of six to twelve months prior to November 10," Clawson wrote later, "the white citizens of Wilmington prepared quietly but effectively for the day when action would be necessary."

The Secret Nine, with the wealthy Hugh MacRae in charge, decided to set up armed "vigilance committees" and "citizens' patrols," organized block by block. The city was divided into five sections, carved up along ward boundaries. Each section was commanded by a captain assisted by a lieutenant. The military designations were intentional, for the patrols were well stocked with pistols, rifles, and shotguns. By late summer, gunmen identified by strips of white cloth tied around their upper arms patrolled the city's neighborhoods. Just as in a military operation, sentries were posted, and gunmen patrolled on set schedules.

Captains kept lists of white women and children in their wards. Many whites believed newspaper reports and local gossip that blacks were plotting to rape white women and burn white homes and shops.

Safe houses were established in churches or storefronts. Some white men made plans to ship their families out of town for safety. Others grumbled about being forced to march through neighborhoods on peaceful, balmy summer evenings, fully armed and primed for threats that never seemed to emerge. But many whites seemed convinced that the black menace, so clearly confirmed in each morning's newspapers, was quite real and alarming, reviving pained memories of Nat Turner's rebellion six decades earlier.

Whites sought a man of military experience to confront the anticipated black rebellion. Rountree and other leaders turned to an obvious candidate to direct what was now formally known as the Vigilance Committee: Colonel Roger Moore, the Wilmington Ku Klux Klan commander whose white-robed men had been routed by Abraham Galloway and his fence rail–toting followers thirty years earlier.

Moore was now fifty-nine, but he still maintained a military bearing. He was tall, with wavy hair brushed back from his forehead and a well-trimmed silver beard. He was regarded by fellow whites as a born leader, despite his uneven performance as commander of the city's Klan. He was considered an honorable Confederate who had demonstrated courage and loyalty as commander of the Forty-First North Carolina Regiment during the Civil War. He was also a prominent politician—a former city alderman, and, in the summer of 1898, a New Hanover County commissioner.

Despite Moore's efforts, not all whites were convinced that blacks were plotting an uprising. Jane Cronly, whose brother had been compelled to patrol the family's neighborhood as a member of the local white citizens' patrol, spent the summer closely observing the behavior of her black neighbors in the face of white provocations. She found no sign of militancy or violent intent, only the slow, prosaic rhythms of constrained black life in a small Southern city amid the stifling heat of a coastal summer.

"The negroes here are an excellent race," Cronly wrote in her dairy. "And under all the abuse which has been vented upon them for months they have gone quietly on and have been almost obsequiously polite as if to ward off the persecution they seemed involuntarily felt to be in the air. In spite of all the goading and persecuting that has been done all summer the negroes have [been] doing nothing that could call down vengeance on their heads."

CHAPTER FOURTEEN

A Dark Scheme

I N MID-SEPTEMBER 1898, the Winchester Repeating Arms Company of New Jersey received a handwritten request from two men in Wilmington who sought to purchase two dozen Winchester rifles and 16-shot pistols. The Winchester agent referred the request to the company's North Carolina agent, the Odell Hardware Company in Greensboro, seventy-five miles west of Raleigh.

Charles H. Ireland, the Odell company manager, received a follow-up request from the Wilmington men, also handwritten, for twelve .38-caliber, 16-shot pistols and several Winchester rifles. "You need not bee oneasy [uneasy] . . . we will send you a check for the amount charged," the letter concluded. It was signed by Wm. Lee and M. H. McAllister of 504 South Church Street in Wilmington.

Ireland, like most white North Carolinians, had read newspaper accounts predicting a race war in Wilmington. A request for guns from Wilmington aroused his suspicions. He decided to check with two white merchants he knew in Wilmington. The merchants responded almost immediately: the men who sent the letter were Negroes.

Ireland refused to supply the guns. But the matter didn't end there. Ireland took the unusual step of forwarding the weapons request to the *News and Observer* in Raleigh. Josephus Daniels was delighted by the fortuitous development. All that summer, he had fed his readers a steady diet of conspiracy theories about blacks in Wilmington secretly planning an armed uprising. Now, it seemed, he possessed documented evidence of black men seeking guns.

Daniels sent a telegram to Iredell Meares, a Wilmington lawyer and Democratic Party operative, seeking details. Meares responded with a telegram informing Daniels that M. H. McAllister was "a negro living at the address named" and that Wm. Lee was John William Lee, the black chairman of the Republican Executive Committee in New Hanover County. In fact, the chairman was John *Wesley* Lee, who denied any involvement with the gun order, but that did not deter Daniels.

On October 18, the *News and Observer* published an article headlined: THE WILMINGTON NEGROES ARE TRYING TO BUY GUNS. A subhead read: BUT THE DARK SCHEME HAS BEEN DETECTED. The story included a copy of the gun order, riddled with misspellings that confirmed for many white readers that the authors were indeed ignorant Negroes.

"So, it seems that the Negroes of Wilmington, and perhaps at other places in Eastern North Carolina are determined to retain control of affairs if it takes Winchester 38 caliber sixteen shooters to do it," the article concluded.

The Wilmington papers picked up the story, offering it as confirmation of a black plot to retain political control at gunpoint. "Sambo is seeking to furnish an armory here," the *Messenger* reported. The newspaper warned the city's blacks that if it was violence they wanted, Wilmington's whites would provide it.

The attempted purchase prompted George Rountree to hire a black detective to investigate what sort of mayhem blacks were planning for Election Day. The detective canvassed black neighborhoods and reported his assessment of black intentions. "We ascertained, I believe, that they were doing practically nothing," Rountree wrote.

Separately, the Group Six, one of the two secret white committees, hired two black Pinkerton detectives to conduct a similar investigation.

The detectives seemed to understand what the white men were seeking. They reported that female servants in white homes intended to burn down their employers' houses if white supremacists prevailed in the election. And several black men, the detectives claimed, had told them they planned to "burn the town down" if the Democrats won.

The detectives' report, spread by newspaper coverage, spurred more gun purchases among whites. As far away as Baltimore, gun merchants reported shortages of Winchester and Colt rifles and revolvers after filling large orders placed by whites in eastern North Carolina. The *Baltimore Sun* reported that the guns were stockpiled for "the threatened race war in North Carolina." In Richmond, gun dealers shipped more than a thousand shotguns, Winchester repeating rifles, and .32-caliber and .38-caliber revolvers to Wilmington and other Black Belt towns.

A *Washington Post* reporter who visited Wilmington in October described a white citizenry primed for battle. The newsroom of the *Wilmington Messenger*, he reported, was "a veritable arsenal, a large closet being stored with revolvers and rifles." The reporter described armed guards posted at the cotton warehouses and turpentine wharves along the Cape Fear. He noted the careful arrangements made for white men to muster with their guns at the sound of an alarm. "There is, doubtless, not another city in the country where business men, lawyers, doctors and even preachers retire at night with Winchester rifles at their bedsides and loaded revolvers within easy reach," he wrote.

On a single block in Wilmington, a reporter for the *Richmond Times* counted thirty-two white men armed with twenty pistols, eighteen rifles, and ten shotguns. "To tell the truth, the whites, or some of them, would welcome a little 'unpleasantness.' They are ready for it," he wrote. Another visiting journalist reported that there were "enough small arms imported in the state in the last sixty days to equip an entire division of the United States army." The reporter also mentioned, in passing, that the city's blacks possessed only "old army muskets, shotguns, or pistols."

To prepare for Election Day, a committee of white merchants led by members of the Secret Nine raised $1,200 to purchase the Colt rapid-fire gun, ostensibly to protect the city's cotton wharves from riot-prone black men who worked on the riverfront as stevedores and laborers. It was a formidable weapon, ideal for riot control if the intent was to kill or maim large numbers of people within a compressed time frame.

John D. Bellamy, a slaveholder's son and the scion of one of Wilmington's leading aristocratic families, later said of the merchants: "They were apprehensive of an uprising of the negroes. They knew how prone they were to have and carry weapons. And even at this late day they have not forgotten the terror and horror of the Nat Turner insurrection."

The merchants wanted the city's black community to appreciate the Colt's lethal capabilities. They rounded up several of Wilmington's leading black citizens and took them aboard a tugboat, where the rapid-fire Colt had been mounted on the deck. Gunners were recruited from the Wilmington Light Infantry.

The black men were brought aboard the tugboat not only to witness a fusillade from the rapid-fire gun but also to be reminded that well-trained soldiers fueled by white supremacist propaganda were on call to confront any black troublemakers at election time. The contingent of gunners was commanded by Captain William Rand "Buck" Kenan, a Civil War veteran who had left his studies at the University of North Carolina at age eighteen to join the Confederate war effort. Wounded in battle, Kenan returned to Wilmington after the war to work in a brokerage house. He had lost his lucrative appointment as port customs collector to a black man, John C. Dancy.

Now, at age fifty-three, Kenan was presented with an opportunity to intimidate the city's black leadership. A photo of Kenan later appeared on the front page of the *Philadelphia Times*, above a caption that read, "The man who was in command of the rapid-fire gun stationed in Wilmington, N.C., to overawe Negroes."

Captain Kenan was in command as the tug pulled up across from a marshy isle between the Cape Fear and Brunswick Rivers called Eagles Island. His Light Infantry soldiers lined up beside the weapon. As the black men looked on, quiet and observant in dark suits and hats, the uniformed gunners took turns lacing the opposite riverbank with bursts of gunfire that ripped through the brush and gouged out holes in the soft earth.

The gun "shot 500 cartridges so quickly and with such visible destruction to the small trees and shrubbery on the river banks that the Negros on the tug were visibly frightened," one account reported. "When these Negro witnesses returned to Wilmington they told members of their race that the gun had death dealing qualities and that the gunners, including Captain Charles H. White, of the Wilmington Light Infantry, were fine marksmen."

Later, Captain White strenuously denied that the gun had been fired to intimidate anyone. The sole purpose of the powerful weapon, he said, was "for the protection of life and property." There was no need to specify that the captain meant white life and white property.

CHAPTER FIFTEEN

The Nation's Mission

S HOPKEEPERS WERE UP EARLY in downtown Wilmington on the sunny morning of September 20. They strung red-white-and-blue bunting across their storefronts and hung billowing American flags from their awnings. At the Fishblate clothing store, former mayor Silas Fishblate mounted an enormous Stars and Stripes next to a fluttering display of flags from several nations. At the entrance to the Wilmington Light Infantry armory, the Wilmington Gaslight Company erected a panorama of American flags with incandescent lights that spelled out the word "Welcome" in red, white, and blue.

Company K, the United States Volunteers of the Wilmington Light Infantry, was due to arrive home from the Spanish-American War on the 5:40 p.m. train. More than a hundred local white men had volunteered for active duty in April, after Congress declared a state of war between the United States and Spain. There had been crushing disappointment in Wilmington when the US military decided not to ship Company K overseas, and the men from Wilmington failed to get anywhere near the fighting. The soldiers had drilled and trained in rural Georgia, where they kept abreast of the action in Cuba—and the white supremacy campaign in North Carolina—by reading free copies of the *News and*

Observer distributed by the Democratic Party. Their only casualty was a soldier felled by typhoid fever.

The war lasted ten weeks. On August 12, the United States and Spain signed a provisional peace treaty, ending hostilities. Now, on September 20, the soldiers of Company K assembled in formation in Raleigh on their way back home to Wilmington. They would be formally mustered out of federal service two months later, on November 18, ten days after the election.

One of their captains was concerned that the men were prone to drunkenness and trouble—especially when they encountered blacks. The captain suggested to a fellow officer "that it would be advisable to 'water' any stimulants which may be provided for the boys."

During the summer of 1898, the Spanish-American War was the only topic sufficiently weighty to push news of the white supremacy campaign from the front pages of Wilmington's newspapers. It was "difficult for the readers of the *News and Observer* to tell which was the bloodier, the war against Spain or the war to drive the Fusionists from power," Josephus Daniels wrote years later. The enlistment of local citizens heightened interest in the war, which was embraced by Wilmington's white community as an expression of Anglo-Saxon conquest.

More than two thousand people clogged the narrow streets of Wilmington to welcome the infantrymen home on September 20. Young women in summer dresses prepared a feast of chicken, roast beef, and cake on picnic tables spread across the grassy drill grounds behind the armory. There, the Wilmington Street Railway Company had constructed towering arc lights to illuminate festivities planned for that evening. In the harbor nearby, flags and bunting flew from the four-mast American schooner *William M. Bird* and the British steamship *Hawkhurst*.

At 4:30 p.m., the formal welcoming procession assembled at the armory. At the front, on horseback, was Colonel Roger Moore, the parade grand marshal, tall and silver haired. He was trailed by the Second Regiment Band. Seven horse carriages followed, decorated with banners as they ferried Wilmington's leading dignitaries and their wives. Among them was James Sprunt, the cotton compress baron who was born in Glasgow, now acting as honorary British vice consul. There were US Navy officers, gray-whiskered Confederate veterans, and dark-suited businessmen and politicians. Riding in the last carriage, seated between two white ministers, was Colonel Waddell, the parade's designated orator, who beamed and waved.

At 5:00 p.m., the procession departed for the train depot. The band played stirring military marches as the horses' hooves clipped the white oyster shells that paved the roadways. The carriages arrived in time to watch the soldiers' train clatter into the darkened depot on schedule. Everyone waved and shouted at the sight of the soldiers crammed into train compartments. On Nutt Street a few blocks away, the Naval Reserves gun detachment fired a sleek howitzer round that splashed into the river. In the calm gray waters of the port, the steam vessels blew their whistles. Another sharp whistle sounded from a tower at the Sprunt Cotton Compress on Front Street.

The soldiers hustled down from the train, hauling their gear. People hugged them and shook their hands and pounded their backs. Some soldiers wore red-and-white White Government Union pins that had been distributed to the unit. They marched in formation to the armory, where the men paraded onto the drill grounds. They halted at a decorated piazza where dignitaries had assembled to address the gathering crowd.

Colonel Waddell rose to speak. "All hail! And thrice welcome! Brave sons of brave squires!" he began. Waddell could see that the infantrymen were restless, and he promised to keep his remarks brief. But instead he launched into an interminable speech on politics. The soldiers fidgeted. At last Waddell finished, and the band struck up "Dixie." Men in the audience tossed their hats into the air as the soldiers were escorted to their picnic dinner.

No one was more pleased to see the infantrymen return home than the leaders of the white supremacy campaign. Unlike the rowdy bands of gunmen recruited through the Vigilance Committee, the Wilmington Light Infantry was a sanctioned, professional fighting force. If the time came after the election to forcibly remove blacks and Fusionists from city positions, the infantry could be called to the streets under the pretext of suppressing the widely predicted black uprising. But first, white vigilantes would assault blacks, precipitating a "riot" by any blacks who resisted. Subsequent attacks on blacks or Fusionists could be attributed to the legitimate efforts of the Light Infantry to restore public order.

The infantry's commander, Lieutenant Colonel Walker Taylor, age thirty-four, was the scion of a prominent Wilmington family and a member of the secret Group Six. Tall and lean, with a narrow face and a prominent mustache, Taylor was also a leader of the Democratic campaign committee. His older brother, J. Allan Taylor, was a member of the Secret Nine.

Also back from the war were the uniformed white men of the Naval Reserves in Wilmington. The unit had spent the war at Port Royal, South Carolina, defending the coast while serving on a federal training ship. Like the Light Infantry with its Colt rapid-fire gun, the reserves would, just before Election Day, acquire a rapid-fire weapon of its own—the Hotchkiss gun that could fire eighty to one hundred rounds a minute.

Many black Americans were conflicted by the war in Cuba. They were not motivated to fight for a government that denied them basic rights and opportunities. They felt a kinship with dark-skinned Cubans and Filipinos oppressed by Spanish rule. To fight for the United States for colonial conquest was, for them, to fight to perpetuate the same system of racial segregation and discrimination that had brought misery to millions of blacks. In March, an editorial in the *Washington Bee*, a black newspaper, referred to white supremacist attacks in the South as it advised blacks to stay out of the impending war:

A government that claims to be unable to protect its own citizens against mob law and political violence will certainly not ask the negroes to take up arms against a foreign government . . . The Negro has no reason to fight for Cuba's independence. He is opposed at home. He is as much in need of independence as Cuba is.

But other blacks, particularly the leading preachers and lawyers of Wilmington, considered the war an opportunity. By serving their country in uniform, blacks could demonstrate to whites their courage and patriotism—the building blocks of citizenship. They had fought for the Union during the Civil War. Now they would fight again for their country, no matter how brutally it had treated them.

Because of white opposition, most of the all-black military units established during the Civil War had been disbanded in North Carolina after Reconstruction. But the outbreak of the Spanish-American War in the spring of 1898 presented Governor Russell with an opportunity to muster black units. He turned to James H. Young, the black editor and former Republican state legislator in Raleigh who had helped deliver the black votes that put Russell in office in 1896. Over the vigorous objections of Josephus Daniels, who was still furious that Russell had appointed Young state fertilizer inspector, the governor commissioned Young a colonel and named him commander of the state's new black volunteer regiment.

The unit was nicknamed Russell's Black Battalion. Though Daniels conceded that Young was an "intelligent Raleigh mulatto," he eviscerated the colonel and his battalion in the *News and Observer* as "Russell's birds of prey" and the embodiment of "Negro domination." Daniels had his cartoonist draw Young as a tiny figure on a ladder, whispering in Governor Russell's outsize ear. Another white editor referred to the colonel as "Jim Young of chocolate hue and resplendent regimentals." The young black men of the state responded by providing Young with more volunteers than his battalion could accept.

Some black soldiers in the new unit recognized the responsibility placed on their shoulders. One recruit wrote, "Nobody seriously suggests any want of patriotism, courage, intelligence or boldness on the part of the black soldier boys . . . This war . . . will not end until any and every color of American man will be gladly welcomed into the trenches alongside of the other boys to fight for Christ's peace and justice on earth."

Wilmington, as the state's biggest city, was asked to provide two companies for the black battalion. On April 27, John Dancy, the black customs collector, received a telegram from the state adjutant general in Raleigh authorizing him to recruit volunteers. Dancy announced the news that evening to a large gathering of blacks at Love and Charity Hall. Two days later, the first thirty black recruits signed up. Two black lawyers, William Henderson and Armond Scott, delivered stirring recruitment speeches. By May, the two black companies were at full strength, and all other volunteers were turned away.

On May 30, four months before white soldiers returned to Wilmington in September, hundreds of black residents had filled its city hall to cheer a company of eighty black volunteers before they reported for combat training at Fort Macon, a hundred miles up the coast. A fife and drum corps accompanied the soldiers as they marched to the train depot, trailed by supporters waving flags. The men climbed aboard an Atlantic Coast Line train to a chorus of cheers, sent on their way to Raleigh after a black preacher led a prayer for their safe return.

In Raleigh, Wilmington's other black company linked up with black units from across the state, all bound for Fort Macon. Several thousand black residents of the capital surrounded the train depot to say goodbye. Black church choirs sang spirituals and patriotic anthems. "Old colored mothers cried aloud and without reserve, younger women, whose brothers or husbands were departing, screamed at the top of their voices," the *News and Observer* reported.

A black minister told the volunteers that they need not prove their manhood or patriotism, for that was a given: "The reason negroes have enlisted, are enlisting and want to enlist and are willing to go and fight wherever the country sends them is because they are Americans, and the nation's mission is a Christian mission."

Like the Wilmington Light Infantry, Jim Young's black battalion never made it to Cuba. His soldiers spent the war and the months that followed in training camps in North Carolina, Tennessee, and Georgia. When allowed to visit local towns on weekend furloughs, the black volunteers were drawn into scuffles with white men who objected to the soldiers' demands for equal treatment on streetcars and in saloons. Black units from other states encountered similar abuse. On a train in Atlanta, white police officers clubbed a group of black soldiers, inflicting bloody head wounds. In Macon, a black soldier who insisted on being served in a segregated saloon was shot dead by the white barkeeper. Three other volunteers in the black battalion were killed by white men in separate incidents in Georgia. In each case, the white killer was acquitted by an all-white jury.

When white soldiers were sent home to Wilmington shortly before the election, the black units were kept far away. On November 10, when the Wilmington Light Infantry and the Naval Reserves took to the streets with their rapid-fire guns, the young black men who had left Wilmington to serve their country were still confined to a desolate training camp in the red clay country of rural Georgia.

CHAPTER SIXTEEN

Degenerate Sons of
the White Race

S MALL HANDBILLS BEGAN APPEARING on the streets of Wilmington that autumn, bearing the message: REMEMBER THE 6. The notices featured a hand-drawn skull and crossbones, flanked by a drawing of a pistol. They were printed by the Democratic Party to alert white voters to the six most prominent Republicans in city government branded as race traitors. It was part of the party's two-pronged approach—terrorizing blacks to prevent them from voting, and intimidating white Republicans to undermine their hold on local government. The flyers read:

> *These degenerate sons of the white race who control the republican machine in this county, or those whose positions made them influential in putting negro rule on the whites, will suffer the penalty of their responsibility for any disturbance consequent on the determination of the white men of this county to carry the election at any cost.*

The handbills did not list the six white offenders, but the *Wilmington Messenger* soon did: Mayor Silas Wright, Police Chief John Melton, Deputy Sheriff George Z. French, businessmen William H. Chadbourn, Flavel W. Foster, and a lawyer, Caleb B. Lockey. The three public officials were advised to resign. The others were instructed to pledge support to white supremacy.

The prime target was Mayor Wright. The mayor had committed two grave offenses. First, he was a Northerner from Massachusetts and thus a carpetbagger. Second, he had helped put black men in office. Wright had moved to Wilmington after the Civil War, in 1870, to take a job as revenue collector. Along with Chief Melton, Wright owed his position to changes in the city charter made by Republicans after 1894. That year, the party won control of the state legislature with the help of black votes. State Republicans awarded themselves control of the board of aldermen in Wilmington, which elected Wright as mayor and appointed Melton police chief.

Wright was ridiculed by white supremacists as foolish and pompous. He lived not in a proper home but as a boarder at the downtown Orton Hotel. He was not known to be particularly wealthy, but he dressed like a duke, often appearing in a black felt hat and white gloves. He sometimes rode his carriage through the city behind a pair of prancing black horses.

Chief Melton, by contrast, was considered common and unsophisticated. Unlike most white officeholders, he did not own a home or property. Melton, then forty-eight, lived with his wife, Augusta, and three daughters in a modest rental home. He worked as a butcher, a lowly trade Democrats cited as evidence that Melton was unqualified and for law enforcement work. He had also committed the offense of hiring the ten black officers on his force. Perhaps not coincidentally, Melton's rented home was set ablaze that summer, forcing the chief to leap from a window to escape.

By October, Melton had received several anonymous letters containing the REMEMBER THE 6 handbills. Friends, including a member of a White Government Union, warned him that he was, as he put it, "liable to be killed." Melton understood that the Big Six white Fusionists represented "six of us that was to be killed," he said. He understood, too, that they would be murdered "if there was any trouble with the negroes." And the Big Six were not the only citizens targeted for murder. As Melton recalled later, "White men had told me that they would carry the election or kill every negro."

If any white Republican was more reviled by Democrats than Wright or Melton, it was Chief Deputy Sheriff George Z. French, an original carpetbagger who had arrived in Wilmington with the invading Union army. French, a native of Maine, had served as a sutler to Union forces during the Civil War, selling supplies to soldiers from a cart that trailed Union wagon trains.

In the chaos of the Confederacy's defeat in Wilmington in early 1865, French had appropriated an abandoned storefront on Market Street. With a partner, he began selling clothing, tobacco, liquor, novels, magazines, "West India goods," and "Yankee Notions." French took out a newspaper ad that offered goods specifically to Union occupiers: "Everything Required in the Army."

French was a complicated figure. He could be a ruthless businessman, but he was also capable of grand acts of compassion. In March 1865, he had been deeply moved by the sight of nine hundred ragged Union officers, freshly released from Confederate prison camps, as they arrived in Wilmington with "barely sufficient clothing left to cover their nakedness." French gave the men food and clothing on credit—four hundred officers during a single two-day period. In all, French advanced officers $4,000 in goods.

Five months later, French had been repaid only $1,500. He threatened to publish the names of the deadbeat officers but never followed through. He was praised by the *Wilmington Herald* as "magnanimous" and for displaying "honor and honesty."

As he settled into hardscrabble postwar Wilmington, French expanded into commodities, land speculation, and ship salvage. For a commission, he marketed naval stores and cotton from farmers and Piney Woods residents for resale at Wilmington's port. He secured a government contract to salvage both Union ships and Confederate blockade-runners that had been sunk in coastal waters outside Wilmington. He also found a way to secure a seat on the city's board of aldermen, where he was known by the nickname "Gizzard."

On a stretch of land he had bought at Rocky Point, sixteen miles north of downtown Wilmington in the wet, sandy lowlands west of the Cape Fear, French built a plantation he named Excelsior. French adhered to a simple operating principle: use more fertilizer than anyone else. At night, as residents of Wilmington sat on their porches to enjoy soft breezes blowing off the Cape Fear, French sent a cart rumbling through the streets to collect excrement from night soil buckets and privies in backyards. This was not well received.

The *Wilmington Journal* complained:

> *Because Gizzard French is a member of the Board of Aldermen, is this any reason that the cart which supplies him at his "Excelsior" plantation with "night soil" should be permitted to disturb the citizens by dragging its filthy load through our public streets?*

French continued to collect night soil, but he soon discovered that his Excelsior property contained limestone deposits that could be quarried for lime, a key ingredient in fertilizer. By 1874, a new quarry produced enough lime for French to package it as French's Agricultural Lime. He had created a viable new fertilizer industry that soon helped rejuvenate Cape Fear farms and plantations devastated by the Civil War.

Wilmington's white aristocracy could tolerate a hustling carpetbagger like George French so long as he busied himself with his plantation and lime. But French, an energetic and garrulous sort, was drawn irresistibly to politics—and to the transactional advantages enjoyed by politicians. He lobbied blacks for their votes, and they helped him win a seat in the state legislature in 1870 and 1894. As chief deputy sheriff, French ignored more than a hundred warrants from a White

Government Union justice of the peace to arrest or remove black police officers French had helped appoint.

French rose to the chairmanship of the county Republican Party. He was irrepressible, glad-handing blacks and whites alike. He was such a "slick talking man," one of his black employees said, that if he were ever "away from home and got strapped, he could preach his way back without the slightest trouble."

By the summer of 1898, French was sixty-six years old, a solidly entrenched politician and businessman. But for all his political skills, he had failed to anticipate the depth of the rage and resentment within the city's white political leadership. He had charmed them, but he had never won them over. As Democrats plotted a violent coup, French realized that his own political position was untenable. REMEMBER THE 6 handbills were filling his mailbox.

Like French, Republican postmaster William H. Chadbourn also recognized that his political stance threatened his livelihood, if not his life. As a postmaster appointed by the Republican Party, he had awarded letter carrier and postal clerk jobs to black men—an unforgivable sin in the eyes of the city's leading white men.

Chadbourn made matters worse for himself by openly denying any "Negro domination" in Wilmington. George Rountree threatened Chadbourn, who backed down and published an apology in the *Messenger* under the headline: HIS EYES OPENED. Chadbourn conceded that there was, in fact, Negro domination in Wilmington. He warned that the city's black men were planning a race riot "of arson and bloodshed."

With Chadbourn's defection, and with the mayor, police chief, and deputy sheriff thoroughly intimidated, the Republican Party in Wilmington was in disarray a month before the election. In Raleigh, Governor Russell was inundated by calls from panicked Republicans in his hometown. They warned him that Democrats were hijacking the election. The governor felt powerless to intervene. His only influence in the city was through Republicans who nominally ran Wilmington but who were now surrendering to Democratic bullying.

After Russell announced that he would give a campaign speech in Wilmington in October, Democrats claimed the visit would trigger a race war. After threats by George Rountree and other Democrats, Russell announced three days later that he was canceling the visit.

But Rountree was not through with Russell. Wilmington's Democrats next demanded that Republicans remove all candidates, black and white, who were seeking New Hanover County offices. Again, Democrats threatened a race war. Russell knew he was being strong-armed, and he resented it. But he could not afford, politically, to be blamed for failing to stop a race war, even one instigated by his political enemies. His reply was noncommittal. He pointed out, to little effect, that all Republicans running for county office were white, except for a black candidate for registrar of deeds.

Democrats in Wilmington responded by dispatching Sprunt, the cotton compress owner, and two other Democrats to Raleigh to confront Russell face-to-face. They took with them a sweetener: if Russell would withdraw local Republican candidates, the Democrats would remove two virulently anti-Russell Democratic candidates who were demanding his impeachment.

An agreement was reached during the final week of October: the two pro-impeachment Democratic candidates and the entire Republican county slate were to be withdrawn. It was lopsided deal. Russell surrendered the county; Democrats gave up virtually nothing. All Russell got were two slightly less hostile Democratic candidates and an empty promise by Wilmington's white supremacists not to interfere with the "rights of lawful voters."

Russell summoned Gizzard French to Raleigh and dumped the ugly deal in his lap, with instructions to sell it to the Republican leadership in Wilmington. The party bowed to the inevitable. Throughout the Black Belt, where Democrats had also threatened white riots, Republicans withdrew local black candidates from the campaign. It was a remarkable demonstration of political thuggery.

Later that week, Wilmington's Democrats again humiliated Russell. They kept their promise to remove the two Wilmington candidates for the state legislature who had been clamoring for his impeachment. But they replaced one of them with a politician even more bitterly opposed to the governor—George Rountree.

Later, in a letter to Wilmington's Fusionists, Russell conceded that he had been intimidated into trading Republican-controlled county offices for peace—a startling acknowledgement that a free and fair election was negotiable. Russell assured his allies that white supremacists in Wilmington "have given their word that there shall be a free and fair and peaceful election."

One by one, Republican county candidates formally announced their decisions to step aside, reluctantly, in the name of election peace. The last Republican to drop out was the county registrar of deeds, Charles Norwood, a black man. Norwood said he had concluded that "a race war was being stirred up." He wanted "no part in any such proceedings." With that, the Democrats' threat of a white riot seemed to be in abeyance, for the moment.

CHAPTER SEVENTEEN

The Great White Man's
Rally and Basket Picnic

E ARLY ON the damp, gray morning of October 20, the foot soldiers of Wilmington's white supremacy campaign trooped across the worn floorboards of the loading platform at the train depot near the downtown waterfront. Men from the White Government Unions were there, dressed in dark suits and carrying banners representing their wards. A detachment of the Cape Fear militia arrived in formation, led through its paces by a uniformed captain. The militiamen were trailed by musicians of the Fifth Ward Cornet Band. Among the high-spirited people on the platform were several women, elegantly dressed and squired by their husbands.

The travelers were bound for Fayetteville, ninety miles up the Cape Fear, to attend the Great White Man's Rally and Basket Picnic. It was to be the state's largest white supremacy campaign event of the year, and white leaders from the state's largest city were eager to add their voices to the white revolution against Negro rule.

By 8:30 a.m., some eighty-two men and women were aboard the Cape Fear and Yadkin Valley Railway train as it chugged out of the Wilmington station, bound for Fayetteville. At each station stop across the coastal plain, more whites boarded. The band played as passengers shouted out hearty welcomes. Food was shared.

By the time the train reached Fayetteville, sloshing through a heavy downpour, every car was full. Even in the cool morning rain outside the train windows, white men and women lined the streets and shouted from office doorways. The men doffed their hats and the women waved handkerchiefs as the Wilmington train pulled into the station. The cornet band played a stirring tune as Wilmington's White Government Union men unfurled their ward banners from the train windows.

At the county fairgrounds outside Fayetteville, crowds had begun to form just after dawn for the largest campaign event ever held by the Democratic Party in North Carolina. People plowed through mud-slick streets in buggies, carriages, and wagons, lashed by rain. By noon, as the downpour eased, nearly eight thousand people had taken seats in the grandstands around a racetrack. They cheered the arrival of a formal procession that had left the Hotel Lafayette late that morning and was now in full view of the eager crowd.

Leading the way was the cornet band, followed by more than two hundred men on horseback, each dressed in a red shirt or jacket. Behind them came a float, mounted on a wagon and decorated with fresh flowers. Aboard were sixteen young white women with names like Pearl and Bessie and Maggie May, each representing a different Fayetteville township. The procession eased to a halt along the grandstand, where the judge's stand had been converted to a speaker's lectern. A cannon boomed out a welcome. A preacher blessed the gathering. Everyone rose to sing the state song, "The Old North State."

The day's featured speaker was a US senator—fifty-one-year-old "Pitchfork" Ben Tillman of neighboring South Carolina, a tall, spade-faced man with a perpetual scowl and a black patch over his left eye. (He had worn the patch since his left eye was destroyed by an inept surgeon who tried to carve a tumor from his face.) Tillman had earned the nickname Pitchfork four years earlier for calling President Grover

Cleveland a "bag of beef" and threatening to thrust a pitchfork through his ribs. Tillman had served as South Carolina's governor for one term and had been considered a potential Democratic presidential candidate in 1896 until a national audience began absorbing his race-baiting speeches.

Tillman was a proud white supremacist. He had once told a colleague that black women were "little better than animals." He said they did not resist the sexual advances of white men, because bearing a half-white child improved their social status. He once declared that he would prefer that one of his daughters be killed by tigers or bears "than to have her crawl to me and tell me the horrid story that she had been robbed of the jewel of her womanhood by a black fiend."

Tillman was born into violence. His father, Benjamin, was a liquor-swilling cotton plantation owner in South Carolina's Edgefield District who was once convicted of riot and assault for his part in a brawl. Young Benjamin's brother, George, shot a man dead during a card game following a dispute over a $10 bet. The Tillman family owned more than thirty slaves and treated them with contempt. Ben referred to his human property as "the most miserable lot of human beings—the nearest to the missing link with the monkeys."

Tillman rose to fame as a leader of a rifle club—a band of armed white supremacists who embarked on a violent campaign against South Carolina's black citizens in the 1870s. His proudest moment came in 1876, a pivotal election year, when he was part of an assault force of rifle clubs that descended on the black hamlet of Hamburg, South Carolina. Tillman later said that the rifle clubs had decided to "seize the first opportunity that the negroes might offer them to provoke a riot and teach the negroes a lesson . . . having the whites demonstrate their superiority by killing as many of them as was justifiable."

The white gunmen provoked a shoot-out with local black militiamen in July 1876, ultimately prevailing with the help of a cannon fired into the militiamen's drill room. Several black men were captured.

The white riflemen lined them up and, one by one, shot five of them dead with bullets to the head.

Tillman often bragged about his role in what came to be known as the Hamburg massacre. "I have nothing to conceal," he said later, adding that whites "had to shoot negroes to get relief from the galling tyranny to which we had been subjected." In 1900, Tillman boasted on the Senate floor of his role in committing election fraud and assaulting black men who attempted to vote in 1876: "We stuffed ballot boxes. We shot them. We are not ashamed of it."

It was quite a coup for Cumberland County's Democratic leadership to secure a prominent, if notorious, national figure like Tillman. The senator was eager to speak in North Carolina. He was convinced that the state's whites were too timid and too accepting of black men in office. He welcomed an opportunity to explain to them how he had helped rid South Carolina of so-called Negro rule and how they could apply the same formula in North Carolina.

From the speaker's stand on that wet October afternoon, Tillman turned his fury on the white men of North Carolina. What sort of "idiocy," he asked the men in the crowd, would permit Negroes to rule a Southern state? Tillman pointed out that the whites of South Carolina had rid themselves of "Negro domination" two decades earlier. He reminded the North Carolinians that whites outnumbered blacks in their state. Why had they succumbed to black rule?

The men and women in the audience were not offended; they seemed chastened, almost thankful for Tillman's challenge. Tillman was interrupted by applause so frequently that the short address he had planned lasted for an hour and a half. Even with the ground soggy and a soft mist settling over the crowd, no one left. Tillman brought several men in the crowd to their feet as he launched into a passionate narrative of the white supremacy campaign of 1876.

"South Carolina had Negro rule fastened on her by bayonets," he told the crowd. "The people stood it for eight years but they grew desperate and donned red shirts and got out their shotguns and took the state!"

More than three hundred Red Shirts were in the audience. They listened raptly, some of them still on horseback and others milling among the onlookers. They hooted and whistled each time Tillman mentioned white supremacy and black capitulation.

Tillman, shouting to be heard over the tumult of the crowd, pointed in the audience to the "very beautiful girls" of Cumberland County in their flowing dresses. He said they represented the purity and chastity of all white women in the state. But they had been defamed, he said, by an editorial published in Wilmington by the black editor Alex Manly.

Tillman pointed to the White Government Union men from Wilmington.

"Why didn't you kill the nigger editor who wrote that?" he screamed. "Send him to South Carolina and let him publish any such offensive stuff, and he would be killed!"

The mention of Manly aroused the Wilmington delegation. They clapped and cheered as Tillman closed his speech by reminding the crowd that there were many ways to win an election—guns and bayonets among them. He departed to a standing ovation.

The men from Wilmington boarded the train home in a festive mood, their bellies swelled with pork barbecue and sweet tea. They felt energized by Tillman's speech and inspired by the example he had set in South Carolina a generation earlier. They were enthralled by the ranks of mounted Red Shirts they had seen—with their gleaming pistols and shotguns and bands of ammunition.

Some of the Red Shirts had ridden up from South Carolina. Others were from Cumberland County surrounding Fayetteville and from other counties in southeastern North Carolina. But very few, if any, were from Wilmington. Some mounted Red Shirts had been sighted in or around the city during the 1896 campaign, but the movement had not yet taken visible hold in Wilmington in the 1898 campaign.

White men on horseback had shot or intimidated blacks in the Cape Fear country that summer. Other white vigilantes had warned blacks in Wilmington not to attempt to vote in November. And armed men were patrolling the city's streets, white kerchiefs tied around their arms. But few of Wilmington's vigilantes had yet begun to wear red shirts or jackets.

The White Government Union men on the train had just witnessed the intimidating effect of red-shirted gunmen, marching in military formation in Fayetteville. Soon after the Cape Fear and Yadkin Valley Railway train rolled back home into the port city, the wives and sisters of the men aboard began sewing shirts and jackets of red calico and silk.

CHAPTER EIGHTEEN

White-Capping

T HE N. JACOBI HARDWARE CO. on Water Street, next to the Cape Fear River, was run by twenty-eight-year-old J. N. Jacobi, a second-generation member of the family that had founded the business in 1868. The Jacobis were part of a small but influential Jewish community that had carved out a niche among Wilmington's merchant class. Until North Carolina's revised constitution in 1868, Jews had been banned from public office by the state's original constitution of 1776. By the 1890s, Jews owned most of Wilmington's dry goods stores and had built comfortable middle-class lives. In many cases, they sought to emphasize their whiteness by adopting their colleagues' white supremacist views. Among them was Silas Fishblate, a merchant and former three-term mayor of Wilmington, who boldly announced that summer: "I am with the white man every time."

So was J. N. Jacobi. He was a prominent synagogue leader who could be counted on to promote the Democratic ticket. Jacobi profited from a record boom in gun sales in the late summer of 1898 at his hardware store, which normally relied on sales of paint, lumber, and tools. Like his fellow white gun merchants, Jacobi refused to sell weapons to blacks. Nor did he sell a single shotgun or rifle or pistol to a white Republican during the campaign. He restricted his gun sales to white Democrats.

All summer, Jacobi had been reading race-baiting newspaper reports that inspired him to action. He helped draft a local resolution that compelled white business owners in Wilmington to notify their black employees that they would be fired if the Republicans won the November election. Jacobi began to take a keen interest in the political leanings of his three black employees—two men named John and Stephen, and a teenager, Richard. Jacobi summoned the workers one morning and told them to choose between their jobs and registering to vote.

"The condition of affairs under the Republican rule were such that it was becoming unbearable, and we could not possibly think of employing people who voted against us and every one of our interests," Jacobi said later.

Across Wilmington and throughout the Black Belt, black employees of white-owned businesses were given similar ultimatums as Election Day approached. On October 20, Alex Manly wrote in the *Record* that he knew of at least thirty black men who had been fired for registering to vote. It is not known whether Jacobi's black workers chose to risk their livelihoods by registering, but many other black employees decided to stay away from the polls. Even black workers not directly threatened by their bosses chose to avoid confrontations by announcing that they did not intend to register, much less vote. Some blacks who had already registered asked white voter registration officers to strike their names from the rolls.

"If a man registered, he would be discharged," John Melton, the police chief, said later. "Colored people . . . said they were not going to vote or register—that they thought more of their lives than they did of their votes or politics."

While many white employers eagerly embraced the practice, some thought it was self-defeating. Robert Mason, a cashier for the North Carolina Cotton Oil Company in Wilmington, called his black workers the "least troublesome labor we can handle . . . their natural disposition when unmolested by mean white people is to know their places and keep in them." Threatening them only drove them to mischief, Mason said.

The men who ran the white supremacy campaign were undeterred. On October 18, the *Star* reprinted Alex Manly's August editorial under the headline: A HORRID SLANDER. To refute rumors that the editorial was secretly written by Democrats to arouse white passions, the *Star* published sworn statements by five white Wilmington men, among them a bat guano merchant and a Confederate veteran. The men confirmed under oath that Manly wrote the editorial, was a Republican, and was, indeed, "a Negro," despite his Caucasian appearance.

Many black workers defied threats by their employers. Black men continued to register to vote, quietly urged on by Fusionists who sought to maximize the city's black majority—11,324 blacks to 8,731 whites. Carter Peamon, a black barber and a Republican activist, defiantly registered to vote in full view of white election officials. He also helped other black men register, confronting whites who attempted to block them.

On October 1, a white clergyman tried to prevent a black man from registering by claiming the man had been declared legally insane. Peamon objected, using what the next day's *Morning Star* described as "insolent language." A white bystander, S. Hill Terry, brandishing a jackknife, challenged Peamon, who wrestled the weapon away. Peamon told Terry he would like to "slap the jaws of every white man." The commotion attracted a crowd of nearly one hundred black men, some of whom cursed and threatened a smaller group of white men gathered at the registrar's office. The whites eventually withdrew. The next day's *Wilmington Messenger* noted the "disgraceful and outrageous conduct of the negroes."

It was the duty of Red Shirts to crush any such black resistance. Throughout the Black Belt, stretching northwest and northeast from Wilmington across the sun-scorched coastal plain, white night riders fanned out into the countryside. Many wore red shirts or vests, along with distinctive white caps, evocative of the hoods once worn by Klansmen. Scores of black farmers and laborers were roused from their beds and threatened with death if they registered to vote. Many were beaten or whipped—attacks that came to be known as "white-capping."

One incident stood out. In rural Stewartsville Township in Scotland County, ninety-five miles northwest of Wilmington, Red Shirts noticed that a forty-year-old black man named T. A. Graham had encouraged other blacks to register—and to vote Republican. Graham worked discreetly, hoping to avoid the Red Shirts who patrolled Scotland County. But one night in mid-October, he drank too much and was spotted ripping down a Democratic election poster. According to one white witness, Graham loudly swore that he would "wade through white man's blood . . . to put a negro in the post-office."

A few nights later, Graham and his wife were asleep at home when a group of white men with pistols pounded on their door. Graham hid under his bed. The men shouted, "Open the door! If you don't, we'll break it open!" Graham's wife told them her husband wasn't home. The men smashed through the door and lit a lamp. One intruder thrust his pistol in the woman's face and told her, "We must have him." They searched the house, finding Graham crouched behind his bed, still in his nightclothes.

The men dragged Graham outside. They beat him with pistol butts and whipped him across his back. Graham begged them to let him speak, but the whipping continued. Finally, the men paused to tell Graham that they had seen him rip down the Democratic poster and knew he had advised black men to vote. They asked him whether he would promise to stay away from the polls in November.

"Yes, sir," Graham responded.

Would he tell other blacks to stay away, too?

"Yes, sir. I swear," Graham said.

One of the men gave Graham five more lashes with a whip, shredding his nightclothes and flaying his back. When the man had finished, he pointed his pistol in Graham's face and told him, "By God, this is white man's country; we are going to rule it if we have to wade in blood."

Graham later said he could not identify his attackers, because it was dark, but he was certain they were Democrats. Asked how he knew, Graham replied, "I know a rat when I see his tail."

Graham did not vote in the election. He also advised his black friends not to vote—a needless gesture for many because they, too, had been whipped and beaten by white men. Graham spoke for them all: "I was whipped out of politics."

CHAPTER NINETEEN

Buckshot at Close Range

T HE RED SHIRT ATTACKS alarmed Jeter Pritchard, North Carolina's Republican US senator. An assault on any voter was an assault on democracy, Pritchard believed, and these were assaults against *his* voters. He owed his seat in Congress, in large part, to the black voters who had helped the Fusion ticket of Republicans and Populists take charge of the state legislature in 1894. He was the only Republican senator from a Southern state; Marion Butler, North Carolina's other senator, was a Populist aligned with Republicans under Fusion.

Pritchard was a heavyset man with a walrus mustache and wavy silver hair parted high on his broad forehead. He was a Tennessean, the son of a Confederate veteran. He had once worked as a newspaper editor. He looked like a prosperous Southern planter, but he had been raised in a Unionist county and staked out relatively progressive political positions. Pritchard was deeply worried about the Red Shirt rampages. If enough blacks were kept from the polls, Republicans would lose the legislature as well as local and county governments across the Black Belt, including Wilmington. On October 21, Pritchard sent a two-page typewritten letter to President McKinley, requesting federal marshals to protect black voters threatened by Red Shirts and other night riders.

Addressing McKinley as "My Dear Mr. President," Pritchard warned that Democrats were stockpiling guns and threatening and whipping blacks, who were attempting to purchase weapons of their own only to defend themselves. He told the president that there was no truth to Democratic claims of "Negro domination." He asked that his letter be kept confidential.

It was immediately leaked, and Josephus Daniels made sure Pritchard's comments were published widely. Furnifold Simmons went further: he sent Pritchard a list of black public officials in eastern North Carolina in a letter that read like an indictment. It listed thirty questions—each one prefaced with "Do you deny . . . ?" The first question: "Do you deny that there is a negro candidate running for Congress in the Second Congressional District?" Indeed, George Henry White was a US representative for the Black Second and was running for reelection. But White was hardly the vanguard of "Negro domination." He was the only black member of Congress.

Simmons's questions continued for several pages. Question four: Did Pritchard deny that Colonel James H. Young, the black commander of the state's Third Regiment of Negro soldiers, had served as fertilizer inspector "with a big salary and with white men working under him?" Question twelve mentioned "FORTY negro magistrates" in New Hanover County and "FOURTEEN negro policemen" in Wilmington.

Governor Russell tried to refute Simmons's claims of black domination. In an interview with a *Washington Post* correspondent, he said that of 170 members of the state legislature, just 17—or 10 percent—were black. For every thirty black voters in the state, Russell said, there were seventy white voters.

The correspondent asked, "What ground is there for fearing negro domination in the state?" Russell replied, "Absolutely none, and the Democrats know it." In fact, the governor said, "The negroes, as a rule, are peaceable, tractable citizens, and any disturbance that may arise on election day will not be of their inauguration."

Daniels had played Pritchard's leaked letter across the front page of the *News and Observer* under the headline: TO INVOKE BAYONET RULE. Daniels wrote, falsely, that Pritchard had requested federal troops, rather than US marshals, "to control the election in North Carolina." The article pointed out that the president could not send federal troops unless Russell requested them. And in any case, the Posse Comitatus Act, passed in 1878, prohibited the armed forces from intervening in law enforcement, with certain exceptions.

Daniels considered the governor weak and compromised. "Russell was in terror for his life," he wrote later. "He feared he might be assassinated." Even within the relative security of the capitol and the governor's mansion in Raleigh, Russell carried a loaded pistol and was accompanied everywhere by a personal bodyguard.

In Washington, Pritchard's letter was discussed during a meeting between President McKinley and his cabinet on October 24. After the session, Attorney General John W. Griggs told reporters that he would approve a request by Governor Russell for federal marshals—*if* Russell requested them. In the meantime, he said, he was dispatching an assistant attorney general to North Carolina to keep him informed on events there.

On October 26, Russell warned the state's voters that "certain North Carolina counties lying along the southern borders have been actually invaded by certain armed and lawless men." These men on horseback had so terrified certain "peaceful citizens"—Russell did not raise the issue of race—that they were afraid to register to vote. He ordered "all ill-disposed persons . . . to immediately desist from all unlawful practices and all turbulent conduct."

Russell's decree only provoked Democrats and Red Shirts. Night riders stepped up their attacks on black homes. Democratic political rallies grew more aggressive and confrontational. Civic leaders in Laurinburg set aside a day on which every male citizen was advised to wear a red shirt "until old North Carolina has been redeemed." In a front-page interview with the *News and Observer*, Democratic Party chairman Simmons promised an end to "corruption, fraud and Negroism."

In Raleigh, Daniels published a front-page cartoon by Norman Jennett depicting a Red Shirt riding a racing stallion labeled "White Rule." He crossed the finish line well ahead of a thick-lipped black man riding a wheezing nag. The caption read: "Pick the Winner."

Later that week, a group of white men confronted a distributor who transported fresh milk into Wilmington for a dairy farm operated by Russell's wife, Sarah. The deliveryman was given an ultimatum: join the white supremacy campaign or be prohibited from selling milk in Wilmington. The man complied, and deliveries of Russell's milk resumed. But the city's white newspapers quickly organized a consumer boycott that sent Sarah Russell's dairy sales plummeting.

On October 28, just two days after the governor's decree, Democrats and Red Shirts held a White Man's Convention at the county courthouse in Goldsboro, a market town on the Neuse River ninety-five miles north of Wilmington. The announced crowd of up to eight thousand was nearly as large as the Democratic gathering in Fayetteville eight days earlier. Special trains ferried white families from every county in eastern North Carolina. Three bands, including Wilmington's Second Regiment Band, greeted arrivals at the Goldsboro train station. The roads leading into the city were clogged with wagons, buggies, and carriages. Mounted Red Shirt brigades rode in procession, Winchesters held high.

The leading Democratic politicians of eastern North Carolina assembled on a grandstand erected on the courthouse lawn. At the front was Simmons, who raised a hand to quiet the music from the Second Regiment Band. He announced that the purpose of the rally was to "consider and devise plans for averting and overthrowing Negro domination." He delivered his familiar accounting of blacks in office in the state—more than a thousand, he said.

"The white people of North Carolina, irrespective of party, have determined that this Negro business has got to be stopped!" Simmons shouted. A man in the audience hollered, "We will stop it!" as others in the crowd hooted and applauded.

Simmons mentioned that Alex Manly, in his August 18 editorial, had "insulted and assailed the purity of the white women of North Carolina." There were cries of: "Lynch him! Lynch him!" Simmons went on, "We say we will protect our women with our ballots, but if we can't protect them from insults and slander, and aggression and lust, we will protect them with our strong arms." There were more cheers and shouts of: "We will rule it!"

Democrats held similar rallies almost every day across the Black Belt in the two weeks before Election Day on November 8. In Tarboro, on the Tar River 150 miles north of Wilmington, several thousand whites sat through a downpour to hear Simmons speak on October 29. In Charlotte, nearly a thousand armed Red Shirts on horseback rode in a parade that ended with a speech by Pitchfork Tillman, who proclaimed once again that Alex Manly should be food for catfish at the bottom of the Cape Fear. An overwhelmed Republican reported that "not a single colored man slept in their houses at night . . . they were afraid that they would be white-capped by the Red Shirts."

On November 1, a procession of four hundred mounted Red Shirts a mile long rode to a rally attended by several thousand whites in Laurinburg. Other Red Shirts arrived riding mules or bicycles. They wore homemade red flannel shirts sewn by their wives and daughters, with collars trimmed in blue or white.

A Northern journalist wrote: "For ten miles through pine-forest and cotton plantations these men rode, singling out the Negro hamlets as the special object of their visitation; while in the afternoon they listened to an impassioned address in which they were advised to win the election—peaceably if they could, forcibly if we must."

Red Shirts paraded through black neighborhoods and farms, brandishing their Winchesters. Several times, riders broke from the main column and galloped in circles around the cabins of black families, shouting racial slurs and unfurling a banner that read: "White Supremacy."

At the Laurinburg rally, Claude Kitchin, a Simmons deputy on the Democratic Executive Committee, told the gathering that any white man who sought the support of black voters was "a negro inside." A man in the crowd shouted, "White niggers!" Everyone laughed. Courting black votes was pointless, Kitchin told the crowd. "We don't need the nigger vote. All that we need for victory is election day."

Kitchin drew the loudest cheers of the day when he announced that any black constable in his Black Belt home county, Halifax, who attempted to arrest a white man would be lynched. "We cannot outnumber the negroes," he said. "And so we must either outcheat, outcount or outshoot them!"

In early October, the Secret Nine met at a private home at Seventh and Market Streets in Wilmington to set a date for the forced removal of the city's Fusionist government. The group operated on the assumption that Democrats, through intimidation and ballot box stuffing, would win local races for judge, solicitor, US representative, and seats in the state's house and senate on November 8. And Democrats would, of course, sweep all New Hanover County races because they had forced Governor Russell to withdraw all Republican county candidates. That would leave only the mayor's office, the police chief, the sheriff, and the board of aldermen in Fusionist hands.

The Secret Nine did not intend to wait until municipal elections in March 1899 to seize those positions. The group decided to allow two days to pass peacefully after Election Day, in order to solidify Democratic control of the state and county. The revolution, as the Secret Nine called it, was scheduled for November 10, a Thursday—to be confirmed after a day of "watching and waiting" on November 9. The group decided that on the morning of November 10, the full firepower of the Red Shirt brigades, the gunmen of the Vigilance Committee, and, if required, the Wilmington Light Infantry and the Naval Reserves would be unleashed against Negro rule.

CHAPTER TWENTY

A Drunkard and a Gambler

OLONEL WADDELL was not part of the Secret Nine's planning. Nor was he a member of Group Six, the other clandestine group of white supremacists. The Colonel had made political enemies in Wilmington with his imperious personality and grating pontification. Not all of the city's leading Democrats were pleased by his prominent role as a long-winded speaker at Democratic campaign rallies. He called himself a lawyer, but he didn't have a functioning law office. In fact, he didn't hold a job of any type. His wife, Gabrielle, taught music lessons to earn cash for the household.

Waddell's political enemies joked that his only real accomplishment was marrying well. His first wife, Julia Savage, was the daughter of a wealthy Wilmington family. In 1878, after Julia died, Waddell married her sister, Ellen Savage. A year after Ellen died in 1895, Waddell married Gabrielle DeRosset, a member of a prominent slaveholding rice plantation family in Wilmington, who had been sent to live with her father's family after her mother died of a self-administered opium overdose. She was thirty-three; he was sixty-two. DeRosset brought to the marriage an unassailable Confederate pedigree. Her parents were Confederate stalwarts who paid blockade-runners to supply goods to a family company in Wilmington from their base in Bermuda during the war. As an infant, Gabrielle had been aboard a blockade-runner shattered by Union cannonballs and rockets just off the coast. She and her mother were rescued by an ambulance dispatched from the Confederate garrison at Fort Fisher.

Waddell was a calculating man who carefully weighed his choices. He often waited to act until he determined that circumstances were fully in his favor—as he had just before the war, when he transformed himself from Unionist to Confederate. He knew how to fill a political vacuum—as he had done in Wilmington just after the war, when he wrote to the governor to complain about freed slaves and colored troops, then lectured the city's blacks in public, even as Union troops controlled the city.

Waddell's best years were the 1870s, when he was elected to Congress for four terms. He rose to prominence in 1871 as a member of a US congressional committee investigating Klan lynchings and murders in the South, known to the committee as "the late insurrectionary states." The committee documented hundreds of abuses by the Klan in Waddell's home state, North Carolina. Testimony at the committee's hearings described a ghastly onslaught of hangings, floggings, burnings, clubbings, and throat slittings. Waddell, who had supported the Klan, worked hard to undermine his own committee.

The committee concluded that the leader of the Klan in North Carolina was Colonel William L. Saunders, the former Confederate officer from Wilmington, where the Klan first appeared in the state. Saunders, called to testify, was confronted by several committee members. But he repeatedly refused to answer when asked about his membership in or leadership of the Ku Klux Klan—or the Invisible Empire or the White Brotherhood or any "secret political organizations" in North Carolina. Saunders told the committee that he was not obliged to answer questions, because, in doing so, "I may criminate myself." He was excused.

While in Washington, Saunders stayed at the home of a committee member—Congressman Waddell. Waddell stoutly defended his fellow

Confederate cavalry officer and old friend from Wilmington. Waddell called his own committee "a body of relentless prosecutors . . . trying to extort evidence that would convict prominent citizens of the South." He complained that Saunders "was badgered and bullied, and threatened with imprisonment . . . but with perfect self-possession, and calm politeness he continued to say 'I decline to answer.'" He considered Saunders "as brave and true a man as ever lived." He informed the committee that its final report on the Klan was "a waste of paper and ink."

The two men from Wilmington left the hearings in triumph.

Waddell was a man who fought back when challenged. In 1876, he had enlisted friends in Wilmington to ambush a Republican newspaper editor who had criticized him. Writing in the *Wilmington Post*, the editor, Jesse J. Cassidey, had accused Waddell of welshing on a gambling debt, describing him as "a drunkard and a gambler." Cassidey challenged the colonel to deny "being drunk at a public dinner" or that he "rode down Pennsylvania Avenue with a woman that *he knew* had a questionable character." These were startling accusations against a US congressman, even one as abrasive as Waddell. They stung even more sharply after Cassidey mocked Waddell as "the cultivated gentleman, the ripe scholar, the rare statesman."

Waddell rushed home to Wilmington from Washington to respond in person. He laid a trap for Cassidey. On the night of May 1, 1876, while a group of Waddell's friends stood by in the shadows, Waddell attacked Cassidey on a Wilmington street. "Without notice or warning," Waddell poleaxed the unsuspecting editor with a club, the *Post* reported the next day. To ensure that no one came to Cassidey's aid, Waddell's friends emerged from alleyways—"as if by magic," the *Post* said. Cassidey later complained that he was prevented from "placing a pistol ball in [Waddell's] carcass" by the congressman's "ruffians and bullies." Waddell was hauled into court and fined $10. He paid on the spot, then returned to Washington.

The feud did not end there. The *Post*, questioning why the penalty for an assault with intent to kill was a mere $10, condemned Waddell for a "cowardly and scoundrelly attack." Cassidey tracked down Waddell in Washington on May 13 and, he claimed, thumped him twice with a cane. Waddell's brother and friends retaliated by breaking Cassidey's nose and blacking his eye. Cassidey later reported that he gave Waddell a solid kick during the melee.

Again, Cassidey was not finished with Waddell. Back in Wilmington, he wrote in the *Post* that he had earlier called Waddell a "gambler, a drunkard and a defaulter." He went on: "I now make the statement that he is a liar." The episode added another layer of uncertainty to Waddell's muddled reputation in Wilmington. For much of his life, he fought to reconcile his stature as a member of the Cape Fear gentry in good standing—a respected lawyer and an admired orator—with the nagging sense among some in town that he was a man who could not be fully trusted and would, literally, club you from behind.

Two years later, Waddell's political career was derailed. He lost his 1878 reelection campaign to his Republican rival in Wilmington, Daniel Russell, the future governor. Waddell had been slowed by illness, and he was outmaneuvered by Russell, who elicited the support of black voters while also attracting the votes of poor white farmers frustrated by their lot under Democratic politicians. Waddell recovered his health and rebounded from his defeat by editing a newspaper in Charlotte for two years, until 1882, but then fell on hard times.

By the summer of 1898, Waddell was desperate for political relevance in Wilmington. John Melton, the police chief, thought Waddell was clinging to the past, struggling to retain the status and influence he had enjoyed in the years after the Civil War.

"I think the biggest object Colonel Waddell had was to get a position and office," Melton said. "He had been out of public life for a long time, and that was his opportunity to put himself before the people and pose as a patriot, thereby getting to the feed trough." Waddell seemed to be forever reaching for that moment, that singular event that would restore him to a position of respect and even reverence. With the white supremacy campaign of 1898, he had found it.

Waddell had begun to earn his way back to prominence by volunteering to deliver white supremacist campaign speeches in the Cape Fear countryside. In October, he offered to give a rousing speech downtown denouncing Negro rule, but he was rebuffed by the city's Democratic leadership. The party did not want to provide Waddell with a prominent public platform inside the city; several leading whites seemed threatened by Waddell's oratory skills.

One day in mid-October, the Colonel encountered George Rountree on the street. Waddell complained that the white men in charge of the campaign didn't seem to want or need his help. They didn't think he had any value to them, he said. Rountree was wary of Waddell, but he also believed Waddell could be useful in rousing white men to action with Election Day approaching.

Later that week, Rountree suggested to the city's Democratic leadership that the time had come for Waddell to deliver a "red hot speech." There was some resistance, but Rountree ultimately prevailed. Most Democrats acknowledged that if anyone could fire up the city's white men, it was Waddell. The Colonel would be permitted to deliver a speech.

Rountree took the offer to Waddell, who eagerly accepted. But he was still stung by earlier rejections by the city's white leadership. He insisted—and Rountree agreed—that the Democratic campaign committee make a formal written request. The committee grudgingly complied. Waddell later bragged to friends that he had been begged to make a speech by the men who ruled Wilmington.

CHAPTER TWENTY-ONE

Choke the Cape Fear
with Carcasses

O N THE MILD AUTUMN EVENING of October 24, 1898, Colonel Waddell stood on a worn wooden stage inside Wilmington's antebellum Thalian Hall, basking in applause beneath an ornately carved ceiling and bathed in the silver glow of a chandelier. In front of the stage, a throng of white men raised their arms in celebration and implored the Colonel to speak. Waddell was pleased to hear them chanting his name: "Colonel! Colonel Waddell!"

Nearly a thousand men and a few women had squeezed into Thalian Hall. Clusters of grimy young men swarmed onto the parquet and across the galleries, packed alongside fellow citizens dressed in dark suits. Large audiences weren't unusual at this majestic New Revival–style hall on Chestnut Street, built by slaves and free blacks. "Buffalo Bill" Cody, Frederick Douglass, Oscar Wilde, the dwarf Tom Thumb, and other late-nineteenth-century luminaries had performed to full houses there; for a while it was the largest theater south of Richmond. But this gathering was different. Its members had a common cause. They had assembled to plot a white revolution. And Colonel Waddell, scion of slave owners, ineffectual army officer, struggling lawyer, aspiring newspaperman, and former Democratic congressman, was to show the way.

This was the night when all the rage and resentment simmering in white men in Wilmington since Reconstruction would be stoked by the words of a former Confederate officer. Waddell, more than any other member of the city's white leadership, believed he was the man best suited to articulate the fears and grievances of his race. And now, thirty-three years after the end of the Civil War and twenty-one years after the close of Reconstruction, Waddell urged the white men of Wilmington to take back the privileges of race that they believed, deep in their hearts, were rightfully theirs.

In the gallery directly below the Colonel's gaze stood several dozen young men crammed into the front rows. They were in a festive mood. Many of them wore red shirts or vests of calico or silk. Earlier that evening, the Red Shirts had marched to Thalian Hall in military formation. They could not help being seen by the firemen of the all-black Company Three of the Cape Fear Steam Fire Engine station along the way. The black men watched in silence. Then the Red Shirts paraded loudly up Front Street, past the swirling brown Cape Fear River amid the sharp stench of turpentine and the sour smell of rotting vegetation and sewage.

Inside Thalian Hall, the men's rough faces were slick with sweat. They wanted inspiration—not a routine campaign speech but an impassioned tribute to white supremacy. They wanted to hear it from the man the local newspapers were now calling the "silver-tongued orator of the East." The next day's *Wilmington Messenger* described Waddell's address as "a sizzling talk . . . that will ring for all time in the ears of those who heard it." The Colonel was sixty-five and slightly stooped, but he could still deliver a mesmerizing speech.

Waddell stood upon the Thalian Hall stage, absorbing the cheers as the county Democratic Party chairman offered a florid introduction.

Seated around the Colonel were sixty men who considered themselves the leading white citizens of Wilmington, dressed in suits and sober neckties. Some had brought their wives, who dressed as if for a formal occasion. Waddell spoke for them all.

The Colonel typically delivered orations without copious notes, for he considered himself an accomplished orator who spoke from conviction, not rote. He could go on without pause for an hour or more, rarely tiring, his voice perfectly modulated and rising when he described the nobility and purity of the white race.

On the stage, Waddell waited for the men below him to stop shouting and whistling. And then he spoke:

"It is just, and right, and absolutely best and wisest for both races that the white people who settled this country, and civilized it . . . and who have done more for the Negro race than all the other peoples who have ever lived upon the earth, should alone govern it . . . It is their country and they have a right to rule it. It will be absolutely suicidal for the Negroes to continue to resist this inevitable result . . .

"The Negro was a slave and was brought here as such," Waddell went on. "Is this his country? For 3,000 years the Negro has had a whole continent to himself, and it is in the same condition now as it was at the beginning, except where white settlements have been made. He has never, during all these 30 centuries, exhibited any capacity for self-government . . . Whenever he has been civilized by white men and then left to himself, he has invariably reverted to a condition of savagery."

His voice was drowned out by a torrent of shouts and applause.

After speaking for nearly an hour, Waddell still held the audience's attention. Most of the Red Shirts and the white patricians and their wives knew what he intended to say next; they had read newspaper accounts of his speeches in the countryside. Waddell had carefully honed his own white supremacist message to dovetail with their vision of an imaginary white utopia, and it thrilled them to hear their deepest convictions expressed so elegantly, and with such passion.

"Here, in the most quiet and conservative of the original 13 states and at the end of the 19th century," he said, "we are reduced to the pitiful necessity of choosing whether we will live under the domination of Negroes led by a few unprincipled white men, and see the ruin of all that we hold dear—or prove ourselves worthy of the respect of mankind by restoring good government at all hazards or any cost."

If violence was required, he said, "I trust that it will be rigidly and fearlessly performed."

Waddell's voice strained to reach a higher pitch. "If a race conflict occurs in North Carolina, the very first men that ought to be held to account are the white leaders of the Negroes!" he shouted. And the leader of those white men, Waddell said, was Governor Russell—"the engineer of all the deviltry and meanness!" There were more shouts.

For several more minutes, the colonel railed against black voters and black domination. He complained that blacks throughout the South now looked to the black men of North Carolina for leadership and inspiration. Regrettably, Wilmington now stood before the nation as a shameful "Negro paradise."

The colonel's voice was like an engine that had reached top cruising speed. His words flowed effortlessly, powered by the certainty of his beliefs and fanned by the passions of those who shared them. The men in the crowd begged for more.

"The people are aroused!" Waddell said, shouting now. "Shall we surrender to a ragged rabble of Negroes, led by a handful of white cowards . . . No! A thousand times no! . . . We will have no more of the intolerable conditions under which we live. We are resolved to change them if we have to choke the Cape Fear with carcasses!"

The image of black corpses floating in the river all the way to the sea brought the white men to their feet at the close of Waddell's address.

They roared and raised their fists. Some of them rushed the stage to shake the Colonel's hand and slap him on the back.

The men shouted for lawyer George Rountree to deliver a few remarks. Rountree had been sitting among the sixty select white men on the stage. He was tall and slender, with a bald skull and a narrow face adorned with an unruly mustache. He waved away the request to speak. He possessed no words to improve upon what he had just heard. He knew it was foolish to follow an orator like Waddell. Rountree could only say what every white man in Thalian Hall was thinking that night: "The time has come to quit talking. The time has come to act."

The next morning, the *Messenger* declared Waddell's speech "the most remarkable delivery ever heard in a campaign here in the memory of this generation." Waddell later boasted that the speech had "started the fire" that restored white supremacy in Wilmington. It was reprinted in several North Carolina newspapers. Even white women were inspired. "These blond women are terrible when their fighting blood is up," Waddell's cousin, Rebecca Cameron, wrote to the Colonel.

Journalist Henry Litchfield West, dispatched to Wilmington by the *Washington Post* to report on an anticipated "race war," described the city that week as an armed camp:

> Wilmington might be preparing for a siege instead of an election. The citizens are armed and make no secret of that fact. There is a new Gatling gun in the local armory, and 2,000 Winchester rifles are said, on reliable authority, to be distributed among private residences. In each block of the city is a lieutenant, while every six blocks is in charge of a captain. Each block has its place of refuge already selected, to which the women and children can flee for safety when the race war breaks out.

West provided a succinct summary of white intentions: "(1) The Negro must either be frightened away from the polls or else (2) he must be forcibly resisted when he undertook to deposit his ballot."

On November 3, just five days before the election, Red Shirts held their first formal rally in Wilmington. Some of their shirts and jackets had been provided by the local Democratic Party, which also supplied food and drink. Rosin and tar were set alight in barrels at dusk in a public square known as Hilton Park, coating the park's twisted live oak branches with an oily sheen. The fires sent up curls of colored smoke and bathed the gathering of several hundred families in a crimson glow. Women arrived with picnic baskets heaped with chopped pork barbecue. Children, let out of school for the day, ran through the grass.

Directing one of the Red Shirt brigades that evening was Mike Dowling, a hard-drinking, brawling Irishman who found occasional work as a laborer. Dowling lived in Dry Pond, a working-class neighborhood populated by Irish immigrants and a smattering of black workers. Some blacks called poor Irishmen *buckra*, or *bocra*, which roughly meant "white nigger." Men of both races competed for unskilled jobs, and the Irish often complained that the city's white merchants favored black workers over whites because blacks accepted lower pay and made fewer demands. Dowling and other Red Shirts often pressed leaders of the white supremacy campaign for public guarantees of white preference in hiring.

A parade of nearly one hundred mounted Red Shirts rode from the downtown business district through the predominately black neighborhood of Brooklyn. The commander of the city's armed white men was Roger Moore, who had adopted the title of chief marshal and rode the streets on horseback. When the procession passed the modest home of the mayor, Silas Wright, some of the Red Shirts pointed their Winchesters and hollered, "Hang Wright!"

Most black residents stayed home, their doors locked, as the Red Shirts whooped and shouted in the dim light. A few black men lined up on the sidewalks, watching sullenly. One Red Shirt rode an oxcart, pistol in hand. "Nearly every man produced a pistol from his hip pocket, pointed it in the air and pulled the trigger. The air was blue with smoke," a correspondent from the *Richmond Times* wrote. Shots were fired into the home of at least one black family and, later, into a schoolhouse for black children that was closed for the evening.

The procession ended at Hilton Park, where plates of barbecue were served picnic style. The mood was festive, like a carnival. Democratic politicians delivered sour speeches complaining of the "negro problem."

Mike Dowling organized a chant: "Three Cheers for White Supremacy!" Some of Dowling's men were drunk. Dowling once bragged that he provided his Red Shirts with whiskey prior to parades to "fire them up, and make them fiercer and more terrorizing in their conduct." A Republican poll watcher chased out of Wilmington at gunpoint by drunken Red Shirts called it "fighting whiskey."

Josephus Daniels was not in Wilmington that day, but he had seen plenty of Red Shirt rallies that summer and fall. He was thrilled by the singularly terrorizing effect on black families of armed white men on horseback:

If you have never seen three hundred red-shirted men towards sunset with the sky red and the red shirts seeming to blend with the sky, you cannot conceive what an impression it makes. It looked like the whole world was carmine. They usually rode horses and had weapons, and their appearance was the signal for the Negroes to get out of the way, so that when the Red Shirt brigade passed through the Negro end of town it was as uninhabited to all appearances as if it had been a graveyard. That was the psychology of the Red Shirt parade . . . many Negroes either did not vote or made no fight in the affected counties on election day.

The next evening, November 4, a gang of Red Shirts from the Fifth Ward encountered a handful of black men on Front Street in downtown Wilmington. The white men were still energized by the rowdy parade the previous night. Two black men were stabbed with swords. Several more were clubbed and pistol-whipped. A white resident named James S. Worth wrote to his wife that the Red Shirts "tackled every nigger that came along regardless and ran several across the street and into nearby alleys."

The next day, one of the city's Democratic newspapers complained that the Red Shirts had "ran amuck," and thus preempted carefully laid plans by the secret committees to forestall violence until after Election Day. The Red Shirts were quietly advised that the opportune time to incite a race riot had not yet arrived.

CHAPTER TWENTY-TWO

The Shepherds Will Have
Nowhere to Flee

I N THE WEEKS LEADING up to the November election, some blacks
in the Black Belt attempted to fight back against white intimidation. On the night of October 31, for instance, black residents
of Williamston, a farm market town on the Roanoke River 143 miles
north of Wilmington, marched through the streets and fired guns to
protest attacks and intimidation by white supremacists. In response,
the town's white leaders called an emergency meeting to authorize the
formation of a white militia, which promptly restored control.

In Edgecombe County, five counties north of Wilmington, a black
candidate for statewide office urged a gathering of blacks in early October to confront white supremacists: "Go to the elections well armed,
with rocks in your pockets, clubs in your hands, and carry your pistols.
And don't allow any officer to arrest you after you have registered until
the day after the election, unless you have stolen something or killed
somebody."

And in New Bern a week before the election, a black-run weekly
published an editorial that infuriated the white supremacists who dominated the city: "Every lover of political liberty, every negro who loves his
mother and father, his wife and children, and is opposed to Democratic

slavery, bury white supremacy next Tuesday face downwards in order that it may never rise again to vilify the negro."

These and other displays of resistance by black men in the autumn of 1898 were quickly crushed by white men with guns. No attempt by black men to register to vote or to defy white authority or to exercise rights guaranteed by the Constitution lasted very long—not in Williamston or Edgecombe County or New Bern and certainly not in Wilmington.

Simply registering to vote required supreme courage and sustained fortitude in the face of white intimidation inflamed by newspaper coverage. Whites seemed more menacing every day. On many nights, small bands of Red Shirts rode through black neighborhoods, firing Winchesters into the air. White gunmen intensified their patrols through the city's predominately black neighborhoods. Black families who normally sat outside on sweltering summer evenings, when sluggish breezes drifted in from the Cape Fear, remained indoors, sweaty and afraid.

Blacks struggled to maintain a veneer of normalcy as they braced for violence. The *Daily Record* offered little solace. Alex Manly's newspaper reported the news of the day but did not delve deeply into sensitive matters of race and politics after the August 18 editorial. Manly and his brother Frank continued to receive death threats. At evening meetings of White Government Unions, white citizens spoke openly of lynching both men.

The Manlys received no support from the state Republican Party, which denied any connection to the "negro named Manly." On November I, a party statement denounced Manly's "impudent and villainous" editorial. It dismissed the *Record* as "a kicking, disorganizing concern . . . edited by an irresponsible upstart."

The black ministers who had previously defended Manly had now abandoned him. In churches, ministers advised their parishioners not to provoke whites. They recited biblical verses about peace and reconciliation.

Manly himself refused to believe that his white neighbors would turn their weapons on blacks. In a front-page commentary titled "What Is There to Fear?" on October 20, he urged *Record* readers to register to vote despite intimidation by white vigilantes. Manly seemed convinced that the better element among the city's white men would not condone violence. "Don't get mad at all the white people . . . we have friends among them yet and they are not all in the Republican Party," he wrote. He reprinted sections of the state's election laws prohibiting violence or intimidation, as if North Carolina's laws applied equally to whites and blacks.

Manly instructed his readers to put their faith in the city's white men of honor: "We have here a class of people who delight in law and order, who will not lend aid to any act of violence . . . Sober, honorable white people in this city, are not at all responsible for these threats and happily they constitute the large majority of our white citizens."

Nor should blacks be alarmed by the threats issued almost daily in the city's white newspapers, Manly wrote. He seemed to have persuaded himself that white men who stockpiled guns and promised to clog the Cape Fear with black carcasses were merely spouting inflammatory but ultimately harmless campaign rhetoric.

"They have talked freely of forcing their way to election, and to those who are not familiar with the people of this city they get the impression that there is danger of bloodshed and riot," Manly wrote on October 20. "We say now as we have said: that there is no danger in this sort of thing."

Manly's assurances had little effect. During the first week of November, black leaders organized a public gathering in response to the fears and anxieties coursing through black neighborhoods. They turned to the city's leading black lawyer, William Henderson, who had built a reputation as a man willing to challenge white authority. Earlier that summer, he had urged blacks to register, telling them: "We have a Republican

Sheriff, a Republican Mayor, the Governor is with us, and we have a Republican President. If we can't get protection now, we can never get it."

But now, surrounded by his frightened neighbors the week of the election, Henderson counseled caution. He suggested that life might return to normal after the election if whites could somehow be appeased. For the sake of "peace and good order," he said, blacks should accept the deal imposed on Governor Russell by Democrats—the abject surrender of county Republican elected offices in return for vague promises of electoral peace.

"Go to the polls and cast ballots quietly and go home," Henderson told the crowd. Some in the gathering accepted his advice, though reluctantly. Others grumbled and made plans to collect as many old revolvers and shotguns as they could find in the very likely event that they had to defend their homes.

Henderson's pleas caught the attention of the Reverend Peyton Hoge, pastor of the First Presbyterian Church, where many members of Wilmington's planter aristocracy worshipped. Hoge was an ardent white supremacist who often carried a gun. At the request of Democratic politicians, he and other white ministers preached white supremacy to their congregations. Hoge cited two Bible chapters recommended by the politicians:

In the evening—sudden terror! Before morning—it is gone! This is the fate of those who plunder us and the lot of those who ravage us.
—Isaiah 17:14

The shepherds will have nowhere to flee, the leaders of the flock no place to escape.
—Jeremiah 25:35

On November 5, Hoge mentioned Henderson's speech in a letter to Governor Russell. He assured the governor that the election would pass peacefully "if negroes do as Henderson advised them: go to the polls and cast their ballots quietly and go home; I have no idea that there will be any disturbance."

* * *

Black citizens assaulted by Red Shirts had nowhere to turn for help. Ten black men served on the city police force, and four more were deputy sheriffs, but they were in no position to confront white authority. The city's newspapers accused black officers of harassing law-abiding white men while permitting blacks to flout the law. "The Sambos do not wait to be threatened or assaulted but they take the initiative and assault to kill from the start," the *Messenger* wrote.

In September, five black Republicans had approached Gizzard French, the chief deputy sheriff, proposing that he fire his four black deputies. By sacrificing a few blacks, they hoped, they might save the jobs of the rest. French had reluctantly fired all four deputies, hoping that would satisfy the city's white leadership. But his capitulation only encouraged leaders of the white supremacy campaign to pressure Governor Russell to fire even more black officers. Russell succumbed. He gambled that removing more black officers would help blunt Democratic charges of "Negro rule." He ordered Mayor Wright to fire "incompetent" black police officers. Wright suspended six black officers and replaced them with five white men chosen by Democrats.

Fusionists tried to fight back. They distributed circulars urging black men to defy Red Shirt threats and register to vote. Democrats responded by threatening to revoke their county election deal with Governor Russell if the circulars continued. Russell decided to keep the circulars, but he softened their message. New circulars dictated by the governor ordered blacks to honor an election deal that had betrayed them:

> *Listen to us! Do not encourage any attempt to depart from the agreement made with the merchants and business men . . . These merchants and business men have given their word that there shall be a free and fair and peaceful election . . . Do not hang around the polls on Election Day, vote and go to your homes.*

The boldest public challenge to white supremacists came from a group of black women who banded together as "An Organization of Colored Ladies." They were workingwomen—maids, nannies, laundrywomen—exasperated by black men who were too cowed by whites to register to vote. Some of the same women had organized an earlier campaign to compel white streetcar conductors to extend their arms to assist black women on and off the cars. White conductors typically stood aside as black women carrying packages struggled on the streetcars' high steps. Their campaign had no effect; white conductors continued to assist white women only.

On October 21, the women turned their attention to black men and the vote. They delivered an indignant letter to Alex Manly at the *Record* office, venting their anger not on white supremacists but on their own menfolk. They recognized that their husbands and brothers had been emasculated by the white power structure—at home, in the workplace, in politics. The women challenged them to reassert their manhood.

Whereas, since it has become apparent that there is a disposition to intimidate the voting element of our race by discharging them from various places of employment in the event that they register to vote, and whereas it has come to the notice of us, the colored ladies—the laboring class . . . we have therefore resolved that every negro who refuses to register his name next Saturday that he may vote, we shall make it our business to deal with him in a way that will not be pleasant. He shall be branded a white livered coward who would sell his liberty and the liberty of our whole race to the demons who are even now seeking to take the most sacred rights vouchsafed to any people.

We are further resolved that we teach our daughters to recognize only those young men who have the courage and manhood to stand up for the liberty which under God he now has . . . Be it resolved further that we have these resolutions published in our Daily Record, the one medium that has stood up for our rights when others have forsaken us.

On the afternoon of November 5, the Saturday before the Tuesday election, Mayor Wright called a special meeting of the city board of aldermen. He announced that temporary measures would be required to maintain order on Election Day. Liquor was one issue; the mayor wanted to make it difficult for Red Shirt brigades to obtain alcohol. The board unanimously passed an ordinance closing all saloons and taverns from Saturday at 6:00 p.m. until the following Thursday at 6:00 a.m.

The city's small police force was another concern. To bolster the force, the ordinance authorized Mayor Wright to appoint one hundred special police officers for the five-day period. How the officers were to be selected—or their race or political party—was not specified.

The city's white newspapers continued to warn of a black riot on Election Day. They reported that black preachers were exhorting their congregations to stockpile weapons and attack whites in their homes. Some articles claimed that black servants planned to burn down their masters' homes, as the black Pinkerton detectives had reported. The *Messenger* predicted a "bloody conflict between the races" and the specter of "terrified women and children flying from burning houses."

Visiting Northern reporters shared meals and drank whiskey with the city's leading white supremacists, absorbing their indignation and rage. The correspondents were often met at their hotels by a "welcoming committee" of white men who handed out cigars and offered to facilitate their reporting. Some reporters accepted invitations to stay in white homes. The whites made sure the correspondents did not interview black leaders—not that the white journalists, even the Northerners, were inclined to seek out black viewpoints.

Washington Post correspondent Henry Litchfield West was cheered with cries of "Hip, hip, hooray!" while covering a Red Shirt rally in Wilmington the first week of November. West reported white men's musings as fact. He published a rambling account, "Race War in North Carolina," in *Forum* magazine, a current-events monthly in New York. The typical black man of North Carolina, West concluded, was "thriftless, improvident, does not accumulate money, and is not accounted a desirable citizen." Black men also were prone to violence, he wrote.

[I]t was expected that the Negroes, when they learned that the right of suffrage was to be denied to them, would resist. From their churches and their lodges had come

reports of incendiary speeches, of impassioned appeals to the blacks to use the bullet that had no respect for color, and the kerosene and the torch that would play havoc with the white man's cotton in bale and warehouse.

It was this fear of the Negro uprising in defence of his electorate—of a forcible and revengeful retaliation—that offered an ostensible ground for the general display of arms; but if the truth be told, the reason thus offered was little more than a fortunate excuse. The whites had been determined to regain their supremacy . . . There would have been rapid-fire guns and Winchester rifles if every church had held a silent pulpit, and every lodge-room where the Negroes met had been empty.

The night before the election, black ministers attempted to refute claims that they were inciting mob violence. They called on all black residents of Wilmington to observe a day of fasting and prayer, intended to assure whites that their black neighbors sought a peaceful election. Even as white gunmen patrolled their neighborhoods, the preachers went home that evening and retired to their beds, still trusting that prayers alone might achieve a lasting peace.

In Washington, DC, black leaders had received reports of an imminent white riot in Wilmington. Even from 360 miles away, they correctly interpreted white supremacist intentions. They had only to read Wilmington's white newspapers, whose breathless accounts were reprinted in Northern newspapers. The fate of black voters in North Carolina, and elsewhere in the South, was a national issue because of widespread attacks and intimidation. In Washington, a committee of black leaders wrote to President McKinley warning of a catastrophe unless the federal government intervened with a show of force.

North Carolina's black congressman, George H. White, visited the White House to personally inform McKinley of white supremacist plans to violently overthrow Wilmington's Fusionist government. White described for the president "the unholy war that Democrats are making on the color line." He explained that white supremacists had concocted spurious claims of Negro rule to incite whites to violence.

"The cry of negro domination is a bugaboo. There has never been Negro domination in any county in the State," White told reporters as he left the meeting with McKinley.

During the first week of November, the Second Baptist Church in Washington, DC, held a symposium titled "The Race War at the South: Its Effects upon the Nation." A committee of black ministers was appointed to appeal to McKinley to intervene in "the farce that is about to be enacted in the state of North Carolina."

There was no response from the White House. The *Wilmington Messenger* quoted an official at the War Department in Washington as saying that no federal marshals would be sent to North Carolina. President McKinley, the official said, believed any federal intervention would be a "fatal mistake."

In Wilmington, White Government Union clubs from the city's white wards gathered at the courthouse on Monday, November 7. A correspondent for the *Washington Evening Star* called it "the most remarkable political meeting which has been held in the United States in this campaign." Several hundred men jammed the main meeting room. After a rousing speech by Colonel Waddell, the clubs requested that all businesses employing Democrats close for Election Day to allow workers to vote.

Separately, twenty-five club members were assigned to spend Election Day as "observers" at each polling place in the city. For white wards, they were told to round up every white man they could find and escort him to the polls with instructions to vote Democratic. They were told to "never look a man square in the face, even if they knew that John Smith was voting as Willie James and the latter was dead and buried in Oakdale cemetery for lo many years."

For the city's two gerrymandered black wards, they were instructed to challenge any black man attempting to vote. Finally, club members were assigned to go to each ward in the evening, when ballot boxes were to be opened and votes counted by election officials of both parties. They were drilled on the most efficient ways to remove Republican ballots and replace them with phony Democratic ballots.

After Waddell left the White Government Union meeting that Monday evening, he walked to Thalian Hall, where he had been asked to reprise his October 24 "Cape Fear carcasses" speech. This time, the gathering was even larger, with armed Red Shirts joined by White Government Union men and throngs of white sentries from the nearby wards. The cheers for the Colonel were deafening.

"Men, the crisis is upon us," Waddell began. "You must do your duty. This city, county and state shall be rid of negro domination, once and forever. You have the courage. You are brave. You are the sons of noble ancestry. You are Anglo-Saxons."

He was interrupted by shouts and applause.

"You are armed and prepared, and you will do your duty," he continued. "Be ready at a moment's notice. Go to the polls tomorrow and if you find the negro out voting, tell him to leave the polls. And if he refuses, kill him! Shoot him down in his tracks!"

As Waddell walked off the stage to a standing ovation, a steamship from New York slipped into the port of Wilmington a few blocks away. On board was the Hotchkiss rapid-fire gun.

The weapon was delivered late that night to the Naval Reserves billet, where members of the unit were asleep on the floor, their rifles stacked nearby, loaded and ready. Among them were White Government Union members who had cheered Waddell's speech. Some still wore white WGU buttons on their lapels.

At the Wilmington Light Infantry armory on Market Street, a few blocks away, the Colt rapid-fire gun had been mounted on a wagon, ready for service the next morning. Inside, in the dark, so many militiamen were spread across the floor, using overcoats as pillows, that their officers could not walk across the armory without stepping on their sleeping forms.

CHAPTER TWENTY-THREE

A Pitiful Condition

ELECTION DAY dawned bright and clear in Wilmington on Tuesday, November 8. It was a typical early autumn day in the Cape Fear country, with the warm residue of summer carried by a mild breeze off the river and the sun low and brilliant in the sky. Voters were out early, walking in small groups toward the polls for the 7:00 a.m. opening. Both blacks and whites were tentative and anxious, but for different reasons. Many whites believed newspaper accounts of black plots to attack and burn white homes and businesses. Black men, who had endured intimidation and beatings all summer, braced for more as they made their way to the polls.

White newspapers advised black men not to vote. Under the headline GONE TO THE NIGGERS, the *Messenger* published the lyrics to "Rise Ye Sons of Carolina," the anthem of the White Supremacy Campaign.

Proud Caucasians one and all . . .
Hear your wives and daughters call . . .
Rise, defend their spotless virtue
With your strong and manly arms . . .
Rise and drive this Black despoiler from your state.

Red Shirts paraded on horseback, occasionally firing Winchesters into the air. They were careful not to show their rifles and shotguns at polling places, where weapons were prohibited. Some white sentries gathered unarmed at the polls. Others tucked pistols in their belts and tied white handkerchiefs to their biceps as they patrolled predominantly black neighborhoods.

White gunmen accosted blacks at gunpoint in some wards, forcing them to turn back as they tried to reach polling stations. "Pistols were held in the faces of Negro poll holders who had to leave to save their lives . . . and they knew not what moment they would be killed," the Reverend J. Allen Kirk, a black minister, wrote later.

A correspondent for the *Washington Evening Star*, after a walking tour of black wards, wrote in a front-page dispatch: "There were not a half dozen Negroes to be seen in the vicinity of the polls. It was said that in former years they would gather in hundreds about the voting places. There is no doubt that the negroes have been thoroughly overawed by the preparations which have been made by the whites to carry the election."

Several black men later complained to federal officials that they had been accosted and turned away before they could vote or were told by white election officials that they were not properly registered. Many others chose to avoid confrontation and stayed home. Benjamin Keith, a white Populist grocer, described his black neighbors as "frightened into a pitiful condition, asking their white friends not to let them be hurt."

But other black men gambled, hoping to avoid white gunmen by voting early and then quickly retreating—as the lawyer William Henderson had advised. All morning, black figures hustled down side roads and ducked through alleys to reach voting sites. Many managed to vote, especially in predominately black wards, where white sentries were less eager to patrol. By the *Washington Evening Star* reporter's count, 1,419 black men had registered in the gerrymandered black First Ward, with

820 casting votes. In the other black ward, the Fifth, 538 black men voted out of 763 who had registered.

The man from the *Evening Star*, along with other Northern correspondents—from the *New York Times*, the *Washington Post*, *Collier's Weekly*, and others—braced for the anticipated black riot. They reported that the Wilmington Light Infantry and the Naval Reserves were on alert, with some men billeted in private homes. But as the morning passed, the reporters were surprised that at least some black men had managed to vote. They were surprised, too, that the black men they encountered were neither hostile nor violent, as the city's newspapers had predicted.

The sight of black men voting enraged Mike Dowling, the Irishman who commanded a brigade of Red Shirts from Dry Pond. Though bars and taverns were closed, Dowling and his men had helped themselves to liquor provided at the office of John D. Bellamy, the Democratic candidate for the United States House. Fifty Red Shirts had gathered on horseback under Dowling's command that morning.

Dowling had wanted to lynch Alex Manly the day his editorial appeared in August, but he had been dissuaded by Furnifold Simmons's order to postpone violence until after the Democrats had carried the election. But now Dowling believed he had waited long enough. At midday on Election Day, he ordered his Red Shirts to mount up and ride to the *Record* office to lynch the editor.

As the Red Shirts rode down Market Street they encountered Hugh MacRae, the cotton mill owner and a leader of the Secret Nine. He was sitting on his porch, watching white voters walk past. Dowling dismounted and walked over to tell MacRae of his plans. MacRae surprised him by objecting. He reminded Dowling that the plan was to forestall any violence until after the election.

Dowling protested, so MacRae invited him and a few other Red Shirts to Sasser's Drug Store a block away. The store was owned by L. B. Sasser, another member of the Secret Nine. Sasser backed MacRae, telling Dowling that his plan was premature. Dowling persisted. Finally, MacRae showed Dowling and his men a document he had prepared—a "White Declaration of Independence." MacRae said the declaration was to be read the next day, November 9, at a mass meeting of whites to be held at the county courthouse. Whites would formally demand that Manly shut down his newspaper and leave the city, and that the Fusionist mayor and police chief surrender their posts to Democrats.

After looking over the document, Dowling still was not satisfied. To placate him, MacRae let Dowling listen as he telephoned the city's newspapers and told them to print a notice of the white declaration meeting in the next morning's editions. Finally convinced that Manly would be dealt with, Dowling suspended the Red Shirt lynching party.

If the Red Shirts had made their way to the *Record* office that afternoon, they would not have found Alex Manly. He had disappeared.

His mother and other family members, alarmed by death threats against Manly, begged him to flee the city. Earlier that week, a white friend had warned Manly that he was about to be lynched. The friend gave Manly $25 in gold coins and the password needed to cross checkpoints set up by Vigilance Committee sentinels. "May God be with you, my boy. You are too fine to be swung up a tree," the man said.

The man was never identified by Manly, but he may have been the Reverend Robert Strange, the rector of St. James Episcopal Church. The church stood at Fourth and Market Streets, just five blocks from the *Record* office. Strange was a small, slender man—five foot six and 135 pounds—who was respected by blacks and whites for his rectitude and sense of moral justice. One newspaper called him "a man of charming dignity." Strange was also the chaplain for the Wilmington Light Infantry, a position that would have provided access to the password.

Thomas Clawson, the reporter and city editor for the *Wilmington Messenger*, was also looking for Manly on Election Day. He wanted his Hoe press back. According to Clawson, the Manly brothers had made only a small down payment on the press and still owed him the bulk of the $600 cost. Clawson claimed the press as his property, while also publishing a small item in the *Messenger* on November 10: "The *Daily Record* has suspended publication. The outfit of the company will be turned over to creditors, and the affairs of the paper will be closed up at once."

Alex Manly had already fled Wilmington, possibly the night before Election Day, with the password and $25 in hand. He had loaded a horse and buggy, planning to bluff his way through checkpoints with the help of the password. Despite his notoriety due to the August 18 editorial, few whites in Wilmington knew what Manly looked like. And because he easily passed as white, he believed he would not be questioned closely. He dressed in a dark suit and hat, looking like a prosperous white merchant.

Manly's buggy managed to reach the outskirts of the city, where he encountered a Vigilance Committee checkpoint set up at a small bridge. Beyond the bridge, a dirt road led out of Wilmington and into the longleaf pine forests. One of the white gunmen asked Manly where he was headed. Manly mentioned a small town north of Wilmington and said he was on his way to buy horses at a farm auction. He recited the password.

The white men told him they were planning "a necktie party" in Wilmington for Alex Manly, the black editor.

Manly had a ready reply. He told the men that he, too, was "going after that scoundrel Manly."

One of the men told him: "If you see that nigger Manly up there, shoot him."

Noticing that Manly was unarmed, he handed him a rifle.

Alex Manly nodded and snapped the reins. The wagon lurched forward across the bridge, headed north.

CHAPTER TWENTY-FOUR

Retribution in History

B Y MIDDAY ON NOVEMBER 8, so many citizens—black and white—
had gone to the polls early to avoid trouble that most of the
voting was over. Ballots were to be counted by hand after the
polls closed at 5:00 p.m. That gave Democrats most of the day to carry
out their plan to stuff ballot boxes at selected precincts. They were not
concerned about the special police officers recruited by Mayor Wright
for Election Day security. The mayor had persuaded only fifteen officers
to serve, not the hundred he had hoped for.

One targeted black precinct was the Fifth Precinct of the First Ward,
where 313 blacks and 30 whites had registered. The polling station had
been set up inside a stable at the corner of Tenth and Princess Streets,
in a cramped room about sixteen feet by twenty feet. That evening,
ballots were being counted by six men—two black Republicans, two
white Populists, and two white Democrats. The gerrymandered precinct
had voted overwhelmingly for the Republican ticket in 1896. But the
White Government Unions had devised a plan to flip the precinct,
despite the odds.

Shortly before 9:00 p.m., nearly 150 white men, some with white
handkerchiefs tied around their arms, surrounded the stable. They
arrived in darkness, having turned off electric streetlights in the

neighborhood. After some low murmuring and whispering, about three dozen of the men suddenly stormed into the little room and confronted the vote counters.

The first man to step inside was former Wilmington mayor William Harriss, a politician with a grudge. Harriss had been replaced as mayor by Wright after the disputed municipal election the previous March. Harriss barged into the stable, shoving a policeman into a barrel of water. Other men rushed into the room behind Harriss. They upended a table, knocked over an oil lamp, and plunged the room into darkness. Lamp oil spilled onto the floor and ignited. Someone stomped out the small fire.

Some of the white men pulled out pistols. Abram Fulton, a black registrar, stumbled in the dark toward the back of the room, hoping to find a way out. He hid in the back for several minutes until someone lit a candle. Then he ran out the front door. Albert Lamb, a black drayman serving as a precinct election judge, also hid in the darkness. When the candle was lit, he, too, escaped through the front door.

Harriss took advantage of the darkness and confusion. He stuffed Democratic ballots into an unattended ballot box for the state senate race. After the candle was lit, Harriss and the other intruders remained inside as the two white Democratic precinct judges, along with a Populist Democrat, continued counting the vote as if nothing untoward had occurred. When the results were announced, the Democratic candidate, W. J. Davis, had received an astonishing 456 votes—113 more than the total number of registered voters in the precinct.

That same night, a separate gathering of white men surrounded another gerrymandered black precinct—the Second Precinct of the Fifth Ward—and created another disturbance. Democratic ballots were stuffed into boxes. After the votes were counted, Democrat Davis was awarded 251 votes to just 39 for the Fusionist-Republican candidate. This was in a precinct where registered blacks outnumbered whites 242 to 140.

✷　✷　✷

Red Shirts and armed sentries continued to patrol the city streets that night, long after the polls had closed. Sentries searched black passersby for guns or kerosene. Many Wilmington whites were certain that every black man in the city was secretly armed. Bellamy, the Democratic candidate for Congress, later recalled that "they constantly carry concealed weapons . . . the razor, the pistol, the slingshot, and the brass knuckle seem to be their inseparable accompaniments as a class."

In white neighborhoods, rumors spread that black men were lying in wait to attack whites under the cover of darkness. Frank Weldon, a correspondent for the *Atlanta Constitution* who accompanied a Red Shirt patrol through a black section of Wilmington, reported as fact Red Shirts' claims of fifteen hundred black men "hidden in the weeds," armed with shotguns and old army muskets in "Darkest North Carolina." According to Weldon's dispatch, blacks had shot out electric lights and tossed rocks at trolley cars. "It is dangerous to rustle the weeds or make any noise, lest a rock or bullet comes whizzing uncomfortably near," he wrote. He claimed to have overheard armed black men shouting at whites: "I want to wash my hands in these tallow-faces' blood."

An even more credulous account was provided by Guy Carleton Lee of the *Baltimore Sun*. Lee was not a typical correspondent. He described himself as a professor at Johns Hopkins University and an orator, historian, and all-around man of letters. In a dispatch to the *Sun*, Lee spun an ominous tale studded with purported eyewitness details provided by his trusted white sources. His dispatch reported that several hundred black men had been marching and drilling in secret formations, armed with rifles, as part of a planned uprising against whites.

"The negroes drilled in their society halls and in unoccupied dwellings," Lee wrote. "No drums beat. No bugle-calls rang out. In somber silence, with subdued voices, the squads learned the manual of arms and the first lesson in the art of war." There was more: Rifles and pistols were stored at secret locations. A single black man had collected and stored more than three hundred guns, "and the whites have not yet discovered their hiding place." Lee wrote that there was a secret plan, called the "poison and the torch," for black women to poison white children in their care and then set white homes afire.

Lee's account was pure fiction. Virtually all the armed men who remained on the streets throughout the night were white, not black. Black men locked their doors and huddled with their families as white gunmen patrolled their neighborhoods. White wives and daughters stayed up, too, supplying their men with biscuits and coffee. The night passed quietly, save for the low voices of the sentries at their posts, talking and stamping their feet against the autumn chill.

One of the sentries, Michael Cronly, was a reluctant recruit. He had fetched his rifle and set out on patrol late that night, but only because he was obliged as a white man to defend his neighborhood against the anticipated black uprising. His sister, Jane Cronly, who kept a diary of events in Wilmington that fall, thought the patrols were pointless, and she told him so. She wrote in her diary that night:

> After being out in the cold and damp, he came in a moment and four women took hold of him so vigorously that they made him promise to come in before not very long, threatening to go out with him if he did not. He knew what a perfect farce it was to be out there in the damp and cold, watching for poor cowed disarmed negroes frightened to death by the threats that had been made against them and too glad to huddle in their homes and keep quiet. So after a time he came home and went to bed.

In Raleigh, Governor Russell continued to receive death threats. The simple act of leaving the governor's mansion, even accompanied by his bodyguard, was fraught with risk. But there was also a political risk if Russell failed to travel to Wilmington to vote in his home city. He would be ridiculed as a coward. Ultimately, Russell decided to take a train to Wilmington on Election Day. "I realize that I am liable to be murdered," he told a reporter.

As a precaution, Russell arranged for two Wilmington Democrats to accompany him inside the city. Both men were distant relatives of his; one was Lieutenant Colonel Walker Taylor, commander of the Wilmington Light Infantry. But even with Colonel Taylor beside him, Russell was showered with taunts and catcalls when he arrived at the Front Street depot aboard an Atlantic Coast Line train. Amid the din, a cluster of local and out-of-town correspondents shouted questions at the governor about the anticipated "Negro riot." It was "all rot," Russell assured them. The *Messenger*, which referred to the obese governor as "his tubs," quoted Russell as saying that the city's blacks were "unarmed, unorganized and helpless in the face of the formidable preparations made by the whites."

Russell was escorted to his assigned polling station, in the predominately white Fourth Ward, located inside a small shop at the corner of Dock Street and Front Street along the riverfront. Correspondents trailed behind him. One reported that while the governor was not molested, he was "greeted by silence and cold looks" from white men.

At the polling station entrance, Russell asked the Democratic ward captain whether Wilmington's Democrats were inclined to allow him to vote. He seemed to be joking.

"We certainly are," the captain replied, and the governor walked inside. As he deposited his ballot, a registrar announced grandly to the handful of people inside: "The governor of North Carolina!" Before Russell left, he asked the correspondents whether blacks were being permitted to vote in the city. The reporters assured him that they were voting without interference.

The *New York Times* correspondent described a tense but ultimately uneventful Election Day in Wilmington. His dispatch made no mention of the armed Red Shirts who had turned away blacks at polling stations or the assassination threats against Governor Russell.

The whites were in force in each polling place in Wilmington but there were no signs of intimidation and no arms were displayed. Very few negroes were seen standing about the corners, and the negro quarter was very quiet. The colored vote was light, showing a marked falling off from previous elections. The citizens received Gov. Russell coldly.

After a brief stop at his plantation in nearby Brunswick County, Russell boarded an Atlantic Coast Line train back to Raleigh. He had intended to take a direct route, through the town of Goldsboro. But he was warned that several hundred Red Shirts were waiting to intercept him there. Russell decided instead to detour to a much longer route, even though that rail line also passed through Red Shirt redoubts—in the small towns of Maxton, Laurinburg, and Hamlet west of Wilmington.

At the station in Maxton, more than a hundred Red Shirts met the governor's train. A small band of gunmen boarded, led by Cameron Morrison, a white supremacist Democrat and a future North Carolina governor. There was no confrontation. In fact, the Red Shirts joked with the governor, who responded by asking them where all his Populist supporters had gone. The Red Shirts "appeared to be in for a good time. The governor took their visit good naturedly," the *Messenger* reported.

Morrison warned Russell that a larger and more hostile brigade of Red Shirts was waiting for his train at an upcoming stop, in Laurinburg. They were promising a lynching. Morrison and several train employees convinced Russell to hide in the train's baggage car. The governor agreed, reluctantly. He looked ridiculous, a frightened fat man sitting on lumpy mailbags in a darkened railcar. He was the governor, after all, with an entire state militia at his disposal. He sat back, glumly, and sank into the mailbags.

Russell was still in hiding when the train pulled into Laurinburg. A boisterous mob of Red Shirts and other armed white men charged the platform, cursing the governor. Some had been guzzling whiskey while awaiting the train.

"Where's the governor?" someone shouted. "Where is the governor?"

Other men hollered, "Bring him out! Lynch him! Lynch the governor! Lynch the fat son of a bitch!"

Several Red Shirts boarded the train, searching for Russell. The conductor and a few other men stood guard outside the baggage car. They denied that Russell was aboard. One drunken man tried to force his way inside the baggage car but was turned away by the conductor's men. Finally, the Red Shirts gave up and the train moved on, with Russell still inside the stuffy baggage car. The next day, several Democratic newspapers reported, falsely, that the Red Shirts in Laurinburg had punched him in the stomach and pulled his ears.

The last stop through Red Shirt territory was Hamlet, where more Red Shirts greeted the train with insults and curses. But again, the gunmen were unable to find the governor. He remained in the darkened baggage car, listening to the cries of the Red Shirts as the train pulled safely out of the station.

The train eased into the Raleigh station at 2:16 the following morning. Russell was taken to the governor's mansion, where he was escorted past a mob that had surrounded the home and grounds, screaming and cursing Russell and his wife. The governor stormed inside, furious but helpless.

Later that morning, Russell was ridiculed in newspapers across the state. The early edition of the *Messenger* taunted the governor with the opening words of his inauguration address two years earlier: "There is retribution in history."

CHAPTER TWENTY-FIVE

The Forbearance of
All White Men

OUR STATE REDEEMED—NEGROISM DEFUNCT, *Wilmington Messenger*
OLD NORTH STATE REDEEMED FROM NEGRO RULE AT LAST, *Atlanta Constitution*
WHITE SUPREMACY RECEIVES A VOTE OF CONFIDENCE, *News and Observer*

When Josephus Daniels and Furnifold Simmons awoke on the morning of November 9, newspaper headlines confirmed what the two men had begun to realize the night before. Democrats had swept the state. The white supremacy campaign had proved more successful than Daniels and Simmons could possibly have hoped when they first met in New Bern in March to plot a new era of white redemption. In a matter of months, their campaign had intimidated and terrified thousands of black men into staying home from the polls; of the state's roughly one hundred thousand eligible black voters, fewer than half had voted.

White supremacists had stuffed ballot boxes with Democratic votes and destroyed Republican ballots. And the campaign's contrived message of the black beast rapist and corrupt Negro rule had persuaded thousands of whites to abandon the Republican Party. The state's Republican attorney general conceded that up to twenty-five thousand registered white Populists had voted "the white man's ticket." Junius Fortune, a

Republican clerk of court, embraced the shift to white supremacy. "This election ends the negro in politics," he said. "And I am glad of it."

After the election, Daniels published a front-page cartoon depicting Furnifold Simmons wearing a white planter's suit and twirling his mustache, as the victor over a diminutive black figure in a game of checkers. The caption: "The Game Is Over. The White Men Win." The North Carolina writer and essayist W. J. Cash later described Simmons as "the Little Giant of New Bern who, single-handed, had slain the dragon of Nigger Rule."

The campaign had decisively snatched control of the state legislature from Republicans and Populists, who had won a two-thirds majority in 1896. Democrats now held ninety-four seats in the state's house to just twenty-three for Republicans and three for Populists. In the state senate, there were now forty Democrats to only seven Republicans and three Populists.

The results were disastrous for Republicans in Wilmington. The Democratic legislature would soon restore legislative control over local appointed offices, ending the Fusionist experiment with elected local rule that had helped put black men in office. In New Hanover County, Democrats were now in complete control. The county flipped from a 960-vote Fusionist majority in 1896 to a 500-vote margin for Democrats in 1898. With no opposition for county offices, Democrats replaced Fusionists in the positions of sheriff, solicitor, coroner, surveyor, and judge. If Alex Manly had not fled Wilmington, he would have suffered the indignity of surrendering his appointed position as deputy registrar of deeds to a white supremacist. George Rountree was elected to the state house. Roger Moore, the former Klan leader, won a seat on the county Board of Commissioners, now run by fellow Democrats.

Among the celebratory articles in Wilmington's white newspapers was a small notice printed on the back page of the *Wilmington Messenger*. Headlined ATTENTION WHITE MEN, the item announced a meeting of the "White Men of Wilmington" at the courthouse at eleven o'clock that morning, Wednesday, November 9: "A full attendance is desired, as business in the furtherance of White Supremacy will be transacted." This was the notice that Hugh MacRae had dictated as he attempted to persuade Mike Dowling to delay the Red Shirt attack on Alex Manly. The mild language only hinted at the meeting's true purpose—to set in motion the long-standing plan to overthrow city government.

George Rountree did not know the meeting had been scheduled. He had stayed up at the Cape Fear Club until 3:00 a.m., receiving congratulatory telegrams from white supremacists across the state. He was "sleeping the sleep of the just" that morning, he wrote later, when his wife woke him at nine o'clock to tell him of an important meeting at the courthouse. Rountree threw on his clothes and ran through the streets.

"I had never seen more people in the courthouse," he wrote later. Nearly a thousand white men—"Wilmington's very best citizens," the *Messenger* said—had squeezed into the white-columned building. Men jostled for space in the lobby and in the corridors, straining to see what was happening inside. Latecomers clustered on the courthouse steps.

Colonel Waddell, too, claimed to know nothing of the meeting. He was often kept in the dark by members of the secret groups, who resented what they considered Waddell's political opportunism and grandstanding. As soon as Waddell heard about the meeting, he rushed to the courthouse. Inside, he encountered Hugh MacRae, who handed him the printed statement that had been composed by MacRae and the Secret Nine. It was labeled "Wilmington Declaration of Independence."

Waddell saw Silas Fishblate, the former mayor, standing on a rostrum, motioning for Waddell to join him. Waddell mounted the rostrum, where he was instructed to read the declaration. He protested that he had no idea what the meeting was all about. But he told the gathering that he was always willing to answer any call from the white men of his city. There was a ripple of applause.

Waddell began reading from the lengthy document. Below the rostrum, several men transcribed his words. They were newspaper correspondents, appointed as secretaries by the Secret Nine to document what the next day's *Messenger* described as "the most remarkable mass meeting in the history of Wilmington." Thomas Clawson, of the *Messenger*, wrote furiously. Beside him, their heads bent over their notes as they scribbled, were correspondents for the *Washington Star*, the *Chicago Record*, the *Charleston News and Courier*, and the *Wilmington Morning Star*.

The preamble of the "Wilmington Declaration of Independence" said the United States Constitution envisioned a government of enlightened men and "did not contemplate for their descendants a subjection to an inferior race." After reading the preamble aloud, Waddell recited a list of seven resolutions:

One—Because whites in Wilmington paid 95 percent of taxes, they would no longer be ruled by Negroes.

Two—Whites would no longer tolerate "the actions of unscrupulous white men in affiliating with the negroes."

Three—"[T]he negro has demonstrated by antagonizing our interests in every way, and especially by his ballot, that he is incapable of realizing that his interests are and should be identical with those of the community."

Four—"[T]he giving of nearly all the employment to Negro laborers has been against the best interests of this County" and had retarded Wilmington's economic growth.

Five—Most jobs held by blacks were to be handed over to white men.

Six—Blacks were to be treated "with justice and consideration" so long as they obeyed "the intelligent and progressive portion of the community."

Seven—The *Daily Record* would cease publication and its printing press would be shipped out of the city. Alex Manly would be banished from Wilmington as punishment for "publishing an article so vile and slanderous that it would in most communities have resulted in the lynching of the editor." If Manly obeyed within twelve hours, he would be guaranteed "forbearance on the part of all white men." But if the editor did not leave Wilmington within twenty-four hours, he would "be expelled by force."

The mention of Manly prompted a roar from the assembled crowd, now packed shoulder to shoulder in the cramped hall. Every man was standing and cheering. There were cries of "Right! Right! Right!" and shouts of "Lynch Manly!" and "Fumigate the city with the *Record*!" Moments later, newly elected US representative John D. Bellamy Jr. told the crowd that Manly would be dealt with firmly.

"Why didn't you lynch him?" a man shouted.

"That ain't no joke!" someone yelled back.

Bellamy advised everyone to remain calm and to refrain from violence. "The eyes of the world are upon us," he said, pointing to the newspaper scribes.

Several members of the Secret Nine had been told that Manly had already fled Wilmington. But they realized that revealing the truth would cool the passions of the crowd. They wanted Wilmington's white men enraged and aggrieved and primed for violence; they said nothing about Manly's whereabouts. Even so, some men in the crowd seemed to know that Manly had fled.

As Bellamy was discussing Manly's fate, a man interrupted him and shouted, "He's gone now!"

Bellamy replied, "Well, then, Wilmington has been rid of the vilest slanderer in North Carolina."

After Waddell and Bellamy had spoken, Fishblate suggested adding a resolution demanding the resignations of the mayor, police chief, and the entire board of aldermen. That prompted a series of loud arguments. Several men in the crowd demanded to be heard, shouting, "Question! Question!" Rountree caught Fishblate's eye and was granted permission to speak. The crowd settled down. Rountree proposed that a committee of five men be appointed to discuss the resolutions. Rountree appointed himself, along with Fishblate, Hugh MacRae, and two other men.

As the five committee members discussed the resolutions, several men in the crowd yelled for Waddell to deliver a speech. The Colonel told them that the time for speech making had passed. "The pot needs no more fuel to set it to boiling," he said. After preaching violence at campaign rallies throughout the summer and fall, Waddell now advised caution and restraint until the time was right to act. He spoke briefly, ending with an assurance that Manly would be dealt with sternly.

Rountree then read a short statement: "It is the sense of this meeting that Mayor S. P. Wright and Chief of Police Jno. R. Melton, having demonstrated their utter incapacity to give the city a decent government and keep order therein, their continuance in office being a constant menace to the peace and welfare of this community, they ought forthwith to resign."

Attention then turned to the broader goal of the meeting: devising a swift and certain plan to overthrow city government and ensure that black men never again held office in Wilmington. Waddell was selected to lead a committee of twenty-five men to carry out the day's resolutions. The Colonel purposely left Rountree off the committee—"the kind of gratitude he generally displayed," Rountree complained later.

The meeting ended at 1:00 p.m. to rousing applause and cheers. Men shook hands and embraced, then lined up to sign the declaration and resolutions. After 457 signatures, there was no space for more.

Henry Litchfield West, the *Washington Post* correspondent, was impressed by the white men's expressions of entitlement and impunity.

Flushed with victory, they hastened to emphasize their return to power . . . one cannot help but admire the candor of their action. They resorted to no secrecy or mask. What they did was done in broad daylight; and the entire proceeding suggested the stateliness of a Greek tragedy.

Two hours after the meeting adjourned, Waddell led twenty-five of the city's leading white men into a conference room inside the Merchant's Association building on Market Street. The Colonel wanted the committee to act quickly and decisively. His first move was to summon the city's black leaders to inform them of the resolutions.

Under Waddell's guidance, the committee drew up a list of thirty-two men they considered leaders of the city's black community. This came to be known as the Committee of Colored Citizens. It included ministers, lawyers, doctors, businessmen, and politicians. Among them:

William Henderson, the outspoken lawyer who everyone assumed was black but was actually of white and American Indian heritage.

Thomas C. Miller, Wilmington's wealthiest black man, who owned considerable property and, it was said, was owed large sums by white borrowers.

Frederick C. Sadgwar, the successful carpenter and builder who was Alex Manly's father-in-law.

David Jacobs, a barber who served as county coroner.

John Goins, business manager of the *Daily Record*.

Elijah Green, a foreman at the Sprunt Cotton Compress and a Fusionist city alderman.

Thomas Rivera, a mortician active in Republican politics.

Armond W. Scott, a promising young attorney who earlier that same week had confronted prosecutor George Rountree in court while defending a black man accused of stoning a streetcar.

Purposely left off the committee were John Dancy, the federal customs collector; and John E. Taylor, his deputy. Both men were prominent black leaders. Dancy edited a widely read black church journal and Taylor was president of the black-owned Metropolitan Trust Company. Waddell and others feared that their inclusion on the committee might invite federal intervention because of their federal posts.

The white men quickly drafted a letter, marked with the day's date and the time, 3:50 p.m. It read like a legal summons.

The following named colored citizens of Wilmington are requested to meet a committee of citizens appointed by the authority of the meeting of business men and taxpayers held . . . at six o'clock this evening at the Merchants' Rooms, Seaboard Air Line building on Front Street to consider a matter of grave consequence to the negroes of Wilmington.

The committee summoned armed Red Shirts to deliver the demand. Two Red Shirts in a buggy were dispatched to find Henderson. He was strolling down the street when the men in the buggy cut him off. They showed him the list of names, including his own. Henderson was told to attend the meeting that evening, with the proviso that several black men on the list had refused to attend unless Henderson was present. He agreed to go. The Red Shirts checked off his name, then rode away to deliver the ultimatum to the other men on the list.

The six o'clock meeting time left the black men barely two hours to drop everything and rush to the Seaboard Air Line building, an imposing structure that dominated Front Street near the river. The black men were puzzled by the demands. They had nothing left to offer. They had already been bullied into agreeing to the plan to abandon Fusionist campaigns for county offices. Democrats now controlled the county and the state legislature. What more did they want?

Men like William Henderson and Thomas Miller had built successful careers in the city and had much to lose. With the Red Shirts barely contained and talk of lynching in the air, they concluded that they had no choice but to obey the command to meet with Waddell. By six o'clock, almost all thirty-two of the black men named in the letter had reported to the Seaboard building, where the whites waited at a large table set up inside a meeting room.

Most of the black men wore dark suits and ties. They arrived carrying their hats in their hands, respectful and cautious—"cowed and terror-stricken," the Northern correspondent Henry Litchfield West reported. There were no pleasantries or introductions. The men were ordered to sit at the table, directly across from the row of white men. Waddell stood at the head of the table, staring intently at the black men. "Stern and determined, the white[s] looked the masters they proposed to be—anxious and expectant, the negro realized his day of dominancy had passed," the *Messenger* reported.

Waddell read the declaration aloud. His commanding, stern tone made it clear that he considered it an ultimatum. He told the black men that there would be no discussion, and he instructed them to use their influence to satisfy white demands. Waddell seemed to have undergone a physical transformation. He somehow stood taller and more erect, his beard thicker and longer, his gaze more menacing. He had long cultivated a public image of a man in full control of his fate, even when he was out of work and dependent on his wife's money. Now he embraced the thrill of controlling the fate of other men.

One of the black men asked about the meaning of a certain phrase in the declaration. Waddell did not elaborate. He merely read the phrase aloud again.

A minister, W. H. Lee, quietly promised to advise Manly and his brother to leave town at once. Waddell did not respond.

Henderson stood and tried to tell Waddell that according to rumors, the *Daily Record* had ceased publication and Alex Manly had fled Wilmington.

Waddell cut him off. "Sit down," he said sharply. "We don't want to hear a damn word out of you. Give us your reply in writing."

Waddell handed out copies of the white men's declaration, repeating that no discussion or questions would be permitted. He emphasized that the resolutions would be fully enforced. The black men had until seven thirty the next morning, November 10, to deliver a written response to Waddell's home at North Fifth between Market and Princess Streets. The Colonel did not mention that he intended to announce the black leaders' response at an eight o'clock meeting of armed white men the next morning at the Wilmington Light Infantry armory. No matter how the black men responded, the white revolution would proceed as planned.

The black men realized that they could never meet the demands and that any formal response to Waddell was an exercise in futility. A man directly across the table from Waddell spoke up. "Colonel, we are not responsible for this, and we have no authority," he said.

Waddell ignored him. "The meeting stands adjourned," he announced.

The black men filed out of the building and into the fading evening light, uncertain and defeated. They glanced at one another in silence. At last someone proposed holding a follow-up meeting to make sense of what had just happened and to devise a fitting response. The men decided to assemble at the barbershop of the county coroner, David Jacobs, on Dock Street near Front Street, a block from the swirling brown waters of the Cape Fear.

There was animated discussion, but it did not last long. Most of the men in the room agreed that Alex Manly should leave town immediately, though Henderson and a few others believed he had already fled. The next morning, November 10, a curious paragraph appeared at the close of a long article in the *Morning Star* about the white man's courthouse meeting on the ninth. It mentioned, almost in passing, that Alex Manly had left Wilmington "and doubtless will never come back."

Many of the black men in the barbershop did not know much more than the white men of Wilmington regarding Manly's whereabouts or appearance. Manly was intensely private, even among fellow blacks. And although he was active in a black church and served as a deputy registrar of deeds, he avoided public gatherings and let his newspaper speak for him.

The black men selected Armond W. Scott, the young attorney, to pen a handwritten response. Scott was a natural choice. He was twenty-five, well educated, eager, and ambitious. He was a member of a prominent black Wilmington family that counted whites among its friends and neighbors. Scott's father, Benjamin, ran a successful grocery store from his home on Walnut Street. Armond had graduated just two years earlier with a law degree from all-black Johnson C. Smith University in Charlotte.

Scott had represented black clients in the city's courts, and his small law practice was growing. He was not afraid to speak out. In September, while successfully defending two black men charged with assault, Scott had complained to a white judge that Wilmington's whites had conspired to "disregard the first clause of the Constitution of the United States, which declares that all men are born free and equal with certain inalienable rights."

But now Scott had been placed in a precarious position. The black leaders knew from observing Waddell's bullish militancy that the whites of Wilmington were quite prepared, even eager, for violence. They understood that defying or questioning the White Declaration of Independence was dangerous. But they had no authority to banish Manly, much less remove the mayor and police chief. They crafted an equivocal response denying any culpability for Manly's editorial but expressing a reluctant willingness to advise the editor to leave town. They approved a two-sentence letter written in Scott's clear, bold hand on two sheets of lined white paper, addressed to "Hon. A. M. Waddell."

We, the colored citizens to whom was referred the matter of expulsion from the community of the person and press of A. L. Manly, beg most respectfully to say that we are in no wise responsible for, nor in any way condone the obnoxious article that called forth your actions. Neither are we authorized to act for him in this matter; but in the interest of peace we will most willingly use our influence to have your wishes carried out.

Very respectfully, The Committee of Colored Citizens

The note was slipped into an envelope addressed to Waddell. Written on the flap was an instruction: "Please deliver at House." Scott accepted the task of delivering the note. He was the youngest, fittest man in the room, light skinned and with perhaps enough stature as a lawyer to pass through white checkpoints set up throughout the city.

Scott set out on foot from the barbershop. It was a short walk to Waddell's home, just four blocks east and two blocks north. But Scott immediately encountered armed white sentinels. Even in the dark, he could see white handkerchiefs wrapped around their upper arms. He could hear gunshots in the distance—Red Shirts firing Winchesters into the air. He abandoned his mission and instead turned on his heel and made his way to the post office. He deposited the letter and, walking quickly with his head down, went straight home.

On the streets that night, Red Shirts and Vigilance Committee sentinels were eager for confrontation. A group of white men assembled on Market Street in front of the First Baptist Church, whose pastor, Reverend Calvin S. Blackwell, had preached white supremacy from the pulpit. There they signed a formal pledge to burn the *Daily Record* building and lynch Manly the next morning if the Committee of Colored Citizens did not provide a written response to Waddell by 7:30 a.m. Colonel Roger Moore, head of the Vigilance Committee, agreed to personally lead the march to the black newspaper. The gathering broke up as the men hurried off to report for sentinel duty.

In the darkness, the Red Shirts and the sentinels searched in vain for armed black men, but their guns soon fell silent. It was a mild evening, clear and cool and calming, and the city slept. The night passed peacefully.

BOOK THREE

LINE OF FIRE

CHAPTER TWENTY-SIX

What Have We Done?

COLONEL WADDELL awoke early on the morning of Thursday, November 10. He had been planning for this day for months—for years, really. If events played out as he anticipated, he would assume his rightful place as not only the voice but also the physical embodiment of white supremacy in Wilmington. Through the summer and fall, he had aroused and channeled white rage. Now it was a weapon in his hands.

Waddell's greatest challenge came not from black men or even from the white Republican leadership in the city. It came from fellow white aristocrats who had staked their own claims as commanders of white fortunes in Wilmington, ambitious men like Roger Moore, George Rountree, Hugh MacRae, and others. The Colonel knew he had to outmaneuver them.

Waddell made a show of waiting inside his home until past 7:30 a.m., the deadline for the response from the Committee of Colored Citizens. He had been told, probably by George Rountree, that the black men had quickly agreed in writing to white demands. Waddell had been told, too, that Armond Scott had mailed the letter instead of hand-delivering it. The next day's *Messenger* reported that Waddell had "waited in suspense for the reply." A group of agitated white men had gathered at the Wilmington Light Infantry armory on Market Street, just a block from Waddell's home at North Fifth between Princess and Market. Waddell's performance persuaded them that the Committee of Colored Citizens had failed to respond.

Just after 8:00 a.m., Waddell put on his hat and coat and walked down Fifth Street toward the armory, a solidly built Greek Revival structure with a pale marble veneer facade mounted over pressed brick. It was a beautiful autumn morning typical of the Cape Fear country in early November—mild temperatures in the low seventies, sunny, with an occasional gust of moist, salty air from the Atlantic. The mob had grown to more than five hundred men, with more on the way. "Every man brought his rifle and many had pistols also," the *Messenger* reported.

Most of the men were from the working class, with sunburned necks and scuffed work boots. Some had tied cartridge belts around their waists and stuffed them with rifle and pistol bullets. Many wore weathered red shirts or jackets. But others were professional men—lawyers, doctors, and even a few clergymen.

Waddell noted that Colonel Moore was not present at the armory. Moore's absence cleared the way for Waddell to take charge. Moore, as leader of the Vigilance Committee, had posted Red Shirts and other armed men at strategic points throughout the city, with each district commanded by a captain who reported directly to Moore. Moore himself had set up a military command post at Fifth and Chestnut Streets, less than two blocks from the armory. He had given Waddell his location and instructed him to inform him immediately if the mob decided to attack the *Record* office.

Waddell disregarded the order. Although he knew Moore was at his command post nearby, Waddell dispatched runners to Moore's home and office, purportedly to find him. While waiting for the runners to return empty-handed, Waddell told the assembled men that the Committee of Colored Citizens had not responded to his demands. Several men began whooping and hollering and cursing the black men. A chant went up, demanding that Captain Thomas C. James, commander of a Wilmington Light Infantry company posted at the armory, lead the mob to the *Record* building.

Captain James was now in an uncomfortable position. As a state militia ostensibly commanded by the governor, the Light Infantry was charged with preventing violence, not instigating it. But the militia took orders from leaders of the white supremacy campaign, not from Governor Russell. James telephoned Lieutenant Colonel Walker Taylor, the infantry commander stationed a few blocks away, to ask for guidance.

As the state militia commander in Wilmington, Colonel Taylor could not openly lead a mob. The Light Infantry normally would have been dispatched to break up any large gathering of armed men, but Taylor decided to keep his distance from the mob. He anticipated, correctly, that the men were primed to attack the *Record* office on their own. That would provide the opening for the infantry to intervene on the pretext of putting down any black riot prompted by an attack on the city's black newspaper. Colonel Taylor instructed Captain James to stay put but to inform him as soon as the mob left for the *Record* office.

Captain James, with a sense of relief, told the armed civilians at the armory that the infantry would not lead the march. But suddenly the captain's own militiamen objected. They demanded to be part of any attack on the newspaper that had defamed their wives and daughters. James quickly devised a plan to keep the militiamen bottled up at the armory. He ordered them to march, over and over, around the grassy armory grounds.

As soon as they realized that the infantry was standing down, several men in the crowd began to chant for Roger Moore. They had been told that Moore would lead the attack on the *Record*, and now they demanded that he follow through. Waddell intervened. He told the mob that Moore could not be located. There was a long pause, and then a new chant arose: "Waddell! Waddell! Waddell!"

Waddell seized the opportunity to outflank Moore. He ordered seventy-five men to line up and join him in a march to the newspaper. But instead of seventy-five, more than five hundred men began forming columns four abreast that stretched for nearly two blocks.

Waddell walked to the head of the column, joined by Mike Dowling and Silas Fishblate, the Jewish former mayor, who was eager to demonstrate his white supremacist bona fides. Behind Fishblate and Dowling were several members of Waddell's Committee of Twenty-Five, formed a day earlier. Many of the men knew that the Committee of Colored Citizens had agreed to their demands—and that Alex Manly had fled—but they saw an opportunity to unleash the enraged white mob.

Few people realized it, but the final issue of the *Record* had been published the previous day, November 9. With Alex Manly gone, his brother Frank had taken over the operation with the help of John Goins, a twenty-nine-year-old black printer who was a member of the Committee of Colored Citizens. Frank Manly and Goins decided not to publish on November 10, hoping that a few days of silence—and Alex's exit—might cool white resentment.

Frank and Goins were having breakfast near the *Record* office on the morning of November 10 when they heard shouts and gunshots. They were warned that a mob was bearing down on the newspaper, intent on burning the press and lynching Alex Manly. The two men abandoned their breakfast, climbed into a buggy, and fled to the outskirts of the city. They later made their way to Washington, DC, where Frank was told, falsely, that Alex had been murdered by a mob.

Waddell, Dowling, Fishblate, and the committeemen marched in tandem, followed by columns of gunmen. The mob had now grown to nearly a thousand people. Several men fired their Winchesters into the air. The gunshots summoned more white men, who ran from their homes, rifles in hand, to join the march. The columns paraded for three blocks east on Market Street, drawing cheers and whistles from white onlookers. Black residents retreated to their homes and locked their doors.

As soon as Colonel Taylor was informed that the mob had set out for the *Record* office, he rushed to the armory to confer with Captain James. Taylor had already set in motion a plan to induce Governor Russell in Raleigh to authorize the infantry to suppress a purported black riot. The day before, Taylor had told Russell in a telegram that because racial tensions were so high, he was holding the infantry ready while awaiting the governor's orders. Russell had not responded. Now, at about 9:00 a.m. on November 10, Taylor tried again. He sent another telegram to Raleigh: "Situation here serious. I hold military awaiting your prompt orders." If the governor ordered the infantry to intervene, Taylor would then be free to attack blacks as planned.

It was only seven blocks from the armory to the *Record* office on the second floor of Love and Charity Hall at South Seventh and Church Streets. The building, mocked by whites as Free Love Lodge, was owned by the Grand United Order of Love and Charity, a black fraternal organization dedicated to helping poor and sick blacks. Some of the white men later regretted targeting the building, saying it was owned by "respectable negroes."

The marchers had by now entered a black neighborhood, where residents clustered at windows or hid behind outbuildings to watch the procession. The police chief, John Melton, walked out onto Market Street to monitor the mob. The columns were so long—at least fifteen hundred men by now, Melton thought—that they took nearly an hour to pass him. With just a handful of police officers under his command and with his job and perhaps his life in jeopardy, Melton felt powerless to stop them. He did not intervene.

As the columns approached the *Record* office, Waddell recalled the night the previous August when black men, some of them armed, had surrounded the newspaper building to ward off rumored white attacks.

He summoned his military training from three decades earlier: *Protect your flanks.* He dispatched several men to set up checkpoints on street corners to cut off any black men who might rush to the *Record*'s defense.

With the perimeter secured, Waddell marched slowly to the front of the *Record* building, a Winchester on his shoulder. He called out, "Halt!" Gripping his rifle, he knocked on the front door. He waited, then knocked again. There was no reply. With the Manly brothers gone and with white gunmen patrolling the neighborhood, the *Record* staff had fled.

Several men beat the door down. The lead column rushed into the building, the men cheering and hooting. They clambered upstairs and smashed office furniture and began to tear apart the Hoe printing press. As more men crammed into the building, they tossed out items from inside—a beaver hat, a crayon drawing of Alex Manly, a sign that read: RECORD PUB. CO. Broken furniture and fixtures followed, with cheers erupting as each piece of debris sailed through the air and tumbled across the dirt roadway.

Two men discovered a container of kerosene stored in a closet. They poured it across the wooden floor. Other men ripped down oil lamps from the ceiling and dumped the contents. Someone struck a match. Flames shot up.

As the fire spread, men raised their rifles, hollering and laughing. They were amused by the sight of an elderly black woman on the street who flapped her arms and cursed them and by black schoolchildren who raced through the streets, screaming for their mothers. Soon embers from the burning building wafted to surrounding properties. Flames flickered on the roof of nearby St. Luke's AME Church. Small fires broke out on the roofs of surrounding homes. Someone sounded an alarm from a firebox at the corner of Seventh and Nun.

Several men from the mob tried to put out the flames. The nearest fire brigade was the Cape Fear Steam Fire Engine Company, formed in 1871 as the country's first all-black steam engine company. The firefighters rushed with their horse-drawn tanker wagon, their fire bell clanging, up North Seventh Street toward the *Record* building. A white fire chief ordered W. T. "Tuck" Savage, a powerfully built white man with a reputation for brutality, to intercept the black crew. The firemen, alarmed by the size of the mob, halted two blocks from the fire.

After Savage was told that the fire had consumed the *Record* building, the black firefighters were permitted to proceed. They were met by rifle fire and pistol shots aimed over their heads. As men in the mob jeered, the firefighters sprayed water from the tanker, dousing the embers and saving surrounding structures, including St. Luke's AME Church. The entire second floor of the *Record* building was gone, with only a blackened back wall and the charred printing press still standing. The bottom floor was gutted, framed by a rickety picket fence and the spectral remains of a burned, leafless tree.

Before moving on to attack other black neighborhoods, the white men posed for photographs. Many were dressed in dark suits and ties. Others sported red shirts or jackets. Each man wore a stern, satisfied look, as if he had just completed a hard day's labor. And nearly every one stood with a rifle or shotgun resting on his shoulder, like a soldier at a drill.

With the *Record* in ruins, Waddell led the mob back to the armory. In a first-person account he wrote two weeks later for *Collier's Weekly*, he claimed that he ordered the men to disband and go home: "Now you have performed the duty to which you called on me to lead you to perform. Now let us go quietly to our homes and about our business, and obey the law, unless we are forced in self defense to do otherwise." A few men departed, but hundreds of others remained in the streets, still armed.

The sounding of the fire alarm next to the *Record* office could be heard in Brooklyn, and at the two-story brick Sprunt Cotton Compress, about three-quarters of a mile away. The black men who worked at the compress could see gray smoke twisting skyward from the torched newspaper building, and they could hear white men shouting and cheering. Rumors quickly spread that white mobs were torching black homes and businesses—when, in fact, only the *Record* office had been burned. The wives of several Sprunt workers, some with children in tow, ran to the compress to warn their husbands that white mobs were descending on their homes.

The Sprunt Cotton Compress was the city's biggest employer. Its daily output was essential to Wilmington's economy. Even a single day's lost work would prove costly if the highly efficient system of compressing cotton, baling it, and loading it onto ships bound for Europe and the Caribbean was disrupted. James Sprunt, the owner, was one of Wilmington's wealthiest citizens. A tall, narrow-faced man with a white walrus mustache, Sprunt was a committed white supremacist. But he adopted a paternalistic attitude toward his black workers. They belonged to him, and he would permit no one to harm them.

The workday had begun normally. Workers manned the compresses and stacked and hauled heavy bales of cotton. But all worked halted when the fire alarm sounded. White supervisors huddled and whispered. A black man ran among the workers, screaming that Red Shirts had killed a black man. "They are going to get us all!" he shouted.

Several black workers approached Sprunt. They reminded him that they had always been compliant and hardworking. They complained, respectfully, that whites should not be permitted to terrorize them so brazenly. Sprunt climbed onto a cotton bale and ordered his employees to resume work. He promised to protect them.

Some workers abruptly left the compress with their wives, hoping to find a way home through white checkpoints. Several hundred more black employees gathered outside the compress, looking anxiously at the smoke in the distance.

The sight of a large gathering of black men sparked rumors among whites that black mobs were gathering to attack white homes and businesses. Word sped across the city in seconds, in many cases relayed by telephone. The rumors reinforced what many whites had long believed based on newspaper reports: blacks were plotting to take over the city. The white men who had burned the *Record* office now rushed to the Sprunt Cotton Compress on the river.

George Rountree had slept in that morning. He had no reason to rise early because he knew the Committee of Colored Citizens had agreed to white demands the day before. But now, as he sat up in bed, Rountree heard the fire alarm and gunshots. He dressed and ran outside. He was hurrying past the post office when he encountered William H. Chadbourn, the postmaster. Chadbourn was a Republican, but he had bowed to intimidation by Rountree and other whites a month earlier when he apologized in print for saying there was no Negro rule in Wilmington. Now Chadbourn surprised Rountree with an offer: if Rountree arranged for white leaders to select a new Democratic mayor and board of aldermen, Chadbourn would help force Mayor Wright and the Fusionist aldermen to resign. Chadbourn could sense that Wilmington's Fusionists were doomed. He aligned himself with the ascendant Democrats.

Rountree agreed, but on his way back home he heard shouts from the workers at the nearby Sprunt Cotton Compress. He grabbed his Winchester and walked down the street with the gun on his shoulder, "feeling very much like a fool," he wrote later. If there was any trouble with blacks, he realized, there were plenty of whites with guns to handle it. Rountree returned the gun to his home, then walked to the Sprunt building.

At the compress, Rountree saw Sprunt and Roger Moore struggling to calm the black workers while also trying to keep the swelling white mob at bay. Rountree joined in, hoping to persuade the blacks to return to work. One worker glanced at the armed white men assembled on the street and asked Rountree: "What have we done? What have we done?" Rountree did not respond. "I had no answer," he wrote later. "They had done nothing."

Even so, Rountree feared that the workers would go home and arm themselves with whatever guns they could muster. He found a telephone and called the armory, directing the Wilmington Light Infantry to haul its Colt rapid-fire gun to the compress "to have it convenient for use if necessary." Rountree regretted the call almost immediately. He realized he had brought into play a murderous weapon at a time when hundreds of whites were armed with rifles, shotguns, and pistols. It was "a fool thing to do," he admitted later.

The deputy sheriff, Gizzard French, arrived at the armory at considerable personal risk. Mayor Wright and Police Chief Melton had by now ceded control of the city's streets to the white mobs and the Red Shirts. But French, an irrepressible sort, tried to take command of the situation at the compress. He deputized Rountree and several other white men and told them to get control of the black workers. It was a peculiar order. It was the enraged white men, not the cowed black employees, who were threatening violence. But Rountree took advantage of his newly granted authority as a sheriff's deputy. He "read the riot act to the negroes," as he put it. This seem to mollify the white mob but only momentarily.

Soon several white men approached Colonel Moore and pressured him to issue an order to shoot the black workers. If he refused, they said, they would open fire anyway. Moore reminded the men that they had chosen him as their commander and that no one would shoot anybody without being ordered to do so. He warned that anyone who fired a weapon at the compress would be arrested. Most of the men backed down.

But others in the mob persisted. One man told Captain Donald MacRae, the brother of the white supremacist leader Hugh MacRae, that he and his friends planned to "kill the whole gang of Negroes." MacRae was still a federal military officer. He was commander of a militia unit composed of local men from the Wilmington Light Infantry. The unit had joined the US service the previous May for the Spanish-American War. On November 10, the soldiers were still members of the US military. They would not be formally released from federal service until eight days later.

Captain MacRae had rushed that morning to the Sprunt Cotton Compress armed with a riot gun, two pistols, a Bowie knife, and five pounds of riot cartridges. He assumed the black workers were rioting.

But now MacRae realized that any role by his troops in the day's events could prompt federal intervention. Beyond that, he saw that the black men were terrified and wanted only to go home and protect their families. "It was little less than murder that they proposed," he said later of the mob. He refused to get involved.

As Sprunt continued to beseech the black men to return to work, he dispatched a white supervisor and a black worker to tour black neighborhoods in his personal buggy to find out what was happening there. He also ordered his white workers to bring his private boat around to the wharf so that its four guns were pointed at the white mob. The US military had provided weapons to private vessels and steamers during the Spanish-American War.

Soon the two employees returned in Sprunt's buggy and reported that only the *Record* office had been burned. Brooklyn was not on fire. The news seemed to calm the black workers. Sprunt arranged with Colonel Moore for armed white men from the Vigilance Committee to escort small groups of black workers to their homes, past the white sentinels. Coincidentally, the white mob suddenly abandoned its siege of the compress and began rushing to Brooklyn, driven there by yet another rumor: a hostile gang of armed black men was said to be gathering at North Fourth and Harnett Streets.

CHAPTER TWENTY-SEVEN

Situation Serious

THE COMMOTION at the Sprunt Cotton Compress alarmed other black workers along Wilmington's crowded waterfront. These men toiled for low wages at white-owned lumberyards, shipping companies, railroad yards, and turpentine and pitch plants. As rumors of a white riot swept the riverfront, the sight of Sprunt workers running home to head off white gunmen sent other wharf workers sprinting toward their own houses.

At the same time, some of the white men who had torched the *Record* office raced on foot and in streetcars toward North Fourth and Harnett Streets in Brooklyn to confront the black men said to be gathering there. Though Brooklyn was home to both blacks and whites, many sections were almost entirely black, prompting some whites to refer to much of Brooklyn as Darktown. The whites in the mob were still stoked with adrenaline from the *Record* torching and eager for an opportunity to shoot black men. From streetcar windows, they fired rifle shots into black homes and storefronts along Castle Street.

It was just after 11:00 a.m. when several dozen white gunmen arrived at North Fourth and Harnett to find a crowd of anxious and aroused black men gathered outside Brunjes' Saloon. A few were armed with old pistols and rifles. The men were angered by the burning of the

Record. They shouted across the street, cursing the white men who had destroyed the voice of Wilmington's black community.

The whites assembled on the opposite corner, displaying their rifles and shotguns, trying to intimidate the black men. Aaron Lockamy, the middle-aged white police officer on temporary duty, tried to calm the situation. But the two sides continued to exchange taunts and curses. The whites ordered the blacks to disperse. They refused and cursed the white men again.

It did not take long for the standoff to erupt in violence. Moments later, four white men unleashed a fusillade from a .44-caliber navy rifle, two 16-shot repeating rifles, and a double-barreled shotgun loaded with buckshot. Three black men toppled to the wood-slatted walkway. Two bled to death there, one on the walkway beneath the awning of Walker's grocery and the other after tumbling into the gutter nearby. They were later identified as Charles Lindsay and William Mouzon. The third man crawled inside a nearby home and died on the floor. Other men ran from the corner in all directions, pursued by whites shooting wildly at their fleeing figures.

"Kill the niggers! Kill the damned niggers!" they screamed.

The next morning, the city's white newspapers, quoting white witnesses, reported that blacks had fired first. George Rountree claimed he had seen "a half-grown negro boy" fire the first shot, although Officer Lockamy later said later he had seen the white men open fire. Whoever had fired first, the black men of Wilmington were now hopelessly outgunned.

Less than a block from the corner at North Fourth and Harnett, Dr. Bernice C. Moore operated a busy drugstore on North Fourth Street. Dr. Moore was a proud white supremacist whose small shop formed a white island surrounded by a sea of black faces in that part of Brooklyn. Like other white men in Wilmington during the summer of 1898, Dr. Moore had purchased a small arsenal of guns and ammunition—not just for himself but also for other white men in the area. A group of white businessmen and citizens had raised $2,600 for Dr. Moore to purchase riot guns and repeating rifles to distribute to local white men, many of them too poor to afford the weapons.

As the proprietor of a white outpost in Brooklyn, Dr. Moore had been tasked by the city's leading white citizens to serve as trip wire for any trouble arising from black men living there. Along with selected white men elsewhere in the city, Moore had been instructed to notify white leaders if blacks began to riot, as the newspapers had been predicting all summer.

Shortly before noon on November 10, Dr. Moore was inside his drugstore when he heard the sudden rattle of gunshots from North Fourth and Harnett. He rushed to his telephone and called the armory of the Wilmington Light Infantry.

"They're fighting over the road!" he shouted into the receiver.

More gunshots sounded. Five or six black men dressed in workers' overalls fell dead. One wounded man, Samuel McFallon, crawled under a house on North Fourth Street and later bled to death. Clawson, the *Messenger* reporter, ran through the streets, trying to keep up with the wild shooting. "Gunfire rattled all around us and bullets whistled closely," he wrote.

Several black men fired back at the whites while trying to run to safety. William Mayo, a young white man who had been standing on his porch at the corner of North Third and Harnett, took a bullet through his left chest, piercing both lungs. A white correspondent for *Collier's Weekly* reported that Mayo had been shot by "a 'bad nigger,' running amuck." A second white man, George Piner, was struck in the left arm by a .44-caliber round. Another .44-caliber bullet pierced the abdomen of a white man named N. B. Chadwick. The three men, who all survived their wounds, may have indeed been shot by black men. But it is also possible that they were accidentally shot by white gunmen, who were firing in all directions.

ESCAPED SLAVES ARRIVING IN WILMINGTON, N. C.—FROM A SKETCH BY OUR SPECIAL ARTIST.

Fugitive slaves flowed into Wilmington at the close of the Civil War, drawn by the promise of jobs in the city's port and in the naval stores industry in the Cape Fear countryside. Many initially lived in sprawling contraband camps.

An escaped slave, Union spy, and state senator, Abraham Galloway led the fight for black rights in Wilmington and eastern North Carolina. He commanded an ad hoc black militia that drove the Ku Klux Klan from Wilmington in 1868.

Colonel Alfred Moore Waddell was the leading orator for the white supremacy campaign in 1898, inciting whites to attack and terrorize black citizens. He vowed to fill the Cape Fear River with black carcasses.

Alexander Lightfoot Manly was the editor of the *Daily Record* and the grandson of a white North Carolina governor. White supremacists used Manly's scathing August 1898 editorial on race and sex as a pretext to order his lynching and burn his newspaper. Manly escaped Wilmington before the coup.

Furnifold Simmons was the chairman of the state Democratic Party and the political leader of the white supremacy campaign of 1898. His speeches and proclamations incited whites to violence.

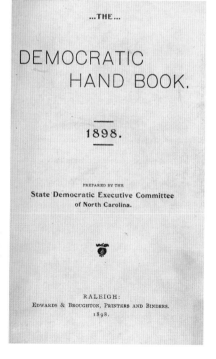

...THE...

DEMOCRATIC HAND BOOK.

1898.

PREPARED BY THE
State Democratic Executive Committee
of North Carolina.

RALEIGH:
EDWARDS & BROUGHTON, PRINTERS AND BINDERS.
1898.

In 1898, the Democratic Party distributed a Democratic Hand Book to warn white voters of the existential threat of Negro rule—"a curse to both races." The pamphlet declared North Carolina "white man's country," where blacks would obey or die.

A SERIOUS QUESTION—HOW LONG WILL THIS LAST?

A WARNING.

Get Back! We Will not Stand It.

THEY ARE RETURNING.

The Goddess of Democracy Welcomes Home All Honest White Men.

The Vampire That Hovers Over North Carolina.

The *News and Observer* fanned white fears that blacks' new political rights emboldened them to rape white women and take white men's jobs. Editor Josephus Daniels incited whites to overthrow "black rule," publishing race-baiting articles—and cartoons aimed at illiterate whites. Daniels called his paper "the militant voice of White Supremacy."

REMEMBER THE

These degenerate sons of the white race who control the republican machine in this county, or those whose positions made them influential in putting negro rule on the whites, will suffer the penalty of their responsibility for any disturbance consequent on the determination of the white men of this county to carry the election at any cost.

REMEMBER THE

Six leading white Republicans and Populists—"degenerate sons of the white race"—were targeted for banishment by the coup's leaders for their political alignment with black Republicans. Three were banished from Wilmington forever.

George Rountree was a Harvard-educated lawyer and a leading conspirator in the murders and coup on November 10, 1898.

William Everett Henderson was a Wilmington lawyer who lived as a black man but was actually the son of a white man and a Cherokee woman. A respected leader among blacks, he was banished from Wilmington at gunpoint after the coup.

John C. Dancy was the highly paid customs collector at the Wilmington port. He counseled fellow blacks in Wilmington to bow to white supremacist threats and blamed editor Alex Manly for the riot and coup.

Wilmington's white businessmen purchased a Colt rapid-fire for the Wilmington
Light Infantry to use against the city's black citizens. On November 10, 1898,
the miltia towed the gun through the streets to terrorize blacks.

State militiamen from Wilmington and three other North Carolina towns.
Seated third from left is George Morton, Naval Reserves commander.
Seated third from right is Lt. Col. Walker Taylor, Wilmington Light Infantry
commander. Seated second from right is Capt. Thomas C. James, commander
of a WLI company. Photo taken November 10, 1898.

Charles Aycock was a former red-shirt supporter whose race-baiting speeches in 1898 incited whites to attack and terrorize black voters. He was elected governor of North Carolina in 1900.

Red Shirts in Laurinburg, about 100 miles northwest of Wilmington. The Red Shirts proved even more effective than the Ku Klux Klan in killing and terrorizing blacks in Wilmington and the Cape Fear country—and stripping most of the right to vote.

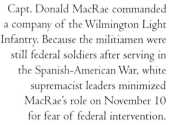

Colonel Roger Moore commanded the Ku Klux Klan in Wilmington in 1868 and the city's Red Shirts in 1898. His gunmen were responsible for killing many of the black men shot dead on November 10, 1898.

Capt. Donald MacRae commanded a company of the Wilmington Light Infantry. Because the militiamen were still federal soldiers after serving in the Spanish-American War, white supremacist leaders minimized MacRae's role on November 10 for fear of federal intervention.

Hon A. M. Waddell.
Chairman Citizens Committee
Wilmington N.C.
            Dear sir
We the colored citizens
to whom was referred
the matter of expulsion
from from this com-
munity, of the person
and press of A.L. Manly.
beg most respectfully
to say that we are
in no wise re-
sponsible for nor
in anyway endorse
the obnoxious
article that called

forth your actions.
Neither are we
authorized to ack
for him in this
matter; but in
the interest of peace,
we will most
willingly use our
influence to have
your wishes carried
out.
    Very respectfully,
        The Committee
        of Colored Citizens.

The leading black men of Wilmington were ordered to obey the terms of the
"White Declaration of Independence" and to banish Alex Manly. In their written
response, they condemned Manly and promised to cooperate with white coup leaders.

The first gunshots fired on November 10, 1898, sounded at the corner of North Fourth
and Harnett Streets after whites and blacks faced off here.

Some oral traditions say Alex Manly (left) and his brother Frank fled Wilmington together before the riot and coup. Alex did leave, but Frank remained at the *Daily Record* until the morning of November 10, when he fled the city to escape the approaching mob.

Members of the white mob pose after burning the black-readership *Daily Record* newspaper and failing to find and lynch editor Alex Manly. Photo taken on November 10, 1898.

Gov. Daniel Russell, a Republican from Wilmington, was bullied by white supremacists into sending white supremacist militias from other cities into Wilmington on November 10, 1898, under the pretext that blacks—not whites—were rioting.

Fusionists of both races were targeted for banishment after the coup, but more blacks were forcibly ejected. On November 11, 1898, armed white militiamen escorted several prominent black men to Wilmington's train station for permanent banishment.

A city ambulance bearing a white cross bounced through the rutted streets, collecting the wounded, both black and white. Fourteen bleeding men, twelve black and two of the three whites who had been shot, were delivered to Wilmington's City-County Hospital. The hospital was understaffed—many of the white nurses and medical assistants had fled, fearing they would be shot by black rioters. The white resident on call, Dr. R. E. Zachary, treated the patients, the whites in the white ward, the blacks in the colored ward. Two of the black men died just after they were admitted. Every other patient survived. Dr. Zachary made a notation: "All except the two white men were shot in the back."

The city's white residents had no doubt who had shot the three white men. Word spread quickly through Wilmington's white community that Negroes were shooting at whites. Wilmington's streets were overrun by white men rushing with their guns to help put down the anticipated black rebellion. The long-planned killing of Wilmington's black population had begun.

Thomas Clawson, the white reporter, followed a wounded black man from North Fourth and Harnett into a home at 411 Harnett Street. He encountered three distraught black women. On the floor behind them was a black man named Bizell, dead of his wounds. On a bed, Clawson found the owner of the house, George H. Davis, also a black man, bleeding from a gunshot wound to the chest, just above his heart, and another to his left thigh. An embedded bullet was visible just beneath the skin of the man's chest. Clawson ran his finger over it. Davis opened his eyes and told Clawson that the white men had fired first. Before returning to his reporting on the street, Clawson sent for both a white doctor and a black one, to tend to the wounded man. Davis survived, though Clawson later remarked that "it appeared impossible for one so desperately wounded ever to recover."

Some of the fleeing black men ran down North Third Street. One of them, Sam Gregory, stumbled upon a group of white men firing into the roadway. He toppled over, dead, between Harnett and Swann Streets. Other black men from the neighborhood, hearing the shots at North Third and Harnett, raced toward the corner. They were intercepted at North Second and Harnett by white gunmen, who warned them to turn back. Several black men opened fire, and the whites shot back. One of the black men, a laborer, was wounded but managed to stumble to nearby railroad tracks before he fell dead.

At the first sound of gunshots, block captains under Colonel Roger Moore's command set in motion a long-standing plan to protect white women and children. White families were escorted to designated collection points, then transferred to the First Baptist Church, located next to the Wilmington Light Infantry armory. Armed guards were posted around the church property. Along the riverfront, the tugboats *Marion* and *Navassa* were ordered to patrol the wharves to prevent black arsonists from setting them afire.

By this time, Colonel Taylor had received a telegram in response to his own earlier "situation serious" telegram to Governor Russell.

Russell knew that whites were predicting a black riot—a highly unlikely event, he reasoned, given his familiarity with the city's cautious black leadership. But the governor was by now thoroughly cowed by the white leaders of his hometown. Once again, he capitulated. Russell accepted, without argument, white supremacist claims that blacks—not whites—were rioting. The governor's response was relayed to Colonel Taylor by the state's acting adjutant general in Raleigh, who wrote: "The governor directs that you take command of Captain James Company at Wilmington and preserve the peace."

At midday on November 10, Russell told his advisers in Raleigh that the Wilmington Light Infantry was unable to put down the purported black riot on its own. Wilmington's white leaders wanted reinforcements. Russell seemed to have accepted, against all evidence, Colonel Taylor's claims of an armed black uprising. He decided to dispatch state militiamen from two nearby towns. The detachments he chose were as committed to white supremacy as the Wilmington units—as Russell knew all too well from his harrowing train ride on Election Day. Russell sent telegrams to state militia units in Clinton and Maxton, two white towns where night riders had threatened and beaten potential black voters throughout the summer and fall.

"Hold your company in readiness to move to Wilmington," Russell instructed. The governor's adjutant general followed up by ordering the Clinton and Maxton units to report to Colonel Taylor in Wilmington. They boarded trains to Wilmington early that afternoon. The Maxton militia left behind a group of disappointed Red Shirts who had just sent a telegram to Wilmington: "*Maxton* has 159 red shirts who want to get on the train."

Colonel Taylor wanted every armed white man available. He telegraphed the governor again: "I need two companies here for patrol duty to-night. Situation still very serious. I need Kinston naval reserves with their rapid-fire gun. Rush assistance."

From towns across the state, white men sent telegrams to the governor's office or to Wilmington's white newspapers, offering to help put down the purported black riot. "Hold your ground. Will carry hundred Winchesters if needed," read a telegram from Rockingham, 130 miles northwest of Wilmington. Whites in Granville County, 170 miles north, offered to send five hundred armed men. Whites in Atlanta and New Orleans also promised armed assistance. And from Washington, DC, came a cryptic offer: "Can bring fifty Tar Heels and Winchesters; if need, wire." In Fayetteville, the men of the Fayetteville Light Infantry, a state militia, did not wait for a reply to their offer of assistance. They grabbed their guns and boarded a train for Wilmington.

Russell's order to the Clinton and Maxton militias was a sideshow. It was his earlier decision to mobilize the Wilmington militia that provided Colonel Taylor with the pretext he needed to launch attacks on blacks. Russell never fully explained his actions that day. But because of his order, Colonel Taylor was able to declare martial law and order the

Wilmington Light Infantry to proceed from the armory to Brooklyn—armed with the Colt rapid-fire gun, paid for by the city's white supremacist businessmen. Before they left, the infantrymen gathered next to the Colt to pose for a photograph.

After telephoning the Wilmington Light Infantry, as he had been instructed by the secret committees, Dr. Moore called the Naval Reserves from his drugstore on North Fourth Street. He reported the gunshots he had heard from the nearby corner. The naval commander, George L. Morton, ordered his men to prepare to deploy to North Fourth and Harnett Streets to assist in "quelling the negro riots," as he put it. But Morton did not want to act without first obtaining formal authorization from a city official. Morton later said he was unable to locate Mayor Wright or Police Chief Melton. He decided to track down the county deputy sheriff, Gizzard French, to persuade him to order the Naval Reserves into the streets.

Morton and his men found French in his room at the Orton Hotel. As one of the targeted Big Six, the sheriff was in no position to turn down Morton's request. But he refused to go out himself to restrain the white gunmen; he had no intention of offering himself as a target. Instead, French provided Morton with a handwritten order instructing him to "use all the force at your disposal to quell the existing violation of the peace in the city." French did not specify who had violated the peace, but it was understood to be black men. The Naval Reserves now had authorization—from a white Republican—to secure the peace with every weapon at Morton's disposal, including the Hotchkiss rapid-fire gun delivered two days earlier.

Before Morton deployed his troops, he sent a telegram to Governor Russell, informing him that the deputy sheriff had authorized the Naval Reserves to restore the peace. The telegraph system proved crucial to the city's white leaders that day. It provided a means of almost instant communication among whites within Wilmington and among their confederates in Raleigh and other towns. Telegraphs had been in use in the United States for half a century, and by the late 1890s telegraph operators were common sights in downtown Wilmington—the gatekeepers of the internet of the day. Visiting white reporters from New York, Chicago, Atlanta, and elsewhere filed their dispatches by telegraph, providing not only moment-to-moment updates but also a nearly unanimous portrayal of the white supremacy campaign as a welcome corrective to corrupt Negro rule. Readers hundreds of miles away kept abreast of events in Wilmington in something approaching real time. A correspondent for the *Washington Evening Star*, for instance, transmitted a detailed account, by telegraph, of the events of November 10 in time to be published in the evening edition that same day.

In response to naval commander Morton's telegram, Russell's adjutant general wired back: "Your action ordering out naval reserves to preserve the peace is approved by the Governor, who directs that you place yourself under orders of Lieut. Col. Walker Taylor." Between them, the infantry and the Naval Reserves were able to deploy 140 trained and armed white men. Russell's decision was pivotal: he gave a committed white supremacist unchecked authority to unleash state troops against black citizens—the very men whose votes had put Russell in office.

Captain Donald MacRae was still resisting efforts by white gunmen to unleash his military unit on black residents in and around Brooklyn. But when several white men told MacRae that whites and blacks were exchanging gunfire near the railroad tracks in Brooklyn, the captain headed toward the site, trailed by an assortment of white men—his Light Infantry soldiers, Red Shirts, and armed citizens.

When Captain MacRae reached the tracks, he saw a crowd of black men on a rise of land known as Dickinson Hill. Men in the mob asked MacRae to take charge. He quickly organized a group of gunmen in a military formation designed to drive the blacks off the hill and toward the river. But just as MacRae's position as a federal officer had compromised his role at the Sprunt Cotton Compress earlier that day, someone again raised an objection.

"I had just gotten the line formed," MacRae recalled later, "when someone came up and said, 'This is not right, Don MacRae [is] an U.S. Army officer and if found in this business, he will be gotten after by the President.' So they said, 'We will put someone else in command and you can get in ranks.'"

A white supremacist leader later explained: "As Captain MacRae's Company . . . had not been mustered out of Federal service, the white leaders realized that his leadership might involve the United States government in the Wilmington Rebellion, and they feared that such a contingency would result in serious complication that might frustrate the objectives of the revolt." MacRae stood down.

Meanwhile, Captain Thomas James had been ordered by Colonel Taylor to lead another Light Infantry unit in Brooklyn—the unit with the horse-drawn wagon fitted with the Colt rapid-fire gun. James marched his men down Market Street to North Third Street, where several white women waved and yelled: "Godspeed!" The column stopped at Princess Street, outside a funeral home, and waited for the Naval Reserves to arrive.

Once the sailors joined the infantrymen, the combined procession of more than a hundred military men marched to the Fourth Street Bridge leading into Brooklyn. Captain James halted the march and told the assembled men: "Boys I want to tell you right now I want you to load and when I give the command to shoot, I want you to shoot to kill."

James and his men marched across the bridge. Members of the Light Infantry later claimed that a large gathering of black men opened fire nearby. The infantrymen raised their rifles and unleashed a volley of shots. George Rountree later recalled seeing "several negroes lying on the street dead and a good many white people about with arms." By some accounts, up to twenty-five black men were shot dead near the bridge.

J. Allan Taylor and Hugh MacRae, Captain MacRae's younger brother, had already made their way to Brooklyn to take charge of the white gunmen there. Both men were members of the Secret Nine. Taylor and Hugh MacRae began by trying to take control of several men who were searching for the black man they believed had shot the wounded white resident, William Mayo. A local man, described by one white man as "a half-breed Indian," approached J. Allan Taylor and told him a black laborer named Daniel Wright had shot Mayo. The man led Taylor and a collection of infantrymen and Red Shirts to Wright's home nearby, at 810 North Third Street.

Wright was regarded by many whites as a troublemaker and an instigator of black rebellion. He had been spotted earlier that morning, chastising blacks who had cowered in their homes rather than going out into the streets to confront white men. The mob descended on Wright's small two-story house. White witnesses later claimed that Wright fired on the whites from his attic, wounding two white men.

Men in the mob fired into the attic, then set the house alight. Wright emerged from the flames and was shot instantly. He fell, his blood soaking the packed earth. Several men yanked him to his feet. Wright begged for mercy. Someone smashed him over the head with a gas pipe, drawing more blood and slamming him back to his knees. Several men yelled for him to be lynched from a nearby lamppost. They searched for a rope. But another man suggested that Wright be given a chance to run for his life. He was released. "Run, nigger, run!" a man shouted.

Bleeding profusely, Wright stumbled through the packed sand at the edge of the street. He struggled about fifty feet before gunshots sounded. He tumbled to the ground, felled by thirteen bullets, five of them through his back. He lay in the dirt bleeding for about thirty minutes before several men took him to a hospital. Wright survived through the night but died early the next morning. Doctors who treated him told the *Messenger*: "They never saw one man with as many shots in him as he had."

By the time Wright was shot, the Light Infantry and Naval Reserves had been deployed as a single military unit, backed by bands of armed white civilians. At the same time, J. Allan Taylor and Hugh MacRae continued to command gunmen roaming black neighborhoods. Separately, Colonel Roger Moore had taken charge of the armed Vigilance Committee groups, which included several Red Shirts. White sentinels acting under various commands set up checkpoints, where they searched every black man, woman, and child they encountered. White housewives walked from one checkpoint to the next, supplying the men with hot coffee, served in fifty-pound lard cans; fried ham and eggs; and buckwheat cakes smothered with butter.

The Reverend J. Allen Kirk, the black minister, saw black men lying dead in the streets and gutters as he tried to make his way home. He planned to load his wife and niece into a carriage and try to flee the city, but he was stopped and searched by white sentinels. Kirk was shocked by the white men's rage. He had assumed that the Committee of Colored Citizens' compliant response to Waddell's demands the day before had soothed their anger.

Kirk had come to Wilmington from Boston and had always assumed that Southern whites would tolerate small measures of black success and achievement so long as blacks ultimately bowed to white authority. But now, it seemed to Kirk, black appeasement had only stoked a more malevolent strain of white ferocity:

The little white boys of the city searched them [blacks] and took from them every means of defence, and if they resisted, they were shot down . . . they went into a colored man's house . . . then took up a stick of wood and bursted his brains out . . .

Colored women were examined and their hats taken off and search was made even under their clothing. They went from house to house looking for Negroes that they considered offensive; took arms they had hidden and killed them for the least expression of manhood . . . One fellow was walking along a railroad and they shot him down without any provocation. White ministers carried their guns to kill Negro Christians and sinners.

At Tenth and Princess Streets, located across the street from the Wilmington Seacoast Railway depot, stood Morro Castle, a well-known whorehouse. The madam asked an officer of the Wilmington Light Infantry to dispatch three militiamen to protect her black prostitutes from attack. Her request was politely refused.

At Second and Castle Streets, J. F. Maunder, a Light Infantry militiaman, stopped a black man and asked him about a bag slung over his back. The man told Maunder he was carrying onions and potatoes. Maunder grabbed the bag and peered inside. "I found onions, potatoes and an old case knife," he recalled. He confiscated the knife and passed the black man on to the next sentinel, who again searched both the man and his bag.

Maunder also told an elderly black woman that he suspected she had concealed a razor in her stocking. When she offered to bare her leg, he passed her on to be searched by a group of white women on the next corner. Nearby, a group of Red Shirts stopped a black woman and demanded to search the soiled laundry in the basket she carried. She showed the men a pair of panties and told them they belonged to the white woman who employed her. The Red Shirts told her to move along.

At another intersection, a black mail carrier in uniform was forced by two white sentinels to kneel at gunpoint. They laughed as the postman begged for his life. One sentinel wanted to shoot the man, but his partner hesitated. They finally set the postman free, with a warning not to return.

At the Sprunt Cotton Compress, Jim Reeves, a powerfully built black man who weighed cotton bales for James Sprunt, was badly shaken by the sight of enraged white men and their Winchesters. He asked his white foreman, James D. Smith, to escort him home past the white sentries. Reeves enjoyed a respectful relationship with the whites who ran the compress and was a personal favorite of James Sprunt. He was alert and quick-witted. He had been raised by a white boardinghouse keeper who taught him to read and write and to speak what he called "proper English." Smith agreed to help Reeves get safely to his home on Eighth Street, just eight blocks from the compress.

The two men crept to the corner of Red Cross and Second Streets, two blocks from the compress. But as they approached, Reeves saw that the corner had been overrun by white men wielding rifles, shotguns, and pistols. He panicked and begged Smith to take him back to the compress. He would try to hide there until the streets were safer. After they had returned, Smith left to try to find something for dinner for himself and Reeves, leaving the black man alone inside the compress office. Reeves tried to remain calm. He sat quietly until he glanced out a window and saw a cluster of armed white men marching toward the compress. He jumped up, leaped over a rail, and tumbled into the private secretary's office, which was not visible from the main office entryway.

Soon Reeves heard a noise. He raised his head and looked out a window to see armed white men milling in the street outside the compress. Some of the men noticed movement through the window and peered inside at Reeves's frightened face. For a moment Reeves stared back. Then he dashed through the office and up a set of stairs that led to the cotton samples room. He burrowed his way fifteen feet deep into a stack of cotton and settled in at the bottom. He tried to control his breathing while listening for sounds on the stairway. He cowered there for a long time—he did not know how long—but the white men from the street did not come searching for him.

At last, Reeves climbed out of the cotton pile and crept silently back down the stairs. The compress seemed empty. The black workers had run home. With production shut down, most of the white supervisors had left as well. Reeves was surprised to encounter one of his white bosses, a man he trusted. He begged the man to escort him home. The boss agreed to accompany Reeves to the first checkpoint, where he said he would arrange for him to be passed safely from there through the final checkpoint nearest Reeves's home.

Reeves managed to pass the first checkpoint, then another. As he approached the next, near a narrow passageway known as Five-Point Alley, he did not see any sentries. But as he entered the alley, two fifteen-year-old white boys with guns emerged from the shadows.

"Halt! Throw up your hands!" one of them shouted.

Reeves felt faint. His legs went weak. He dropped to his knees and raised both hands so that the boys could see he was not armed. He said a silent prayer. "I knew these boys didn't have no better sense than to shoot me dead," he recalled later. "My heart was in my mouth. I thought that my time had come."

The boys asked, "Do you have a pistol?"

Reeves sputtered. "Yes sir . . . No sir . . . Yes sir, no sir."

The boys seemed amused by the big distraught black man cowering before them. Reeves weighed 225 pounds and could easily have throttled the boys under other circumstances. But now he was just a helpless black man at the mercy of white schoolboys. The sentries laughed and told Reeves to go home.

Breathing heavily, he rose and walked away quickly, praying that he boys wouldn't shoot him in the back. He was only a couple of blocks from home. He made his way down the street, trying to spot the next checkpoint. There was nothing. He reached his house, ducked inside, and slammed and locked his front door.

Reeves hid inside his home for the next three days and nights with almost no food or water. On the fourth day, the streets were quiet, and he slipped safely out of Wilmington.

To back up the rapid-fire guns, Colonel Taylor had ordered the Naval Reserves to roll out two howitzers behind his columns. The howitzers were field guns, useless in tight urban quarters, but Taylor found them helpful in intimidating black residents. Given the killing efficiency of the two rapid-fire guns, the howitzers were hardly necessary to send crowds scattering. But Taylor had decided to bring out every weapon in his arsenal.

The crews who manned the two horse-drawn rapid-fire guns were known as flying machine-gun squadrons. A half dozen militiamen sat in the back of each wagon, clutching their hats and their rifles as the horses cut across street corners in pursuit of blacks. In most cases, black residents fled the instant they saw the gun squads—usually before the military men could aim the powerful weapons, much less fire them.

"The appearance of the machine gun was impressive and magical," the *Messenger* reporter Thomas Clawson wrote. "Wilmington's forethought in being prepared with a machine gun to meet any emergency was a display of wisdom . . . The fiery big horses drawing the outfit were cutting corners and racing at a rapid rate through every section of Brooklyn. It was really a dramatic and thrilling spectacle."

As the flying squadrons and white mobs searched for black men, rumors spread that armed blacks had taken up firing positions in several black churches, where guns and ammunition were said to have been stored in anticipation of a black uprising. Colonel Taylor ordered the Infantry and the Naval Reserves to search the churches. At each location, the men lined up in military formation behind the rapid-fire guns, with the barrels aimed at the front doors. In every case, black clergymen quickly opened the doors.

One flying squadron aimed a rapid-fire gun at the entrance of St. Stephen AME Church at Fifth and Red Cross Streets. With sixteen hundred members, it was one of Wilmington's largest black churches. The squadron threatened to blow a hole through the structure. The doors swung open and the militiamen rushed inside. They found no guns or ammunition—only stacks of flyers reading "Vote for Dockery," the losing Republican candidate for Congress.

After their churches were searched, black clergymen were ordered to walk through black neighborhoods and instruct residents to succumb to white authority. Reverend J. Allen Kirk watched his fellow ministers meekly obey.

> *The mob took the leading colored ministers and compelled them to go around the city with them and ask the colored people to be obedient to the white people and go in their homes and keep quiet. This was a great humiliation for us and a shame upon our denominations.*

Although rumors about gunmen and arsenals inside black churches had proved false, Colonel Taylor continued to respond to other unconfirmed reports. When he was told that three hundred to five hundred "fully armed" black men were marching toward Wilmington from neighboring Brunswick County, Taylor ordered the flying machine-gun squadron to set up the gun on the banks of the Cape Fear, aimed at bridges leading into the city from Brunswick County. Later, the rapid-fire Colt gun was hauled to the middle of the span on the river's main bridge, known as Hilton Bridge. Then the drawbridge was raised to block access to Wilmington's waterfront. After waiting in vain for the advancing black columns, the gun squad withdrew in disappointment.

But soon the infantry was summoned again, this time to investigate reports of a gunshot fired at white men from inside a shack at Sixth and Bladen Streets. The militiamen searched the area and found no sign of a black gunman. But across the intersection stood Manhattan Park, a black dance hall that had long been regarded by whites as a den of scoundrels and troublemakers. Someone started a rumor that blacks were firing on whites from inside the hall. The militiamen opened fire on a tall wooden fence that surrounded the hall, tearing ragged holes in the boards. More rounds pitted the wooden walls of the hall and shattered its windows.

From the rear of the hall, a black man emerged from a doorway and raced across the yard. He was trying to climb over a section of fence when he was felled by a fusillade of fifteen to twenty gunshots. One of the militiamen ran over to examine the man's body. "When we tu'nd him ove' Misto Niggah had a look of s'prise on his count'nance," he recalled in an account related by a reporter for *Collier's Weekly*.

A detachment of militiamen wielding axes hacked down the remainder of the fence and pushed inside the hall, where they encountered five terrified black men. The militiamen ordered them to raise their hands. Four complied and were arrested. The fifth man, Josh Halsey, bolted for the doorway and fled into the street. According to some accounts, Halsey was deaf and had not understood the militiamen's commands. A squad was dispatched to track him down. The militiamen searched the area, house by house, until someone provided them with Halsey's address.

Halsey had run home and climbed into bed. When his young daughter spotted the militiamen marching toward the house, she begged her father to run. Halsey ran out the back door and was cut down by a stream of gunfire. "The poor creature jumped up and ran out the back door in frantic terror to be shot down like a dog by armed soldiers ostensibly sent to preserve the peace," Jane Cronly, a white neighbor, wrote in her diary.

In another version of Halsey's murder, recounted by the militiaman J. F. Maunder, Halsey was captured on the street. The militiamen offered to release him if he agreed to run through gunfire. One militiaman, Bill Robbins, was appalled. "I am sick to my stomach," he said. Maunder said he told Robbins not to "show the white feather or I will shoot you myself." Halsey was set free and began to run. The militiamen raised their rifles. Robbins fired over Halsey's head, muttering, "I hope I did not hit that man." But Maunder and others aimed directly at Halsey. Their gunshots tore off the top of his head. He was dead before his body hit the street.

A few white men tried to reason with the mobs and halt the killings. James Sprunt and Mayor Silas Wright drove a carriage through the city, following the sounds of gunshots as they sought to "abate the excitement and prevent needless bloodshed." Some accounts said Wright claimed to be a British subject so that he could seek protection from

Sprunt, who served as the British vice consul in Wilmington. From the moment the mob stormed his compress, Sprunt had been trying, with little success, to convince fellow white supremacists that his workers posed no threat. Now, as he again pleaded for calm, Sprunt and Wright were rebuffed. Some of the gunmen responded by firing at their carriage.

A white Catholic priest, Father Christopher Dennen, confronted Mike Dowling, the belligerent Red Shirt brigade commander. Dowling and many of his men from Dry Pond had been drinking most of the day. They expected all white men, including clergymen, to support them. Indeed, several white ministers had fetched their guns and joined the mob. But Father Dennen calmly prevailed on Dowling, an Irish Catholic, to refrain from killing anyone. Dowling reluctantly agreed.

Buck Burkhimer, a Light Infantry militiaman, was upset that soldiers were shooting at unarmed civilians. He rode on horseback among his fellow militiamen, screaming at them, "Shame, men! Stop this! Stop this!" He pointed to several black corpses. "Don't you see these dead men?" The soldiers responded by pointing their weapons at Burkhimer.

Jane Cronly, the sister of the reluctant white sentinel, witnessed several killings that afternoon, including the bloody execution of Josh Halsey after he fled the Manhattan Park dance hall. In her diary, Cronly described how white men had shot blacks "down right and left in a most unlawful way, killing one man who was simply standing at a corner waiting to get back to his work." She overheard one white man shout to others as they fired at fleeing blacks: "We are just shooting to see the niggers run."

Cronly watched Red Shirts cheer some of the killings and then parade in triumph, rifles on their shoulders, as they searched for more blacks to shoot. She felt ill. "For the first time in my life," she wrote, "I have been ashamed of my State and of the Democratic Party in North Carolina."

As a white woman whose brother had been compelled to serve as a sentinel, Cronly understood, to her horror, the murderous motives of the white supremacists who directed the killings. And she had clearly observed the effect on her black neighbors. "The whole thing was with the object of striking terror to the man's heart, so that he would never vote again," she wrote. "For this was the object of the whole persecution; to make Nov. 10th a day to be remembered by the whole race for all time."

The killings continued throughout the mild, sunny afternoon.

John L. Gregory, a black laborer, was shot dead on North Third Street, between Harnett and Swann, a few blocks from his house on North Fifth Street. He had been trying to reach home from work.

Sam Macfarlane, another laborer, was shot as he crossed the Seaboard Air Line Railroad tracks on Harnett Street on his way home for dinner. He died later in the colored ward of the City-County Hospital of "four terrible wounds."

A black man, possibly a tavern owner named Tom Rowan, was shot and killed on a Cape Fear wharf after he was accused of having "sassed" two white men. His body was dumped into the river.

A black man was shot and killed near a railroad repair shop on North Third Street. White witnesses said he had fired at a group of white men.

A black man was shot dead on the Fourth Street Bridge and fell onto the railroad tracks. White witnesses said he had pointed an old musket at a white man.

A black man was killed on Fourth Street near Red Cross Street for reasons unknown. Another was shot at Tenth and Princess, purportedly for failing to stop for white sentinels.

A black man was shot and killed by a Light Infantry militiaman on a railroad track.

A black man was killed at Tenth and Mulberry Streets for failing to stop for a white patrol.

A member of a Red Shirt brigade saw his comrades shoot six black men at the Cape Fear Lumber Company and bury their bodies in a ditch.

Another Red Shirt watched a single white sniper shoot and kill nine black men, one by one, as they filed out of a shack.

A Red Shirt said he had watched a white gunman in Dry Pond wait four days to shoot a black policeman named Perkins, finally killing the officer when he emerged from his home in an alley near Second and Castle Streets.

A white teenager shot and killed a black "rabble-rouser" as the man spoke to a gathering of blacks near Fourth and Nixon Streets. The city's newspapers did not record the black man's words.

CHAPTER TWENTY-EIGHT

Strictly According to Law

As the pale autumn sun dimmed at midafternoon on November 10, white gunmen were still tramping through the streets. They were in pursuit of black men hiding in the warren of tidy frame homes, cramped yards, and narrow alleys of Brooklyn and nearby neighborhoods. The worst of the killing was over. Black corpses were left where they had fallen, "stretched on their backs with their eyes open as a warning to other blacks," one witness wrote. The black men of Wilmington were trapped. The main roads leading into the city were blocked by Red Shirts intent on intercepting the columns of black rioters rumored to be descending on the city from outlying areas.

Hundreds of black families had begun abandoning their homes and possessions. They fled the city in wagons and carriages or on foot, seeking safety in cemeteries and swamps just outside the city. The Red Shirts and other sentinels did not try to stop them. They were focused on confronting columns of armed black men purportedly invading the city. Other blacks were more than welcome to *leave* Wilmington.

White leaders turned their attention to the Fusionists still holding elected and appointed municipal offices. They began discussing ways to enforce the ultimatum, issued by the coup leaders the day before, that the mayor and police chief resign. Members of the Committee of

Twenty-Five, appointed by Colonel Waddell and others, jockeyed for selection as replacement aldermen as they plotted to forcibly remove the current council.

Colonel Waddell had by now surrendered control of the men who had burned the *Record* office that morning. They had raced away on their own to confront the black men gathered at North Fourth and Harnett Streets. That left Waddell bereft of armed men to command. Seeking to reassert his authority, he called a meeting of the Committee of Twenty-Five at the Seaboard Air Line building.

Under Waddell's direction, the committee issued an order instructing Mayor Wright, Police Chief Melton, and the board of aldermen to report to city hall. Waddell dispatched two emissaries to deliver the news to Wright and Melton. He then led the committee to the nearby Merchant's Association building, just down Front Street, to await responses from the mayor and police chief. It was now just past 3:00 p.m.

When Mayor Wright was tracked down and told to resign, he initially objected, saying he preferred not to step down during a crisis. He was told he had two options: resign or be forcibly removed from office. Nothing in the city charter permitted such an ultimatum, but Wright had just watched white mobs surge through the streets, firing their weapons. Wright's name was among the most prominent listed on the REMEMBER THE 6 placards; the notices were still posted around the city. Reluctantly, he agreed to quit.

Under further duress, the mayor agreed to call a meeting of the board of aldermen for 4:00 p.m. at city hall. He did not need to be told the purpose of the meeting—for Wright and his police chief and aldermen to formally submit their resignations.

When Waddell's two emissaries found Police Chief Melton at the police station at city hall, he was preoccupied by a fresh report from a deputy about "a riot" at the Fourth Street Bridge near the railroad tracks. The deputy told Melton he had just seen "a lot of men killed." Waddell's emissaries interrupted and told Melton not to worry about the dead black men, because he was no longer in charge. He was instructed to resign at once. Melton resisted. He said he would resign only if he were paid the remainder of his salary. There was no reply. The two men simply told Melton to report at once to the Committee of Twenty-Five to submit his resignation.

While Waddell and his committeemen awaited a response from Wright and Melton, they began selecting their own mayor, police chief, and aldermen. An impromptu "election" was held. Eight white supremacists were selected as aldermen—seven of them from the Committee of Twenty-Five itself, including two men who had directed the rioters, Hugh MacRae and J. Allan Taylor of the Secret Nine. All that remained was for them to confront the current Fusion aldermen and force them to surrender their positions.

When the moment arrived to select a new mayor, there was little debate. Waddell had limited the committee's options by ensuring that ambitious men such as Rountree and former mayor Fishblate were left off the committee—reducing the chance that either man would be considered for mayor. At the same time, Waddell had won over some resentful white leaders with his Opera House speech and his leadership of the mob that had torched the *Record* office. The committeemen concluded, with little discussion, that Chairman Waddell was the obvious choice. Waddell, feigning modesty, if not surprise, accepted their appointment as Wilmington's new mayor. There was no objection.

Later, Waddell would insist that his election was entirely legal because Wright had "resigned" on his own volition: "It was certainly the strangest performance in American history, though we literally followed the law, as the Fusionists made it themselves," he wrote. "There has not been a single illegal act committed in the change of government. Simply, the old board went out, and the new board came in—strictly according to law."

Waddell was in a triumphant mood. He decided to lead a procession of committeemen, militiamen, Red Shirts, and armed citizens on a short march to city hall to force the resignations and complete the coup. The committee members made a show of readying their weapons before they left. As Waddell and the rest of the men walked out of the Merchant's Association building, they were greeted with shouts and cheers from rioters. There was a loud call-and-response chant: "Victory!" which was followed by "White men!" and then "Victory!" again. Waddell led the marchers to the city hall chambers inside Thalian Hall, the gunmen still chanting and clutching their Winchesters.

Inside the chambers, five members of the Fusionist board of aldermen were at their posts. They had just received word that rioters were headed to city hall to overthrow the government. They looked helpless. They didn't bother to flee. They chose instead to stay on the job and await their fate. Four aldermen had been there for most of the day. The fifth, John Norwood, a seventy-three-year-old black carpenter appointed to the board by Governor Russell, had just arrived after being ordered by the city clerk to report there.

Three aldermen were absent—two black men and Benjamin Keith, a prominent white Populist who had already left Wilmington. A boycott mounted by Democrats, along with false rumors that Keith advocated sex between blacks and whites, had destroyed his wholesale grocery business. Mayor Wright had just returned to the chambers, as ordered by Waddell's emissaries. Chief Melton was still at the police headquarters inside city hall.

The aldermen could hear rioters thundering through the corridors, shouting insults and hooting and whistling as they approached the chambers. They packed the room and leaned over the rails, heckling the Fusionists. At the head of the pack were J. Allan Taylor and Colonel Waddell. Taylor informed the aldermen that their replacements had been "elected." Waddell ordered Mayor Wright to call a special meeting of the board to submit its resignation. It was just after 4:00 p.m.

DAVID ZUCCHINO

The board convened, with Wright presiding. One by one, the five alder-men who were present resigned. They obeyed instructions to formally approve their replacements—the men selected an hour earlier by Waddell and his Committee of Twenty-Five. The approvals gave the proceedings a veneer of propriety, suggesting that the outgoing aldermen had resigned on their own. "They resigned in response to public sentiment," a front-page *New York Times* article explained the next morning.

Witnessing the resignations was William Struthers, a white city clerk and treasurer who had kept the minutes of the outgoing board's last meet-ing three hours earlier when it had voted to extend the election liquor ban. Struthers, a Democrat, retained his position. He dutifully kept the minutes of the coup, as if it were just another routine board of alder-men meeting. He even read aloud the minutes of the previous meeting.

As each Fusionist alderman "resigned," Struthers wrote that the resignation "was accepted." Then he wrote the name of each replace-ment, noting that each man had been "nominated and elected." Finally, Struthers swore in the new aldermen, who vowed to "support the Constitution and Laws of the United States and the Constitution and Laws of North Carolina not inconsistent therewith."

J. Allan Taylor and Hugh MacRae asked that their appointments as aldermen be delayed for two days because they were needed to com-mand the gunmen still roaming the streets. They did not consider that proper work for aldermen. Their new positions were held open for them. The three absent Fusionist aldermen were then summarily fired and replaced. In a matter of minutes, the eight Fusionists on the board—including three black men—had been replaced by eight white supremacist Democrats.

By midafternoon on November 10, Wilmington's black community was in a state of terror and panic. The limited defensive counterattack that morning had evaporated by the time the sun began to dip behind the twisted live oaks that shaded Wilmington's streets. By late afternoon, the only gunshots that echoed through the street were fired by whites.

"Rumors fly here and there that the negroes are armed," Waddell wrote. "There is no truth to that. They are utterly cowed and crushed, and are not going to interfere with anybody."

Pierre Manning, a member of the Secret Nine, was surprised by how thoroughly the killings had cracked Wilmington's black resistance. He had expected a well-armed black insurgency, not abject surrender. "No people have been so completely terrorized and . . . so completely broken or crushed than has been that of these miserable wretches," Manning wrote.

Outside the council chambers, George Rountree cornered Chief Melton in the Board of Finance meeting room. Melton was still demanding to be paid the remainder of his annual salary. Rountree told Melton that he, Rountree, could not control the white mobs. If Melton did not resign immediately, Rountree warned, he would not be responsible for anything that might befall the chief. Melton understood the meaning of the threat. He told Rountree he would resign without further pay, then left city hall and walked home, unmolested.

Told of Melton's resignation, the new board of aldermen appointed Edgar G. Parmele as the city's police chief. Parmele was a stoutly built man with wavy, short-cropped hair and a black goatee. He was one of Wilmington's most influential Democrats, having served beside Rountree and Colonel Taylor as a director of the Democratic committee. Parmele was sworn in and handed $1,000 in cash—his annual salary, in advance. It was generous pay, about $28,000 in twenty-first-century dollars at a time when Wilmington's black street cleaners earned 10 cents an hour and black maids $2 to $3 a week. Parmele would soon be tasked with restraining the white mobs that had been unleashed by his party.

The time had now come for Mayor Wright to step down. Wright calmly announced that he had decided to resign because Wilmington's leading citizens had expressed "dissatisfaction" with the way he had run the city. The resignation was unanimously approved by the new board of aldermen.

One of the aldermen nominated Waddell as the new mayor. It was a formality; the Committee of Twenty-Five had already "elected" the Colonel. There was a sudden burst of cheering and applause from the aldermen and from Red Shirts leaning over the rails. Each of the new aldermen voted, to more applause, to approve the nomination. Waddell accepted.

Struthers, the city clerk, took up his pen again. He wrote that Alfred Moore Waddell had been elected to fill the unexpired term of the office of mayor of Wilmington. But in the blank space for noting the expiration date of the new mayor's term, Struthers wrote nothing. Then the new mayor was sworn in.

After signing his name below the phrase "So help me God," Waddell felt compelled to speak. Addressing the new aldermen, he claimed he had not sought the office but had been compelled to serve due to the current "grave crisis." He said he hoped to be replaced soon. But for the moment, Waddell said, he intended to put an end to the violence and restore law and order.

"The law will be rigidly enforced and impartially administered to black and white alike," he said. There was no irony in his voice. The aldermen again cheered their new mayor.

One alderman proposed that the new council offer a formal vote of thanks to the outgoing council. The motion was tabled.

Just after the coup was consummated inside city hall, Rountree received a telegram from Governor Russell in Raleigh. The governor had fallen hopelessly behind the swift pace of events in Wilmington. The telegram informed Rountree that if Wilmington's white business leaders selected a new mayor and board of aldermen, Russell would use his influence to persuade the current mayor and board to resign.

Rountree sent the governor a dismissive reply: "Mayor and Aldermen have resigned. Nominees of citizens chosen . . . Law will be maintained and peace restored."

Waddell's first act as mayor was to swear in 250 "special policemen" to restore order. He chose them from among the armed men who had spent the day chasing and killing black men—men who were described by the *New York Times* the next day as "reputable white citizens." Waddell was also authorized to appoint twenty-five armed men to patrol the city on bicycles that night. Another twenty-five gunmen would be selected to patrol on horseback. Several Red Shirts offered their services.

"The new Government will devote its attention to restraining recklessness among the whites, as well as keeping down lawlessness among the negroes," the *Times* reported. "Further trouble of a genuine or serious nature is not expected."

CHAPTER TWENTY-NINE

Marching from Death

A s DARKNESS DESCENDED on November 10, a cold rain began to soak the streets. The wind picked up, slamming shutters and blowing trash through the backyards of Brooklyn. Sheets of rain driven by gusts from the ocean lashed a ragged procession of black men, women, and children trudging along the main avenues leading out of Wilmington. Some families had bolted from their homes without pausing to gather warm clothing, for it had been mild and sunny earlier in the day. Others had collected a few blankets and quilts, which they draped over their heads to ward off the rain. A few people had piled into carriages or horse-drawn wagons, but the rest were on foot, some without shoes.

Children sobbed in their wet clothing. Their mothers scooped them up and carried them. The women's feet sloshed where the hard clay of the roadway had turned slippery in the rain. The procession headed east, away from the river and white neighborhoods, seeking safety in the sandy pocosin swamps and the dense oak and pine forests. Some families broke away and bedded down among the worn tombstones of Wilmington's colored cemetery, known as Pine Forest. They thought white men would not venture there.

Reverend J. Allen Kirk had fought a strong urge to flee along with the families. He had instead decided to keep his wife and young niece in the city for the moment. The Kirks lived in the parsonage of the downtown Central Baptist Church, where Kirk preached. He feared his wife and niece would be swept up by the white mobs, so he sent them to stay with friends on the outskirts of Wilmington. Now, as Kirk watched the exodus of other black families pass him by, he felt forlorn.

It was a great sight to see them marching from death, and the colored women, colored men, colored children, colored enterprises and colored people all exposed to death. Firing began, and it seemed like a mighty battle in war time. The shrieks and screams of children, of mothers, of wives were heard . . . Thousands of women, children and men rushed to the swamps and there lay upon the earth in the cold to freeze and starve.

A Northern reporter, Charles Francis Bourke of *Collier's Weekly*, followed the procession into the forests:

In the woods and swamps innocent hundreds of terrified men, women and children are wandering about, fearing the vengeance of the whites, fearful of death . . . Fearing to light fires, listening for chance footsteps crushing fallen twigs . . . I heard a child crying and a hoarse voice crooning softly a mournful song . . .

"When de battle's ov-er we kin war a crown

In de new Je-ru-sa-lum."

Next day I heard soldiers singing thoughtlessly, in the gayety of their hearts, a savagely suggestive refrain:

"Oh, you niggahs, yo' had better lie low!"

Most of the black families fleeing Wilmington hailed from the working class—stevedores and laborers, maids and washerwomen. Many had witnessed the killings firsthand. The city's black professionals and businessmen had also seen the shootings, but they had made a different calculation. They decided to remain, hoping to outlast the violence.

They prayed that their capitulation to white demands the day before had inoculated them against further retribution. They were convinced the killings would cease once the white mobs realized they had broken Wilmington's black resistance. "They were frightened to death at the threats made against them, and too glad to huddle in their homes and keep quiet," Jane Cronly wrote in her diary.

White Fusionist politicians who had been hounded from office also remained in Wilmington. They assumed that their forced resignations had satisfied the leaders of the coup. But J. Allan Taylor, Hugh MacRae, and others were determined to permanently cleanse the city of any threat, white or black, to the new white supremacist order. They drew up a new list of nearly fifty men to be forever banished from Wilmington. It included the Big Six white Fusionists plus several other Fusionists, white and black, who were considered troublesome.

Late in the afternoon on November 10, Taylor and MacRae took charge of the banishment campaign. Because they had not yet formally taken their positions as aldermen, they were free to act as private citizens. As such, they did not share their plans with Waddell and his new aldermen. They feared that the new mayor and board, now responsible for maintaining law and order, would try to rein in the mobs. Taylor and MacRae quietly sent a police captain, John Furlong, in a horse-drawn wagon to round up the men on the banishment list. They assigned a detachment of Light Infantry militiamen on horseback to accompany Furlong.

The first target was Carter Peamon, the outspoken black barber whose shop was on North Fourth Street, near the center of the day's violence. Peamon had made a great public show of urging blacks to vote. But earlier in the day on November 10, he concluded that further resistance would only get him killed. He had gone from house to house in Brooklyn, accompanied by three white men, pleading with black residents not oppose the white gunmen. At one point, a group of enraged black men seized the three white men and held them hostage.

It was the sort of bold and desperate act that might be expected of Peamon himself. But he surprised everyone by pleading with the black men to release the captives.

After a series of negotiations, the three whites were set free. Peamon escorted them to a nearby gathering of white gunmen, expecting a round of thanks. Instead, several white men in the crowd attempted to lynch him. They were intercepted by two of the freed hostages, who plunged into the mob and pulled Peamon free.

Peamon's daring intercession on behalf of the white hostages did not spare him from the banishment campaign. Just before dark, the infantry detachment sent out by Taylor and MacRae "arrested" Peamon and escorted him to the city jail. A short time later, the Secret Nine issued a formal banishment order for Peamon. The infantry soldiers took him from jail and marched him at gunpoint to the train depot, where he was placed aboard a departing train.

Peamon was terrified. Just before the train departed, two ominous developments made his situation even more dire. First, he was warned by the soldiers that he would be killed on sight if he ever returned to Wilmington. Second, a gang of Red Shirts boarded the train just before it rolled out of the depot. The infantry detachment departed, leaving Peamon alone with the Red Shirts.

A few hours later, Peamon's body, riddled with bullets, was discovered in the woods near Hilton Park on Wilmington's northern outskirts. One account said he had jumped from the moving train and was shot by the Red Shirts. It is more likely that he was executed on board and his body flung from the speeding train.

The men of the infantry detachment turned their attention to George Z. French, the deposed deputy sheriff. French did not fully appreciate just how deeply many whites resented him—as a Northerner, a former carpetbagger, and, as the *Evening Dispatch* put it, "a white politician of influence with the negroes." Many white supremacists had not forgotten that French, at the height of Fusionist influence, had declared in a speech: "I would like to spin a rope to hang every Democrat in North Carolina."

French lived in a large room at the four-story brick Orton Hotel, the city's finest. His Excelsior Plantation had made him a wealthy man. Late on the afternoon of November 10, a clerk at the Orton got word that the rioters were searching for French. He went to French's quarters and persuaded him to hide in a different room.

The infantry soldiers conducted a room-to-room search and soon found French's hiding spot. They marched him from the hotel at bayonet point, bound for the train depot, past throngs of whites drawn to the streets by rumors of the banishment campaign. The gawkers hoped to catch a glimpse of well-known Fusionists who had just hours earlier held positions of influence. Someone shouted, "There's French!" Several Red Shirts sprang from the crowd and chased after the militiamen and their captive, catching up to them near the depot.

"Hang him!" someone cried. A chant rose up: "Hang him! Hang him!"

The infantry soldiers used their rifle butts to push back the throng, but they were quickly overwhelmed. Several Red Shirts seized French and dragged him to Front Street. Someone tossed a rope over the arm of a telephone pole. A noose was fashioned and wrapped around French's neck. A Red Shirt tugged at the rope and French gasped for air. As he choked, he managed to mumble the Masonic cry of distress. "Oh Lord, my God! Is there no help for the widow's son?"

A white man emerged from the crowd. It was Frank Stedman, a member of the Committee of Twenty-Five. Stedman was also a Mason. He told the men in the crowd that they would be pursued and prosecuted if they killed French. It was an effective threat; Stedman knew them all by name. The Red Shirts released their grip on the rope and French dropped to his knees, gasping for air.

Stedman and several other Masons from the crowd surrounded French and half-walked, half-dragged him to the train depot. They were followed by a band of Red Shirts who again tried to seize French and lynch him. Stedman and the other Masons again held them off. At last they shoved French aboard a 7:15 p.m. northbound train.

"French, you are a Mason and I am a Mason," Stedman told the departing sheriff. "I will protect your life with my life, if necessary, but only on condition that you leave town and agree to remain away from Wilmington for the rest of your life."

French bowed his head in assent. He climbed aboard and dropped to his knees, cringing, on the floor between the coach seats as the train left the station.

Armond Scott, the black lawyer who had failed to deliver the Committee of Colored Citizens' response to Waddell's home, had remained inside his house for most of the day on November 10. Some whites were already blaming Scott for the outbreak of violence. They reasoned that if Waddell had received the response on time that morning, he and the mob would have had no cause to burn down the *Record*. Their logic ignored the fact that Waddell already knew the content of the Colored Citizens' response and proceeded to attack the *Record* anyway.

That evening, a white neighbor offered to hide Scott, who took shelter in the man's house, intending to wait out the mob. At the same time, a white lawyer who had been a boyhood friend of Scott's went to the home of Scott's parents nearby. He told Scott's mother that the mob was now "out of hand" and that her son was sure to be lynched if found. The lawyer offered to escort Scott to the train station with the help of several other white men.

Scott was informed of the offer. He was twenty-five, with no wife or children to keep him in Wilmington. His law practice, which defended blacks, was growing, but he could certainly rebuild it in another city—perhaps in the North. He agreed to allow the white men to escort him to the train depot.

When Scott and his protectors reached the station, they saw that it was surrounded by several hundred Red Shirts. Scott regretted his decision. Given the surly mood of the mob, he knew he was likely to be lynched. But the Red Shirts didn't notice him. They were focused on their efforts to lynch French before he was put aboard the same train that now awaited Scott. In the commotion, Scott was able to slip aboard. He and French escaped into the night.

CHAPTER THIRTY

Not the Sort of Man
We Want Here

WILMINGTON'S OTHER LEADING black lawyer, William Henderson, remained in the city, hoping to reason with the white supremacist leadership. On the morning of November 10, he had written a letter addressed to Waddell and other members of the Committee of Twenty-Five.

> *I feel it is my duty to set at rest the public minds as to the action of the colored citizens that was intended to meet the white citizens last evening . . . We discharged the duties entrusted to us by informing the Chairman, Hon. A. M. Waddell, that we would use our individual influence to carry out the wishes of your committee. The same was mailed to Colonel Waddell.*
>
> *We appointed a committee to search for F. G. Manly and inform him of the facts and to urge him to act at once. We were informed and we believed that Editor A. L. Manly is now and has been out of the city for more than a month. Our committee could not find either of the associate editors, but hoped to find them today.*
>
> *Respectfully, W. E. Henderson*

Henderson hid inside his law office downtown most of the day, awaiting a reply that never came. Late in the afternoon, as the shooting seemed to die down, he ventured outside to gauge the degree of danger. On the street, he encountered a white wholesale merchant he knew.

"What does all this mean?" Henderson asked him.

The merchant seemed oddly calm, as if it were just another weekday afternoon downtown.

"Oh, it will be all right, Henderson," he replied. "We have a new form of government now and the new mayor will see to it that order is restored. Tonight the streets will be patrolled by armed men. You go home. It's all right."

Henderson didn't believe him. "How can I go home? I will be shot on the way."

The merchant seemed to consider for the first time that the poisonous racial atmosphere might be perilous for a black man. He offered Henderson a ride home in his buggy. Any gunmen they encountered were likely to assume that Henderson worked for the merchant. The buggy arrived, without incident, at Henderson's home. As Henderson thanked the merchant, the white man told him to reassure his wife that their family would be safe.

Henderson did not feel safe at all, but he had no intention of fleeing Wilmington. He was forty years old, with a successful law practice. He and his wife, Sally Bettie, and their four children lived in a finely appointed home with a parlor and a small veranda. Their outward circumstances differed little from those of their white neighbors. They worked, saved their money, maintained their home, and sent their children to school. William and Sally Bettie, who taught at a colored school, were determined to educate their children for professional careers as teachers or perhaps lawyers.

The couple prospered in Wilmington. They befriended several white neighbors. They convinced themselves that if race troubles arose, their new white friends would protect them. They were devoutly religious, with an abiding belief in the essential goodness of all people, black and white.

By eight o'clock on the evening of November 10, the Henderson children had said their prayers and fallen asleep. William, suffering from a headache brought on by the day's stress, had stretched out across his bed, a pistol close at hand. Only Sally Bettie was awake.

Just after 8:15 p.m., she heard a long, low whistle. She peered through the window blinds and saw a bright light at the guard stand that housed a black sentry the couple had hired.

She heard the sentry ask, "Who goes there?"

A reply drifted from the darkness: "White men."

Moments later, Sally Bettie heard an insistent knocking. She went to the door, and a voice from the veranda demanded that William Henderson step outside.

"He can't come outside," Sally Bettie told the man. "But you can come inside." She did not know what else to say.

William, awakened by the commotion, emerged from the bedroom and shouted at the men through the closed door. "If you want to kill me, you must come inside my own house and kill me here!"

He opened the door. He saw forty to fifty men on the veranda and in the yard. They carried pistols and rifles. White kerchiefs were tied around their arms.

Several men burst inside, filling the hallway and parlor.

"Well, gentlemen," Henderson said evenly. "What do you want?"

He spoke slowly, trying to gain control of an alarming situation inside his own home. He was determined to prevent the men from pushing into the bedrooms where his children slept.

"We have come to tell you that you must leave," one of the men replied in a low voice, as if he were inviting Henderson to a business meeting. "We do not want you to remain here longer."

Henderson tied to remain calm. "Will you tell me what I have done and why I must leave?"

"You are not the sort of man we want here," the man said.

Henderson made a brief attempt to remind the men of his status as a member of the bar and of his unwavering civility toward whites. But he could see that they were unmoved. He decided to bargain for time. He asked for ten days to get his affairs in order. He would have to shut down his law practice and try to sell his home, all under duress.

The man shook his head. He said Henderson had until the following evening to leave Wilmington forever. Otherwise, he and his men could not guarantee Henderson's safety.

The man turned and led his gunmen back out into the night.

Thomas C. Miller, the real estate broker and pawnbroker, also chose not to flee the city. His roots were too deep. Miller had become one of Wilmington's wealthiest men, black or white. He had once served as a deputy sheriff before building a small business empire that included a restaurant and a saloon. He was worth more than $10,000. He outbid whites at courthouse property auctions. Money owed to Miller by whites may have contributed to his inclusion on the banishment list, though his wealth and business acumen alone made him a threat to white supremacy. Some whites spread rumors that Miller had vowed to "wash his black hands in white men's blood."

Captain Furlong and his infantry detachment rode to Miller's house to arrest him that evening. Miller's daughter was on the veranda and tried vainly to send the soldiers away. She told them her father was not home. Furlong pushed past her into the house, pausing for a perfunctory knock on the front door. The captain confronted Miller and ordered him to accompany the soldiers to the city jail. Miller refused. Furlong motioned for several soldiers to seize him. As Miller was led outside, his daughter tried to pull him away. The soldiers shoved her aside.

Miller was loaded onto the gun wagon for the short ride to the jail. Miller's young daughter followed it, begging the militiamen to let her father go. Aboard the wagon, Miller told them that he'd rather be dead than suffer the humiliation of being dragged from his home like a common criminal in full view of his daughter. One soldier told Miller that if he would simply jump from the wagon, he would gladly shoot him and end his suffering. Miller kept talking until one of the soldiers cocked his gun several times. He rode in silence for the rest of the journey to the jailhouse.

The banishment of bold and successful men like Tom Miller had a profound effect on the rest of Wilmington's black men and women. Their world had been upended. A multiracial city government had been overthrown. The city's black middle class, built and nurtured for decades, was collapsing. Hundreds of black families were homeless. Those who remained were by now thoroughly intimidated, accepting of white authority, and thus welcomed by whites to remain in Wilmington. DESERVING NEGROES WILL BE PROTECTED, the *Evening Dispatch* promised.

The *Messenger* elaborated: "The 'colored' folks . . . for the most part are decent, well behaved, intelligent, not given to the dark crimes, fond of official grub but self-respecting in the main. There are not many Tom Millers among them, but when revolutions set in the Toms are politely invited to pack and go and keep going."

After watching drenched black families flee to the forests and cemetery on November 10, Reverend J. Allen Kirk changed his mind about keeping his wife and niece in the city. He decided to get them out immediately. He knew his name was on the banishment list. The *Evening Dispatch* had singled him out as a racial provocateur. It called him "the negro who came from Boston here to lead the Negroes in their depredations." Kirk was warned to "take his departure and shake the dust of the city from his feet."

Just as Kirk was arranging to move his wife and niece from their hiding place at a friend's home on the city's outskirts, a mob of whites barged into the sanctuary of the Central Baptist Church, searching for Kirk, who had vacated the dwelling the day before. He retrieved his

wife and niece, and the three of them began walking on a roadway leading out of town. Kirk hailed a passing delivery wagon and convinced
the driver to take them to join other black families hiding inside Pine
Forest Cemetery.

The Kirks made plans to bed down among the headstones. But Kirk's
wife feared he would be killed if Red Shirts attacked the cemetery that
night. She begged him to flee for his own safety. Kirk was reluctant to
leave his family, but his wife convinced him. He moved them to the
edge of the cemetery, near a swamp, where they would be better able
to hide. He would arrange for them to join him once he had found a
haven far from Wilmington. He kissed them good-bye.

Kirk waded through swampland in the dark for hours, headed north.
He made his way to Castle Hayne, a railroad stop nine miles north of
Wilmington. It was utterly quiet. Kirk camped in Castle Hayne for a
day, then stumbled upon a black family living in a "country hut in the
swamps," he wrote later. Through friends, he sent word to his wife and
niece in the cemetery. They waded through the swamps and joined Kirk
at the hut on November 13. They decided to stay there until Kirk was
able to flee the state, find a place to live, and send for them.

Kirk left the hut on the evening of the thirteenth and walked to the
train depot in Castle Hayne, where he bought a ticket for a northbound
train to Weldon, North Carolina, a few miles from the Virginia border.
He boarded the train, made his way to the smoking car, and sat down.
Within minutes, the car was filled with boisterous Red Shirts carrying rifles. They cursed and threatened Kirk. He was thankful for the
conductor and the other passengers on board.

Kirk decided he would get off at the next stop and try to find a
northbound train with no Red Shirts aboard. When the train pulled
into a station, he got up to leave, but the Red Shirts followed him and
blocked his way. He sat back down.

At the next station, a black man boarded. Kirk recognized him. He
was William A. Moore, an attorney from Wilmington. Kirk assumed

that Moore, too, was fleeing the riot. The two men made eye contact but did not speak, fearing that any interaction might arouse the Red Shirts. One of them cursed at Moore as he sat down.

Moore seemed terrified. When the train pulled in at Wilson, North Carolina, Moore's destination, 120 miles north of Wilmington, he tried to get off. The Red Shirts blocked his path and forced him to sit back down. "This completely unstrung the most pitiful colored lawyer," Kirk wrote later.

Kirk spoke quietly to Moore, trying to calm him. Moore said he had no money to pay for the fare past Wilson. He planned to get off in Rocky Mount, 145 miles north of Wilmington, if the conductor allowed him to ride that far without paying the added fare.

Kirk decided to try to draw out the Red Shirts and ascertain just what they intended to do with the two frightened black men sharing their train. He gestured to the white men and said, loudly, "Perhaps some of these white gentlemen would give you the money to go as far as Rocky Mount."

The Red Shirts cursed Moore and told him they'd rather pay for his ticket to hell.

The white men stood up and made their way to the adjacent first-class car, leaving the door ajar. Kirk assumed they were discussing whether to kill him and Moore. Moore drew the same conclusion. As the train slowed to pull into the next station, Moore bolted from the smoking car, flung open the door, and leaped from the train.

He landed hard, bounced up, and sprinted into the woods that hugged the tracks. The Red Shirts emerged from the first-class car, screaming and cursing, and bounded from the train as it rolled into the station and came to a stop. Rifles drawn, they stomped through the flat, piney woods, searching for Moore. After a while they gave up and returned to the station, where the engineer had stopped the train to wait for them.

Now the Red Shirts watched Kirk more closely. He decided again to try to get off at the next station. But then he noticed that the conductor was talking intently to the Red Shirts. Perhaps, Kirk hoped, the conductor would tell them that Kirk had a ticket to Weldon, several stops north, so they would not need to watch him closely until the train neared the town. After the conductor moved on, the Red Shirts continued to watch Kirk, but they did not speak to him.

At the Rocky Mount station, Kirk quietly rose from his seat and attempted to get off the train. He was surprised when the Red Shirts did not try to stop him. He stepped from the car and hid inside the station. After the train pulled away, he used most of his remaining cash to hire a carriage to take him north to the small crossroads town of Whitakers, North Carolina, where he knew that freight trains embarked daily to Virginia. The carriage ride took all night, through a driving rain, to reach Whitakers. There, Kirk boarded a northbound freight train. He reached Petersburg, Virginia, the next day, November 14, four days after escaping Wilmington.

John C. Dancy, the customs collector, knew that his name was not on the banishment list. The coup leaders did not wish to invite federal intervention by harassing a federal appointee. Even so, Dancy was uneasy. He did not believe the leaders of the white supremacy campaign could control the Red Shirts, especially those who had been drinking.

To complicate matters, Dancy was out of town on November 10. He had gone to Tarboro, North Carolina, the city of his birth, 150 miles north of Wilmington. Whether Dancy had left home because he felt threatened or because he was visiting relatives, his wife and children were left unprotected at the family home in Wilmington.

The first indication of trouble for Dancy's wife, Florence, came when black boys from the neighborhood ran past her home, shouting and waving. The Dancys were one of only two black families on their street, though other blacks lived elsewhere in the neighborhood.

"There's something terrible going on!" one boy yelled. "You'd better stay in the house!"

Florence decided that she and the children should join Dancy at once. She had no way of knowing what was happening downtown, but she knew from reading the papers that whites were primed for violence. She managed to secure a horse and buggy to take the family to the train depot. They took nothing with them. It was only about a ten-block ride, but the buggy was stopped and searched several times by white men at checkpoints. There were more white gunmen at the station, but the family was not harmed. The white men may have recognized Florence as the wife of a federal official. Late that night, the family arrived safely in Tarboro.

Dancy was worried that blacks in Wilmington would meet violence with more violence. The next morning, November 11, he wrote a letter to the *Wilmington Messenger*.

> *Every good citizen of this city regrets the difficulties of the past two days. Every good citizen is also anxious that perfect peace be restored at once. I therefore appeal to my own race to do nothing that will in the slightest degree inflame new passions or revive old ones. Let us be quiet, orderly, submissive to authority and refrain from any utterance or conduct that will excite passion in others.*
>
> *Let us abstain from loud talking or undue excitement and go to and fro from our homes, where the Mayor and city authorities pledge us every protection . . . The whites, led by the Mayor, pledge us their aid in such a direction. Let us keep the peace at all hazards.*

The *Messenger* published Dancy's letter prominently on its front page under the headline: DANCY'S COUNSEL TO NEGROES. On the same page, the headline above the day's main news story read: ORDER IS RESTORED. THE NEW CITY GOVERNMENT IS PROVING THOROUGHLY EFFECTIVE.

Captain Furlong and the Light Infantry detachment continued to round up black men on the banishment list late in the day on November 10. But the six most recent captives were not taken to the train depot, because passenger trains had stopped running for the night. Hugh

MacRae and J. Allan Taylor decided to hold the men in the city jail overnight "for their protection," then put them aboard trains when service resumed the next morning. The captives were charged with "using language calculated to incite the negroes."

Several black men on the banishment list had managed to get out of town ahead of Furlong and his soldiers. Among them was Robert Reardon, a barber so popular among blacks that he was often referred to as a "tonsorial artist." Reardon was a mulatto, the son of an Irishman and a black woman. He had a strong entrepreneurial spirit, operating an advertising agency in addition to his barbershop. He also managed a pavilion on a segregated beach at nearby Wrightsville Beach. He was a member of the Committee of Colored Citizens, and brash and successful enough to warrant banishment. The *News and Observer* described Reardon as "an objectionable negro barber."

Reardon hid inside his home on November 10 until he learned that a squad from the Light Infantry was on its way to search his residence. The soldiers were delayed by confusion over the exact location of Reardon's dwelling. That gave Reardon an opportunity to run out his back door, climb over a fence, and disappear. The soldiers took off in pursuit but never found him. One of them, George Boylan, was amused by Reardon's desperate flight to safety: "All we saw was a flit of his coat tail as he went over the fence . . . that was one badly frightened negro."

The Secret Nine had carefully selected the successful black men whose banishment would most grievously undermine Wilmington's thriving middle class. The *Indianapolis Freeman*, a black newspaper, later wrote: "Four or five of the Negro men whom they made leave are worth from two to eight thousand dollars. They are all business men . . . All were good Negroes, dealing constantly with the whites."

Among the six black men rounded up and jailed by Captain Furlong and his soldiers was Ari Bryant, an enterprising butcher who, according to the *Messenger*, "was looked upon by the negroes as a high and mighty leader. He was of vicious temperament toward the white people and counseled his race to strife . . . inciting the blacks to violence."

Also arrested were Robert B. Pickens and Salem J. Bell, partners in a prosperous fish and oyster wholesale operation. Both men, along with Miller and Bryant, had helped recruit black voters for the Republican Party and were also members of the colored committee. Furlong's men also arrested the Reverend I. J. Bell, a black minister. Bell, obeying orders from white leaders, had gone house to house that morning, trying to persuade blacks not to oppose the mob. The next day's *Messenger* described "commendable efforts" by Bell and other black ministers to "pacify their race." But Bell nonetheless retained a reputation among whites as subversive and thus too dangerous to remain in the city.

Word of the jailed black men soon reached squads of Red Shirts roaming the streets. As the shootings died down, the Red Shirts had grown frustrated. They had certainly shot their share of black men, but they had yet to conduct a single lynching. Many had been disappointed the day before, when the lynching they had planned for Alex Manly was aborted after they learned that Manly had fled. Now, just twenty-four hours later, they were elated by news that the city jail had provided them with a fresh batch of captive black men.

The Red Shirts mounted up and rode to the jailhouse.

CHAPTER THIRTY-ONE

Justice Is Satisfied,
Vengeance Is Cruel

A HARD RAIN was still pounding the city streets after nightfall when a brigade of Red Shirts descended on the city jail late on the night of November 10, cursing and taunting the six black men held inside. The faces of some of the white men were florid from liquor. They hooted as they raised their Winchesters and set up ragged picket lines around the jail. They shouted insults at the white jailers, asking why they were defending criminal Negroes. They demanded the prisoners so that they might be properly lynched.

Word quickly reached Colonel Walker Taylor at the armory, just a block away, that Red Shirts were causing a ruckus. He rounded up a detachment of the Wilmington Light Infantry and led the soldiers to the jail, located next to the county courthouse, across Princess Street from city hall. Though Taylor's soldiers had pursued and shot at blacks all afternoon on November 10 in league with Red Shirts, he now believed circumstances obliged him to bring the Red Shirts under control. In Taylor's view, it was one thing to shoot black rioters, but it was quite something else to lynch unarmed black men arrested under martial law that he himself had imposed.

His soldiers surrounded the jail, creating a buffer between the black prisoners and the Red Shirts. There was no hostility. Many of the Red Shirts and infantry soldiers were relatives or lifelong friends.

At city hall, Mayor Waddell was also undergoing a change of heart. Less than a month earlier, he had vowed to clog the Cape Fear with black carcasses. Now he felt compelled to protect the lives of black men imprisoned under his hours-old authority. Waddell turned for help to his Civil War adversary, Colonel Moore. Waddell no longer had armed men under his direct control, save a city police force that was in disarray with the resignation of its chief and the dereliction of white officers who had abandoned their posts to join the riot. Moore, on the other hand, commanded scores of armed citizens serving in the Vigilance Committee groups.

Waddell found Moore at his home. The mayor explained that any lynching would undermine the new administration and possibly prompt federal intervention and thus needed to be prevented. Moore agreed. He dispatched several armed men to help the Light Infantry soldiers set up posts around the jail. Waddell followed directly behind them. He wanted to prevent Moore from taking control of the standoff.

At the jail, the Red Shirts refused to disband. Whooping and cheering drunkenly in the dark, they continued to demand the prisoners. The Reverend Robert Strange, the white Episcopal minister, told the Red Shirts that if they lynched the prisoners, "it would be a lasting disgrace to the town." Waddell discussed the situation with the minister and Moore, and with Walter MacRae, who had been elected sheriff two days earlier. MacRae was the uncle of Hugh MacRae of the Secret Nine and was a white supremacist himself. But at that moment, in his new position, he was responsible for the safety of prisoners, black or white. Sheriff MacRae agreed that the black men should be kept alive until they could be taken to the train station the next morning.

Waddell decided to deliver a short speech, addressed not just to the Red Shirts but to all his new constituents surrounding the jail.

"My position has been radically changed. I am now a sworn officer of the law. This jail and these people must have protection," Waddell said from the front door of the jailhouse.

Moore stood with his back against the jail entrance. When Waddell had finished, he addressed the Red Shirts directly.

"Men, we may as well understand each other," Moore told them. "You are here to lynch these men and I am here to prevent it. You can only carry out your purpose over my dead body."

Moore's remarks appeared to carry more weight than Waddell's. Some of the Red Shirts began to drift away. Others remained, rifles in hand. For the next few hours, they continued to try to persuade the soldiers and armed guards to abandon their positions just long enough for the Red Shirts to slip inside and seize the prisoners. But the soldiers held their ground throughout the night. Waddell, Moore, and Reverend Robert Strange stood outside the jail door until dawn, when the remaining Red Shirts finally gave up and dispersed.

Early that Friday morning, November 11, Waddell delivered a mayoral proclamation from the jail, signed at midnight and addressed to the "Good People of Wilmington." He wanted to make a public appeal to tamp down the white rage he had been stoking for months.

The undersigned upon whom has been placed a great responsibility by the action of his fellow citizens, takes this method of assuring the good people of this city that all the power with which he is invested will be exercised to preserve order and peace in this community, and that power is amply sufficient for the purpose.

At nine o'clock that Friday morning, a squad from the Naval Reserves escorted the six captives from the jail to the train depot. Waddell accompanied them. The black men were marched through the streets in a straight line and paraded before the town's white citizens. Dressed in dark suits and hats, the prisoners walked with their heads up. There was the moneyman Miller, the fishmongers Pickens and Bell, the butcher Bryant, the preacher Bell, and one unidentified black man, all flanked by khaki-uniformed Naval Reserves militiamen. Some whites on the street jeered and heckled the captives, showering them with racial slurs.

At the depot, Waddell said later, he bought six tickets for Richmond. Surrounded by jeering whites, he referred to the six passengers as "the scoundrels." The black men were loaded aboard the train at gunpoint, accompanied by an armed guard who had been ordered to make sure they were taken all the way to Richmond. Separately, J. Allan Taylor telegraphed mayors along the rail line, alerting them that banished black men would be passing through their towns. Before the train pulled away, its shrill whistle cutting through the chilled air, Waddell warned the six men, one at a time, never to return to North Carolina.

A correspondent for the *New York Times* watched them leave. "The negroes are thoroughly terrorized," he wrote.

The Secret Nine disregarded Colonel Waddell's midnight plea for peace. Hugh MacRae and J. Allan Taylor continued to round up the remaining men on the banishment list. One of the targets was Wilmington's United States commissioner, Robert H. Bunting, a white Republican. Bunting should have been exempt from banishment because of his federal position. But he had committed a grave sin—he had a black common-law wife. Josephus Daniels's *News and Observer* had referred to Bunting as "vermin of the white race" for living "in open adultery with a negro woman." Bunting had also supported black suffrage, another affront.

On the morning of November 11, a white mob surrounded Bunting's home. Some of the men were already drunk. They screamed Bunting's name, demanding that he and his wife show themselves. Bunting, aware that he had been targeted for banishment, had fled the house with his wife the night before. When there was no reply from inside, several men proposed tearing down the house. Others in the mob decided that it would be easier to break in. They crashed through the front door and began smashing furniture and stealing valuables. Someone ripped down gold-framed portraits of Bunting and his wife. These were nailed to a tree at Seventh and Market Streets. A handwritten sign was attached: R. H. BUNTING—WHITE. MRS. R. H. BUNTING—COLORED.

The mob finished ransacking the Bunting home, then moved on in search of the missing commissioner and his wife.

Another target, the deposed police chief John Melton, did not attempt to hide, though he knew his name was on the banishment list. Melton had spent the previous night at his rented home with his wife and children after his forced resignation at city hall. At dawn on the eleventh, he rose and had breakfast, then walked to city hall to turn over his keys to the new police chief, Edgar Parmele. On the way, Melton passed several Red Shirts, who warned him they would later track him down and kill him.

Melton was unnerved, but he convinced himself that the men were drunk and only blowing off steam. He walked to a small corral outside city hall that housed impounded livestock. He told the janitor there to give grain to the animals, which had not been fed the previous day because of the riot. Melton was about to walk inside to his former office when a group of white men armed with Winchesters confronted him.

They told him he was being placed under arrest.

"All right, for what? Where is your authority?" Melton asked.

One of the gunmen said he had been authorized to take Melton to the office of a local magistrate, John J. Fowler.

Melton began to argue, but he quickly realized that he was surrounded by a crowd of nearly three hundred men. He was escorted to the magistrate's office, trailed by the mob.

Melton was brought face-to-face with Magistrate Fowler. Melton considered Fowler a friend who he thought might treat him fairly, perhaps even let him go. He asked Fowler why he had been brought before him. Fowler shrugged. He said he wasn't sure what was going on. He had issued no warrant for Melton's arrest, but he advised Melton to heed the gunmen's demands. It was out of his hands, he told Melton. The city was under new authority.

Melton was dragged outside and marched up Market Street to the armory, where a detachment of Light Infantry soldiers took charge of him. The arrival of the soldiers may have saved Melton's life. The *Morning Star* reported the next day that the military prevented the commission of "grave threats of violence" by the mob against the ousted police chief.

The soldiers ordered Melton to follow them. He was hauled down Front Street, where he noticed a white man with a rifle wearing a special police badge. The man's face was contorted with rage. He sprang at Melton and smacked him in the temple with the rifle butt. Melton was stunned and bloodied by the blow but remained on his feet. The man tried to strike him again, but the sergeant in charge of the detachment reached across Melton and jabbed at the man with his sword. "None of that!" he shouted.

His head pounding, Melton was escorted to the national cemetery downtown. A dozen soldiers remained there with him as he nursed his wound. Though he was a captive, Melton felt relieved when the soldiers told him that part of their duty was to protect him from the mobs until he could be banished from the city. He overheard one of them mutter, "God help Melton."

Just after midday, a group of armed men delivered Commissioner Bunting to the custody of the infantry guards holding Melton. Bunting had been tracked down by J. Allan Taylor and Hugh MacRae, who found him hiding behind city hall. They searched Bunting's backyard nearby and found two pistols buried in the dirt. They later gave these to one of the out-of-town-militias. Bunting and Melton were then marched down Market Street to the armory and told to sit in the yard. A few minutes later, soldiers brought them sandwiches, oysters, and coffee. Melton was too upset to eat, but he sipped some coffee. Bunting wolfed down the oysters and sandwiches.

Melton asked the soldiers several times what they intended to do with him. They did not reply. One of the soldiers felt a stab of pity for the ousted chief.

"I shall never forget how Melton looked as he sat under a tree in front of the Armory," he said later. "He could not eat and when some of the boys went upstairs and took a rope with a noose in it and threw it at his feet, he turned just as white as a sheet."

Shortly after 1:00 p.m., one of Melton's white former police officers, Charles H. Gilbert, rushed into the armory yard and asked the soldiers for protection. He said he had just escaped capture by a band of Red Shirts. Gilbert, too, was placed under guard.

At about 2:00 p.m., Melton, Bunting, and Gilbert were ordered to accompany the soldiers back down Market Street. Melton caught a glimpse of his wife and children in the throngs of whites watching the spectacle. He was not permitted to stop and say good-bye. He felt humiliated, and he feared the Red Shirts would torment his family now that he was in custody.

The procession turned up Front Street, where white bystanders hissed and mocked the three Fusionists, sarcastically waving good-bye. At one point, several men in the crowd broke through the soldiers' lines and tried to beat Melton with clubs. One of them shouted: "White nigger!" The soldiers shoved the men aside and continued to the depot.

There were more jeering whites at the station, but the soldiers pushed past them and put Melton, Bunting, and Gilbert aboard a train bound for New Bern. They were ordered to sit inside a compartment where they were confronted by a tall, muscular white man who began screaming at Bunting, warning him that if he ever returned to Wilmington, he would kill him on sight. The man then turned on Melton and Gilbert, cursing and threatening both men before abruptly exiting the compartment.

At 3:30 p.m., as the train rumbled out of the station, the roar of the locomotive was drowned out by a crescendo of cheers and taunts from white men and women gaily waving good-bye. Bunting and Gilbert began to weep.

✣   ✣   ✣

With almost all leading Fusionists removed from the city, the soldiers of the Wilmington Light Infantry assembled on Market Street to celebrate later in the day on November 11. They were joined by uniformed men of the Naval Reserves, as well as the state militiamen deployed from other towns by Governor Russell the day before. Led by Colonel Taylor on horseback, the soldiers paraded through downtown in military formation, rifles on their shoulders and pistols on their hips. They were trailed by horse-drawn wagons pulling the heavy Colt and Hotchkiss rapid-fire guns. White families lined the streets, cheering and singing. Women waved white handkerchiefs and delivered coffee and sandwiches for the soldiers.

The *Atlanta Constitution* correspondent on the scene wrote that the parade served "the double purpose of teaching the negroes the utter foolishness of further resistance and would inspire the white people with confidence in the city government and its ability to protect them and their property."

Mayor Waddell now turned his attention to the black families hiding in the swamps and cemetery. He feared they were becoming a political liability for his new city government. Wilmington's white business leaders, though certainly satisfied by the banishment of troublesome black leaders, complained that their best black workers were among the terrified people who had fled to the countryside. Several businessmen went to Waddell and asked him to try to lure the blacks back into town.

Among them was James Sprunt. More than a third of his black employees had failed to report for work at the cotton compress following the November 10 killings. Sprunt needed them to restart his export operations. Seven steamships were backed up at the port, awaiting cargoes of cotton. Nonetheless, Sprunt told a reporter he was confident that the city's blacks would be reassured by Mayor Waddell's public declarations of equal treatment for both races.

But before black families were likely to feel safe enough to return, Waddell realized, he had to first rein in the Red Shirts. Some remained in the streets, drinking and carousing and brandishing their guns. Waddell called a board of aldermen meeting on the afternoon of November 11 to address the matter. It was the new board's first formal meeting. Waddell disparaged the Secret Nine, complaining that "self-appointed vigilantes are responsible for much of this misery because of the indiscriminate way they have gone about banishing objectionable persons." Though Waddell had helped put six innocent black men aboard a train to Richmond earlier that day, he had not been involved in the banishment selection process. As mayor, Waddell felt entitled to some say in the process.

That night, Waddell wrote a statement advising "all good citizens" to remain in their homes and allow the Wilmington Light Infantry and Naval Reserves to patrol the streets unhindered. Waddell singled out the Red Shirts, telling them that no other armed patrols would be allowed.

Waddell was also authorized to appoint another temporary police force, to serve for thirty days. Many of the new officers he selected had been part of the mob that he had led to the *Daily Record* two days earlier. Their task now, he told them, was to help the military men restore order.

The only prominent Fusionist politician who remained in the city was the deposed mayor, Silas Wright. Like Melton and other former office-holders, Wright assumed that his resignation had satisfied Wilmington's new leaders. But on the morning of November 11, a delegation from the Secret Nine confronted Wright at his home. He agreed to leave the city but pleaded for another day to wrap up his affairs. He was granted a twenty-four-hour grace period.

That afternoon, Wright learned that his fellow Fusionist politicians had been marched through the city, harangued by white onlookers and shoved aboard trains at gunpoint. He decided to leave that night under the cover of darkness. Wright had lived in Wilmington for nearly three decades, having arrived from Massachusetts in 1870, but he had no time to gather his possessions or say good-bye. He abandoned his home and bought a ticket to New York City.

That evening, Wright was boarding a northbound train when he heard shouting and laughing. He saw a squad of Wilmington Light Infantry soldiers escorting a tall, unsmiling man to the waiting train. It was William Henderson, trailed by his wife and children. A crowd of whites taunted them.

Earlier that day, Henderson had gone to Colonel Waddell to ask for protection from the white mob that had barged into his home the night before. He told the new mayor that he had been given twenty-four hours to flee the city. Waddell surprised Henderson by informing him that he could remain in Wilmington under his personal protection.

Henderson had dealt with Waddell long enough to know that he could not trust him.

"No, you will not protect me," he told Waddell flatly. "I ask for protection today while I am settling up my business."

Waddell agreed to provide one of the newly deputized temporary policemen as Henderson's escort for the day. The officer went home with Henderson and stood by as the family packed several suitcases and locked up the house. They left behind almost all their possessions, taking just a change of clothes each.

Henderson went ahead to the train station to buy tickets for Richmond. But by two hours before the departure time, Sally Bettie and the children had not yet arrived. Henderson sent word to Waddell, who dispatched three more temporary police officers to escort the family to the station. At dusk, the officers pushed past a jeering crowd of whites and put the black family aboard the train.

Henderson led Sally Bettie and their four children to a sleeping car. He felt safer there than in an open day coach. Everyone crowded inside. Henderson pulled down the shades and stepped into the passageway.

In the next sleeping car, he discovered former mayor Wright, sitting alone. Wright said he wanted to get as far from Wilmington as possible. A reporter from the *Messenger* caught a glimpse of the crestfallen mayor. "A worse scared man I have seldom seen," he wrote the next day.

Although Wright had bought a ticket for New York City, he had been told that mobs of Red Shirts were waiting at several stations north of Wilmington. Henderson had heard the same reports. The two exiles commiserated as the train pulled away, headed north through the night.

Later that evening, Waddell was told that Red Shirts were still patrolling the city, drinking and brandishing their rifles. He was annoyed that his two proclamations had been disregarded, first by the Secret Nine and now by some of the same gunmen he had inspired to violence on November 10. He did not note the obvious irony—that some of the new police officers charged with restoring order carried the same weapons they had fired at black men the day before.

Word of Waddell's hypocrisy reached John Spencer Bassett, a history professor at Trinity College in Durham, later renamed Duke University. In a letter to a friend, Bassett wrote: "The first act of the new government was to elect the leader of the mob Mayor of the town. He who had just led a mob issues a proclamation commanding that 'all further violence' shall stop. If he had any sense of humor he must have split his undergarments laughing at his own joke."

No matter what had taken place previously, Waddell now considered himself Wilmington's rightful custodian of law and order. He wrote yet another proclamation, this one more peevish, and had it delivered to the city's newspapers.

The comparatively few persons in the city who seem disposed to abuse the opportunity of carrying arms which recent events afforded and who are doing some very feverish talking are hereby notified that no further turbulence or disorderly conduct will be tolerated. They are notified that a regular police force will preserve order and every peaceable citizen, white and black, will be protected in his person or property.

No armed patrol except those authorized by the Chief of Police will appear on the streets.

Justice is satisfied, vengeance is cruel and accursed.

CHAPTER THIRTY-TWO

Persons Unknown

A FEW HOURS after the shooting erupted at North Fourth and Harnett Streets on November 10, David Jacobs had gone to the scene in a wagon. Jacobs was a barber, with a popular shop on Dock Street. Under the Fusionist city government, he had been appointed county coroner. It had now fallen to him to collect the dead so that a proper inquest could be conducted.

It had not occurred to anyone in the Secret Nine or the new city government to replace Jacobs, a black man who was a member of the Committee of Colored Citizens. No one was thinking about an inquest. There was no mystery, after all, regarding the cause of death of the black men who had been shot. Only the identities of their white killers were in question, and no one in the city's new power structure intended to pursue the matter.

Jacobs dutifully carried out his coroner's duties, rolling his wagon from one body to the next. He loaded at least six corpses; one account put the number at fourteen. On some, dark circles of dried blood marked the wounds in their backs. Others lay faceup, their eyes open. Some of the dead had already been collected by family members after the shooting stopped and then secretly buried. Other bodies, concealed in underbrush or under houses, were left to decompose; it was later estimated that more than sixty black men were killed on November 10. "Some were found by the stench and miasma that came forth from their decaying bodies," Reverend J. Allen Kirk wrote.

Jacobs hauled the dead men to the D. C. Evans Funeral Home, a rough shanty on Second Street near Princess Street. A throng of whites and blacks jammed the doorway, craning their necks to catch a glimpse of the dead black men laid in a neat row on the floor. Some of the whites wanted to confirm that black rioters had indeed been shot dead. Some of the blacks were searching for missing relatives.

The dead men wore work coveralls stained with dried blood. Above the corpses, three black men sawed pine boards to build crude coffins. Sawdust drifted to the floor. A reporter for the *News and Observer* pushed his way inside:

> On the bare floor stretch six dead negroes. Their stark bodies and staring faces tell the story of the previous day. They were dressed in their working clothes, just as they were shot down on the streets. Around them stood Negro women with sad faces. There were no men present, for the men feared to leave their homes.
>
> I could but feel pity for these poor, deluded creatures, and a certain amount of honor for them. No doubt they believed they were right . . . They were no brave men, these leaders of yours who incited you to murder and deeds of lawlessness, and they forsook you in your hour of need.

Jacobs scheduled an inquest for the morning of November 11, the day after the shootings. When no officials from the new city government appeared, the inquest was rescheduled for 3:00 p.m. Again, no one in authority showed up. The inquest was moved to the courthouse and rescheduled for the following morning, November 12.

"The coroner is a negro," the *Atlanta Constitution* reported. "This fact, perhaps together with the possibility of getting witnesses, prevented the inquest being held."

At 9:00 a.m. on Saturday November 12, the inquest was convened at last, inside the courthouse on Princess Street. The bodies of the black men were brought over from the funeral home a block away. A coroner's jury had been selected—four white supremacists, some of whom may have participated in the killings, and "two leading negroes."

The proceedings were brief and perfunctory. Just ten witnesses were called. "Their testimony was couched in profoundly vague terms," a correspondent for the *Charleston News and Courier* wrote. White witnesses were able to recall clearly that black men fired first, but they said they could not provide the names of the white men they said returned fire. Though many whites in Wilmington were connected by blood, marriage, or work, the witnesses claimed not to know the killers.

Dr. Bernice C. Moore, who had telephoned the armory after the first shots were fired, testified that he had seen "two pistol shots fired from the crowd of negroes" at North Fourth Street and Harnett. He said they were aimed at a group of white men who were "standing peaceably."

Aaron Lockamy, the white special police officer who had failed to persuade the blacks to disperse, testified that he was walking away from the corner when he heard a volley of shots. He said he did not know who fired them, and he did not go back to find out. (In a court hearing the following April, Lockamy would testify that he saw the white men fire first.)

Dr. C. D. Bell, a white man, testified that he saw the bodies of two black men in front of Walker's Store near North Fourth and Harnett, but he did not know their names. In his medical opinion, he said, their deaths were caused by gunshot wounds.

Dr. J. T. Schonwald, another white physician, testified that he heard one or two pistol shots, then saw "a posse of whites fire a volley" that felled two Negroes. He said he felt for the pulse of each man and determined that they were dead.

A lone black witness, Mildred Clinton, the sister of the murdered Josh Halsey, confirmed that the body she had been shown was indeed her brother. No one was charged with killing Halsey. (Waddell went to court five days later and charged a black man who had accompanied Halsey with attempted murder for allegedly shooting at whites).

"For the most part," the *Morning Star* told its readers the day after the inquest, testimony had been provided by "good reputable citizens." Their accounts, the paper said, "prove conclusively that the negroes were the aggressors in the unfortunate affair and that the white men were forced to fire as a matter of protection."

It did not take the coroner's jury long to render a verdict and put a hasty end to the first and only investigation of the killings of November 10: "The said deceased came to their deaths by gunshot wounds inflicted by some person or persons to this jury unknown."

For the remainder of Saturday, November 12, the streets were quiet. The last of the Red Shirts had finally gone home. Some had heeded Waddell's proclamations. Others were weary and needed sleep. Aside from the Light Infantry soldiers and the uniformed men of the Naval Reserves, the only armed men in sight were a few white civilians wearing temporary police badges.

Colonel Taylor, still operating under martial law, decided that the state militiamen called in from other towns were no longer needed. He sent them home. Then he sent a telegram to Governor Russell, his nominal boss, telling him that the situation in Wilmington was calm: "No probability of further race conflict. Military needed for some days to aid civil authorities in restoring peace and order."

Russell turned the matter over to his acting adjutant general, who sent a telegram telling Taylor he could keep the Light Infantry deployed for as long he thought necessary.

By the next day, November 13, Waddell was convinced that neither the Red Shirts nor the city's terrorized black community posed any threat of further violence. "I do not think there is any further need for the presence of the military forces in this city," he told Colonel Taylor. Without consulting the governor, Taylor demobilized the two militia units in Wilmington. The infantrymen and sailors marched back to their barracks to the cheers of white bystanders and the sounds of "Dixie" played by a band.

The two Secret Nine leaders, Hugh MacRae and J. Allan Taylor, relinquished their command of the city's armed citizens, who in any case had already gone home. The board of aldermen then voted to formally install MacRae and Taylor as aldermen.

With Red Shirts off the streets, Waddell believed he could now persuade "frightened darkies," as one newspaper described them, to return to the city.

He dispatched several men he considered "well known negroes" to the woods and the cemetery to relay his assurances. A newly appointed white assistant police chief and several white officers made a separate foray, with little success. Black children ran screaming at the sight of armed white men.

Waddell was undeterred. If the black families would simply return to their homes, he announced, they would see for themselves that Wilmington's new white leadership intended to protect them. In his view, the white supremacist coup had made the city safer for both whites and blacks. "I believe the negroes are as much rejoiced as the white people that order has been evolved out of chaos," he declared.

Waddell and other white leaders did have one regret: the attack on the *Record* office had destroyed the building that housed the small newsroom. The structure was owned by "a worthy charitable association of colored women," one newspaper reported. A group of white businessmen promised to raise money to pay to rebuild it.

Like Waddell, the editors of the *Messenger* suggested that the city's blacks had benefited from the white riot. It was the beginning of a myth that would last a century. "We must hope that by far the greater part of negroes in this city are anxious for the restoration of order and quiet and 'the old order'—the rule of the white people," the editors wrote. The *Messenger*, which proudly proclaimed just after the killings that it was "edited for the White Men," now expressed sympathy for the cold and hungry families. One headline read: NEGROES WHO FLED TO THE WOODS SUFFERING.

Some whites felt a Christian duty to aid their black neighbors; several families ventured into the woods, bearing food and clothing. A *Messenger* reporter wrote that he had provided shelter to three black women he had hidden, as well as to a black man who had been threatened by one of the reporter's own relatives. And, according to the *Messenger*, the few blacks who had returned from the swamps had been protected by their white neighbors. But hundreds more remained in hiding, too afraid to return home.

With the killings completed and their enemies banished, Wilmington's whites began crafting a lasting narrative of a heroic victory over dark and malevolent forces. The city's white ministers led the way. The Reverend James W. Kramer, a member of the Committee of Twenty-Five, had fetched his rifle from home on the morning of November 10 and joined the mobs in the streets. Another prominent white minister, Peyton H. Hoge, had carried a Winchester on his shoulder during the shootings. But by Sunday morning, November 13, both ministers had put away their weapons and prepared their sermons for a momentous day—the first Sunday since white rule had been redeemed in their city.

The pews were filled at Brooklyn Baptist Church that morning. Well-dressed white families were eager to hear their minister's reflections on the violence that had played out in the streets of their city just three days earlier. Kramer, gazing from the pulpit at his congregation, told the men seated before him that they were the vanguard of a dominant race chosen by the Creator.

"God from the beginning of time intended that intelligent white men should lead the people and rule the country," Kramer said. "I am not a friend of lawlessness and have put forth indefatigable efforts to prevent bloodshed, but the expected has happened. In the riot the negro was the aggressor. I believe that the whites were doing God's services, as the results for good have been felt in business, in politics and in the church. We will give the negro justice and will treat him kindly, but never again will we be ruled by him."

Nearby, at the First Presbyterian Church, Hoge opened his sermon by speaking not as a minister but as a member of the Committee of Twenty-Five.

"Since we last met in these walls we have taken a city," he told his congregation. "That is much."

Hoge described the events of November 10 as a pivotal battle. He invoked the recent Spanish surrenders in Cuba and the Philippines and compared the conquest of Wilmington to that of Jerusalem.

"This city we have taken, not by investment and siege, not by shot and shell, but [taken] as thoroughly, as completely, as if captured in battle. It has been redeemed for civilization, redeemed for law and order, redeemed for decency and respectability . . . For these things, let us give God glory."

Hoge urged his congregants to show compassion for "our colored neighbors," whom he considered ill equipped for citizenship and misled by white carpetbaggers. When properly guided, blacks were a simple, agreeable, and obedient people, Hoge said. "[W]ho can quietly and dispassionately consider their history and conditions and not pity them, not sympathize with them, not lend them a helping hand?" he asked, and his congregation murmured in agreement.

Earlier that Sunday morning, the new police chief, Edgar G. Parmele, spoke privately with the ministers and deacons of several black churches in Wilmington. By the standards of the white men who now ruled Wilmington, Parmele was a moderate. On November 10, he had complained of what he called the "atrocious treatment of colored citizens" and had tried to restrain several drunk and belligerent Red Shirts. Now the chief advised the black ministers to tell their congregations to help lure their friends and neighbors from the woods and back to their homes and jobs. Parmele also instructed them to preach acceptance of the new racial and political order in Wilmington.

The ministers needed little prodding. They were deferential men who had survived on November 10 by bowing to white demands. They had been spared the banishment inflicted upon more obstinate preachers like Reverend J. Allen Kirk and Reverend W. H. Lee. The ministers seemed buoyed; they had assumed the white authorities would ban them from preaching that first Sunday for fear they would stir black passions so soon after the killings.

Guy Carleton Lee, the white correspondent for the *Baltimore Sun*, visited several black churches that morning. Lee had falsely reported a week earlier that blacks were stockpiling weapons in churches. Now he was surprised at the ministers' utter lack of resentment toward a white outsider who had spread lies about them and their congregations. Lee was greeted warmly. He was invited to attend services.

"The sermons were generally moderate in tone," he reported. "The congregations were large and orderly."

Lee then stopped at St. Luke's AME Church in Brooklyn, which had escaped the flames that consumed the *Record* office next door. He reported that Deacon Briscoe Harris assured his congregation that "if the negro trusted in God and minded his own business, all would be well. If not, terrible consequences would follow."

At another Brooklyn church, Mt. Zion Afro-American AME, Lee watched Pastor J. K. Telfy preside over a solemn funeral service for Sam Macfarlane, one of the black men shot dead three days earlier. The killings that day were a mark of God's wrath, Telfy explained, and must not be avenged. "The people must obey the law and keep the peace," he instructed his congregants.

Nearby, at Central Baptist Church, Lee listened as Pastor A. S. Dunston advised acquiescence and silence: "Let the past bury the past . . . Be still, be quiet; all will be well."

CHAPTER THIRTY-THREE

Better Get a Gun

A S WILMINGTON'S WHITE MINISTERS celebrated the return of white supremacist rule, and as black preachers counseled obedience, the city's Democratic newspapers continued to frame the coup not as a violent overthrow but as a return at last to law and order and responsible government.

At the forefront was the *Messenger*, edited by Theodore B. Kingsbury, who claimed that he was "the man who had brought about the revolution." Kingsbury complained to his friends that Colonel Waddell had appropriated "undue credit" for the coup. Kingsbury had placed his newspaper at the center of the white revolution and accepted words of thanks from white citizens. In print, the *Messenger's* coverage of the killings celebrated both white superiority and white benevolence.

> *Never more shall Sambo and Josh rule rough-shod over the white men who helped and befriend them. Henceforth the rule of the White Race will not only be asserted but with benignancy and mercy. The rule of the Master Builders will be full of goodness and charity.*

A few blocks away, at the *Morning Star*, the editors insisted that "not the hair of any man's head was hurt" on November 10 but quickly backtracked to clarify that no *unarmed* black man had been shot. "It was not a *mob*, it was simply the unanimous uprising of the white people against conditions that had become intolerable," the *Star* reported.

In Raleigh, the *News and Observer* compared the coup in Wilmington to the French Revolution.

> *In this Wilmington upheaval, just as in Paris, there was a frantic crowding toward town-halls, dethroning of those who mis-rule, a banishment of those who are obnoxious and a destruction of places hated for their association. But unlike the French Revolution everything was done in Wilmington in due form and strictly in accordance with law.*

In their haste to justify the violent outcome in Wilmington, some Democratic newspapers, including the *News and Observer*, did not always hew to the version of events dictated by the city's white leaders—that the coup was a spontaneous eruption of white rage. Instead, they described how white leaders had instructed their followers to refrain from overthrowing the city government until Democrats had first won county and state elections. "They bided their time," the *News and Observer* reported. "'After the election,' they said."

The *Wilmington Messenger* reprinted an article from the *Charleston News and Courier*, whose correspondent had shared drinks and meals with Wilmington's white supremacists in the days leading up to the killings. Under the subhead: IT WAS ALL PLANNED IN ADVANCE, the Charleston reporter detailed the secret white strategy in Wilmington:

> *All of this sounds very cold-blooded, but nevertheless it is grounded on mighty good horse sense.*

One of the few Southern newspapers to express remorse at the loss of life in Wilmington was the *Richmond Times*. "Some negroes were killed by lawless white men for the sport of the thing," the paper reported.

Waddell arranged to have his version of events published in *Collier's Weekly*, which described itself as a source of "fiction, fact, sensation, wit, humor, news." *Collier's Weekly* was a useful tool for disseminating the white narrative that the killings were necessary to remove a corrupt government dominated by blacks plotting an armed insurrection. That version was virtually unassailable in the South, but it had not yet been fully embraced in the North, where *Collier's* was widely read.

Waddell's bylined article was published on November 26, just two weeks after the killings. It was spread over two pages, with a cover illustration depicting two black men firing revolvers, flanked by other blacks wielding pistols and clubs. The headline read: THE STORY OF THE WILMINGTON, NC, RACE RIOTS. Waddell wrote that he had been swept up by events, as though he had been standing idly by when gunshots rang out.

"When the crisis came, there was universal demand that I should take charge . . . I never dreamed the time would come when I would lead a mob," he wrote.

Waddell wrote that he reluctantly led armed men to Alex Manly's newspaper office, intent solely on destroying the printing press inside. He had nothing to do with smashing down the front door, he wrote, "For I have not the strength." Nor did he take part in setting the building on fire. The torching was "purely accidental," he wrote.

In Waddell's account, no black men were shot. Indeed, no shots were fired at all. Anyone reading his article would have assumed that the day's only untoward event was the accidental burning of the *Record* office. It was a tidy, efficient little coup, Waddell wrote. He quoted a United States Army officer he said had witnessed the day's events: "It's the most orderly performance I ever witnessed!"

Northern newspapermen seemed torn between their scorn for Southerners and their widely held contempt for black capabilities. Most deplored the violence in Wilmington but not the outcome. Many Northern editors wrote that they did not consider blacks, in the North or the South, capable of holding public office. They welcomed the return of what they regarded as the natural order in America—whites ruling blacks. They seemed aggrieved only by the way Wilmington's whites went about it.

DAVID ZUCCHINO

The *Washington Post* said whites were justified in rebelling against an "insufferable situation" in Wilmington. But the newspaper asked why they weren't resourceful enough to avoid violence: "There has been too prompt use of the rifle, too swift a wreaking of angry vengeance . . . the revolution in Wilmington, which could have and should have been accomplished by peaceful means, is stained with blood."

The *Philadelphia Record* called the white riot "deplorable" and "disgraceful." But it said bloodshed could have been avoided if the United States had not "armed the ignorant negro with the right of suffrage." That miscalculation served only "to halt negro advancement by making the white population antagonistic as a matter of self-preservation . . . The weaker race must bend to the stronger. This is a law that no act of Congress can repeal."

The *New York Herald* declared the Fifteenth Amendment all but dead in North Carolina. The *Washington Evening Star* and *New York Journal* were among the few white-run Northern newspapers to express unreserved outrage. The *Evening Star* headlined its editorial on Wilmington: NORTH CAROLINA'S SHAME. It said the violence "had the desired effect of keeping the negroes away from the polls on election day."

The *New York Journal* correspondent on the scene equated the killings of November 10 to mass murder:

The 10th was a bloody day in this one-horse town. They talk of culture and refinement. But could you have seen them on Thursday you would have thought them the bloodhounds of hell turned loose. There was no riot; simply the strong slaying the weak and helpless. The negroes had no firearms of any kind but every white man from 12 to seventy was handling guns . . . From every town around the whites poured in to exterminate the Negroes.

The nation's black newspapers roundly condemned Wilmington's white supremacists, but from a distance. It had been too dangerous to send black correspondents to Wilmington. Most black papers had relied on reports from blacks still in Wilmington or from relatives who had taken in blacks who had fled.

In Virginia's capital, black journalists at the *Richmond Planet* relayed eyewitness accounts provided by black refugees from Wilmington:

> *It was a slaughter, useless slaughter, and A. M. Waddell was the leader of this murderous outrage . . . Does anyone doubt that if the men killed at Wilmington had been white instead of colored that the government at Raleigh, N.C., and Washington, D.C., would have stumbled over itself in suppressing the "insurrection"?*

The black-readership *Washington Bee* asked why Governor Russell had failed to aid not only his fellow Republican officeholders, but the black voters who had helped put him in the governor's mansion: "The Governor of North Carolina was no more than a baby in the hands of the hot-headed rebels of the South. He was not man enough to exercise his authority as governor of a great State."

The *Indianapolis Freeman*, which billed itself as "the Highest Mark of Negro Journalism," ridiculed pious whites in Wilmington and urged blacks to take up arms:

> *The shotgun and the Bible have never been separated by the Caucasian . . . It is not the Christianity that makes the Negro forgiving, it is two hundred and fifty years of forced coercion, cowardice and damaging instructions to play into the favor of the white man. Better get a gun for Christmas. Insure your lives Negroes, and then you are in line of equality.*

In Washington, DC, and in Pittsburgh, Chicago, East St. Louis, and Denver, black leaders organized rallies to spread the word about the killings in Wilmington. They sent resolutions of protest to President McKinley, to the Justice Department, and to members of Congress. The National Anti Mob-and-Lynch Law Association, formed in 1897 by black residents of Columbus, Ohio, wrote to the president's 1896 campaign manager to seek help persuading the Justice Department to investigate the killings: "The treatment of the Armenians by the Turks and the cruelties of the Spaniards is nothing to the willful murders at Wilmington, N.C." In Brooklyn, a black minister suggested that someone lynch Colonel Waddell.

In New York, T. Thomas Fortune, a former slave who cofounded and edited the black newspaper *New York Age*, organized a mass meeting at the Cooper Union, coordinated with similar gatherings in Philadelphia, Baltimore, and other Northern cities. Before a large crowd of blacks and a few whites, Fortune condemned the "mobocracy" in Wilmington and urged blacks to resist white violence. Another speaker proposed a constitutional amendment that would allow the president to send federal troops, without a formal request from a governor, to any state where mobs violated the rights of citizens.

Organizers of the Cooper Union meeting sent a resolution to every member of Congress "condemning the white people of Wilmington for the shooting of unoffending black men and their cruelty toward fleeing negroes."

There was no response.

On November 15, five days after the killings in Wilmington, Josephus Daniels welcomed thousands of white men and women from across the state for a parade his newspaper called the "Victory, White Supremacy and Good Government" jubilee. A front-page headline called the celebration in Raleigh: THE MOST REMARKABLE DEMONSTRATION EVER SEEN AT THE CAPITAL.

White visitors arrived on special reduced-fare trains. They were greeted by hundreds of flaming tar barrels and bonfires that sent dark orange flames skyward. Fireworks lit up darkening skies on a crisp autumn evening. "Every man had a torchlight which gleamed and blinked like the eye of some mighty Cyclops," the *News and Observer* reported.

The tar fires illuminated American flags fluttering from offices and shops, and red-white-and-blue bunting draped over storefronts. An orange glow lit up the *News and Observer* building, where Daniels had affixed brooms to the facade to commemorate the sweeping Democratic victory.

At city hall, the ladies of the Chrysanthemum Committee had decorated a towering arch with a crest of fresh white mums. On Fayetteville Street, two thousand men carried torches to light the way for a hundred men on horseback, followed by a marching band and dignitaries in horse-drawn carriages.

The torchlit line of men and horses and carriages stretched for two miles. More than an hour passed before the procession made its way from the Carrollton Hotel to the capitol building at the head of Fayetteville Street. The men on horseback were trailed by men and boys on bicycles decorated with patriotic bunting and by men who toted brooms and pitchforks. Several white men pushed through the crowds packed along the sidewalks to raise handmade signs for all to see.

White Supremacy Means Work for All
Down with Negro Rule
No More Crucifixion on Colored Crosses

One man held aloft a sign taunting Russell, who remained holed up inside the Queen Anne–style governor's mansion: *It's a Hard Pill, Governor, but Shut Your Eyes and Swallow It.*

There were more fireworks as the procession ended at Nash Square, two blocks southwest of the capitol. Thousands of white men and women gathered on the brown grass beneath bare branches of oak trees to eat and listen to speeches. A troupe of Democratic politicians took turns denouncing "Negro rule" and "race traitors" and "the alien and servile Negro race." Then came the event's featured speaker, Furnifold Simmons. As Daniels mounted the speaker's stand to introduce Simmons, several men grabbed the editor and hoisted him onto their shoulders. The crowd roared.

Simmons took the stage to cheers so loud they could be heard over the thumping of a brass band and the popping fireworks overhead.

People shouted white supremacist slogans. Simmons raised a fundamental question that was on the minds of the white citizens gathered before him: "What shall we do with the negro?"

There were hisses and groans. Simmons answered his own question.

"The Democrats intend that the Negro shall know his place," he said. "Today, as always, the Democrat is his best friend. We will do all we can to promote his best interests but by the eternal gods he shall not rule over white men!"

CHAPTER THIRTY-FOUR

The Meanest Animals

ON THE MORNING of Sunday, November 13, after two days and three nights in the forest and swamps, hundreds of black families began gathering up their belongings for the long trek home. They did not believe the guarantees of fair treatment promised by Mayor Waddell or the police delegation, but they could no longer tolerate sleeping on the damp ground at night, when temperatures dropped to near freezing. Some children and elderly people had fallen grievously ill; a black minister reported that several infants born under the pines had died of exposure. The *New York Times* reported that many families "were in a starving condition." All that Sunday morning, they emerged from the tree line sodden, hungry, and exhausted. Their clothing was streaked with rust-colored mud. Children were sobbing and begging to go home.

Some families returned home only long enough to gather their belongings and borrow enough money to purchase train tickets out of Wilmington. Others waited until tickets mailed by relatives reached them. Most did not have a destination in mind; they sought to travel as far north as their money permitted. Some bought tickets to Washington, Baltimore, and Philadelphia to join relatives or find lodging in black neighborhoods there.

Those who owned homes or small businesses in Wilmington also bought train tickets. But they delayed their departure until they could wrap up their affairs and plan for new lives elsewhere. It was clear to them that Wilmington's brief interlude as a mecca for blacks in the South had come to a decisive end.

Dozens of black families had begun fleeing the city on November 10 to escape the white mobs. Instead of retreating to the woods and swamps, they boarded wagons, carriages, and trains headed north out of the city.

Day by day, Wilmington's newspapers chronicled the exodus: "about 50 negroes left here yesterday"; ". . . more than a dozen families . . . about sixty persons . . . left on the S.A.L. [Seaboard Air Line] train"; ". . . last week 150 took their departure from the city."

The *Atlanta Constitution* reported two days after the killings that thousands of blacks had abandoned Wilmington. A black church newsletter edited by John C. Dancy put the number at more than fourteen hundred in the four weeks after November 10. Over that same period, fifty-five houses rented to blacks were vacated in Brooklyn, where the first black men were shot on November 10. White real estate agents reported, with some satisfaction, that most of those homes had since been rented to whites.

The passage of so many black families through white towns along the rail lines north of Wilmington alarmed some local whites. In New Bern, white men climbed the town's water tower to spot black families arriving by wagon or cart from Wilmington so that they could turn them away. "They will be promptly and summarily shipped," they warned. In Richmond, police threatened to arrest six black men aboard a train from Wilmington if they tried to get off. The men continued their journey north.

A few blacks who had fled sought permission to return to Wilmington. F. P. Toomer, a fired black policeman, wrote to Mayor Waddell from New Bern to inquire about going home. Waddell delivered a disingenuous reply, asking Toomer what possibly could have prompted him to flee his hometown. But then Waddell answered his own question: he said he had been informed that Toomer "was very obnoxious to many persons here." Perhaps, for his own safety, Toomer should stay away. But if he insisted on returning, Waddell promised, he would do his best to protect him. Of course, the mayor added, he had no authority to prevent Toomer or other "obnoxious persons" from "being assaulted and probably treated with violence by private persons." Toomer stayed away.

When the editors of the *Messenger* learned that some blacks were considering returning, they published a warning in the form of an anonymous letter signed with an X: "If the occurrences that day meant anything, they meant that the white men were determined to govern this city and county . . . and should any disturbances arise . . . the 10th of November will prove to be child's play to what the consequences will be to the negroes."

Over the next few months, the pace of the exodus quickened. On a single day in April, sixty-two black men, women, and children fled the city for Norfolk, Baltimore, and New York. They were among more than three hundred black people who departed that month. By the end of April, an estimated twenty-eight hundred blacks had left since November 10. In an uncharacteristically neutral tone, the *Messenger* explained why: "Under the policy of our business men to give white labor the preference, hundreds of negroes have been thrown out of employment and they are forced to seek homes elsewhere."

The departure of black workers was initially welcomed by the new city government. Waddell and his aldermen were determined to carry out the resolution passed at the mass meeting of whites on November 9—"to give to white men a large part of the employment heretofore given to Negroes."

The board of aldermen went to work. They fired the black day jani-tor and black messenger at city hall. They dismissed the city's black cattle weigher, the black superintendent of city streets, and the black lot inspector. The all-black health board was disbanded and the vacated posi-tions were awarded to whites. The city's ten black police officers, already suspended, were formally dismissed and replaced by white men, among them Red Shirts or other participants in the November 10 killings.

The new board fired every firefighter serving in the two all-black fire companies in the city and county. The black men's gear and equip-ment were awarded to white companies. The fourteen black firemen who had been permitted to work for otherwise all-white companies were replaced by white men. Among the white replacement firefighters was Mike Dowling, the Red Shirt brigade leader, who was appointed foreman of Hose Reel Co. No. 3 at a generous salary of $45 a month. Four months later, Dowling was suspended for "incompetency, drunk-enness, and insubordination." Rather than attend a formal inquiry to plead his case, Dowling told the board of aldermen to go to hell. The aldermen fired him.

Various city boards and commissions were purged of Republicans and Fusionists, most of them white men. Gone were Fusionist members of the Board of Audit and Finance, the county Board of Commission-ers, and the Board of Education. Frank Dempsey, a white Republican jettisoned from the Board of Education, begged for his job, writing: "I do not propose to let myself be let off . . . and intend not to serve in any office in which a negro is with me in said office." He was fired anyway.

Some service jobs were also taken from blacks. But other black work-ers were able to remain in those positions, primarily because whites lacked the skills or inclination to perform them. Blacks continued to work, for $2 or $3 a week, as domestic servants—as maids, cooks, waiters, stablemen, and laundrywomen—in the homes of whites or in exclusive white clubs. Since the antebellum era, black waiters and other household servants had cultivated traits prized by their white employers—a formal bearing, a cultured appearance, and proper diction. A few days after the killings of November 10, Waddell told a New Jersey reporter that Southern whites had long embraced "a certain class of black labor that we could not well get along without."

Working-class whites, many of whom had joined the mobs on November 10, began demanding that blacks be removed from positions as laborers, stevedores, and draymen, and from other semiskilled jobs. A White Laborer's Union was organized "to aid and assist white men in obtaining situations and work which previously had largely been occupied by negroes." Members wore lapel pins stamped with the union name. They visited white-owned businesses to demand that merchants hire only whites. The union set up a makeshift night school to educate white children who worked during the day.

White farmhands drifted into the city from the countryside, drawn by the promise of steady pay; many offered to perform "disagreeable and arduous work" previously carried out by black men. That included working in the holds of ships, a hot, filthy job traditionally reserved for blacks. In the first days after the coup, more than sixty white men were awarded unskilled or semiskilled jobs previously held by blacks, with many more promised.

The Wilmington Chamber of Commerce announced a white-labor campaign. The city's Democratic newspapers began printing the names of white job applicants and their qualifications. A White Labor Bureau was established for the same purpose.

Waddell and his board of aldermen did not always cooperate with the Chamber of Commerce. They instituted a program of spending cuts in response to what Wilmington's white leaders claimed had been profligate spending under "Negro rule." The city proposed reducing the wages of street cleaners to 8 cents an hour, from 10 cents an hour paid under Mayor Wright. But now the cleaners were white. At a meeting on November 23, with Mike Dowling presiding, the White Labor Union declared that it was "shocked and surprised" at the proposed wage cut. Union members accused the new government of conspiring to "cramp and grind down the poor sons of toil." Did the mayor and board need to be reminded whose efforts had put them in charge?

The wage cuts were abandoned.

There were other complications. The *Messenger* complained that the whites-only labor policy had by no means solved "the negro problem," because many blacks still held jobs in the city. "It is proposed to organize White Men's Unions throughout the south for the purpose of encouraging the employment of white men and . . . cause the negro to segregate or emigrate to other sections of the United States, which is all the more desirable," the paper suggested.

Not all white employers were pleased with the turn of events. Owners of lumber mills complained that whites weren't up to the standards set by longtime black workers. Some whites were unable to properly count and pile lumber. It sometimes took two white men to perform the same job previously held by a single black man. On the waterfront, it was difficult to replace some black draymen, who owned their own wagons and mules and horses and who had learned to unload and deliver cargo quickly and efficiently. Some white employers said they missed their fired black workers, who had provided "the least troublesome labor."

Other whites made exceptions for deferential blacks who had worked for them for years. James S. Worth, a white banker and insurance executive, was pleased when a black worker named George returned to work on November 16 after hiding out for five days. Worth wrote that George was "back at work again and is happy as can be whistling at his work—I am quite satisfied that he as well as all the best darkies are glad the change has been made." Worth added that he was "glad that 'dark town' has been taught a lesson, as one bad nigger will harm the rest."

The most notorious exile from Wilmington was Alex Manly, who had not been heard from since he fled the city shortly before November 10. Manly was by now a nationally known figure. "Wilmington, N.C., is far too small for such a celebrity," the *Indianapolis Freeman* reported. Newspapers published purported eyewitness sightings of the fugitive editor—in Raleigh, Norfolk, Richmond, Washington, Philadelphia, and New York City. He was hiding in a swamp. He had fled the country. He was plotting a return. Josephus Daniels first said Manly was hiding in New Bern but then conceded he could not be found: "He seemed to have disappeared off the face of the earth."

Southern white men stood ready to capture the elusive editor. In Norfolk, a gang of whites thought they had spotted Manly when they encountered a light-skinned black man inside the local post office. One of them asked the man where he was from. When he replied "Wilmington," the white men punched him, knocked him to the floor, and kicked him in the ribs. The bloodied black man was one George W. Brown, who had arrived in Norfolk that day from Wilmington on the same train that carried the city's fired police chief, John Melton. Brown had gone to the post office to buy a stamp. He was rescued by white police officers, who took him to a police station—for his own safety, they said—before shoving him aboard a northbound train that night.

News of the missing black editor raced across the Atlantic. One newspaper account reached Carrie Sadgwar, Manly's fiancée, who was performing at Covent Garden in London with the Fisk University Jubilee Singers. She saw a photograph of the torched remains of the *Record* building. A headline caught her eye: BURLY NEGRO PURSUED BY BLOODHOUNDS.

"I read in the *London Chronicle* that trouble was brewing, and it would only be a matter of time before they would catch the editor, as he had escaped to the swamps and the bloodhounds were on his trail," Carrie wrote years later. She was so distraught that she was unable to perform. "I stood on the stage that night to sing my solo and my voice quavered and stopped." A doctor was summoned. She did not sing again for a week.

As it turned out, there had been no bloodhounds, no swamps, no manhunt. Manly had safely boarded a train just north of Wilmington after leaving the city in a carriage. He had made his way to Asbury Park, New Jersey, where his brother-in-law, Reverend I. N. Giles, was a prominent member of the town's large and vibrant black community. Word spread among black leaders in the North that Manly had survived. Black ministers in New York City sent word to him in New Jersey, inviting him to speak at the protest rally planned for the Cooper Union. He agreed. But later he backed out. He offered no public explanation.

The *Wilmington Morning Star*, in an unsigned dispatch sent by telegraph from New York, speculated that rally organizers feared Manly was too provocative. The truth was more alarming. Manly had received several hate letters warning that he would be shot dead if he attended the rally. The threats meant that Manly's presence in Asbury Park was no longer a secret. His friends and in-laws panicked after a "rough looking white man" arrived in town by train late one night and asked where he could find Manly. They began providing bodyguards to accompany the editor everywhere he went.

Three days after the killings in Wilmington, a reporter for the *Baltimore Sun* tracked Manly down and secured the fugitive's first interview since he had fled the city. Manly was not particularly forthcoming. He answered questions perfunctorily, providing no details of his flight from Wilmington. He did, however, attribute "the trouble" in Wilmington to his August 18 editorial. He said he wrote the piece to defend "defamed colored men" who had been libeled by Rebecca Felton in Georgia. His words had been misquoted and distorted by white newspapers and politicians "to scare the white voters who were likely to support the populist candidates," Manly told the reporter.

"Flaming mutilations of this article were published all through the South, and I was charged with slandering the virtue of white women," he went on. "Such a thought never entered my head."

Manly seemed puzzled by the delayed response to his editorial that summer. He told the man from the *Sun* that few whites in Wilmington had mentioned the article to him in the days after it was published in August. It was only weeks later, after white newspapers republished the editorial and politicians delivered threatening speeches, that Manly was blamed for inflaming the white men of North Carolina by defaming their women.

The *Sun* reporter pressed Manly for more. Manly declined to say whether he intended to return to Wilmington. He feared his presence there would endanger others. But Manly did engage in a moment of personal refection. He told the reporter that he had lost everything—his home, his business, his printing press, his church, his friends. It was of little consolation that his properties were covered by insurance, he said, for the policy contained an exception. It did not cover the "fury of a mob."

Manly's interview was reprinted by newspapers up and down the Eastern Seaboard. On November 15, Rebecca Felton delivered a furious response from Georgia. In her original speech more than a year earlier, she had suggested lynching any black man caught with a white woman. Now she wanted Manly lynched.

"When the negro Manly attributed the crime to intimacy between negro men and white women of the South the slanderer should be made to fear a lyncher's rope rather than occupy a place in New York newspapers."

Against the advice of his friends and in-laws, Manly granted a follow-up interview to the *New York World*. He spoke elliptically. Referring to Felton's charge that black men were sexual predators, he mentioned that some male slaves left in charge of plantations during the Civil War protected white women and girls from harm. Refuting Felton's claims that blacks were inherently inferior, Manly said any black man provided the same opportunities as white men could obtain "as high a standard of intelligence and morality as his white brother."

But Manly refused to address Felton's threat to lynch him. "Any utterance of mine at this time must necessarily increase the race friction in Wilmington, and I do not care to be responsible for further violence or subject my friends and relatives to possible maltreatment or death," he said.

Manly was weary and disillusioned. He was homeless and in hiding. His life was in danger. His fiancée was half a world away. Many of the black leaders he had expected to rally to his defense had forsaken him. His life as a crusading editor in the post-Reconstruction South was over.

Manly had expected venom from the likes of Rebecca Felton. But he had hoped that even obsequious black men like John C. Dancy, the federal customs collector, might offer some support. He was bitterly disappointed.

Dancy had traveled to New York City after he and his family left Wilmington. He took up temporary residence with a black AME minister in Manhattan. Unlike Manly, Dancy was not in hiding. In fact, he denied that he had been forced out of Wilmington, pointing out that he still had a federal appointment there. Dancy seemed to consider himself distinct from the quarrelsome blacks he believed had provoked white wrath in Wilmington. He had counseled cooperation, and he remained true to his conciliatory and accommodating nature even after the killings.

On November 20, Dancy granted an interview to a reporter from the *New York Times* who had approached him after a church service in Manhattan. Without prompting, Dancy blamed Manly and his editorial for unleashing bloodshed.

"Manly is responsible for the whole unfortunate condition of things," he said. "When he published his editorial reflecting upon the white women of the State, I with other leading colored men of Wilmington held a conference with him and urged him to retract the article. We even went so far as to write an editorial retracting the one written by Manly, but he would not take our advice and publish it. If he had done so there would have been no race war in Wilmington."

Dancy said the city's black leadership had failed to understand that "the intelligent colored people of the State" were deeply offended by Manly's views on race and sex. Prior to Manly's editorial, Dancy said, relations between blacks and whites were "most cordial and amicable . . . but the white men of the South will not tolerate any reflection upon their women."

Dancy was not a politician, but he understood the importance of quickly carving out a public position to reflect prevailing political currents. Through the *Times*, he was telling the white supremacists ruling Wilmington that he was *their* Negro. As a federal appointee, he would retain his lucrative custom collector's position while hundreds of blacks in Wilmington were losing their jobs. But to do so Dancy would have to return to Wilmington, and he wanted to ensure a cordial welcome.

Later that week, Dancy wrote an editorial for his AME church newsletter that justified the white violence in Wilmington. "The manhood of a race that will not defend its womanhood is unworthy of the respect of that womanhood," he wrote.

Dancy was hardly the only prominent black man to abandon Manly. John Edward Bruce, a former slave who gained a reputation as a journalist and orator under the name Bruce Grit, suggested that Manly was foolhardy in matters of race because he was a mulatto. Blacks and whites could coexist peacefully, Bruce wrote, if only "these gentlemen with large Caucasian reinforcement would cease in their efforts to revolutionize the social order."

Cyrus D. Bell, editor of the *Afro-American Sentinel* in Omaha, also denigrated Manly's white ancestry. He attributed the violence in Wilmington to "that element that are so nearly white that they are miserable anywhere except in the white race. They are the meanest animals unhung."

Other leading black men proceeded carefully. The National Afro-American Council declared a nationwide day of fasting to commemorate the victims in Wilmington. But rather than condemn the city's white supremacists, the council asked blacks to embrace "a hearty confession of our own sins."

And then there was Armond Scott. Manly had been buoyed when he read in the press that Scott, the black lawyer who had mailed the Committee of Colored Citizens' statement to Waddell's house, had reached Washington, DC, after fleeing Wilmington. Down to his last hundred dollars, Scott rented a top-floor room in a cheap apartment building for $3 a month and slept on a secondhand couch.

Several newspapers reported that Scott intended to petition President McKinley for federal action on behalf of Wilmington's beleaguered blacks. Scott had read the same reports, but he was not inclined to take a public stand. He intended to build a new life as a lawyer in the capital. He wanted to bury the past. He did not want to risk stirring up racial animosities by appealing to the president for help that was unlikely to materialize.

Scott wrote a short statement and delivered it to the Associated Press.

It has been stated in the several newspapers of this city that I am here preparing to present the Wilmington race trouble to the President, and I desire through your courtesy to make a correction of the same. I am here in no official capacity whatever and have no intention of saying anything to the President or taking any action in the matter at all.

It would be left to other exiles to petition the president.

CHAPTER THIRTY-FIVE

Old Scores

J OHN MELTON, Robert Bunting, and Charles Gilbert sat slumped in a train car, staring out the windows at the coastal plain of eastern North Carolina late in the day on November 11. They had no baggage and few possessions. They were hungry and exhausted as they approached New Bern, where Melton knew the local sheriff and hoped he would rescue them. But the sheriff didn't want any trouble in his city—and he refused to intervene.

At the New Bern station, the three exiles were abducted from the train, manhandled, jeered, and paraded through town by a white mob, then put aboard a boat headed north. A telegram was sent to their next stop, Elizabeth City, warning town leaders there of the impending arrival of the "Dirty White Republican scoundrels." Before the boat pulled out, a futile search was mounted for Alex Manly, who was rumored to have stowed away.

That same evening, the sky above the New Bern waterfront lit up with fireworks as the ship slid down the Neuse River toward Pamlico Sound. New Bern was welcoming its native son, Furnifold Simmons. The Democratic Party chairman had returned home that evening on a postelection victory tour. He was met at the depot by the city band, which escorted him to his hotel with a blast of marching music, trailed by wisps of gray smoke from the fireworks.

The three exiles traveled from New Bern to Elizabeth City to Norfolk and across the Mason-Dixon Line to Washington, DC, where they arrived on Monday, November 14. For the first time on their journey, there was no mob to confront them. They found lodging at a cheap hotel on Pennsylvania Avenue and, for the first time in four days, were able to sit quietly and ponder their future. They decided to keep their location secret for fear they were being stalked by Washington confederates of Wilmington's white supremacists.

As seasoned politicians and public servants, the three men believed they possessed the credentials to demand the attention of United States attorney general John W. Griggs and perhaps McKinley himself. On their first day in the capital, they lodged a complaint at the US attorney general's office, then met with reporters. They complained that they had been seized without charge or warrant "and told in forcible language that if ever again they set foot in Wilmington they would be shot on sight." They demanded federal intervention.

Back in North Carolina, Democratic newspapers taunted the three Republicans. A front-page headline in the *Morning Post* of Raleigh read: MELTON, BUNTING ET AL. TELL THEIR TALE OF WOE TO UNSYMPATHETIC EARS. With no attribution, the newspaper reported that the McKinley administration had decided not to act on the men's request for federal intervention.

There is no record that McKinley ever met with Melton, Bunting, or Gilbert. The president had other matters on his mind. The bloodshed in Wilmington was overshadowed by several crises confronting McKinley that week. Negotiations with Spain in Paris for a peace treaty to formally end the Spanish-American War were proceeding poorly. Some American troops who had fought in Cuba were dying of yellow fever, prompting an investigation into the War Department's combat tactics in Cuba and its handling of food and sanitary facilities for troops. In the Philippines, insurgents were defying American occupation. An American general, serving as military governor, sought to ease tensions with the natives by ordering his troops not to refer to Filipinos as "niggers," at least to their faces.

McKinley did not publicly address events in Wilmington, but the killings had commanded the attention of one member of his cabinet. On the evening of November 10, a correspondent for the *Charlotte Observer* had interviewed Secretary of War Russell A. Alger as he emerged from a meeting with the president. Asked about the Wilmington killings, Alger called them "a disgrace to the State and to the Country." McKinley was "much exercised over the startling reports" from Wilmington, the *Observer* correspondent reported, citing his conversation with Alger. But Alger emphasized that federal troops could not be dispatched unless Governor Russell requested them.

The next day, November 11, the killings in Wilmington were discussed at the day's cabinet meeting. "Cabinet officials, in their remarks, greatly deplored the situation, and unhesitatingly stated that the white people had gone too far," the *Washington Evening Star* reported. The *Star* reporter speculated that McKinley would send federal troops if the killings continued.

A day later, on November 12, McKinley convened a rare Saturday cabinet meeting to discuss tensions at the peace talks in Paris and a troubling military report on the botched evacuation of American troops from Puerto Rico. The situation in Wilmington was mentioned only in passing. Questioned by Southern reporters after the meeting, Attorney General Griggs said he had heard nothing from Governor Russell or anyone else to warrant dispatching federal troops to North Carolina.

Back in Raleigh, Russell's political position was precarious. He could not risk antagonizing the white supremacists who now controlled the state legislature and who had already threatened to impeach him.

Russell feared for his life and kept a loaded pistol close at hand. He wrote to a colleague that his "friends in Wilmington" were plotting to assassinate him. For the first three days after the Wilmington killings, Russell and his wife, Sarah, barricaded themselves inside the governor's mansion as jeering whites paraded up and down the streets of the capital.

Russell was trapped. He did not dare return to Wilmington to investigate the killings or to check on his home and plantation. Both had been vandalized. "Devils are breaking up our business and it looks like we will be driven from our home," he wrote. Finally, on November 14, the Russells retreated to the mountain city of Asheville in western North Carolina. Russell cited Sarah's condition: "Mrs. Russell has been through such a terrible ordeal that I am getting uneasy about her."

The respite in Asheville gave Russell time for a sober assessment of his predicament. He was more than halfway through his term as governor and would face reelection in a hostile political environment. He began considering other employment. He wrote to a friend, the tobacco and textile baron Benjamin Duke, to inquire about a job with Duke's American Tobacco Company in New York. Russell complained to Duke that "the irritations incident to being a Republican and living in the South are getting to be too rank to be borne."

The killing of blacks in Wilmington was not the only Southern racial violence to make headlines in Northern newspapers that month. On Election Day, November 8, a bloody racial confrontation had erupted in the hamlet of Phoenix, South Carolina. A white Republican, Thomas Tolbert, had spent the day taking depositions from black men at a polling station in Phoenix, documenting attacks by white vigilantes. White supremacist Democrats had confronted Tolbert. He was beaten, then shot and wounded. In the ensuing melee, the local Democratic Party boss was shot and killed. In retaliation, white supremacists burned Tolbert's home and killed at least eight black men.

On November 11, McKinley met at the White House with Tolbert's brother. Robert "Red" Tolbert was a prominent Republican politician who had been appointed federal customs collector in Charleston. "The President listened attentively to the recital, but gave no indication of what action, if any, might be taken," the *New York Times* reported in a front-page dispatch.

Encouraged by Tolbert's visit with the president, Melton, Bunting, and Gilbert persisted in their efforts to secure their own meeting with McKinley. But on Christmas Eve, they finally abandoned their pleas for federal intervention. They sent a plaintive letter to McKinley, begging him to appoint them to federal positions in Washington. They reminded the Republican president that they had been loyal Republican officeholders.

> *We the undersigned, were driven from Wilmington, N.C. our home for the reason, we were republicans and stood up for the Republican Party . . . We can't return to our families, and have been notified through the public press at Wilmington, N.C. that if we return we would be killed . . . We would have called on you and laid our troubles before you, but we know your time is too valuable, hence we take this method of reaching you.*

McKinley did not respond.

The president was petitioned by other citizens across the country who demanded justice in Wilmington. Many of the letters came from blacks asking McKinley to send federal troops to Wilmington—letters from Asbury Park and Elizabeth, New Jersey; Mount Vernon, New York; Washington, DC; Pittsburgh; East Saint Louis; Chicago; Cincinnati; and elsewhere.

Harry Jones, a black man, wrote from Denver to remind McKinley that black soldiers from Wilmington and elsewhere had served during the Spanish-American War that summer: "Is it possible we must leave our homes and go and fight a foreign foe and not get any protection at home by the government we are defending?"

Another black man, Samuel E. Huffman, wrote from Springfield, Ohio: "The Republican party always posed as a friend of the Negro, and the Negro has so regarded that party, and he allyed himself with that party, believing it to be his friend, yet that friend stands by and sees him robed [robbed] of both his political and civil rights, without making a protest Against such treatment."

There were letters from Wilmington, too. Most were from black citizens, who left many of them unsigned for fear of retribution. A black woman from Wilmington, who did not sign her name, wrote: "[T]hat old confradate flage is floating in Wilmington North Carolina. The city of Wilmington is unde the confradate laws. We are over powered with the rapid fire of the guns, and they had cannons, in wagons, and they set fie to the almost half of the City."

Perhaps the most anguished letter from Wilmington was sent by a black woman who wrote that she was afraid she would be murdered if she identified herself: "The outside world only knows one side of the trouble here, there is no paper to tell the truth about the Negro here, in this or any other Southern state. The Negro in this town had no arms (except pistols perhaps in some instances) with which to defend themselves against from the attack of lawless whites."

The woman described Waddell's leadership of the mob that burned the *Record* office, adding: "The Man who promises the Negro protection now as Mayor is the one who in his speech at the Opera house said the Cape Fear should be strewn with carcasses." She mentioned the Colt and Hotchkiss guns and provided details of the attacks on blacks by white Spanish-American War veterans in the Wilmington Light Infantry: "The men of the 1st North Carolina were home on a furlough and they took high hand in the nefarious work also. The Companies from every little town came in to kill the negro. There was not any Rioting Simply the strong slaying the weak."

The woman concluded: "I cannot sign my name and live. But every word of this is true. The laws of our state is no good for the Negro anyhow. Yours in much distress."

McKinley also heard from whites who asked him not to interfere in Wilmington. He met privately with Mrs. A. B. Skelding, the wife of a prominent white supremacist in Wilmington. Mrs. Skelding, who had been a neighbor of McKinley's in Ohio, told the president that the Wilmington rebellion, as she called it, had been necessary to eliminate a corrupt and incompetent city government and to return the city to white rule. She reported that McKinley had responded: "Daughter, I understand the conditions and have neither the wish nor intention to interfere."

The president also heard from Julian Shakespeare Carr, the financier who had bankrolled Josephus Daniels's purchase of the *News and Observer*. Carr wrote to McKinley the day after the Wilmington killings:

> *Sir:*
>
> *Men with white skins, sons of revolutionary ancestors, who drafted the original Magna Charter of American Independence, lovers of the Union and the constitution . . . are leading the victorious column this morning, and will rule North Carolina ever hereafter. No need of troops now.*
>
> *Praise God!*

A day later, Carr followed up with a telegram to McKinley sent from a hotel in New York City. Carr told the president that he employed hundreds of black men, "and they would die for me." He claimed that he paid $1,000 a year in federal taxes to cover "every day in the year, including Sundays." He said he had read newspaper reports that McKinley was considering sending federal troops to North Carolina.

"Don't do it," Carr wrote. "It is the lawless, vicious, bad element of the negro race that is being suppressed . . . the property-owners and the taxpayers will not submit to the domination of the vicious element of the black race."

Another telegram, sent to federal officials in Washington, DC, by an anonymous white supremacist in Wilmington, warned that if federal troops were sent, "Caskets should be included in their equipment."

It would have been out of character for McKinley to be unmoved by the Wilmington killings and the suppression of black voting rights in North Carolina. He was the son of Ohio abolitionists who imbued in him a visceral hatred of slavery. As a young man, McKinley confronted Democratic-voting workers at a local tannery and challenged them to spirited debates about slavery. At Allegheny College in Pennsylvania, he responded to a student who raised a glass to Jefferson Davis by vowing to fight treason on Southern soil. In 1861, McKinley joined the Union army as a private, rising to major and leading troops in battle. His final promotion was for "gallant and meritorious service."

Later, as a national political candidate, McKinley courted black votes. In 1879, he accused Southern Democrats of stealing elections by suppressing the black vote. At the 1888 Republican National Convention, he received a standing ovation after he condemned violence against Southern black voters. McKinley later championed a proposed "force act" that would require federal supervision of elections in the South to protect black voting rights. During his run for the Republican presidential nomination in 1895, McKinley became the first presidential candidate of either party to campaign before black voters, at a church in Savannah.

During the 1896 campaign, McKinley focused on reconciliation to heal the lingering wounds of the Civil War. He invited thousands of Confederate veterans to Canton, Ohio. He gave each man a knife engraved with the message: "No East, No West, No North, No South, the Union Forever." He told them: "Patriotism is not bound by State, or class, or sectional lines . . . we are a reunited country. We have but one flag."

In the second year of McKinley's presidency, the Spanish-American War blurred distinctions between North and South as young men from all parts of the country volunteered for service. By the autumn of 1898, as Spain challenged the United States in peace talks and American troops served in Cuba and the Philippines, a spirit of nationalism and patriotism—and often jingoism—prevailed over sectional interests. In this climate of reconciliation, McKinley was reluctant to antagonize Southerners by intervening in their affairs, even on behalf of black voters whose interests he had defended in the past. He did not make a single public reference to the killings in Wilmington.

While McKinley was silent on the killings and coup in Wilmington, he did support black advancement within his administration. In his first seven months in office, he appointed a record number of blacks—179—to federal positions. Blacks served in almost every government agency, including the Treasury and the State Department.

On New Year's Eve of 1898, two dozen black leaders from the Afro-American Council, formed three months earlier to promote black advancement, met with McKinley for fifteen minutes at the White House. The group was led by North Carolina congressman George White, who had campaigned tirelessly for McKinley in 1896. White hoped to persuade the president to publicly acknowledge that white supremacist Democrats had violently overthrown an elected Republican government. But White was overruled by the rest of the council, which merely asked McKinley to "use his good offices in presenting to Congress the subject of the recent lynchings of colored men in the Carolinas that the perpetrators may be brought to justice." McKinley did not comply.

Attorney General Griggs quietly pursued the matter. Griggs was a handsome, distinguished lawyer from New Jersey with a reputation for rectitude. He had turned down an nomination by President Harrison to the United States Supreme Court, then mounted a successful campaign in 1895 for governor of New Jersey. He resigned in January 1898 to become McKinley's attorney general.

That fall, Griggs had received a letter—written November 9, the day before the bloodshed in Wilmington—from the United States commissioner in the Justice Department's Eastern District of North Carolina. Griggs was told that armed white men had formed White Unions and had raided black homes in around Wilmington, "yelling and shooting in the houses of innocent Negroes."

"Are not these people liable for indictment?" the commissioner asked.

Griggs had taken no action then. But now, several weeks after the bloodshed in Wilmington, the situation commanded his attention. He sent a letter to the US attorney for eastern North Carolina in Raleigh, Claude M. Bernard, ordering him to investigate any "acts of lawlessness and violence." He told Bernard to consider a grand jury and bills of indictment.

Bernard was a loyal Republican functionary, a lawyer whose support for McKinley had been rewarded with an appointment as US attorney for the Eastern District of North Carolina. It was a dramatic reversal for the office. Bernard had replaced Charles Aycock, the white supremacist who had been one of Josephus Daniels's leading "men who could speak" during the white supremacy campaign.

Bernard was a political realist. He knew that any prosecution of a Democrat in eastern North Carolina would invite retaliation—political and physical. In the case of the Wilmington killings, he would have to persuade white witnesses to testify against fellow whites; the testimony of black witnesses held little value in a North Carolina courtroom, even a federal one.

Bernard wrote to Griggs that as a Republican US attorney in a hostile Democratic state capital, he was "powerless without a complaint from somebody, or a witness or witnesses." He had nothing: "I have no information reliable from any witness except from newspaper reports, and the letters I now have from your department. No one has made complaints to me."

Nonetheless, Bernard promised Griggs that he would press ahead, despite the obstacles. But he did not intend to act without help from Washington: "I will thank your department to assist this office in every way possible in bringing every violation of the US laws in the recent high handed revolutionary methods employed in this state in the recent election, to justice."

Griggs responded by traveling to Raleigh to help guide Bernard. Griggs was accompanied by his deputy, Assistant Attorney General James E. Boyd of North Carolina, whose arrival reassured Wilmington's white supremacists. Boyd was a former Confederate soldier and had secured a footnote in Civil War history as the courier at Appomattox who had delivered a message from Robert E. Lee to Ulysses S. Grant requesting a meeting to arrange a surrender. A few years later, federal marshals arrested Boyd in North Carolina and charged him with membership in the Ku Klux Klan.

Griggs seemed inclined to let Boyd take charge of the Wilmington investigation, perhaps because of his North Carolina roots. Boyd was also supervising the federal investigation into the South Carolina Election Day killings of black voters. His involvement ensured that whites who had killed blacks in either state would not be prosecuted.

Boyd and Griggs did not spend enough time in Raleigh to help Bernard accomplish anything. They departed for Washington on December 12 without locating a single witness, much less convening a grand jury.

Left on his own, Bernard gamely pursued his investigation. He was unable to locate Melton, though he could have read in the newspapers that the former police chief was holed up in Washington. Nor was Bernard able to locate former mayor Wright, who had disappeared but was rumored to be in Knoxville, Tennessee.

Bernard wasn't sure where the former deputy sheriff, Gizzard French, had fled after escaping the lynch mob but issued a subpoena for him nonetheless. French was not eager to return to Wilmington. He had sent a check to the Orton Hotel to settle his bill and to pay for his belongings to be forwarded to him in Pender County, north of Wilmington. Meanwhile, Wilmington's white "citizens' committee" issued a statement to North Carolina newspapers warning French and other banished Republicans to stay away: "French can never return to this city. If he comes secretly he will not be allowed to stay twelve hours . . . We did not send these fellows away for fun, but because they are a menace to the peace and prosperity of our community and we don't intend that they shall ever come back."

Bernard managed to persuade French to venture to Raleigh for an interview. Reporters cornered Bernard afterward and pressed him for details, but Bernard was circumspect, saying only: "He was able to give me some valuable information." But after speaking to French, Bernard had realized that he was too terrified to testify candidly. He dismissed French, and the former sheriff quickly left Raleigh.

Bernard then issued a subpoena for Bunting, the banished US commissioner. As a federal official, Bunting was crucial to Bernard's investigation. But Bunting feared for his life if he returned to North Carolina. He ignored the subpoena.

Bernard also issued a subpoena for Flavel W. Foster, a white businessman and former Union soldier who was still living in Wilmington. Foster was one of the "Big Six" Fusionists targeted by the skull-and-crossbones handbills. He had helped engineer the Republican surrender in the county, sparing himself from attack by Red Shirts. They allowed him to remain in Wilmington, even as other Big Six politicians were banished.

Reluctantly, Foster agreed to meet Bernard at the US attorney's office in Raleigh. Bernard wanted to interview Foster before putting him in front of a grand jury. He hoped to elicit crucial details of the attacks on Republican officeholders and the killings of black men. But Foster stunned Bernard by denying that there had been any violence on

November 10. Bernard pressed him for nearly an hour but got nowhere. It was obvious that Foster had been thoroughly intimidated. Bernard was not about to let him testify before the grand jury. He sent the frightened businessman home.

After the session with Bernard, Foster granted an interview to a reporter from the *Morning Post* of Raleigh, a white supremacist newspaper. He said he had been "interrogated" by Bernard, who demanded that he provide the names of whites who had intimidated Republicans.

"I told him that I did not know of any intimidation during the election," Foster said. "I informed him that I never heard of an insult offered or an unpleasant word spoken during the day of the election. The day the killings occurred, I was frequently to and from my home and to my factory, which is centrally located in the city. I heard the firing of guns, but never saw any disorder or anything of the riot. I never witnessed any disturbance whatever during the day and I moved about freely."

Foster said Bernard had asked him whether any Republicans had been banished from Wilmington. Foster replied that he had not seen any such thing. "I informed him that the first I heard of it, I read in the newspapers," he said.

The *Morning Post* mocked Bernard over his failure to squeeze the truth out of Foster: "Little Bernard is frightened near unto death, less Griggs bounce him from his failure to have indictments returned . . . The opinion prevails in court circles that Mr. Foster gave the contemplated indictments a knock out blow."

Without French or Foster or Bunting, Bernard had no eyewitnesses. And with no eyewitnesses, he had no grand jury testimony and no case. On December 17, just hours after he questioned Foster, Bernard discharged the grand jury. From Washington, Attorney General Griggs continued to urge Bernard to press ahead. But after a few months, Bernard reported that he did not have enough evidence for an indictment, much less a conviction.

On April 1, 1899, Bernard made one final attempt to collect evidence for the grand jury. He asked Griggs for two Secret Service agents or private detectives to operate undercover in Wilmington and ferret out eyewitness testimony. Bernard suggested the men "go into and associate with the roughs and toughs in certain wards of the city, who were incited and led and directed, by other men of higher official and social standing, and who have profited by this work, and who should be made examples of."

Griggs did not respond. After waiting more than two weeks for a reply, Bernard wrote to Griggs once more, begging for guidance. Again, Griggs did not reply; he never explained why he had suddenly lost interest in the investigation. Bernard was left adrift. The investigation withered.

More than a year later, on August 30, 1900, Bernard finally received an artfully bureaucratic reply, not from Griggs but from a midlevel official with the Justice Department in Washington. It hit Bernard like a hammer blow:

> *This Department is in receipt of your letter of April 1st, 1899 . . . In reply I have to say that the Department deems it inexpedient at this time to grant . . . [Bernard's] request. You are, however, at liberty if, in your judgment, the facts at the present time still justify the application, to renew it, in which event you will please state in detail and fully the circumstances upon which the application is based, so that the Department may judge of its necessity.*

It was clear to Bernard that Washington wanted nothing to do with any credible investigation into the Wilmington killings. He was all alone in Raleigh, 280 miles from the capital. Attorney General Griggs, who had once seemed so eager to hold someone accountable for the violence in Wilmington, had been silent for months. As it turned out, Griggs's tenure as attorney general was coming to an end. He would resign six months later.

Abandoned and adrift, Bernard was a beaten man. He realized that his investigation had been stillborn. He closed his files and shut down the investigation for good.

For Alex Manly, the collapse of the investigation was hardly a surprise. He had no faith in Russell, McKinley, Griggs, or any other Republican to pursue the killings and coup. He had watched Republicans, cowed by the Democrats' intimidation tactics, abandon blacks in Wilmington. He had predicted that Republicans in Raleigh and Washington would turn their backs on them as well.

After escaping Wilmington, Manly first went to Washington, DC. He spoke to federal officials—he never said who—and pleaded with them to prosecute the white supremacists responsible for the killings of November 10. According to his son, Milo Manly, Alex managed to secure an interview with McKinley, who assumed from Manly's light complexion that he was a white man. After Manly asked the president for federal intervention, it dawned on McKinley that he was speaking to the black editor who had caused all the trouble in Wilmington.

"When he realized that Manly was a Negro—and worse, the alleged instigator of the riot—the President ordered him out of the White House," Milo Manly told a historian in 1977.

Alex Manly never mentioned a meeting with McKinley, but for the rest of his life he spoke bitterly of his interactions with white Republican officials in Washington. In January 1899, at the same time that Bernard's investigation was floundering, Manly abandoned all hope of federal assistance. In a speech to a black audience organized by a black minister in Providence, Rhode Island, he spoke caustically of the McKinley administration and told black men that they were now on their own.

"I bought a ticket and went to Washington, there putting my case before the administration. I was told that the country was powerless,"

Manly told the gathering. "Besides, it was too busy settling questions in the Philippines, and could not stop such pastimes as shooting down 'niggers,' or words to that effect. I said I was sorry that the nation had such a wide spirit of humanity that it could fight for the Cubans, but let the negroes be massacred at home."

CHAPTER THIRTY-SIX

The Grandfather Clause

WELL BEFORE US Attorney Bernard shut down his investigation in Raleigh, Josephus Daniels and Furnifold Simmons had concluded that the federal government had no interest in punishing election violence in North Carolina. They knew that no white man in the state would be prosecuted for killing blacks. No Red Shirt would face justice for threatening blacks or whipping them in their homes. No Democratic poll worker would be held accountable for stuffing ballot boxes. Murder, fraud, and voter intimidation had been effectively legalized, so long as the targets were black.

The success of the 1898 campaign energized the careers of the white supremacist politicians who helped direct it. George Rountree was elected to the state legislature. Simmons won the Democratic nomination for the US Senate. Aycock became the Democratic candidate for governor.

North Carolina's black vote seemed nearly vanquished. Thousands of blacks were afraid to register, much less vote. But the black population of the Black Belt was still large enough to sway elections if they could somehow manage to vote in significant numbers. Daniels and Simmons sought a legislative tool to snuff out that vote without infringing on white voting rights. To provide a veneer of legality, they turned to the new, Democratic-led legislature of 1899, which Daniels predicted would "garner the fruits of the white supremacy victory."

One of the legislature's first acts was to grant broad discretion to the state's voting registrars—now all white Democrats—to decide who was eligible to vote. A new voter registration law gave registrars authority to ask a potential voter any "material" question regarding identity and qualifications. To help identify blacks for disqualification, the law required registrars to write down applicants' race. The law enhanced opportunities for fraud and intimidation, but it did not eliminate the black vote altogether. The next challenge was to find a legal framework to suppress the black vote.

The Democratic legislature created a special joint committee to devise ways to legally strip blacks of the vote. The committee was in experienced hands. Its chairman was George Rountree, whose role in the Wilmington coup had brought him statewide notoriety. He told his fellow legislators—among them three black politicians who had survived the Democratic election wave—that "the ignorant, debased negro, in power, is the same arrogant and insolent animal he was in the Reconstruction period." He received a thundering ovation.

Rountree's committee seized on two schemes to help disenfranchise black voters: the poll tax and the literacy test. Both had been imposed in other Southern states. The US Supreme Court had upheld Mississippi's literacy test and poll tax in 1898; it ruled that both satisfied the Fifteenth Amendment because they applied to all voters, not just black men. But white politicians in North Carolina realized a poll tax would create financial hardships for poor whites, and a literacy test would disenfranchise illiterate whites at a time when nearly a quarter of the state's whites could not read or write. Rountree began exploring creative ways to exempt whites from both provisions, thus freeing Democrats to bring the full weight of the poll tax and literacy test down on black men.

The committee looked south to Louisiana, where in 1898, the state legislature had passed a constitutional amendment that carved out an ingenious loophole for white voters. Men who had voted before 1867—the year Reconstruction laws instituted universal suffrage—or whose fathers or grandfathers had voted before 1867 were exempted from the state's poll tax and literacy test. White Louisiana legislators argued that their grandfather clause did not explicitly discriminate against blacks, because it applied to both races. But it punished only black men, of course, because the black vote did not exist before 1867.

Rountree and his committee added a virtually identical grandfather clause to the North Carolina suffrage amendment. Rountree explained that the clause was designed to deny the vote to "those negroes who are unfit for citizenship." A few Republicans and Populists objected, but it hardly mattered. Republicans held only thirty seats, the Populists just six. Democrats had 134.

Black leaders scrambled to defeat the amendment. In desperation, John Crosby, a black educator, offered to sacrifice the rights of some black men but not all. "You want to disenfranchise enough Negroes to make it certain good government will prevail," he told white politicians. "Do that and stop. Do not go to the extent of persecution."

Crosby estimated that perhaps 25,000 of the roughly 125,000 eligible black voters in the state could read and write. (He shortchanged North Carolina's blacks; the 1900 US Census listed 59,597 literate blacks of voting age.) Crosby hoped to head off the grandfather clause by conceding poll taxes and literacy tests but nothing more. He suggested disenfranchising 100,000 blacks but allowing 25,000 literate black men to vote. He was ignored.

Other black leaders hastily formed a State Negro Council that met in Raleigh. It was led by Congressman White, who advised blacks to leave the state if the amendment passed. Such an exodus would deprive whites of cheap black labor. But John C. Dancy, serving as the council's secretary, hustled to outmaneuver White. Dancy rammed through a tepid resolution requesting that Democrats not pass any laws that might "blunt our aspirations, ruin our manhood, and lessen our usefulness as citizens."

Even that watered-down resolution was rebuffed. On February 21, 1899, just seven weeks after the legislature convened, it approved the suffrage amendment and the grandfather clause by overwhelming margins: 42 to 6 in the state senate and 81 to 27 in the house.

Louisiana's grandfather clause had been passed by the state legislature as an amendment to the state constitution, but Charles Aycock wanted the North Carolina amendment approved by a popular vote. Confident that Democrats could once again rely on intimidation and fraud to restrict black voting, he argued that the amendment would carry greater weight nationally if passed by the state's white citizens and not just its politicians. The legislature approved the amendment as a referendum to be put to a statewide vote in an August 1900 election that would also select a governor. The voting was moved up from the customary November date to give the federal government less time to intervene.

Daniels and Simmons launched a campaign to build public support. The entire amendment hinged on support for the grandfather clause. Without the clause, the amendment would disenfranchise too many white voters. The two men decided that Daniels would take an extended trip through Louisiana "to make a calm study of this question," as Daniels put it. But it was no study. It was a propaganda campaign to convince North Carolina's white voters that the white men of Louisiana had devised an unassailable tool to disenfranchise many blacks without punishing poor, illiterate whites.

Daniels, always alert for opportunities to pursue political gain under the guise of journalism, would publish reports on his journey in the *News and Observer*. He did not want to pay his own expenses, so Simmons arranged for the state Democratic Party to cover the cost of the trip. That eliminated any pretense that Daniels was on an objective newspaper pursuit. But he had not bought a purely journalistic enterprise when he purchased the *News and Observer*. He had bought a political weapon.

Daniels began his mission in the spring of 1900 with the drive and curiosity of a journalist and the cool calculation of a politician. In Louisiana, he met with white farmers and reporters and county sheriffs. His reputation as an unyielding white supremacist had preceded him, and the state's leading politicians lined up to greet him. Daniels stayed in private homes and was served sumptuous meals. He described his trip as "one of the most pleasantest of my life."

Without telling his readers that the trip had been paid for by the Democratic Party, Daniels filed dispatches from New Orleans, Baton Rouge, and Thibodaux. Few readers were surprised when he reported that his "investigation" had found widespread support among Louisiana's white voters for the amendment and the grandfather clause.

Daniels reported that Louisiana had found a way to protect "uneducated voters . . . of old American stock." He interviewed Judge E. B. Kruttschnitt, a bombastic white supremacist who had helped draft Louisiana's amendment. The judge said of the law: "It does not deprive anyone of the right to vote on account of race, color, or previous conditions of servitude but it catches the ignorant Negro just the same."

The Louisiana law had been in effect for several months—long enough for Daniels to judge how thoroughly it disenfranchised blacks not just on paper but also in practice. He traveled to New Orleans, where he interviewed the parish registrar. He was delighted when the registrar opened his books to reveal that in the most recent city election the new law had helped reduce the number of black voters from 14,117 to 1,493.

Buried deep in Daniels's story the next day was a curious aside related by the registrar. He mentioned that seven mulattoes had been permitted to vote after signing affidavits attesting that their white fathers or grandfathers had voted prior to 1867. "No questions were asked," the registrar told Daniels. The exceptions had potential consequences for North Carolina, where many blacks with white ancestors might be able to prove that their fathers or grandfathers had voted three decades earlier. Daniels did not address the issue.

The next day, Daniels's article celebrated the salutary effects of the grandfather clause in New Orleans. The story was headlined: IT HAS ELIMINATED THE NEGRO——BUT THE AMENDMENT IN LOUISIANA GUARANTEES TO EVERY WHITE MAN THE RIGHT TO VOTE.

In his next dispatch a day later, Daniels reported that the amendment had not permitted *every* illiterate white man in Louisiana to vote. A group of immigrants, many of them Italian, had been stricken from the polls by the new law. Previously, immigrants had been permitted to vote if they promised to pursue citizenship. Now, only citizens could vote. Daniels amended his previous article to specify that no *native-born* white man in Louisiana had been denied the vote. The headline above his article injected a note of nativism into North Carolina's white supremacy campaign of 1900: IT IS AN AMERICAN WHITE ROLL.

For his next installment, Daniels traveled to the sugar-industry town of Thibodaux to speak to "the Acadians," known in Louisiana as Cajuns. He reasoned that because Cajuns had high illiteracy rates, their voting experience would provide the ultimate test of the grandfather clause. Daniels interviewed four white men—a judge, a lawyer, a sheriff, and a former US congressman. Each man assured Daniels that the grandfather clause had been a boon to illiterate Cajuns by exempting them from literacy tests because their fathers or grandfathers had voted prior to 1867.

Daniels was told that the amendment had improved race relations by sharply reducing black votes, which whites considered divisive. In one parish that contained twenty-five hundred black men of voting age, not one had dared register to vote in the most recent election, he reported. In a neighboring parish, where blacks had held a five-hundred-vote advantage prior to the amendment, only forty blacks had registered to vote. "The election was perfectly fair," a white judge assured Daniels.

The next day, a front-page headline above Daniels's story read: CRE-OLES LIKE THE AMENDMENT. A subhead added: IT WORKS TO PERFECT SATISFACTION OF THE EDUCATED AND UNEDUCATED WHITES IN THE SUGAR DISTRICT.

To test how ruthlessly the grandfather clause had robbed blacks of the vote in rural areas with large black populations, Daniels traveled to St. Joseph, a black farming town. He sketched the history of the surrounding parishes, set in what he described as Louisiana's black belt. During Reconstruction, he reported, whites in the area had suf-fered the same indignities of Negro rule endured by whites in North Carolina in the 1890s:

> Government was just as bad as could be. There were negro sheriffs, negro clerks, a negro State Senator—negroes were in complete control of everything until it grew intolerable. It was only by an almost superhuman effort in 1876 that the white people were able to wrest control of the government from the blacks . . . they had a revolution not unlike that in Wilmington . . . They took their ballots and their guns and they drove out the negro politicians and carpet baggers just as the people of Wilmington did in 1898.

C. C. Cordill, a state senator, told Daniels that prior to the amend-ment, 3,000 blacks and 380 whites had registered to vote in his local parish. In the most recent election after the amendment, registered white voters had outnumbered blacks 369 to 14. "The negro being eliminated," Cordill said, "the election was perfectly fair."

It certainly seemed so to Daniels. His dispatch the next day reported that eliminating the black vote had eliminated fraud. Only black voters committed fraud, he argued. And with no prospect of black voters or black officials, he wrote, white men were assured of free and fair elec-tions. And with blacks removed from both the polls and public office, there was no need for white men to resort to violence.

What the amendment has done for this black belt of Louisiana, it will do for the black belt of North Carolina, and make unnecessary the strenuous struggle which the white men had to adopt in 1898 to secure their counties from negro domination.

In his final dispatch from Louisiana, Daniels summarized the achievements of the grandfather clause:

1. *Eliminating the Negro.*
2. *Guaranteeing the right to vote to every white man, whether educated or not.*
3. *Purifying politics.*

The grandfather clause "works like a charm" in Louisiana, he told his readers. "Why should not North Carolina 'go and do likewise'?"

CHAPTER THIRTY-SEVEN

Leave It to the Whites

A S DEMOCRATS AWAITED the August 1900 vote on the amendment, another election had played out in Wilmington more than a year earlier. This one was preordained. By overthrowing the city government and crushing black aspirations in November 1898, the state's white supremacists had guaranteed a sanctioned electoral municipal victory in Wilmington in March 1899 that validated their coup four months earlier. Once again, they threatened and intimidated black voters—this time with even greater success. Only twenty-one of Wilmington's black citizens registered to vote, and only five turned up at the polls.

No Republican or Populist dared run against the aldermen appointed by the coup leaders. Running unopposed, the white supremacist aldermen who had been "elected" in November were "reelected" to two-year terms by the city's white voters. Among those candidates were two of the men who had directed the mobs on November 10, Hugh MacRae and J. Allan Taylor.

Mayor Waddell was challenged by two white supremacist Democrats, John J. Fowler and Frank Stedman, in the race for mayor. Fowler was a former Wilmington mayor who, while serving as a magistrate, had declined to protect Police Chief Melton from the mob on November

10. Stedman was a member of the Committee of Twenty-Five who nonetheless had helped the young black lawyer Armond Scott get safely out of Wilmington. Stedman had also rescued Deputy Sheriff French, a fellow Mason, from the lynch mob on November 10. But neither Fowler nor Stedman possessed Waddell's white supremacist pedigree, burnished by his central role in the November coup. And neither was a match for him as a public speaker. Waddell cruised to victory for a full term as mayor with an annual salary approaching $2,000, nearly double the $1,000 paid to his predecessor, the exiled Mayor Wright.

Waddell continued to deliver speeches throughout 1899, reveling in his notoriety. He dared federal authorities to interfere in North Carolina's white supremacist citadel along the Cape Fear. If the suffrage amendment passed, Waddell assured white voters, "there aren't enough soldiers in the US Army to make whites give up the vote."

Waddell's new city government erased lingering vestiges of the black experience in Wilmington. His aldermen took aim at the annual African holiday, Jonkonnu, in which blacks paraded during the Christmas holidays, wearing costumes and masks as they sang, banged drums, and knocked on doors seeking candy and coins. Six weeks after the November 10 killings, the aldermen had passed a law prohibiting the wearing of costumes or masks, with a hefty fine of $10. Jonkonnu ended. Whites soon appropriated the holiday. Young white boys began mocking blacks by dressing in wild costumes and darting through the streets, begging for coins.

The annual Emancipation Day celebrations also ended abruptly. They had been a widely attended New Year's Day spectacle for the previous three decades, with parades, music, and speeches celebrating black freedom and achievement. But there was no parade on New Year's Day in 1899. Blacks marked the day quietly indoors, in their homes and churches.

* * *

In Raleigh, the new Democratic state legislature of 1899 moved quickly to codify segregationist customs into law. Like other Southern states, North Carolina had practiced an ingrained, if generally unlegislated, system of segregation for decades. White supremacists who had been advocating legally mandated segregation since the early 1890s had been blocked by Fusionist control of the legislature. In Wilmington, blacks in the 1880s had defied custom by mixing with whites in public places. In 1885, a visiting black journalist from Boston, T. McCants Stewart, was surprised when he was able to eat beside whites in restaurants in Wilmington.

But in 1899, the Democratic legislature passed the state's first formal Jim Crow law, requiring segregated train compartments. Railroad companies complained that the law would require them to build separate cars for each race. They also pointed out that whites would lose the services of their black servants while riding on trains. The bill was amended to allow the use of partitions within train cars and to permit black servants to sit with their employers in white sections.

Democrats also proposed a bill to punish "fornication and adultery between the negros and whites," punishable by a prison sentence of up to five years. The proposal was mocked mercilessly by Republicans. A white legislator from western North Carolina pointed out a fatal flaw: if the law passed, he said, almost every man in the state house would have to plead guilty. A white Republican judge joked that "nine times out of ten, if you will chase down the fellows who are trying to stir up race prejudice, you will find that the most vigorous one is sleeping with a negro woman." In Washington, Congressman George White invited members of the US House to accompany him to North Carolina to see for themselves the state's preponderance of mulattoes—evidence, White said, of the widespread crime of sex between the races. The bill died without a vote.

The train car segregation law was just the beginning of a deluge of Jim Crow laws in North Carolina. Over the next few years, new legislation would mandate separate black and white facilities from the cradle to the grave—from hospitals to schools to cemeteries. Jim Crow laws soon required segregated toilets, water fountains, cinemas, swimming pools, and public parks—among them whites-only Hugh MacRae Park in Wilmington. Black cadavers could be sent only to black medical schools. White and black children used different textbooks.

In June 1899, Wilmington's new city government rushed to implement the Jim Crow train law locally. Trains were fitted with partitions that divided coaches by race. The board argued that the law was not discriminatory, because black passengers would be given a choice of segregated first- or second-class seating.

Several more Jim Crow laws followed. One required whites to sit in the front of streetcars and blacks in the rear. Exceptions were made for black nurses or attendants caring for white children or the infirm. (The first passenger charged under the new law was a white man who insisted on sitting in his favorite seat at the back of a car.) Another Jim Crow law mandated that black and white witnesses swear oaths on separate Bibles in city courtrooms. A white judge had complained that "both races have kissed the same Bible."

North Carolina's Republican US senator Jeter Pritchard twice offered resolutions demanding that the Senate declare the grandfather clause a violation of the Fourteenth and Fifteenth Amendments. Both attempts failed. Governor Russell advised Republicans not to worry about the suffrage amendment; he predicted that the courts would declare it unconstitutional. Russell went to Washington to try to persuade the McKinley administration to mount political and legal challenges to the suffrage amendment, but he was rebuffed. Dejected, he returned to Raleigh and decided not to run for reelection in the August 1900 voting.

On his way out of office, Russell suggested that the state's black citizens accept the inevitable. "My advice to the colored people is to let the amendment thing alone," he told black Republicans. "They are helpless. Let them leave it to the whites."

Charles Aycock, campaigning for Russell's job, ridiculed the jowly governor. Aycock was the opposite of the phlegmatic Russell. He was slender and vigorous, with a prominent chin, a receding hairline, and a commanding stage presence. He had been a popular public speaker at the University of North Carolina, graduating with honors in essay writing and oratory. During the white supremacy campaign of 1898, Aycock had rivaled Waddell in his ability to rouse white supremacists to violence.

On the campaign trail in 1900, Aycock's supporters rolled out an intimidating symbol of white violence: one of the rapid-fire guns from the Wilmington riot. Aycock was often greeted by Red Shirt brigades and young women who wore white dresses to symbolize purity. In the eastern North Carolina town of Laurinburg one oppressively hot day in July 1900, several hundred sunburned Red Shirts welcomed Aycock's train. The Red Shirt commander wore a white hat, white trousers, and a brilliant red blouse as he rode a cantering horse at the head of a column of mounted men. Aycock stepped out of the train and was swept from the platform by several Red Shirts, who carried him off on their shoulders.

On the day Aycock accepted the Democratic nomination for governor in April 1900, he delivered a memorable tribute to white supremacy at the Academy of Music in downtown Raleigh. Two thousand white Democrats howled and cheered for several minutes after the nomination was announced. A band played "Dixie" as men tossed hats and handkerchiefs into the air.

"When we say the negro is unfit to rule we carry it one step further and convey the idea that he is unfit to vote," Aycock told the crowd. "To do this we must disenfranchise the negro."

Republicans could be as ignorant as blacks, Aycock went on, to more shouts and foot stomping. "We have taught them much in the past two years in the University of White Supremacy," he said. "We will graduate them in August next with a diploma that will entitle them to form a genuine white man's party. Then we shall have no more revolutions in Wilmington."

Aycock understood that white voters appreciated simple concepts and straight talk. He framed the suffrage amendment as the inevitable—and perfectly legal—outgrowth of the terror and fraud of the white supremacy campaign two years earlier.

"There are three ways in which we may rule—by force, by fraud or by law," he said in a one speech. "We have ruled by force, we can rule by fraud, but we want to rule by law."

To reassure white voters, Democrats published an amendment catechism, a question-and-answer propaganda sheet that described the goals of the amendment with brutal honesty.

> Question: Will the Amendment, if adopted, disfranchise the Negro?
> Answer: The chief object of the Amendment is to eliminate the ignorant and irresponsible Negro vote.
> Question: Will the Amendment disfranchise the uneducated white man?
> Answer: Why certainly not. The object of the Grandfather Clause is to protect forever the entire body of the uneducated white vote of the state in their right to vote.

On the hot, suffocating evening of Election Day, August 2, 1900, several hundred men and women gathered on the sidewalk along Princess Street in downtown Wilmington. As the night wore on, the crowd swelled. By 11:00 p.m., people were forced to spill into the street to avoid being trampled. They jostled and craned their necks to get a clear view of images flickering on a canvas sheet hung outside the newsroom of the *Wilmington Messenger*.

The images were projected by a marvelous device called a stereopticon, popularly known as a magic lantern. Viewers typically paid 10 cents for the privilege of watching the machine's twin lenses project images from a glass plate. On this evening, a newspaper clerk slid the day's suffrage amendment voting returns under the plate, and the lenses projected them onto the sheet screen. With each burst of light upon the canvas, a cheer of delight rose up from the onlookers—for the beauty of the magic lantern and for what the results revealed.

The suffrage amendment had easily passed into law statewide, 182,852 to 128,285, or nearly 60 percent to 40 percent, if the reports of Democratic poll officers were to be believed. Of North Carolina's ninety-seven counties, sixty-six were reported as voting in favor of the new law. In the Black Belt, every single county reported decisive vote totals for the amendment. It somehow passed even in Black Belt counties with black majorities of up to 68 percent.

It seemed that North Carolina's blacks had voted to disenfranchise themselves. In fact, they had barely voted. Many who tried were beaten, threatened, or intimidated, just as they had been in 1898. Others were turned away by Democratic registrars on various pretexts. In Snakebite, a township in the Black Belt's Bertie County, several black men who had tried to register were rejected because they could not cite the day and month of their birth. In another Black Belt county, a black man was told he could not register until he produced two witnesses who could prove that he had been born in the county.

In many counties, black ballots were thrown away by Democratic registrars and replaced by phony Democratic ballots. Some registrars used ballot boxes with false bottoms to discard black votes that had been cast. In the Black Belt town of Scotland Neck, registered Republicans outnumbered Democrats nearly two to one, but ballot stuffing produced a stunning eleven-to-one margin for the amendment, with 831 "yes" ballots reported in a city where only 539 residents had registered to vote.

After black men won the right to vote in the state in 1868, nearly eighty thousand registered. By 1900, the two white supremacy campaigns had whittled that number to just fifteen thousand. Perhaps half of them were able to vote. For the first time since just after the Civil

War, no black man was elected to either the state house or the state senate in the 1900 election. Not a single black man was elected to a local office in the Black Second.

In Wilmington, the pro-amendment margin reported by Democratic officials strained credulity. In a city where the number of males of voting age was evenly divided between whites and blacks, at about 3,100 each, there were a remarkable 2,967 "yes" votes. Officials reported that just two people had voted against it. The *Messenger* claimed that only five black men voted, all five to disenfranchise themselves.

In addition to deciding the suffrage amendment, voters also selected their new governor. Charles Aycock won easily, defeating the Republican candidate by 60 percent to 40 percent. Aycock probably did not need fraud to win, but widespread fraud took place nonetheless. Polling stations run by Democrats reported margins of 91 and 88 percent for Aycock in two Black Belt counties with black majorities of 60 percent or more. In Halifax County, the recorded vote count exceeded the total population of voting-age men by nearly 250 votes. In three other Black Belt counties, the recorded vote for Aycock exceeded the total number of white men of voting age by several hundred.

In Wilmington, Democratic officials reported that Aycock had won New Hanover County by a preposterous 2,960-to-3 margin. Just four years earlier, Republican Daniel Russell had easily carried the county by a 3,145-to-2,218 margin over his Democratic opponent.

The following January, the Democratic legislature elected Furnifold Simmons to the US Senate with a vote of 124 to 26. (State legislatures elected US senators until the 1913 passage of the Seventeenth Amendment, which provided for a direct popular vote.) Simmons routed the state's leading Populist, Marion Butler, who failed to persuade the legislature that Simmons had committed widespread voter fraud. "The stench is awful," Butler said of Democratic race-baiting.

The white supremacy campaign launched long, fruitful political careers for Simmons, Aycock, and Daniels. Simmons served thirty years in the US Senate, building and nurturing the Simmons machine, a relentlessly efficient system of patronage and bare-knuckle politics. Aycock was nicknamed North Carolina's "Education Governor" for his campaign to build separate and decidedly unequal school systems. Josephus Daniels became a national political figure. He was appointed secretary of the navy in 1913 by Woodrow Wilson, a segregationist who had lived for eight years in Wilmington as a young man. In 1933, President Franklin D. Roosevelt appointed Daniels ambassador to Mexico.

For many white Southerners, the 1900 election results were a validation of white privilege—"a glorious triumph for white supremacy," the *Messenger* proclaimed. Democrats had seized control of North Carolina's largest city, its capital, its legislature, its governor's mansion, and one of its US Senate seats. White supremacists had eliminated most blacks from the voting booth and from public office. They had hardened segregation into law. And with the help of Daniels and his influential newspaper, they continued to promote white rule through the pages of the state's most persistent voice of white supremacy.

The killings in Wilmington inspired whites across the South. The white supremacy campaign demonstrated that determined whites could whittle down the black vote and black officeholders, first through terror and violence and then by legislation. Wilmington's whites had proved that the federal government would reproach them but not stop them. Inspired by the sweeping success of North Carolina's grandfather clause, other Southern states adopted variations of the law—Alabama in 1901, Virginia in 1902, Georgia in 1908, and Oklahoma in 1910.

Even Charles Aycock was awed. "It's a glorious victory that we have won," he said. "And the very extent of it frightens me."

CHAPTER THIRTY-EIGHT

I Cannot Live in North Carolina
and Be Treated Like a Man

T HEY NEVER WENT BACK. Not Tom Miller or Armond Scott or William Henderson or Alex Manly. Not the white mayor, Silas Wright; or the white police chief, John Melton; or the white deputy sheriff, Gizzard French. Wilmington was dead to them.

Tom Miller wanted to return home, but he knew his life in Wilmington was over. He had fled to Norfolk after his banishment. He almost certainly had been the wealthiest black man in Wilmington and one of the richest men of either race. He had grown accustomed to respect and deference in Wilmington, even from whites. But Miller had been arrested like a criminal and tossed aboard a train, stripped of everything—his home, his saloon and restaurant, his pawnbroker shop, his real estate properties, his manhood. Miller endured a miserable exile in Norfolk, depressed and in poor health.

In 1902, Miller wrote to Colonel John D. Taylor, clerk of the superior court in Wilmington, pleading for help with a stalled real estate transaction.

I have been treated not like [a] human but worse than a dog and someday the Lord will punish them that punished me without a Cause. I am Well and doing Well the

only thing that worries me is just to think that I were not allowed to come to my
Mothers funeral she being 95 years of age and the oldest Citizen on Wrightsville
sound [outside Wilmington] just to think of it will last me to my grave if I were
guilty of any Crime or was a Criminal it would not worri me in the least but oh
my god just to think it is enough to run a sane man insane.

Col I hope you will pardon me for the way I write you but when I think about
it all knowing I am not Guilty it almost drives me mad—just to think how my
own people could treat me as they have with out a Cause knowingly. Oh my god.

A year later, Tom Miller was dead at fifty-two, felled by a stroke.
His family was permitted to bring his body back home to Wilmington.
He was buried in the black cemetery of Pine Forest where, five years
earlier, black families had sought shelter from marauding Red Shirts.

After fleeing Wilmington at age twenty-five, Armond Scott escaped to
Washington, DC. But he struggled to find enough clients for his law
practice there and soon gave up law and left the capital. He borrowed
$5 from a friend and moved into the home of the friend's mother in
Germantown, Pennsylvania, outside Philadelphia. He found a job as
a butler, earning $5 a week. "I was desperate and I needed to eat," he
recalled years later.

Scott hated the dreary, servile life of a butler, and soon he decided
to try his luck elsewhere. He moved to New York City, where he took
a job as a janitor in an apartment building on Morningside Drive. For
$5 a week, he emptied trash and ran the elevator. He slept in a packing
room. Later, he left the city and took a position as a bellman at the
Grand Hotel in Saratoga, New York. One day Scott delivered a pitcher
of ice water to a hotel guest—a justice of the North Carolina supreme
court. The judge recognized Scott, whom he had appointed to the
state bar in 1898. He reprimanded the younger man for abandoning
his law career. "Is this what you're doing after we gave you a license to
practice law?" he asked.

Stung by the upbraiding, Scott decided to move back to Washington, DC, to again try to make a living as a lawyer. He slowly built a successful practice, then married and bought a home. In 1935, President Franklin D. Roosevelt appointed Scott a judge in the District of Columbia court system—Roosevelt's first black judicial appointment. Scott served as a judge for two decades, expressing sympathy for poor or alcoholic defendants and handing down harsh sentences to convicted bootleggers. He built a reputation as a theatrical courtroom figure who delivered homilies from the bench. When he died in 1960 at age eighty-seven, an obituary described Scott as "colorful, often fiery."

John C. Dancy, who was permitted to return to Wilmington and resume his duties as federal customs collector, often teased Scott about his post-Wilmington success, telling him: "Wilmington did you a favor by running you out of town; they ran you right into a judgeship." Scott, too, seemed to recognize that his banishment, though devastating at the time, had delivered him from a small Southern city ruled by white supremacists and on to success in the North. "Had it not been for the riot," he once said, "I might have remained a corn-field lawyer."

William Henderson also recovered from the loss of his home and law practice in Wilmington. After he was put aboard a northbound train the week of the riot, he and his wife and children sought shelter with relatives in Brazil, Indiana. The family later moved to Indianapolis, where Henderson established a flourishing law practice and became active in civic affairs. Many of his clients were freedmen. Henderson defended them vigorously, "his gray head wagging emphatically before the jury, his finger driving home his facts as his voice boomed all over the courthouse," a local newspaper reported. He waged losing battles against lynching, voter disfranchisement, and segregation. Indianapolis established segregated public high schools despite Henderson's vigorous protests. He remained a defiant activist the rest of his life. A newspaper obituary described him as a resolute man "long recognized as an able barrister, convincing talker and for the bull-dog tendency with which he was known to cling to his convictions."

The white riot in his hometown left Henderson embittered until the day he died in 1932. He never forgave his white neighbors. In December 1898, after a Northern newspaper called Wilmington's blacks "cowards who lacked a leader," Henderson reminded a black church congregation in Indianapolis that blacks from Wilmington had served during the Spanish-American War "while their parents at home were being murdered."

In his unpublished memoir, Henderson described the betrayal by and cruelty of whites in Wilmington. He singled out John D. Bellamy, the Wilmington white supremacist elected to Congress in 1898 through terror and fraud. Bellamy, Henderson wrote, "walks cheerfully to his seat over broken homes, broken hearts, disappointed lives, dead husbands and fathers, the trampled rights of freedmen and not one word of condemnation is heard."

The passage of the suffrage amendment in 1900 soon ended the political career of US representative George White, the only black man in Congress. If the black vote in the Black Belt could be suppressed even before the amendment went into effect, then White could hardly expect to muster enough black votes to be reelected to Congress.

Not only had White fought the suffrage amendment and lost, but he also failed in his long struggle to outlaw lynching. In January 1900, with support from Attorney General Griggs, he had introduced a bill to make lynching a treasonable offense punishable by death. Like Alex Manly, White declared that white men committed more sexual assaults against black women than black men committed against white women. In fact, White told Congress, only 15 percent of lynchings involved a black man who had attacked a white woman. The clear implication was that most lynchings punished consensual sex between black men and white women.

White's argument was too much for Josephus Daniels. The editor had always despised White, primarily because he was black but also because he was intelligent and effective. The *News and Observer* described White's "unworthy mind" and his "coarse and low utterances." Daniels's newspaper also falsely claimed in November 1898 that White's wife, Cora Lena, had ordered rifles through the mail and that his daughter Della had instructed black women to stop working for white families.

"It is bad enough that North Carolina would have the only nigger Congressman," a *News and Observer* editorial complained after White's antilynching speech. "Thus does Manleyism of 1898 show its head in 1900. Manley [that was how the paper spelled Manly's name] slandered white women in a scurrilous negro newspaper having a local circulation; White justifies assaults by negroes on white women by slandering white men in a speech in the Congress of the United States."

Several days later, White responded on the House floor. He asked that the editorial be read aloud and reprinted in the public record to provide wide circulation for "that vile, slanderous publication." To a round of applause, he said he regretted that men like Josephus Daniels were now ascendant in his home state.

White also told Congress that he agreed with Daniels that any man who assaulted any woman should be hanged, "whether he be a white brute or a black brute." He went on: "I think such a man ought to be hung—hung by the neck until dead. But it ought to be done by the courts, not by an infuriated mob such as the writer of that article would incite."

White's performance did little to advance the prospects of his antilynching bill. It was buried in the House Judiciary Committee, where it languished and died. Yet Daniels continued to taunt White, publishing a cartoon in May that depicted the congressman as a black-faced elephant with a long tongue slurping from a jug labeled "Term in Congress Worth $5,000 a Year." The drawing was headlined: HE DOESN'T LIKE TO LET GO. The caption read: "But most people think our only negro congressman has had it about long enough."

Three weeks after the suffrage amendment was approved in August 1900, White gave a long, rueful interview to a *New York Times* reporter. He announced what everyone already suspected: he would not run for reelection. He was also leaving North Carolina for good, he said, and he advised other blacks to do the same. "May God damn North Carolina, the state of my birth," he said.

White told the reporter that the blatant racism in the state and the newspaper attacks on his character had ruined the health of his wife, Cora Lena.

"I am certain the excitement of another campaign would kill her," White said. "My wife is a refined and educated woman, and she has suffered terribly because of the attacks on me." He predicted that fifty thousand blacks would follow him out of North Carolina over the next decade because of the suffrage amendment and "the general degradation of the Negro" in the state.

The *Times* story, headlined: SOUTHERN NEGRO'S PLAINT, described White as "the only colored man now in Congress . . . a stalwart, good-looking man, and a good speaker." White told the *Times* that he feared he would be the last black man in Congress for a very long time. And given the violence and racism in his home state, he said, "I cannot live in North Carolina and be treated as a man."

Whites rejoiced at the news. On March 4, 1901, as the clock struck noon inside the Greek Revival capitol building in Raleigh—the precise moment when Representative White's term formally ended—Alston Watts, a Democrat, celebrated along with other white legislators.

"George H. White, the insolent negro . . . has retired from office forever," Watts announced to cheers. "And from this hour on no negro will again disgrace the old State in the council of chambers of the nation. For these mercies, thank God."

Before George White left Congress, he hired Alex Manly as his private secretary in Washington. The editor was distraught and desperate for

323

work after months on the run. The new job helped stabilize his life. More than any other black man exiled from Wilmington, Manly had reason to fear for his safety. His editorial had made him a notorious public figure in the South, and his movements were constantly tracked by North Carolina newspapers. White men in Wilmington still threatened to murder Manly as revenge for his editorial.

Manly had left his brother-in-law's home in New Jersey to accept White's job offer in Washington, where he was reunited with his brother Frank. The two men lived together and briefly published the *Daily Record* in the capital beginning in March 1899, with Alex as editor and Frank as manager. The effort soon collapsed for lack of public support. Alex continued to work for White, who presided at his marriage to Carrie Sadgwar in the parlor of White's home on Eighteenth Street in Washington.

As White's tenure in Congress neared its end, Manly and Carrie moved to Philadelphia in search of work. The couple rented an apartment on the roof of a downtown building at Eleventh and Walnut Streets, where Manly took a part-time job as the building's janitor. He also sought work as a housepainter, his first profession. It was difficult for a black man to find semiskilled work with white employers, even in a Northern city like Philadelphia. But when Manly applied in person at a white-owned painting company, he was mistaken for a white man and hired on the spot. He said nothing to suggest otherwise—a startling departure from his lifelong refusal to pass as white.

Later, Manly tired of the pretense. He began to identify himself as a black man, saying, "I'd rather be a Negro and hold up my head rather than to be a sneak." He started a one-man business as a painting contractor. He and Carrie later moved to an Irish neighborhood in Philadelphia, where most people assumed that Alex was white and that Carrie was his maid. When neighbors realized that Carrie was Manly's wife, they erected a spiked fence across from the Manly home. It was taken down a short time later, after Carrie rushed next door to resuscitate a white woman who had been choking and gasping for air.

For the rest of his life, Manly devoted himself to assisting blacks who, like him, had left the South to seek new lives in the North. He formed a boys' club in his neighborhood, then began helping newly arriving black men find jobs in the city. He encountered a prominent Quaker, John Thompson Emlen, who was helping some of the same black men find work. Together, Manly and Emlen established the Stationary Engineers Association to teach black men industrial skills. To promote black employment, the two men also set up the Armstrong Association of Philadelphia. It was later absorbed by the National Urban League, which sent Manly and others on a nationwide campaign to raise money and help establish chapters in other Northern cities with black enclaves.

Until the day he died in 1944, Manly refused to speak to anyone— not his wife, his son, or his friends—about details of his time in Wilmington in 1898. His memories of his life in North Carolina were harsh and painful, and he wanted nothing more to do with the South. He never moved back to Wilmington, although he did return at least once, probably in disguise, to attend the funeral of his father-in-law, Frederick Sadgwar, in 1925.

In January 1899, two months after he fled Wilmington, Manly agreed to speak to a group of black men and women at a music hall in Providence, Rhode Island. The event had been organized by a black minister to discuss race relations and to explore ways to aid the "helpless colored people of the south." Perhaps Manly felt more comfortable addressing middle-class blacks rather than the white reporters who had cornered him for interviews. He seemed calm and reflective, and he allowed several details of his final days in Wilmington to slip out. He spoke in the matter-of-fact cadence of a journalist, but his voice simmered with anger and resentment.

"Intimidation, arson and murder are crimes that the good people of Wilmington, N.C., have been guilty of," he began. "The mayor and governor were in collusion with them . . . The white southern press then tried to stir up the citizens against the colored men. They drew cartoons, they published stories of crime, and they printed editorials that tried to make out that the colored men were beasts prowling the streets in search of white women.

"The democratic campaign began in September, and the whole basis for it was 'negro domination,'" Manly went on. "Indecent literature was scattered, and red shirt clubs were formed. Senator Tillman came into North Carolina and made a speech in which he said that he heard that they had a big black negro editor who had insulted the women of the south. He asserted that if I were in his state, I would be lynched before the ink was dry on my paper . . . Bullets, he said, were better than ballots in the case of negroes."

And then, for the only time in public, Manly provided an account of certain events up to and including November 10.

"On the evening of October 21st, after a speech by Colonel A. M. Waddell, a well known citizen, armed mobs patrolled the streets," he told the audience. "No stores would sell the colored men any powder . . . A friend came to me to tell me to leave, for they had decided to put a bullet through me."

He said that armed white men had been posted outside his home. His family persuaded him to flee—though he thought he would be gone only a few days. He planned to return the following week. He assumed "there would be no cause for any crimes." Whites would realize he had done nothing to warrant a lynching.

Manly described the decisive meeting of the city's leading white men on the night of November 9, the burning of his newspaper office the following morning, and the standoff at the Sprunt Cotton Compress.

"Gatling guns were placed to sweep the streets and a Colt's gun was placed . . . so that it was impossible for a negro to leave the compress without being shot down," he said. "Colored men and women ran in great numbers to the woods, carrying their bedding. There, mothers gave birth to children and both mothers and babies died.

"On the corner the mob met a number of colored men. The white men ordered the frightened black men to disperse and began firing upon them, killing three and wounding others. Caleb Halsey, a highly respected colored man, was driven out of his own house and into the yard and there shot down and his brains beaten out with a club before the terrified eyes of his wife and children."

Manly mentioned his editorial and the death threats he had received. "If any editorial brought enmity upon me," he said, "why should it have also caused the death of 25 innocent men?" He did not explain how he arrived at that number.

That was the most Manly would ever say in public about Wilmington. He wanted the matter buried. He had made that clear just six days after the killings, when the reporter for the *New York World* tracked him down at his brother-in-law's home in Asbury Park. Manly spoke to the correspondent despite objections from the friends accompanying him.

"The editor is guarded wherever he goes and is reluctant to express himself regarding the riots," the reporter wrote.

He pressed Manly nonetheless, but Manly stood firm. He seemed to carry a great burden of responsibility, as if all the blame cast upon him by whites in Wilmington had pierced his heart.

"Any utterances of mine [at] this time must necessar[il]y increase the race friction in Wilmington," he told the reporter. "And I do not care to be responsible for further violence or subject my friends or relatives to possible maltreatment or death."

Manly was far from home, weary, and on the run. He wanted to lose himself, to shed the cloak of the blasphemous editor Alex Manly, at least for a moment, and become a man without a history.

"I feel as though I would give worlds to lose my identity, and, like the chrysalis, expand into some other being and forget all the bitterness of the past," he said. He started to say more, but his friends pulled him away, afraid that he had said too much.

EPILOGUE

THE KILLINGS and coup in Wilmington inspired white supremacists across the South. No one had ever seen anything like it. Wilmington's whites had mounted a rare armed overthrow of a legally elected government. They had murdered black men with impunity. They had robbed black citizens of their right to vote and hold public office. They had forcibly removed elected officials from office, then banished them forever. They had driven hundreds of black citizens from their jobs and their homes. They had turned a black-majority city into a white citadel.

The white supremacy campaign had demonstrated to the nation that the federal government would reproach whites for attacking and killing black citizens, but it would not punish them or even condemn them. No one was ever charged, much less convicted, of a crime stemming from what whites called their "white revolution." Wilmington's leading white citizens had pioneered a formula that was soon duplicated across the South: deny black citizens the vote, first through terror and violence and then by legislation.

When white supremacists in Georgia conspired to suppress black voting rights in 1906, they consulted Wilmington's coup leaders for advice. M. Hoke Smith, a white supremacist elected governor after a race-baiting campaign, said of Georgia's blacks, "we can handle them as they did in Wilmington," where he said the woods were "black with their hanging carcasses."

North Carolina's suffrage amendment and grandfather clause were marvels of political opportunism. Four other Southern states quickly passed their own grandfather clauses between 1901 and 1910. The United States Supreme Court struck down those laws in 1915, ruling that a grandfather clause in Oklahoma violated the Fifteenth Amendment. But the systematic suppression of black voting rights had by then been set in stone in Wilmington and elsewhere in the South. White supremacists soon found creative new ways to snuff out the black vote.

After 1898, North Carolina's white supremacists suppressed the black vote through poll taxes, literacy texts, violence, intimidation, whites-only Democratic primaries, and voter-roll purges. The number of registered black voters in North Carolina quickly plummeted—from 126,000 in 1896 to 6,100 in 1902. The state's black citizens did not vote in significant numbers for at least six decades, until the rise of the civil rights movement in the 1950s and, ultimately, after passage of the Voting Rights Act of 1965.

For seven decades after 1898, black citizens were denied political or appointed office in Wilmington and elsewhere in North Carolina. George Henry White was the last black U.S. Representative from North Carolina for ninety-one years—until Eva Clayton was elected in 1992 in a district that contained parts of the old Black Second. In Wilmington, local offices were reserved for whites for three-quarters of a century. After black carpenter John Norwood was forced to resign as alderman in 1898, no black man served on the council until Kenneth McLaurin in 1972. Ten years later, Joseph McQueen Jr., a police detective, was elected New Hanover County's first black sheriff.

Almost overnight, the coup transformed Wilmington from an American mecca for blacks to a bastion of white supremacy virulently hostile to its black citizens. Before the 1898 coup, Wilmington was 56 percent black. That percentage dropped precipitously in the years after 1898.

The 1900 federal census listed Wilmington as 49 percent black. The rate continued to plunge—from 47 percent in 1910 to 40 percent in 1930, 35 percent in 1950, 33 percent in 1990, and just 18.3 percent by 2018.

After Daniel Russell left office in 1900, North Carolina did not elect a Republican governor for nearly three-quarters of a century—until 1972. By that time, the Republican Party's ethos had shifted completely: the civil rights movement of the 1950s and 1960s had driven Southern white conservatives from the Democratic Party into the segregationist states-rights wing of the Republican Party. In 1972, North Carolina elected its first Republican US senator in seventy-four years—Jesse Helms, an ardent segregationist who once mailed postcards to black residents warning that they could be prosecuted for fraud if they tried to vote.

Nearly four decades passed before the evolution of white conservatives from Democrats to Republicans was reflected in North Carolina's electorate. But by 2010, Republicans controlled both houses of the state legislature for the first time since 1898. In 2012, voters elected a Republican governor. From that power base, white legislators reprised a tactic perfected by their forebears in 1898: suppressing the black vote. They began searching for ways to restrict voting among groups that traditionally voted Democratic—especially African Americans, who had abandoned the Republican Party during the civil rights era. Republicans spent months unearthing obscure statistics on black voting patterns, searching for vulnerabilities. They inundated the state elections board with data requests. How many black voters lacked a driver's license? How many took advantage of early voting hours? How many voted during early voting on Sundays?

The legislators proposed a voter ID law that included a set of restrictions aimed at black voters. But they were thwarted by the Voting Rights Act, which targeted states like North Carolina with a history of racial discrimination in voting. The law required forty of North Carolina's one hundred counties to seek federal preclearance for any changes to voting procedures. But in 2013, the United States Supreme Court, in *Shelby County v. Holder*, gutted the law and eliminated the preclearance requirement.

Within hours of the *Shelby* decision, a Republican leader of the voter ID effort told reporters: "Now we can go with the full bill" for voter ID—because the "legal headache" of preclearance had been removed. The state's conservatives were now free to invoke the spirit of 1898 via a twenty-first-century voter suppression law nearly as effective as the suffrage amendment and grandfather clause 115 years earlier.

The so-called voter ID bill was passed into law in late 2013. It reduced early voting and Sunday "souls to the polls" voting, both used disproportionately by African Americans. It eliminated same-day registration and straight-ticket voting, two other provisions especially popular among African Americans. The new law also required a state-issued ID to vote. That requirement imposed a special burden on African Americans voters, many of whom lacked a driver's license, birth certificate, or other official documents required to obtain a state-issued ID.

In 1898, suppression of black voting rights went unchallenged. But more than a century later, the US Justice Department and civil rights groups sued to block voter ID. In July 2016, a three-judge federal appeals court struck down the law, ruling that its provisions "target African-Americans with almost surgical precision." The panel added: "Because of race, the legislature enacted one of the largest restrictions on the franchise in modern North Carolina history." The court pointed out that Republican politicians had crafted the law after collecting data showing that African Americans would be disproportionately burdened by its requirements. The judges emphasized "the inextricable link between race and politics in North Carolina."

Twenty-first-century white conservatives reprised another tactic of Wilmington's white supremacists: they said the voter ID law was designed to eliminate widespread voter fraud, the same accusation leveled against the state's black voters in the 1890s. But the 2016 federal court panel, noting that voter fraud was extremely rare, said voter ID restrictions "impose cures for problems that did not exist."

Two years later, the state's Republicans found a way around the court ruling. Rather than passing a revised voter ID law, they proposed a constitutional amendment to require citizens to show an ID to vote. The state's voters approved it by a margin of 56 to 44 percent. In December 2018, the Republican-dominated state legislature voted the amendment into law.

Meanwhile, white conservatives had adopted yet another tool of Wilmington's white supremacists: gerrymandering. In the 1890s, Wilmington's white leaders herded blacks into black-majority wards to dilute their voting power. In 2011, Republicans crammed black voters into two contorted, serpentine congressional districts with the aid of sophisticated computer models. At the same time, they created several safe Republican districts dominated by conservative white voters. The changes produced remarkable results. In 2012, Democratic congressional candidates won 51 percent of the vote in North Carolina. Yet Republicans won nine of thirteen congressional districts, erasing the previous 7-to-6 Democratic advantage.

In February 2016, a federal three-judge panel ruled that the two majority-black congressional districts had been racially gerrymandered in violation of the Fourteenth Amendment. The panel found that "race was the legislature's paramount concern."

In August 2016, a different three-judge panel ruled that dozens of North Carolina's gerrymandered state house and senate districts also were racial gerrymanders that violated the Fourteenth Amendment. The ruling said Republican legislators had created the districts "through the predominant and unjustified use of race."

In both cases, the state legislature was ordered to redraw the districts.

Victors indeed write history. From the moment the first black men fell dead at the corner of North Fourth and Harnett Streets on November

10, 1898, Wilmington's white leadership portrayed the day's events as a justified, spontaneous response to a black riot. The white supremacy campaign itself was depicted as a legitimate corrective to corrupt black politicians and the "black beast rapist." More than a century would pass before those narratives were successfully challenged—and only after a long and divisive debate in modern Wilmington over the true legacy of 1898.

In memoirs and letters, the coup leaders boasted of their roles in crushing black aspirations. Colonel Waddell wrote that the coup "set the pace for the whole south on the question of white supremacy." He described it as "the spontaneous and unanimous act of all the white people . . . in behalf of civilization and decency." In the weeks after the killings, Waddell received letters of congratulations from whites across the nation; a man from Baltimore praised him for cleansing whites of "the slough of black mud and degradation." Even James Sprunt, who had tried to protect black workers at his cotton compress, wrote that "the results of the Revolution of 1898 have indeed been a blessing to the community."

In 1936, Harry Hayden, a white supremacist writer who was a boy in Wilmington in 1898, solidified the white narrative in a pamphlet titled *The Story of the Wilmington Rebellion*. Hayden's account was based exclusively on interviews with the perpetrators of the coup. Writing in an elegiac tone, Hayden's narrator regrets that "the better elements" of the city's white aristocracy were obliged, reluctantly, to "remove the stupid and ignorant Negros" from elected office. "Black rapists prowled the city . . . attacking Southern girls and women, those pure and lovely creatures who graced the homes in Dixie Land," Hayden wrote. He sold the pamphlet for $1 a copy to a new generation of whites in the city, many of them born after 1898.

J. Allan Taylor, who helped lead white rioters in 1898, added a typewritten postscript to Hayden's account. Taylor described white rule in Wilmington as "an inherent and traditional right." Confronted in 1898 by "negro domination," he wrote, the city's white men "pledged our manhood, at whatever sacrifice necessary, to reestablish white supremacy on a firm and enduring basis." He boasted of stuffing ballot boxes and intimidating black voters. He scribbled a handwritten comment that read: "masterful duplicity."

The state's school textbooks, presided over by white supremacists, ensured that the enduring myths of 1898 were passed down to each new generation of white pupils. A 1933 textbook placed the blame for the killings on elected black officials: "There were many Negro office-holders in the eastern part of the state, some of whom were poorly fitted for their tasks. This naturally aroused ill feeling between the races." The textbook described Charles Aycock, whose speeches incited white supremacists at rallies in 1898 and 1900, as "one of the best friends that colored people had." One passage suggested that black citizens were deprived of the vote for their own good: "Though Aycock was in favor of an amendment to take the vote away from illiterate Negroes, he had no ill feeling toward their race."

A 1940 public school textbook blamed black citizens for the mis-fortunes that befell them: "The mass of negroes became poor citizens. To keep their vote, the Carpetbaggers and Scalawags allowed them to do very much as they pleased. The worst crimes were not punished. The white people of the South were no longer safe."

The 1940 textbook went on to describe how the Ku Klux Klan and, later, the Red Shirts, addressed the problem:

To put an end to this terrible condition white people all over the South joined together in a sort of club which they named the Ku Klux Klan. Members of the Ku Klux Klan, dressed as ghosts, scared lawless men into acting decently. On moonlit nights these men could be seen on horseback, riding to bring order back into the lives of their people . . . Such sights frightened the negroes into living better lives.

The names of those men, negro or white, who had done wrong were listed. The next moonlit night the Ku Klux Klan would visit these men and punish them according to the wrongs they had done. After this, lawless men were not so bold and crime became less and less.

In 1949, another North Carolina public school textbook glossed over white supremacist violence and portrayed black men as aggressors and whites as defenders of law and order in Wilmington. It ignored the killings and coup, describing instead an orderly change of government. "A number of blacks were jailed for 'starting a riot' and a new white administration took over Wilmington's government," one summary read.

In 1951, for the first time since 1898, a North Carolina historian challenged the white narrative. Helen Edmonds, a black scholar at North Carolina Central University in Durham, debunked the white myths of 1898 in a meticulously researched doctoral thesis, "The Negro and Fusion Politics, 1894–1901." Edmonds revealed that the purported spontaneous white response to a black riot was instead a carefully planned coup d'état that restored white supremacy. She demonstrated that the number of black officials in Wilmington and eastern North Carolina was far too small to constitute "Negro domination." She exposed race-baiting by white politicians and newspapers. "The *News and Observer* led in a campaign of prejudice, bitterness, vilification, misrepresentation and exaggeration to influence the emotions of whites against the Negro," she wrote.

Edmonds's thesis incensed the white guardians of Wilmington's 1898 legacy. Louis T. Moore, chairman of the New Hanover Historical Commission, wrote an aggrieved letter to the president of the University of North Carolina, which had published Edmonds's account.

"The assumption is that this Dr. Edmonds is a Negress," Moore informed the university. He described her account as "inflammatory, not in accord with real facts, distorted and sensational." What happened in Wilmington in 1898, Moore wrote, "was distinctly a REVOLUTION and not a race riot as she terms it."

Edmonds's revelations had no lasting effect on Wilmington's white mythology, which had hardened like shellac in the years after 1898. It would take more than the determined research of a lone historian to dismantle the carefully constructed narrative that had sustained white Wilmington for nearly a century.

✳   ✳   ✳

As the hundredth anniversary of the 1898 coup approached, the faculty and staff at the University of North Carolina, Wilmington, tried to bring black and white citizens together to discuss ways to commemorate the centennial. Organizers invited residents to express their views of 1898 at centennial events. Racial participation was carefully balanced. The white cochairs of the 1898 Centennial Foundation included Hugh MacRae II, the grandson of coup leader Hugh MacRae; and Katharine Taylor, the great-granddaughter of Colonel Walker Taylor. Among the black cochairs was Frankye Manly Jones, Alex Manly's niece.

The foundation trod carefully, coaxing whites and blacks into talking openly about the legacy of 1898. For many descendants of either race, it was an incendiary topic. More than a few whites said they bore no personal responsibility for their ancestors' actions. Some asked why the city was heightening racial tensions by dredging up ancient history. But many black residents resented white descendants who refused to acknowledge the lasting damage inflicted on Wilmington's black community. Some demanded reparations and a monument to the 1898 victims. Many whites dismissed reparations as a nonissue. One white man vowed to tear down any monument to the dead.

Wilmington's black weekly newspaper, the *Wilmington Journal*, protested the centennial effort. Founded in 1927 by Robert S. Jervay, a printer who was the son of a slave, the *Journal* succeeded the *Record* as the voice of the city's black community. First published as the *Cape Fear Journal*, the weekly is published today by Jervay's descendants from a white clapboard building on South Seventh Street, directly across from the spot where the *Record* was torched in 1898.

In an editorial in November 1998, the *Journal* announced that it would have nothing to do with the 1898 commemoration. "The first step on atonement cannot take place," the editorial said, "until an all out effort is made to determine all who were killed on that bloody night, all who fled the city, by force or by will because of fear, and all who lost their businesses and other property."

Even the very definition of what had happened in 1898 was disputed. For decades, it had been called a race riot. But by 1998 other terms were under consideration—revolution, rebellion, coup d'état, massacre. Centennial organizers sought a compromise. They cobbled together an artfully worded statement: "No one living in Wilmington today was a participant in the events of 1898." Consequently, "none of us bears personal responsibility for what happened," the statement said. Even so, the statement stressed that "all among us—no matter our race or history . . . all are responsible for 1898." Organizers also settled on a compromise term for the events of 1898: "Racial violence."

In early 1998, there was a breakthrough of sorts. George Rountree III, the grandson and namesake of a coup leader, George Rountree, agreed to attend a "Wilmington in Black and White" lecture at St. Stephen AME Church. Built in 1866 by ex-slaves, the church stood just five blocks from where the first shots were fired in 1898. It was pivotal moment. Rountree was the first direct descendant of a riot leader to agree to speak at a commemorative event. The lancing of a century-old wound had raised old grievances and challenged long-held myths, but the participation of a prominent white descendant like Rountree suggested one possible path to frank discussion, if not reconciliation.

Nearly every pew was filled at St. Stephen the night Rountree spoke. There was silence as he rose from his seat. He began by describing his lasting affection for a black nanny, then quickly absolved his grandfather, saying he was merely a product of his times. The disappointment was palpable among those in the audience who had expected a moment of racial healing. Inez Easom, a descendant of black residents targeted by white mobs in 1898, responded with a call for reparations. Rountree countered by suggesting that Wilmington's citizens address racial inequalities by donating to local charities. Then he emphasized that he, personally, bore no responsibility for the events of 1898.

In 2018, I spoke with Rountree inside his law office on Market Street in Wilmington. Like his grandfather, he was tall and imposing; he played varsity basketball at the University of Arizona. Rountree was eighty-five, a wealthy admiralty law attorney who had for years donated to charitable causes in the community. Among them were charities that benefited African Americans, he pointed out.

Rountree told me that he had attended the centennial lecture in search of racial healing but instead felt unfairly harangued to apologize for 1898. "What role did I have in creating the environment that produced the hostilities which generated this anvil in which all kinds of frustrations were forged?" he asked.

Rountree described his grandfather, who died when he was eight, as a powerful influence on his life—"a gruff, imperious, articulate, bright man," he said. He remembered the old man telling him of his own father, Robert Rountree, a slave owner, who returned from the Civil War to find his plantation sacked. That seemed to instill a sense of grievance in the family, nursed by George Rountree Sr. as he helped plot the 1898 coup. Rountree said his grandfather had simply returned control of the city to men of property with a vested stake in society.

"I am asked frequently: 'Don't you know all that occurred in 1898 was horribly wrong?'" Rountree told me. "My answer has always been, compared to today's notions of propriety and lawfulness, yes. On the other hand, if you want me to criticize my grandfather a hundred and twenty years later, I am not going to do that. If you want me to take a detached view of whether maltreatment of other people is wrong in any civilized society, I would of course concur."

Rountree said he believed the events of 1898 had inhibited the commercial growth of Wilmington because they decimated the black middle class and "entrenched the old-line [white] families, maybe twenty or twenty-five of them."

I asked whether Wilmington had been able to move past 1898.

"I think people under forty have basically moved on," Rountree said. "I think people my age, eighty-five, might think they have, but they haven't, not totally. I'm talking about whites *and* blacks. They haven't forgotten."

Ultimately, the centennial groups reached an uneasy accommodation with 1898. There were several poignant moments. Two nieces of Alex Manly held polite, if painful, discussions with descendants of whites who had carried out the killings and coup. In November 1998, inside Thalian Hall, where Colonel Waddell delivered his notorious "Cape Fear carcasses" speech, black and white musicians and actors performed a play based on the events of 1898. Afterward, the audience joined in a dramatic counterpoint to the "White Declaration of Independence," signed by white supremacists at Thalian Hall a century earlier. This time, more than a thousand people of both races lined up to sign a "People's Declaration of Racial Interdependence." The document asked the city's leaders to "declare openly their common commitment to the path of interracial dialogue, inclusion and reconciliation."

On November 10, 1998—one hundred years to the day since the coup—whites and blacks held another ceremony at Thalian Hall. The combined choirs of the predominately white First Presbyterian Church and black St. Luke's AME Church sang "Amazing Grace" and "Let There Be Peace on Earth." It was a richly symbolic moment—not just for its exquisite timing but also for the painful legacy of First Presbyterian Church. Its white minister a century earlier had celebrated the coup by proclaiming: "We have taken a city."

In 2000, North Carolina's legislature passed a bill, sponsored by two black legislators from Wilmington, to create a state commission to investigate the causes and impact of the 1898 coup. The commission spent the next five years trying to dig beneath the dominant white narrative and produce a historically accurate account.

Achieving a balanced account was challenging. The coup's leaders left a wealth of written accounts that justified and celebrated their own roles in the violence. But leaders of Wilmington's black community, under attack and fleeing for their lives, produced far fewer letters, journals, diaries, or memoirs. And while white newspapers published minute-by-minute narratives, the *Record* had shut down before the riot. Few of its back issues survived the torching of November 10. The commission's authors acknowledged the historical imbalance—and their reluctant dependence on white accounts.

"Although white leaders attempted to justify their actions in every word and deed after November 10, the truth of what happened lies within their clouded narratives," the commission wrote in its final 480-page report, published in 2006.

The report upended white myths a century old. It concluded that the coup was a "documented conspiracy" by Wilmington's white elite to overthrow a legitimately elected government "through violence and intimidation." White supremacists statewide were incited to violence by Josephus Daniels and his *News and Observer*, the report said. Federal and state authorities failed "at all levels" to respond to the violence or punish the perpetrators. The report concluded that the coup and killings led directly to strict residential segregation in Wilmington, decades of Jim Crow discrimination, and the disenfranchisement of the state's black citizens.

The report also challenged an enduring black myth—that whites seized the property of hundreds of black residents who fled after the coup. Based on a detailed study of deeds and tax records by researcher Sue Ann Cody, the commission found no evidence of widespread property seizures. Wilmington's whites sought to rob blacks of their civil rights, not their property.

The commission also upended the myth that blacks in Wilmington's city government in 1898 were corrupt, incompetent, and complicit in street crimes. It cited a 1997 study by the Research Branch of North

Carolina State Office of Archives and History, which found "no con-clusive evidence that the town's finances were in danger of default" in 1898. The study also concluded that the city government, rather than presiding over corruption, had produced a "meticulous and fair tax code." In addition, the study found no evidence of a significant increase in street crime and concluded that the judicial system tried and convicted both blacks and whites.

The commission estimated that twenty-one hundred black residents fled Wilmington during and after the violence. It documented twenty-one citizens banished by the coup's white leaders—fourteen blacks and seven whites. It identified, by name, thirteen black men killed during the riot and listed nine more dead men whose identities could not be confirmed. Noting that the bodies of many black victims were either quickly buried or never recovered, the commission estimated that the total number of blacks killed was at least sixty.

The report noted "the ability of white leadership in Wilmington to develop long-range plans for instigating violence, a strategy to quell that violence and their subsequent ability to call the affair a riot—implying a sudden break in peacefulness rather than reveal its true character, that of a planned insurrection."

On November 8, 2008—110 years after the stolen election of 1898—an 1898 Memorial Park was installed. The memorial stands just a block from where the first black men were shot dead at North Fourth and Harnett Streets. An inscription describes the white mob, the burning of the *Record*, and the restoration of white supremacy. Two short sentences engraved on the monument unraveled the city's white mythology:

Wilmington's 1898 racial violence was not accidental. It began a successful statewide Democratic campaign to regain control of state government, disenfranchise African-Americans, and create a system of legal segregation which persisted into the second half of the 20th century.

As Wilmington struggled to address the legacy of 1898, the *News & Observer* also confronted its central role in the riot and coup.

After the death of Josephus Daniels in 1948, the newspaper continued to be published by the Daniels family. It remained loyally Democratic editorially, even after Southern segregationist Democrats migrated to the Republican Party. The *News and Observer* generally supported the civil rights movement and school desegregation. By the 1970s, it had earned a national reputation for strong local and regional reporting that held state government and powerful business interests accountable. Editorially, the paper was solidly Democratic and hewed to mainstream liberal positions. It remains so today; the *News & Observer* editorial page repeatedly condemned efforts by the Republican-led legislature to suppress black votes through voter ID laws and to dilute black voting strength through gerrymandering schemes.

In 1995, the *News & Observer* was sold to the McClatchy newspaper chain, ending 101 years of Daniels family ownership. In 2006, the paper's new owners published a sixteen-page special edition titled "The Ghosts of 1898—Wilmington's Race Riot and the Rise of White Supremacy." The eleven-chapter series punctured the white supremacist narrative, describing the events of 1898 as a "carefully orchestrated campaign that spread white supremacy across North Carolina and the South."

In an accompanying editorial, the *News & Observer* apologized for its actions in 1898, referring to the murders and coup as "a milestone of shame." The paper outlined the pivotal role of the white press "in firing the hatreds that led white vigilantes to overthrow Wilmington's elected municipal government and wantonly to kill black residents. This newspaper was a leader in that propaganda effort under editor and publisher Josephus Daniels." (The *Charlotte Observer* issued a similar apology and published the same special edition, written by historian Timothy Tyson.)

The *News & Observer* editorial described how racial hatreds unleashed in 1898 helped contribute to the spread of lynching: "And cynical, ruthless politicians rose to authority by fanning white fear and loathing of blacks. This, sadly, was Josephus Daniels' stock in trade during those years in which he used The N&O to further the white supremacist cause and advance his party's fortunes."

The editorial referred to Daniels as "someone we continue to salute in a different context on this [editorial] page." That was a reference to the newspaper's motto, derived from Daniels's will and printed daily at the top of the editorial page: "If the paper should at anytime [*sic*] be the voice of self-interest or become the spokesman of privilege or selfishness it would be untrue to its history."

Josephus Daniels never apologized for his actions in 1898, even as he built a twentieth-century reputation as a progressive on such issues as labor, public education, women's suffrage, and open government. In a 1941 memoir, *Editor in Politics*, he expressed mild regret for manipulating news coverage. He wrote that the *News and Observer*, as the "militant voice of White Supremacy," was guilty of "sometimes going to extremes in its partisanship." He added, "We were never very careful about winnowing out the stories or running them down."

At times, Daniels acknowledged, the *News and Observer* unfairly savaged his political enemies. "The paper was cruel in its flagellations," he wrote. "In the perspective of time, I think it was too cruel." He conceded that the bias bled into news coverage. "The *News and Observer's* partisanship was open, fierce, and somewhat vindictive, and was carried in news stories as well as in editorials," he wrote.

While Daniels may have regretted some of his tactics, he made no apologies for what they achieved. Even with the benefit of forty-three years of reflection, he wrote glowingly of the white supremacy campaign in his memoir. He boasted that white supremacists had crushed "Negro domination." He glorified Red Shirt attacks on black neighborhoods and praised white gunmen for creating "a reign of terror" among blacks in Wilmington.

* * *

Frank A. Daniels Jr., Josephus Daniels's grandson, was the last member of the Daniels family to serve as publisher of the *News & Observer*. I spoke to Daniels at his office in Raleigh in 2018. Daniels, then eighty-six, had retired as publisher twenty-two years earlier, but he kept an office in a downtown building, decorated with newspaper mementos and photos of his grandfather.

Daniels told me that as publisher he had never considered an apology for the actions of his grandfather. "I didn't think it was necessary," he said. "No one ever talked about it. It never came up."

Like George Rountree III, Daniels described his grandfather as a man who both defined and reflected the ethos of his time. He said Josephus sincerely believed that blacks in the 1890s were not qualified to vote or hold public office. In his grandfather's view, Daniels said, only educated white men of property could create the conditions to properly educate blacks.

"It was primarily driven by the fact that blacks didn't have the education," Daniels said of his grandfather's role in 1898. "He always said, not directly, but he clearly implied, that the main thing was to get the right people in office."

Did Josephus ever express regret?

"He did," Daniels said. "But there is a difference between apologizing and regret. At the time he did it, it made good sense."

Daniels said that during his quarter century as publisher he made a point of hiring black employees. He mentioned the 1970s, when the newspaper had no black employees in the advertising department. Daniels said that under his instruction his classified advertising manager hired a black candidate with the next job opening.

Daniels also told me he was proud of the *News & Observer*'s modern role in advocating for civil rights, its support for the Democratic Party and progressive issues, and the Daniels family's charitable donations to civic causes. Whatever the paper stood for in his grandfather's era, he said, it stood for something completely different in modern times.

I asked Daniels for his thoughts on the state commission report, particularly its criticism of his grandfather's racial incitements and demagoguery. Did he agree with the report's conclusions?

"I never read it," he replied.

Another North Carolina institution, the University of North Carolina at Chapel Hill, also faced a reckoning. Nearly thirty buildings on the school's campus were named for white supremacists or supporters of white supremacy, among them Josephus Daniels, Charles Aycock, and William Saunders, the Ku Klux Klan leader in North Carolina in the nineteenth century.

After years of protests by student activists, Saunders Hall was renamed Carolina Hall in 2015. The school also altered the name of its football stadium, Kenan Memorial Stadium, which had honored William Rand Kenan Sr., who commanded a rapid-fire gun squad during the 1898 coup. In 2018, the stadium was renamed for Kenan's son, William Rand Kenan Jr., an industrialist who had donated the money to build the stadium.

Those changes did not quell decades of turmoil over a Confederate Civil War monument erected on campus in 1913 by the United Daughters of the Confederacy. Nicknamed Silent Sam, the statue of a young Confederate soldier honored UNC students who had fought and died in the Civil War. The 1913 dedication speech was delivered by Julian Shakespeare Carr, the wealthy businessman who had described the Wilmington coup as "a grand and glorious event" and had warned President McKinley not to punish the city's white supremacists. Carr had left the university to join the Confederate army. In his 1913 speech, he said the school's fallen soldiers had "saved the very life of the Anglo-Saxon race in the South" and preserved the "purest strain of the Anglo Saxon."

Carr also told of flogging a black woman near campus shortly after he returned from the war: "I horse-whipped a negro wench until her skirts hung in shreds, because upon the streets of this quiet village she had publicly insulted and maligned a Southern lady." He called it "a pleasing duty."

Campus protests over Silent Sam had erupted from time to time during and after the civil rights era. In 2017, after white nationalists staged a deadly rally in Charlottesville, activists in North Carolina began staging frequent, raucous rallies next to Silent Sam, demanding the statue's removal. They sometimes clashed with whites committed to commemorating the Confederate cause.

In April 2018, in a symbolic protest, an African American graduate student poured a mixture of red paint and her own blood on Silent Sam. Four months later, a group of about 250 protesters gathered to support the student, who faced criminal charges. Shortly after nightfall, several protesters strung a rope around the statue's head and neck, then dragged Silent Sam to the ground. People stomped on the bronze head and whacked it with clubs. The toppled statue was placed in storage while the university struggled to decide whether to erect it again, display it elsewhere, or remove it permanently from the campus.

In 2018, a North Carolina state historical marker was installed in Wilmington to commemorate the events of 1898. The marker stands near the corner of Market Street and Fourth Street, outside the Wilmington Light Infantry Armory, where the white mob gathered before torching the *Record* office.

It was only the second state historical marker to address the killings and coup. The other is a marker for Alex Manly, installed in 1998 during the 1898 centennial. The Manly marker stands four blocks from the old *Record* site. Its brief inscription does not mention that black citizens were shot dead or that the city's multiracial government was overthrown by white supremacists:

Alex Manly, 1866–1944. Edited black-owned Daily Record four blocks east. Mob burned his office Nov. 10, 1898, leading to "race riot" & restrictions on black voting in N.C.

In 2007, the Manly marker was ripped from its metal post and stolen. A replacement was soon installed. I visited the marker more than a decade later, in 2018. It was listing and partially obscured by overhanging tree limbs as traffic whizzed by on South Third Street, a busy four-lane artery.

A few blocks north, the 2018 installation of the second 1898 state marker addressed the shortcomings in the inscription on the Manly plaque. After considerable debate, agreement was reached on the new marker's text:

WILMINGTON COUP

Armed white mob met at armory here, Nov. 10, 1898. Marched six blocks and burned office of Daily Record, black-owned newspaper. Violence left untold numbers of African-Americans dead. Led to overthrow of city government & installation of coup leader as mayor. Was part of a statewide political campaign based on calls for white supremacy and the exploitation of racial prejudice.

Faye Chaplin never met her great-grandfather, Thomas C. Miller, Wilmington's wealthy black entrepreneur, who died before she was born. But the weight of Tom Miller's life—from his triumphs as a businessman to his humiliating eviction from his hometown—still bears down on Chaplin 120 years later. Scraps of Miller's existence live on inside her home—in the plaintive 1902 letter in which he says he was treated worse than a dog, and in a letter begging for permission to attend his mother's funeral in Wilmington.

When I spoke to Chaplin in 2018, she was sixty-five, a retired bank manager living in Raleigh, the state capital, where she was born and raised. She had never lived in Wilmington, but what happened there in

1898 is never far from her consciousness. She told me she felt cheated out of her great-grandfather's legacy.

"He was this great businessman and he had all this wealth, but where is it and what happened to it?" Chaplin told me. "Did they make him leave and just take everything from him? What happened? That's what I want to know."

Chaplin attended several centennial events in Wilmington in the late 1990s. She visited Miller's two-bedroom home, which still stands on North Sixth Street. The tidy yellow frame structure is part of a historic homes tour. But Chaplin's visits to Wilmington only compounded the pain and longing that the events of 1898 have instilled in her.

"The way they did things just because of the color of your skin," she said. "He came out of slavery and built things for himself. So he was a threat to them. He was a successful black man and they couldn't stand that. He was a black man who was doing well and who wouldn't close his mouth. He'd speak his mind and stand up for what was right. He wasn't afraid of them. And that's why they went after him."

Chaplin's grandmother—her mother's mother—was Lula Miller, Thomas Miller's daughter. She was almost certainly the young girl who ran after the gun wagon that hauled her father from his home to the city jail in 1898, begging the white gunmen to release him. That event is part of a straight line of sorrow that connects Thomas Miller to his great-granddaughter.

That same connection also leads to the letters inside Chaplin's home, among them Miller's plea to attend his mother's funeral. His letter mentioned that his mother had been the oldest resident of a sound-side community south of Wilmington—as if that somehow buttressed the case for allowing him to return to Wilmington to bury her. The white men who ran Wilmington were unmoved. Miller's request was denied.

Alex Manly never revealed all that had befallen him in Wilmington— not to his wife or his two sons, his nieces, his sisters-in-law, or any friend or colleague. He died in 1944 at age seventy-five, nearly silent until the end, a weary man haunted by the past. His Pennsylvania death certificate listed his race as colored, his profession as painter, and his cause of death as carcinoma of the bladder. He had told his wife that he did not want to be buried in Wilmington—or anywhere in North Carolina. Alex's secrets were buried with him, in an unadorned grave beneath a tombstone of Vermont granite in Fairview Cemetery in Willow Grove, Pennsylvania, outside Philadelphia. Beneath his name are the words: "At Rest." Alex's wife, Carrie, is buried beside him.

Alex Manly's grandson, Lewin Manly Jr., was born eleven years before Alex died. Young Lewin lived with his grandfather until he was three years old. He remembers little of the man, except a vague notion, formed in Lewin's youth, that something terrible had wrecked his grandfather's life—so terrible that no one in the family spoke of it. Lewin later asked his father—Lewin Manly Sr., the younger of Alex's two sons—what had happened to Alex in Wilmington. His father refused to discuss the matter. Only years later did Lewin Jr. realize that his father knew little more than he did.

Lewin Manly Jr. was born in Philadelphia and raised in Savannah, but he often visited his great-aunts, Felice and Mabel, the sisters of Carrie Sadgwar Manly, young Lewin's paternal grandmother. The two women survived the riot and lived in Wilmington for the rest of their lives, though Mabel also spent several years in Philadelphia. Lewin Jr. pressed his elderly aunts for details about his grandfather's life in Wilmington. If they knew anything, they did not share it. They regaled Lewin with family lore unrelated to events in Wilmington in 1898, but when he raised the subject, they fell silent. "As soon as I would mention 1898, they would just clam up," Lewin Jr. told me in 2018.

As an adolescent and later as a young man, Lewin Jr. often visited his grandmother Carrie in Pennsylvania. Lewin sometimes asked her about Alex's time in Wilmington. Carrie shared nothing. But in 1954, when Lewin Jr. turned twenty-one, Carrie wrote several letters to her sons, Milo and Lewin Sr. She briefly described the harrowing escape by Alex, then her fiancé, from Wilmington in 1898, and her own shock when she heard the news while preparing to sing onstage in London.

Carrie's letters mentioned Alex's 1898 editorial, but only to describe its explosive effects: "It turned the Southern cities from N.C. to Ala. upside down." She offered little else regarding the events of 1898. "I should let the 'dead past bury its dead,'" she wrote. For Carrie and her late husband, the past was weighted with pain and regret, eased only by death. Carrie mentioned that she kept a yellowed, crumbling copy of the *Record* from 1898. "Every man connected with that paper," she wrote, "has gone to his rest where there will be no more sorrow or riots."

In a single sentence, Carrie reflected on the lifelong impact of her husband's near-death experience in Wilmington: "How my poor boy went through all he did and came out cheerful and forgiving is a wonder to me." And she offered a glimpse of Alex's state of mind, relaying an arch comment he muttered one night in 1918 after reading that "Pitchfork" Ben Tillman had died. "Carrie, here is a notice of the death of old Ben Tillman," he told her. "I wonder who is making hash out of him in hell tonight?"

Lewin Manly Jr. did not learn the full truth of the events of 1898 until 2006, when the state commission released its report. It pained him that his own family had kept so much from him, but he didn't blame them. He concluded that his father and grandmother and great-aunts sought to spare him the burden that Alex had carried to his grave.

When I spoke to Lewin Manly Jr. in 2018, he was eighty-five years old. He was retired and living in Atlanta, where he tended a garden, dabbled in photography, and read voraciously. He had spent forty years as a dentist in Atlanta after graduating from Howard University's dental school. He was so intrigued by his family's refusal to discuss the events of 1898 that he wrote an essay for his college alumni newspaper about his attempts to pry details from relatives. I asked him why he thought his grandfather and other relatives so adamantly refused to dredge up the past.

"The stress from what they saw, they never got over it," Lewin told me. "It scared the hell out of them. That's why they never talked about it. My grandfather probably blamed himself for all the deaths in Wilmington and it probably sent him to an early grave. He had to deal with all that evil. Those were evil people."

Lewin said he had no desire to spend time in Wilmington, except to visit his great-aunts. For him, the residue of 1898 is lasting and corrosive. In the late 1990s, he read news accounts of blacks and whites in Wilmington attempting to reconcile as the city prepared to commemorate the centennial in 1998. He said he did not believe true reconciliation was possible or that black descendants could ever recover from the crushing dislocation and racism stoked by the events of 1898. Nor did he believe that descendants of the white supremacists of 1898 would ever acknowledge the inherited status and privilege afforded them by the actions of their ancestors.

"There's no hope for them," Lewin told me. "You're never going to change them."

I asked whether he was prepared to forgive the white men who led the riot and drove his grandfather from Wilmington 120 years earlier.

Lewin thought for a moment, then said, "I'm not a very religious person, and I don't forgive. If there's a hell, I hope they're burning in it, all of them."

ACKNOWLEDGMENTS

T HIS BOOK is a work of journalism, but it has relied extensively on a foundation laid by historians. I approached this project by attempting to transport myself back to 1898, seeking out the written record left by Wilmington's white conspirators and their black targets—letters, diaries, memoirs, articles, proclamations, telegrams, and various official communications. There was also a rich, if deeply biased, record provided by the many national white journalists dispatched to Wilmington to report on what they described as "the race war," as well as articles by white supremacist reporters for Wilmington's newspapers.

But a full and accurate account would not have been possible without the work of academic researchers whose patient digging undermined the false narrative crafted by white supremacists. Helen Edmonds, an African American scholar at North Carolina Central University, was the first to expose the white myth of 1898 in her groundbreaking 1951 work, *The Negro and Fusion Politics in North Carolina, 1894–1901.* I am also indebted to another African American historian, H. Leon Prather Sr., for his detailed 1984 account, *We Have Taken a City: Wilmington Racial Massacre and Coup of 1898.*

Equally essential was the extensive research conducted by the state of North Carolina's Wilmington Race Riot Commission under the auspices of the North Carolina Department of Cultural Resources, Office of Archives and History. The commission produced the definitive *1898 Wilmington Race Riot Report,* led by principal researcher LeRae Umfleet, whose companion book, *A Day of Blood,* was also an invaluable resource. In addition, LeRae guided me to other important sources of information. Also especially helpful was Michael Hill, research supervisor at the North Carolina Office of Archives and History.

Robert Wooley graciously shared extensive archival material on the life and work of Alexander Manly and offered suggestions for the manuscript. Wooley's 1977 PhD dissertation, "Race and Politics: The Evolution of the White Supremacy Campaign of 1898 in North Carolina," was an indispensable guide. I relied, too, on other dissertations, especially Jerome McDuffie's "Politics in Wilmington and New Hanover County, North Carolina, 1865–1900: The Genesis of a Race Riot," as well as academic works by Sue Ann Cody, Hayumi Higuchi, and Evelyn Underwood.

For the life and times of Abraham Galloway, I relied heavily on David S. Cecelski's intriguing and deeply researched book, *The Fire of Freedom: Abraham Galloway & the Slaves' Civil War*. Equally valuable was *Democracy Betrayed: The Wilmington Race Riot of 1898 and Its Legacy*, edited by Cecelski and Timothy B. Tyson.

Much of my research was conducted at Wilson Library at the University of North Carolina at Chapel Hill. The staffs of the North Carolina Collection and the Southern Historical Collection fielded countless requests with professionalism and courtesy. I want to especially thank John Blythe at the North Carolina Collection, who took a special interest in this book and guided me through the collection. Also helpful was the staff at the David M. Rubenstein Rare Book and Manuscript Library at Duke University.

In Wilmington, Beverly Tetterton was the perfect guide, walking the streets with me and pointing out important landmarks while enriching my understanding of the events of 1898. The staffs of the New Hanover County Public Library and the Cape Fear Museum were helpful and patient. Malcolm McLaurin provided essential background on the struggle in modern Wilmington to commemorate the riot and coup. He also offered a thoughtful critique of the manuscript.

ACKNOWLEDGMENTS

Several descendants of historical figures caught up in the tumultuous events of 1898 graciously agreed to speak with me about the painful legacy of the killings and coup. I thank Lewin Manly Jr., Lisa Adams, George Rountree III, Faye Chaplin, and Frank A. Daniels Jr. for sharing their memories with me.

I also thank Sasha Mitchell for her genealogical research on the families of Alexander Manly, Abraham Galloway, and Thomas C. Miller. Thanks, too, to the Logan Nonfiction Program at the Carey Institute for Global Good for providing living quarters, writing time, and good company.

Many friends read all or portions of the manuscript or the book proposal and offered insightful suggestions. I want to thank Rick Nichols, Nancy Szokan, Kevin Maurer, Errol Somay, Jim Wann, Bruce Siceloff, Greg Boyden, and my brothers Vince and Larry Zucchino. I'm especially grateful to Bland Simpson, who knows as much about the people and history of the Carolina coast as anyone alive. Bland took an early and abiding interest in this book. Our regular conversations over BLT sandwiches at Merritt's Grill in Chapel Hill were always enlightening.

My agent, Flip Brophy at Sterling Lord Literistic, has always believed in my work and fought hard to have it published. She is a trusted and lasting friend.

At Grove Atlantic, Morgan Entrekin took a chance with this book, despite my disjointed proposal. Morgan recognized the significance of this forgotten chapter of American history and pushed me to place the events of 1898 in the proper historical context. Two talented and sharp-eyed editors, Allison Malecha and Brenna McDuffie, made valuable improvements to the manuscript. They offered constructive advice that helped sharpen the writing and streamline the narrative. Additional editing by Paula Cooper Hughes and Julia Berner-Tobin corrected my many factual errors, grammatical mistakes, and misspellings. Sara

Vitale made sure everything connected to this project was accomplished professionally and on time. Deb Seager worked diligently to promote this book.

Finally, I owe everything to the four most important people in my life—my wife Kacey and our daughters Adrien, Emily, and Natalie. My favorite editor, Kacey, was the first person to read my early draft. She is a voracious reader, with a remarkable ability to spot holes and flaws in a narrative. She flagged confusing passages, narrative inconsistencies, and excess verbiage, helping me polish and focus the manuscript. Kacey instilled in our daughters a lifelong love of books and reading. They, too, took an exceptional interest in this book and provided astute critiques. It is a blessing to have my family's love and support. Every writer should be so fortunate.

NOTES

Prologue

xv **The killers came** 1898 Wilmington Race Riot Report, 1898 Wilmington Race Riot Commission, North Carolina Department of Cultural Resources, Office of Archives and History, LeRae Umfleet, principal researcher, May 31, 2006, 133. (Hereafter cited as Riot Commision Report.)

xv **Many of them** *Washington Evening Star*, November 10, 1898.

xvi **Murchison also sold** Contested Election Case, *Oliver H. Dockery v. John D. Bellamy*, from the Sixth Congressional District of the State of North Carolina (Washington, D.C.: Government Printing Office, 1899), 13, 14.

xvi **When pressed on** Ibid., 11.

xvi **Years later, one** Harry Hayden, *The Wilmington Rebellion*, North Carolina Collection, University of North Carolina at Chapel Hill, 1952, 10.

xvi **Wilmington, with a** William M. Reaves, *Strength Through Struggle: The Chronological and Historical Record of the African-American Community in Wilmington, North Carolina, 1865–1960*, ed. Beverly Tetterton (Wilmington, N.C.: New Hanover County Public Library, 1998), 496.

xvi **They telegraphed emergency** *Wilmington Semi-Weekly Messenger*, reprint of *Baltimore Sun* article, November 8, 1898.

xvii **"Nigger lawyers are"** Helen G. Edmonds, *The Negro and Fusion Politics in North Carolina, 1894–1901* (Chapel Hill: University of North Carolina Press, 1951), 164.

xvii **In 1898, a** Robert H. Wooley, "Race and Politics: The Evolution of the White Supremacy Campaign of 1898 in North Carolina," thesis, University of North Carolina, 1977, 161.

xvii **There were black** Reaves, *Strength Through Struggle*, 489. Sue Ann Cody, "After the Storm: Racial Violence in Wilmington, North Carolina and Its Consequences for African-Americans, 1898–1905," thesis, University of North Carolina Wilmington, 2000, 26–27.

xvii **Black merchants sold** John C. Dancy, *Sand Against the Wind: The Memoirs of John C. Dancy* (Detroit: Wayne State University Press, 1966), 66.

xvii **A black barber served** LeRae Sikes Umfleet, *A Day of Blood: The 1898 Wilmington Race Riot* (Raleigh: North Carolina Office of Archives and History, 2009), 181.

xvii **The county jailer** Edmonds, *The Negro and Fusion Politics*, 163.

xvii **The county treasurer** Ibid.

xvii **In 1891, President** Ibid., 89.

xvii **A white newspaper** H. Leon Prather Sr., *We Have Taken a City, Wilmington Racial Massacre and Coup of 1898* (Wilmington, N.C.: Associated University Presses, NU World Enterprises Inc., 1984), 23.

xvii **Black businessmen pooled** Jerome A. McDuffie, "Politics in Wilmington and New Hanover County, 1865–1900: The Genesis of a Race Riot," PhD diss., Kent State University, 1979, 342.

xvii **A black alderman** Edmonds, *The Negro and Fusion Politics*, 164.

xviii **In fact, Wilmington's** Ibid., 173, 200. McDuffie, "Politics in Wilmington," 324.

xviii **The planters, lawyers,** Alan D. Watson, *Wilmington, North Carolina, to 1861* (Jefferson, N.C., and London: McFarland and Company, 2003), 9–15.

xviii **The armed men** Minutes of the Organizational Meeting of the Association of Members of the Wilmington Light Infantry, Lumina, Wrightsville Beach, December 14, 1905, North Carolina Collection, University of North Carolina at Chapel Hill, 10.

xviii **The white men** *Wilmington Messenger*, November 11, 1898.

xviii **One of the** Hayden, *The Wilmington Rebellion*, 30

xix **Some of the** Prather, *We Have Taken a City*, 115.

xix **The compress was** Andrew J. Howell, *The Book of Wilmington* (Published privately, 1930), 165. Edmonds, *The Negro and Fusion Politics in North Carolina*, 169.

xix **The white men** *Wilmington Messenger*, November 11, 1898.

xix **A city newspaper** Ibid.

xix **They were "going"** Jane Cronly, *Account of the Race Riot in Wilmington, 1898*, unpublished diary, Cronly Family Papers, Duke University Libraries.

xx **"I'm as brave"** *Wilmington Messenger*, November 11, 1898.

xxi **He had walked** Contested Election Case, 342.

xxi **Prospective members had** Umfleet, *Day of Blood*, 57–58, 220. Alfred Moore Waddell, *Some Memories of My Life* (Raleigh, N.C.: Edwards and Broughton Printing Company, 1908), 45–46. Reaves, *Strength Through Struggle*, 335–336.

xxii **Under optimum conditions** *Wilmington Messenger*, November 1, 1898. *Washington Post*, October 29, 1898. Umfleet, *A Day of Blood*, 96.

xxii **Most were from** Umfleet, *A Day of Blood*, 58, 220.

xxii **Like the men** Report of the Commanding Officer of Naval Battalion, Headquarters, N.C. Naval Battalion, Wilmington, December 1, 1898, Reports on the Riot at Wilmington, November 22, 1898, North Carolina Public Documents, Document No. 9, North Carolina Collection, University of North Carolina at Chapel Hill, 28.

xxii **The gun's bore** Umfleet, *A Day of Blood*, 98.

xxii **One of Wilmington's** *Wilmington Messenger*, November 8, 1898.

xxii **Just before midday** Umfleet, *A Day of Blood*, 92.

BOOK ONE: DAYS OF HOPE

One: Cake and Wine

3 **General Braxton Bragg** William McKee Evans, *Ballots and Fence Rails: Reconstruction on the Lower Cape Fear* (Chapel Hill: University of North Carolina Press, 1966), 35.

3 **The US Navy** William S. Powell, *Encyclopedia of North Carolina* (Chapel Hill: University of North Carolina Press, 2006), 460.

4 **Portions of the** Evans, *Ballots and Fence Rails*, 35–36.

4 **Corn sold for** Ibid., 21.

4 **Many Union soldiers** Ibid., 38.

4 **Carpenters struggled** Ibid., 39.

4 **One visitor claimed** Ibid, 71.

4 **"There is not"** *Wilmington Herald*, June 14, 1865.

5 **Just a few months earlier** *Wilmington Daily Journal*, December 26, 1864.

5 **Dick was considered** Ibid.

5 **Barely six thousand** Gregory P. Downs, *After Appomattox—Military Occupation and the Ends of War* (Cambridge, Mass.: Harvard University Press, 2015), 103.

5 **And by the** Steven Hahn, Steven F. Miller, et al., *Freedom, A Documentary History of Emancipation 1861–1867, Series 3: Volume 1, Land and Labor, 1865* (Chapel Hill: University of North Carolina Press, 2008), 173.

5 **The mayor quickly** Report of the Joint Committee on Reconstruction, at the First Session, Thirty-Ninth Congress (Washington, D.C.: Government Printing Office, 1866), 267.

6 **"The people boast"** W. E. Burghardt Du Bois, *Black Reconstruction: An Essay Toward a History of the Part Which Black Folk Played in the Attempt to Reconstruct*

Democracy in America, 1860–1880 (New York: Harcourt, Brace and Company, 1935), 136.

6 **In September, Ames** Evans, *Ballots and Fence Rails*, 58.

6 **But the Freedmen's** Hahn, Miller, et al., *Freedom*, 759–761.

6 **A general order** *Wilmington Herald*, July 17, 1865.

6 **One leading black** Evans, *Ballots and Fence Rails*, 65.

6 **Most of the new** Report of the Joint Committee, 271.

7 **In the countryside** Evans, *Ballots and Fence Rails*, 68.

7 **Colonel Beadle had** Hahn, Miller, et al., *Freedom*, 183.

7 **"They would endeavor"** Report of the Joint Committee, 266–272.

7 **"All look bad"** Ibid., 271.

7 **One day, he** Ibid., 271–272.

8 **The reporter wrote** *Philadelphia Inquirer*, August 9, 1865.

8 **"By colored man"** John Richard Dennett, *The South as It Is* (Tuscaloosa: University of Alabama Press, 2010), 125–126.

9 **After the war** Evans, *Ballots and Fence Rails*, 71.

9 **"Houses of colored"** Report of the Joint Committee, 272.

9 **In Charleston in** Downs, *After Appomattox*, 58.

9 **In Mississippi that** Hahn, Miller, et al., *Freedom*, 122.

9 **Across the South** Ibid., 122.

9 **But blacks were** Du Bois, *Black Reconstruction*, 99.

9 **The city's white** Hahn, Miller, et al., *Freedom*, 131–132.

10 **They stormed the** Evans, *Ballots and Fence Rails*, 81, 250.

10 **Ultimately, federal military** Ibid., 81.

10 **The *Wilmington Journal*** Umfleet, *A Day of Blood*, 12.

10 **"Blood is thicker"** *Wilmington Journal*, April 17, 1868.

Two: Good Will of the White People

11 **"My health was"** Waddell, *Some Memories*, 54–57.

12 **He moved to** Ibid., 7–8, 28, 39–45.

12 **He pointed out** *Wilmington Herald*, January 11, 1861.

13 **They "insult and"** Evans, *Ballots and Fence Rails*, 76.

13 **Other whites complained** David S. Cecelski, *The Fire of Freedom: Abraham Galloway & the Slaves' Civil War* (Chapel Hill: University of North Carolina Press, 2012), 176.

13 **Though Governor Holden** Ibid.

13 **Both blacks and** Powell, *Encyclopedia of North Carolina*, 1,047.

14 **Waddell announced that** *Wilmington Herald*, July 27, 1865.

14 **One of Wilmington's** *Wilmington Journal*, March 13, 1874.

14 Seated on the *Wilmington Herald*, July 27, 1865.

14 He stood five Military identification card, Alfred Moore Waddell, North Carolina Collection, University of North Carolina at Chapel Hill.

16 A few hours *Wilmington Herald*, July 27, 1865.

Three: Lying Out

17 In the spring *Wilmington Herald*, October 26, 1865.

18 He participated in *Wilmington Herald*, October 21, 23, 1865.

18 A fellow Confederate *Wilmington Herald*, October 12, 1865.

18 There was a *Wilmington Herald*, October 13, 1865.

19 They then stabbed *Wilmington Herald*, October 11, 12, 1865. *Wilmington Daily Dispatch*, October 11, 1865.

20 One side of *Wilmington Herald*, October 12, 13, 19, 1865.

21 It pronounced the *Wilmington Herald*, October 14, 18, 25, 26, 1865.

21 But there was *Wilmington Dispatch*, February 24, 1866. Waddell, *Some Memories*, 89–92. Evans, *Ballots and Fence Rails*, 25–32.

Four: Marching to the Happy Land

22 He was described *New York Times*, September 17, 1865.

22 Frederick Douglass's abolitionist *New National Era*, September 22, 1870.

23 Copies of the *New York Times*, September 17, 1865.

23 "The time has" *Wilmington Herald*, September 8, 1865.

24 He returned to Cecelski, *The Fire of Freedom*, 189.

24 Galloway was born Ibid., 2–4. William Still, *Still's Underground Rail Road Records, with a Life of the Author. Narrating the Hardships, Hairbreadth Escapes and Death Struggles of the Slaves in Their Efforts for Freedom. Together with Sketches of Some of the Eminent Friends of Freedom, and Most Liberal Aiders and Advisers of the Road* (Philadelphia: William Still, 1886), 150. Galloway Family Files, New Hanover County Public Library, Wilmington, N.C. *New National Era*, September 22, 1870.

24 Abraham later said Still, *Still's Underground Rail Road*, 150.

24 Abraham was the Cecelski, *The Fire of Freedom*, 6. Still, *Still's Underground Rail Road*, 150. (Still, perhaps misunderstanding what Galloway had told him, identified Galloway's master as Milton Hawkins.)

24 "He always said" Still, *Still's Underground Rail Road*, 150.

25 Hankins required Galloway Ibid., 151.

25 "Times were hard" Ibid., 150–151.

25 They arranged with Ibid., 151.

26 The photo showed Ibid., 151–152.

26 Galloway had found Ibid., 152.

26 **Posing as a** Cecelski, *The Fire of Freedom*, 49–52.

26 **In Union territory** *New National Era*, September 22, 1870.

26 **Thousands of fugitive** Cecelski, *The Fire of Freedom*, xiii–xiv. Judkin Browning, *Shifting Loyalties: The Union Occupation of Eastern North Carolina* (Chapel Hill: University of North Carolina Press, 2011), 88

27 **Union officers called** Eric Foner, *A Short History of Reconstruction* (New York: Harper & Row, 1990), 3.

27 **Raised as the** Edward W. Kinsley Papers, *A Little More About Mary Ann Starkey*, University of Massachusetts Amherst Libraries.

27 **But because there** Edward W. Kinsley Papers, *Ordered to Newbern*, University of Massachusetts Amherst Libraries.

27 **"You will allow"** Bowdoin S. Parker, *History of Edward W. Kinsley Post, No. 113* (Norwood, Mass.: Norwood Press, 1913), 144.

27 **"Among the blacks"** Albert W. Mann, *History of the Forty-Fifth Regiment Massachusetts Volunteer Militia*, New York Public Library, 301.

28 **Galloway wanted an** Edward W. Kinsley Papers, *Raising the First North Carolina Colored Regiment*, University of Massachusetts Amherst Library. Mann, *History of the Forty-Fifth Regiment*, 301–302. Cecelski, *The Fire of Freedom*, xv.

29 **Yet some Union** Robert Dale Owen, James McKaye, and Samuel G. Howe, "Preliminary Report of the American Freedmen's Inquiry Commission," to E. M. Stanton, 30 June 1863, in U.S. Adjutant General's Office, Negro in the Military Service, roll 2, vol. 3, pt. 1: Military Employment 1863.

29 **Under existing North** *Douglass' Monthly*, July 1862. Browning, *Shifting Loyalties*, 78.

29 **It was little** *Douglass' Monthly*, July 1862, 678. Browning, *Shifting Loyalties*, 79.

30 **Kinsley repeated Galloway's** Edward W. Kinsley Papers, *Raising the First North Carolina Colored Regiment*.

30 **The next day** Mann, *History of the 45th Regiment*, 302.

30 **"It seemed to"** Edward W. Kinsley Papers, *Raising the First North Carolina Colored Regiment*.

30 **They enlisted in** Cecelski, *The Fire of Freedom*, 80.

30 **Galloway would soon** Library of Congress, *African American Soldiers During the Civil War*. Cecelski, *The Fire of Freedom*, 80.

Five: Ye Men of Unmixed Blood

31 **He built a reputation** *New National Era*, Washington, D.C., September 22, 1870.

31 **He attracted national** Cecelski, *The Fire of Freedom*, 103–114.

32 **Lincoln assured the** *North Carolina Times*, New Bern, May 21, 1864. Cecelski, *The Fire of Freedom*, 115–117.

32 **He was neither** Cecelski, *The Fire of Freedom*, 204.

32 **The *Wilmington Post*** *Wilmington Post*, August 13, 1867.

32 **"His power of"** Dennett, *The South as It Is*, 152.

32 **He referred to** *Wilmington Daily Journal*, February 14, 1868.

32 **A secretive band** *Report of the Joint Select Committee to Inquire into the Condition of Affairs in the Late Insurrectionary States, Made to the Two Houses of Congress February 19, 1872* (Government Printing Office, 1872). J. G. de Roulhac Hamilton, *Reconstruction in North Carolina* (Gloucester, Mass.: Peter Smith, 1964), 461. Stanley F. Horn, *Invisible Empire—The Story of the Ku Klux Klan, 1866–1871* (Montclair, N.J.: Patterson Smith, 1969).

33 **After the Civil** William Lord deRosset, *Pictorial and Historical New Hanover County and Wilmington, North Carolina, 1723–1938* (Wilmington, N.C.: William Lord deRosset, 1938), 30.

33 **Moore's Klan camp** Ibid.

33 **Many of Wilmington's** McDuffie, "Politics in Wilmington," 300.

33 **"He did yeoman's"** deRosset, *Pictorial and Historical New Hanover County*, 30.

33 **Moore, just thirty** *Wilmington Journal*, December 15, 1865.

33 **The robes were** *Report of the Joint Select Committee*.

34 **The penalty for** *Weekly Standard*, Raleigh, N.C., September 7, 1870.

34 **"You solemnly swear"** *Report of the Joint Select Committee*.

34 **"A friend to"** Ibid.

34 **"To keep down"** Otto H. Olsen, "The Ku Klux Klan: A Study in Reconstruction Politics and Propaganda," *North Carolina Historical Review* 39, no. 3 (July 1962): 352.

35 **"My people stand"** *Wilmington Evening Star*, September 25, 1867.

35 **Galloway promised that** *New National Era*, Washington, D.C., September 22, 1870.

35 **In 1866, North** James E. Bond, "Ratification of the Fourteenth Amendment in North Carolina," *Wake Forest Law Review* 20, no. 89 (1984): 101.

35 **Black children could** Laura F. Edwards, "Captives of Wilmington," in David S. Cecelski and Timothy B. Tyson, eds., *Democracy Betrayed: The Wilmington Race Riot of 1898 and Its Legacy* (Chapel Hill: University of North Carolina Press, 1998), 120–121.

35 **The codes relied** Du Bois, *Black Reconstruction*, 167–177, 434.

35 **White-run newspapers** *Wilmington Journal*, March 17, 26, 1868.

36 **For a dollar** Dancy, *Sand Against the Wind*, 66. Powell, *Encyclopedia of North Carolina*, 1,046.

36 **For a time** Evans, *Ballots and Fence Rails*, 195.

37 **"Decidedly they are"** Frederick Law Olmsted, *A Journey in the Seaboard Slave States, with Remarks on Their Economy* (London: Sampson Low, Son, and Co., 1856), 338–348.

37 **North Carolina's thirty thousand** Du Bois, *Black Reconstruction*, 526.

37 **By 1880, Wilmington** Lawrence H. Larsen, *The Rise of the Urban South* (Lexington: University Press of Kentucky, 1985), 38.

38 **Five railroads set** Hayumi Higuchi, "White Supremacy on the Cape Fear: The Wilmington Affair of 1898," thesis, University of North Carolina at Chapel Hill, 1980, 4.

38 **paid white brakemen** McDuffie, "Politics in Wilmington," 320.

38 **Congress denied the** Stephen Marc Appell, "The Fight for the Constitutional Convention: The Development of Political Parties in North Carolina During 1867," thesis, University of North Carolina at Chapel Hill, 1969.

38 **In North Carolina** Foner, *A Short History of Reconstruction*, 30.

38 **It would be** Ibid., 191.

39 **His hometown *Daily*** *Wilmington Daily Journal*, February 26, 1868.

39 THE NIGGER CONVENTION Ibid.

39 THE GORILLA CONVENTION Ibid.

39 THE KANGAROO KONVENSHUN *Wilmington Daily Journal*, February 19, 1868.

39 **One newspaper editor** *Raleigh Sentinel*, March 18, 1868.

39 **Galloway had the** *Morning Star*, Wilmington, N.C., March 27, 1868; *Wilmington Daily Journal*, March 27, 1868.

39 **He was.** *Wilmington Daily Post*, February 4, 1868.

40 **"If I could"** *Wilmington Journal*, February 23, 1868.

40 **"As I have"** *Wilmington Post*, April 21, 1868.

40 **In 1868, blacks** Reaves, *Strength Through Struggle*, 496.

40 **"Shall MARRIAGE BETWEEN"** *Wilmington Journal*, April 14, 1868.

40 **"Arise then, ye"** *Wilmington Journal*, April 21, 1868.

Six: The Avenger Cometh

41 **"The Shrouded Knight"** *Morning Star*, Wilmington, N.C., March 24, 1868.

42 **"Terrible was the"** *Daily Journal*, Wilmington, N.C., April 18, 1868.

42 **These black militias** Otis Singletary, *Negro Militia and Reconstruction* (Austin: University of Texas Press, 1957), 16.

42 **Whites called it** Ibid., 118.

43 **A white lawyer** *Daily Journal*, April 21, 1868.

43 **On the rain-swept** *Wilmington Star*, April 21, 1868.

43 **Another newspaper complained** *Wilmington Post*, April 21,1868.

43 **During three days** *Wilmington Star*, April 24, 1868.

44 "Galloway ought to" *Daily Journal*, April 21, 1868.

44 "Niggers, white and" *Daily Journal*, April 24, 1868.

44 Still, they held *Daily Journal*, April 21, 1868.

Seven: Destiny of the Negro

45 Newspapers speculated that *New National Era*, September 22, 1870. Cecelski, *The Fire of Freedom*, 213.

45 Six thousand people *New National Era*, September 22, 1870.

45 It was described *Morning Star*, Wilmington, N.C., September 4, 1870.

46 The church was Ibid.

46 The newspaper displayed *New National Era*, September 22, 1870.

46 His paternal grandfather Manley Family Genetic Genealogy Project via FamilyTreeDNA. Prather, *We Have Taken a City*, 69. Descendants of Governor Charles Manly (1795–1871) confirmed through DNA testing that Samuel Trimetitus Grimes Manly, nicknamed "Trim," born in the 1830s, was the son of Governor Manly and that Samuel Manly was the father of Alexander Lightfoot Manly, born 1866.

46 His grandmother, possibly Ibid.

46 Among the black Milo Manly, interview with H. Leon Prather, Philadelphia, May 25, 1977.

47 Alex's mother, Corrine United States Census, 1870, Raleigh Township, Wake County, N.C., June 16, 1870, 48.

47 In 1880, the United States Census, 1880, Selma Township, Johnston County, N.C., June 3, 1880, 7.

47 Alex's teachers were Hampton University Archives, research by Robert Wooley.

47 He never graduated Ibid.

47 He struck out Charles Hardy III, interview with Milo Manly, September 11, 1984. Prather, *We Have Taken a City*, 70.

48 Around 1893, the Thomas W. Clawson, "The Wilmington Race Riot in 1898, Recollections and Memories," manuscript, Southern Historical Collection, University of North Carolina at Chapel Hill.

48 Two other Manly Manly family research by Robert Wooley.

48 "My father's family" H. Leon Prather, interview with Milo Manly, Philadelphia, May 25, 1977.

48 "The young editor" *Chicago Record*, November 13, 1898.

48 Alex refused to Ray Stannard Baker, *Following the Color Line: An Account of Negro Citizenship in the American Democracy* (Williamstown, Mass.: Corner House Publishers, 1973), 161.

48 **He was the** Henry Louis Gates Jr., "Who Really Invented the 'Talented Tenth'?" in *The Root*, at https://www.theroot.com/who-really-invented-the-talented-tenth-1790895289.

49 **Manly printed an** Prather, *We Have Taken a City*, 70–71. Jack Thorne, *Hanover: Or Persecution of the Lowly—Story of the Wilmington Massacre*, published by M. C. L. Hill, copy in the North Carolina Collection, University of North Carolina at Chapel Hill, 13.

49 **"We will wait"** *Daily Record*, September 28, 1895.

49 **The Raleigh *Gazette*** Raleigh *Gazette*, August 28, 1897.

49 **"We have been"** *Daily Record*, September 28, 1895.

50 **The paper carried** *Daily Record*, November 15, 1897; March 26, 1898; August 18, 1898.

50 **"a very creditable"** Clawson, "The Wilmington Race Riot."

50 **"The Only Negro"** *Daily Record*, November 15, 1897.

51 **"There is but"** *Raleigh Gazette*, August 28, 1897.

51 **"Be careful, young"** Ibid.

Eight: A Yaller Dog

52 **Alex Manly wrote** Reaves, *Strength Through Struggle*, 5.

53 **White citizens gathered** Ibid., 7. Research by Robert Wooley.

53 **These and other** Reaves, *Strength Through Struggle*, 34–36. Watson, *Wilmington, North Carolina, to 1861*, 140. Hahn, Miller, et al., *Freedom*, 801.

53 **The justices noted** Supreme Court of the United States, *Plessy v. Ferguson*, 163 U.S. 537 (1896).

54 **By 1897, Wilmington's** Riot Commission Report, 457.

54 **In 1898, black** Ibid., 330, 332.

54 **Black children typically** *Indianapolis Freeman*, December 3, 1898.

54 **In 1897, at** Riot Commission Report, 292, 326.

54 **Black homeowners often** *Indianapolis Freeman*, December 3, 1898.

54 **Horsecar lines began** Howell, *The Book of Wilmington*, 175.

54 **After complaints about** Reaves, *Strength Through Struggle*, 215.

55 **As early as 1880** *Star-News*, Wilmington, N.C, June 29, 2016.

55 **It was a hardened** Prather, *We Have Taken a City*, 24, 161. Umfleet, *A Day of Blood*, 186.

55 **It was a small** Cody, "After the Storm," 100.

56 **He lived the** Lisa Adams, great-granddaughter of William Everett Henderson, address to symposium, University of North Carolina, Wilmington, November 1998. Lisa Adams, telephone interview with author, January 12, 2016.

56 **He lost the** *Indianapolis Register*, June 25, 1932.

56 **He fled with** Lisa Adams address, University of North Carolina, Wilmington, November 1998.

56 **"Wilmington was a"** Ibid.

57 **His prominence** Umfleet, *A Day of Blood*, 111–112.

57 **"The colored man"** Wooley, "Race and Politics," 32–33.

58 **He required his** Dancy, *Sand Against the Wind*, 60.

58 **"If I had"** Ibid., 61.

58 **He sent his** Ibid., 61, 64.

58 **"I had never"** Higuchi, "White Supremacy on the Cape Fear," 37.

59 **"I'd rather be"** Lisa Adams address, University of North Carolina, Wilmington, November 1998.

59 **"a nightmare constantly"** Alexis de Tocqueville, *Democracy in America*, trans. George Lawrence (New York: HarperCollins, 2006), 358.

59 **His bones were** Thomas R. Gray, *The Confessions of Nat Turner, the Leader of the Late Insurrection in Southampton, Va., as Fully and Voluntarily Made to Thomas. R. Gray* (Baltimore: Lucas and Deaver, 1831; electronic version, Documenting the American South, North Carolina Collection, the University of North Carolina at Chapel Hill. *Atlantic*, August 1861. Herbert Aptheker, *American Negro Slave Revolts* (New York: Columbia University Press, 1943), 294–295.

59 **"invasion and slaughter."** Charles Edward Morris, "Panic and Reprisal: Reaction in North Carolina to the Nat Turner Insurrection, 1831," *North Carolina Historical Review* 62, no. 1 (January 1985): 32.

60 DISTURBANCES AMONG THE SLAVES! *Raleigh Register*, September 22, 1831.

60 **Their heads were** Morris, "Panic and Reprisal," 40–42.

61 **"quite in the"** Diary of Moses Ashley, September 1831, M. A. Curtis Papers, Southern Historical Collection, University of North Carolina at Chapel Hill.

62 **"If ever stern"** *Cape-Fear Recorder*, September 21, 1831.

62 **From that day** *Star-News*, Wilmington, N.C., May 27, 2009. *Morning Star*, Wilmington, N.C., November 11, 1945; December 15, 1945; May 13, 1947. Leslie H. Hossfeld, *Narrative, Political Unconscious and Racial Violence in Wilmington, North Carolina* (New York: Routledge, 2005), 133, 153. Powell, *Encyclopedia of North Carolina*, 785–786.

BOOK TWO: RECKONING

Nine: The Negro Problem

65 **Josephus Daniels and** Rachel Marie-Crane Williams, "A War in Black and White: The Cartoons of Norman Ethre Jennett and the North Carolina Election of 1898," *Southern Cultures* 19, no. 2 (2013): 7–31.

NOTES

65 **"The Negro shall"** Wooley, "Race and Politics," 258.
66 **The Black Belt** Alexander Weld Hodges, "Josephus Daniels, Precipitator of the Wilmington Race Riot of 1898," honors essay, University of North Carolina at Chapel Hill, 1990, 39. Edmonds, *The Negro and Fusion Politics,* 120.
66 **For the next** Edmonds, *The Negro and Fusion Politics,* 8–9.
67 **"Men who a"** Josephus Daniels, *Editor in Politics* (Chapel Hill: University of North Carolina Press, 1941), 123.
67 **The next year** Prather, *We Have Taken a City,* 34.
68 **Another black man** Edmonds, *The Negro and Fusion Politics,* 234–236.
68 **He was ridiculed** *Wilmington Messenger,* November 13, 1898.
68 **In a city** Riot Commission Report, 33. Reaves, *Strength Through Struggle,* 495.
69 **A close friend** Wooley, "Race and Politics," 70–71.
69 **His straight hairline** Josephus Daniels, *Tar Heel Editor* (Chapel Hill: University of North Carolina Press, 1939), 47.
69 **"he was also"** Lee A. Craig, *Josephus Daniels, His Life and Times* (Chapel Hill: University of North Carolina Press, 2013), 188.
69 **Daniels was born** Ibid., 2–3.
70 **Daniels was grievously** Ibid., 10–13.
71 **He gave young** Ibid., 77–78. Daniels, *Tar Heel Editor,* 248.
71 **That earned him** Craig, *Josephus Daniels,* 78–79. Daniels, *Tar Heel Editor,* 437.
71 **"persistent, cold-blooded"** Daniels, *Tar Heel Editor,* 344–354.
71 **When the *News*** Craig, *Josephus Daniels,* 78–79. Daniels, *Editor in Politics,* 85–93.
72 **After meeting with** Daniels, *Editor in Politics,* 284.
72 **The men who** Leonard Rogoff, "A Tale of Two Cities: Race, Riots, and Religion in New Bern and Wilmington, North Carolina, 1898," *Southern Jewish History* 14 (2011): 67.
72 **According to local** Umfleet, *A Day of Blood,* 54, 213.
72 **"He might be"** W. J. Cash, "Jehovah of the Tar Heels," *American Mercury,* July 1929, 312
72 **Even one of** Ibid.
73 **This was the** Richard L. Watson Jr., "Furnifold M. Simmons: 'Jehovah of the Tar Heels'?" *North Carolina Historical Review* 44, no. 2 (Spring 1967): 169–171.
73 **Simmons was born** Wooley, "Race and Politics," 204. Fred J. Rippy, *F. M. Simmons, Statesman of the New South* (Durham, N.C.: Duke University Press, 1936), 3.
73 **"No white person"** Rippy, *F. M. Simmons, Statesman of the New South,* 4.
74 **"I did not"** Ibid., 17–18.
74 **The Democrats coasted** Ibid., 20.
74 **Simmons's reward was** Ibid., 20–21.
74 **"Simmons made the"** Cash, "Jehovah of the Tar Heels," 313.

75 **"Rise, ye sons"** Glenda E. Gilmore, "Murder, Memory and the Flight of the Incubus," in Cecelski and Tyson, *Democracy Betrayed*, 74.

75 **"It is useless"** *The Democratic Hand Book*, 1898. Prepared by the State Democratic Executive Committee of the North Carolina Democratic Party, State Executive Committee (Raleigh: Edwards and Broughton, 1898). North Carolina Collection, University of North Carolina at Chapel Hill.

76 **Shortly afterward, in** Daniels, *Editor in Politics*, 147–148.

76 **"We would decide"** Ibid., 148.

76 **But in July** Rob Christensen, *The Paradox of Tar Heel Politics: The Personalities, Elections and Events That Shaped Modern North Carolina* (Chapel Hill: University of North Carolina Press, 2008), 18–19.

76 **Daniels assured his** Daniels, *Editor in Politics*, 147–150.

Ten: The Incubus

78 **"concentrated lye given"** *News and Observer*, January 21, 1898; March 18, 1898. Hodges, "Josephus Daniels," 28–29.

78 **"A reign of"** Daniels, *Editor in Politics*, 288.

78 **"described the unbridled"** Ibid., 285.

79 **"The propaganda was"** Daniels, *Editor in Politics*, 254, 295–296.

79 **Simmons raised the** Ibid., 244, 285.

80 **"assert your manhood"** *News and Observer*, September 23, 1898.

80 **"One of the"** *News and Observer*, October 8, 1898.

80 **"the prevalence of"** *News and Observer*, February 13, 1898.

80 AN INCUBUS MUST *New Berne Daily Journal*, August 10, 1898. (The paper continued to use the spelling *New Berne* even after the town became New Bern.)

80 **In fact, there** Glenda E. Gilmore, "Murder, Memory and the Flight of the Incubus," in Cecelski and Tyson, *Democracy Betrayed*, 75.

80 **In New Hanover** Public Documents of the State of North Carolina, Session 99, Document #8, 5. Research by Robert Wooley.

80 **Years later, Daniels** Daniels, *Editor in Politics*, 254.

80 **To help pay** Christensen, *Paradox of Tar Heel Politics*, 17.

80 **The main topic** Daniels, *Editor in Politics*, 244.

81 **Daniels worked until** Ibid., 295.

81 **In Wilmington, the** *Morning Star*, Wilmington, N.C., September 27, 1898.

81 **"The Negroes about"** Higuchi, "White Supremacy on the Cape Fear," 29.

81 **The *Atlanta Constitution*** Edmonds, *The Negro and Fusion Politics*, 148.

81 **They were no** McDuffie, "Politics in Wilmington," 351–352.

81 **"It was horrible-looking"** Daniels, *Editor in Politics*, 303.

82 **"And in such"** *News and Observer*, September 22, 1898.

Eleven: I Say Lynch

83   **She suggested that** *Atlanta Journal,* August 12, 1897.

83   **"The black fiend"** *Macon Telegraph,* August 20, 1897.

84   **"suffering of innocence"** *Morning Star,* Wilmington, N.C., August 18, 1898.

84   **"They cheered me"** *Atlanta Constitution,* December 22, 1898.

84   **He read the** Prather, *We Have Taken a City,* 71. Thorne, *Hanover,* 13, 14.

85   **His editorials helped** Thorne, *Hanover,* 13.

85   **"the usual friendly"** *Charlotte Observer,* November 16, 1898.

86   **Manly charmed her** Carrie Sadgwar Manly, letter to sons Milo A. Manly and Lewin Manly, La Mott, Pa., January 14, 1954. Alex L. Manly Papers, East Carolina University Manuscript Collection, Collection 0065.

87   **"the retort which"** Thorne, *Hanover,* 13.

88   **"You sow the"** *Daily Record,* August 18, 1898. (The *Daily Record's* associate editor, William L. Jeffries, later claimed to have written the editorial. But Alex Manly consistently said that he had written it, and he is widely credited as the author.)

Twelve: A Vile Slander

90   **"when that article"** Minutes of the Organizational Meeting of the Association Members of the Wilmington Light Infantry, Lumina, Wrightsville Beach, December 14, 1905. North Carolina Collection, University of North Carolina at Chapel Hill.

91   **"apologize for that"** Prather, *We Have Taken a City,* 73.

91   **"You are the"** Unsigned letter, August 27, 1898, Carrie Manly Scrapbook, New Hanover County Public Library, Wilmington, N.C., courtesy of Robert Wooley.

91   **Some carried clubs** Contested Election Case, 377.

91   **Others took up** *News and Observer,* August 26, 1898.

91   **He and his** Contested Election Case, 377.

91   **A butcher by** Umfleet, *A Day of Blood,* 185.

92   **"Let the white"** Contested Election Case, 385.

92   **With the help** *News and Observer,* August 26, 1898.

92   **Manly had "inflamed"** Daniels, *Editor in Politics,* 286, 289.

92   **But as the** Jeffrey J. Crow and Robert F. Durden, *Maverick Republican in the Old North State: A Political Biography of Daniel L. Russell* (Baton Rouge: Louisiana State University Press, 1999), 2.

92   **"all Negroes are"** Reaves, *Strength Though Struggle,* 241.

93   **"The negro who"** *Morning Post,* Raleigh, N.C., August 24, 1898.

93   **The structure, called** Thorne, *Hanover,* 14. Umfleet, *A Day of Blood,* 221.

93   The issue was Wooley, "Race and Politics," 196.

93   The *Wilmington Messenger* Prather, *We Have Taken a City*, 81.

93   "Resolved, That the" *News and Observer*, August 26, 1898.

94   "without any thoughts" *Wilmington Messenger*, October 21, 1898.

95   "Manly is responsible" *New York Times*, November 21, 1898.

95   "The intelligent colored" Ibid.

Thirteen: An Excellent Race

96   But they proved Umfleet, *A Day of Blood*, 41.

96   "to announce on" Ibid., 53.

97   He had married Ibid, 209.

97   "It soon became" George Rountree, "Memorandum of My Personal Recollection of the Election of 1898," Connor Papers, Southern Historical Collection, University of North Carolina at Chapel Hill, 2.

98   In all, the Ibid., 3.

98   "I started to" Ibid., 4.

98   "Simmons might go" Ibid., 6.

98   At the same Hayden, *The Wilmington Rebellion*, 9.

99   "For a period" Clawson, "The Wilmington Race Riot."

99   By late summer Umfleet, *A Day of Blood*, 56. Contested Election Case, 360.

100 He was also Samuel A. Ashe, Stephen B. Weeks, and Charles L. Van Noppen, *Biographical History of North Carolina, Vol. VIII* (Greensboro, N.C.: Charles Van Noppen, 1917), 381–389.

101 "In spite of" Jane Cronly, *Account of the Race Riot*, Cronly Family Papers, Duke University.

Fourteen: A Dark Scheme

102 It was signed *News and Observer*, October 8, 1898. *Morning Star*, Wilmington, N.C., October 9, 1898. *Wilmington Messenger*, October 9, 1898.

103 In fact, the Umfleet, *A Day of Blood*, 60.

103 "So, it seems" *News and Observer*, October 8, 1898.

103 The newspaper warned *Wilmington Messenger*, October 9, 13, 1898.

103 "We ascertained, I" Rountree, "Memorandum of My Personal Recollection," 5.

104 "burn the town" Umfleet, *A Day of Blood*, 60.

104 In Richmond, gun *Baltimore Sun* article, reprinted in *Semi-Weekly Messenger*, Wilmington, N.C., November 8, 1898. *Richmond Times*, November 5, 1898.

104 "There is, doubtless" *Washington Post*, October 20, 1898, reprinted in *Wilmington Messenger*, November 1, 1898.

104 **"To tell the"** *Richmond Times*, November 5, 1898.

104 **The reporter also** Riot Commission Report, 92.

105 **"They knew how"** Ibid., 249, 257.

105 **"The man who"** *Philadelphia Times* article, reprinted in *Charlotte Observer*, November 16, 1898.

106 **There was no** Riot Commission Report, 344–345.

Fifteen: The Nation's Mission

107 **At the entrance** *Wilmington Messenger*, September 21, 1898.

107 **The soldiers had** Umfleet, *A Day of Blood*, 220.

108 **They would be** *Wilmington Messenger*, September 7, 1898.

108 **The captain suggested** Umfleet, *A Day of Blood*, 220.

108 **It was "difficult"** Daniels, *Editor in Politics*, 283.

109 **Men in the** *Wilmington Messenger*, September 21, 1898.

110 **Tall and lean** Umfleet, *A Day of Blood*, 47.

110 **His older brother** Ibid., 229.

110 **The unit had** Ibid., 35.

110 **Like the Light** Ibid., 98.

111 **"The Negro has"** *Washington Bee*, March 5, 1898.

111 **Over the vigorous** Edmonds, *The Negro and Fusion Politics*, 99.

111 **The unit was** Willard B. Gatewood Jr., "North Carolina's Negro Regiment in the Spanish-American War," *North Carolina Historical Review* 47, no. 4 (October 1971): 375.

111 **Though Daniels conceded** Daniels, *Editor in Politics*, 275.

111 **"Negro domination."** Gatewood, "North Carolina's Negro Regiment," 377.

111 **Daniels had his** *News and Observer*, September 30, 1898.

111 **Another white editor** Gatewood, "North Carolina's Negro Regiment," 378.

112 **"Nobody seriously suggests"** *News and Observer*, May 22, 1898.

112 **On April 27** *Morning Star*, Wilmington, N.C., April 28, 1898.

112 **Two days later** *Morning Star*, Wilmington, N.C., April 30, 1898.

112 **The men climbed** *Morning Star*, May 31, 1898.

112 **"The reason negroes"** *News and Observer*, May 31, 1898.

113 **On a train** Gatewood, "North Carolina's Negro Regiment," 385.

113 **In Macon, a** *Atlanta Constitution*, November 30, 1898.

113 **In each case** Gatewood, "North Carolina's Negro Regiment," 383–385.

Sixteen: Degenerate Sons of the White Race

114 **"These degenerate sons"** Prather, *We Have Taken a City*, 86.

115 **He sometimes rode** Ibid., 50.

115　Melton, then forty-eight Ibid.

115　Perhaps not coincidentally Contested Election Case, 369–372.

116　"White men had" Ibid., 360–361.

116　French, a native Evans, *Ballots and Fence Rails*, 114.

116　"Everything Required in" *Wilmington Herald*, March 7, 1865.

116　He was praised *Wilmington Herald*, August 4, 1898.

116　For a commission *Daily Dispatch*, Wilmington, N.C., October 20, 1865.

117　He secured a *Wilmington Post*, August 13, 1867.

117　He also found *Daily Journal*, Wilmington, N.C., September 25, 1869.

117　"Because Gizzard French" Ibid.

117　He had created Evans, *Ballots and Fence Rails*, 116.

117　As chief deputy Contested Election Case, 222.

118　He was such *Wilmington Post*, January 1, 1882.

118　He warned that *Wilmington Messenger*, October 21, 1898.

119　After threats by Rountree, "Memorandum of My Personal Recollection," 8.

119　"rights of lawful" McDuffie, "Politics in Wilmington," 640–643.

120　But they replaced Prather, *We Have Taken a City*, 91.

120　"have given their" Edmonds, *The Negro and Fusion Politics*, 159.

120　Norwood said he *Wilmington Messenger*, November 4, 1898.

Seventeen: The Great White Man's Rally and Basket Picnic

122　The cornet band *Wilmington Messenger*, October 22, 1898.

122　"The Old North" *Fayetteville Observer*, October 22, 1898. *News and Observer*, October 22, 1898. *Wilmington Messenger*, October 22, 1898.

122　He had worn Stephen Kantrowitz, *Ben Tillman and the Reconstruction of White Supremacy* (Chapel Hill: University of North Carolina Press, 2000), 39.

122　Tillman had earned Francis Butler Simkins, *Pitchfork Ben Tillman, South Carolinian* (Baton Rouge: Louisiana State University Press, 1944), 315.

123　He said they Kantrowitz, *Ben Tillman*, 241.

123　"than to have" Simkins, *Pitchfork Ben Tillman*, 397.

123　"the most miserable" Kantrowitz, *Ben Tillman*, 16, 23.

123　"seize the first" Ibid., 67.

124　The white riflemen Ibid., 65–71.

124　"I have nothing" Ibid., 261.

124　"We stuffed ballot" Ibid., 400.

124　"South Carolina had" *Fayetteville Observer*, October 22, 1898.

125　"Send him to" *Wilmington Messenger*, October 22, 1898.

125　He departed to *Fayetteville Observer*, October 22, 1898.

126　But few of Prather, *We Have Taken a City*, 84–85.

Eighteen: White-Capping

127 **In many cases** Rogoff, "A Tale of Two Cities," 41.

127 **"I am with"** Ibid., 51.

128 **"The condition of affairs"** Contested Election Case, 8–9.

128 **On October 20** *Daily Record*, Wilmington, N.C., October 20, 1898, courtesy of a project to preserve copies of the *Daily Record*. John Jeremiah Sullivan and Joel Finsel, University of North Carolina, Wilmington, Cape Fear Museum, Williston Middle School, Friends School of Wilmington, cited in *Star-News*, Wilmington, N.C., July 21, 2017.

128 **Some blacks who** *Winston-Salem Union-Republican*, March 15, 1900. Cronly, *Account of the Race Riot*, 4.

128 **"Colored people . . ."** Contested Election Case, 363.

129 **Threatening them only** Riot Commission Report, 103.

129 **The men confirmed** *Morning Star*, Wilmington, N.C., October 18, 1898.

129 **Black men continued** Reaves, *Strength Through Struggle*, 495.

129 **The next day's** *Wilmington Messenger*, October 2, 1898. *Morning Star*, Wilmington, N.C., October 2, 1898.

131 **"I was whipped"** Contested Election Case, 138–141.

Nineteen: Buckshot at Close Range

132 **He looked like** United States Congress and O. M. Enyart, *A Biographical Congressional Dictionary, 1774–1903* (Washington, D.C.: Government Printing Office, 1903).

133 **It was immediately** H. Leon Prather Sr., "The Red Shirt Movement in North Carolina, 1898–1900," *Journal of Negro History* 62, no. 2 (April 1977): 177.

133 **Question twelve mentioned** Edmonds, *The Negro and Fusion Politics*, 234.

133 **"Absolutely none, and"** *Morning Star*, Wilmington, N.C., November 3, 1898.

133 **"The negroes, as"** *Weekly Star*, Wilmington, November 4, 1898.

134 **The article pointed** *News and Observer*, October 25, 1898.

134 **"Russell was in"** Daniels, *Editor in Politics*, 303.

134 **Even within the** Prather, *We Have Taken a City*, 101–102. *News and Observer*, October 25, 1898.

134 **In the meantime** *News and Observer*, October 25, 1898.

134 **"all ill-disposed persons"** *Wilmington Messenger*, October 26, 1898.

134 **"until old North"** *News and Observer*, November 6, 1898.

134 **In a front-page** Ibid.

135 **"Pick the Winner"** Ibid.

135 **But the city's** *Semi-Weekly Messenger*, Wilmington, N.C., November 4, 1898.

136 **"We will rule"** *Wilmington Messenger*, October 29, 1898. *News and Observer*, October 29, 1898.

136 **In Tarboro, on** Prather, "The Red Shirt Movement in North Carolina," 178.

136 **In Charlotte, nearly** *Wilmington Messenger*, October 22, 1898.

136 **"not a single"** Contested Election Case, 136.

136 **"For ten miles"** Prather, "The Red Shirt Movement in North Carolina," 178.

137 **"White Supremacy"** *Wilmington Messenger*, November 3, 1898.

137 **Kitchin drew the** Ibid.

137 **"We cannot outnumber"** *Semi-Weekly Messenger*, Wilmington, N.C., November 4, 1898.

137 **The group decided** Hayden, *The Wilmington Rebellion*, 16. McDuffie, "Politics in Wilmington," 622.

Twenty: A Drunkard and a Gambler

139 **His wife, Gabrielle** Glenda Elizabeth Gilmore, *Gender and Jim Crow: Women and the Politics of White Supremacy in North Carolina, 1896–1920* (Chapel Hill: University of North Carolina Press, 1996), 206.

139 **She was thirty-three** Ibid., 217.

140 **She and her** James Sprunt, *Chronicles of the Cape Fear, 1660–1916* (Raleigh: Edwards and Broughton Printing Co., 1916), 450–451.

140 **He was excused** *Report of the Joint Select Committee to Inquire into the Condition of Affairs in the Late Insurrectionary States, Made to the Two Houses of Congress, February 19, 1872* (Washington, D.C.: Government Printing Office, 1872), 354–361.

141 **"a waste of"** Waddell, *Some Memories of My Life*, 109–112.

141 **"the cultivated gentleman"** *Wilmington Post*, May 5, 1876; June 2, 1876.

141 **Waddell poleaxed the** *Wilmington Post*, May 19, 1876.

141 **"as if by magic"** *Wilmington Post*, May 5, 1876.

141 **"placing a pistol"** *Wilmington Post*, May 19, 1876.

141 **Waddell was hauled** *Wilmington Post*, May 5, 1876.

142 **Waddell's brother and** *Daily Journal*, Wilmington, N.C., May 17, 1876.

142 **Cassidey later reported** *Wilmington Post*, May 19, 1876.

142 **"I now make"** *Wilmington Post*, June 9, 1876.

142 **He lost his** Prather, *We Have Taken a City*, 87.

142 **"He had been"** Contested Election Case, 378–379.

143 **Waddell later bragged** Rountree, "Memorandum of My Personal Recollection."

Twenty-One: Choke the Cape Fear with Carcasses

144 **"Colonel! Colonel Waddell!"** *Wilmington Messenger*, October 25, 1898.

144 **Large audiences weren't** Bennett L. Steelman, "Black, White and Gray: The

Wilmington Race Riot in Fact and Legend," *North Carolina Literary Review* 2, no. 1 (Spring 1994): 73.

144 **"Buffalo Bill" Cody** *Star-News*, Wilmington, N.C. April 8, 2009.

145 **"a sizzling talk"** *Wilmington Messenger*, October 25, 1898.

148 **"The time has"** Ibid.

148 **"the most remarkable"** Ibid.

148 **Waddell later boasted** Riot Commission Report, 81.

148 **West provided a** *Washington Post* article, reprinted in *Wilmington Semi-Weekly Messenger*, November 4, 1898.

149 **Some of their** *Winston-Salem Union Republican*, March 15, 1900.

149 **Children, let out** *Wilmington Messenger*, November 4, 1878.

149 **Some blacks called** Prather, *We Have Taken a City*, 21.

149 **Dowling and other** Ibid. McDuffie, "Politics in Wilmington," 625. *Wilmington Messenger*, October 8, 1878.

149 **"Hang Wright!"** *Winston-Salem Union Republican*, March 15, 1900.

149 **The air was** *Richmond Times* report, reprinted in *Wilmington Messenger*, November 5, 1898.

150 **Shots were fired** Contested Election Case, 362.

150 **The mood was** *Wilmington Messenger*, November 3, 1898.

150 **"fire them up"** Riot Commission Report, 83.

150 **"fighting whiskey"** Contested Election Case, 388.

150 **"That was the"** Daniels, *Editor in Politics*, 293–294.

150 **"tackled every nigger"** Riot Commission Report, 84.

151 **The Red Shirts** *Wilmington Evening Dispatch*, November 5, 1898.

Twenty-Two: The Shepherds Will Have Nowhere to Flee

152 **In response, the** *Wilmington Messenger*, November 3, 1898.

152 **"And don't allow"** *News and Observer*, October 8, 1898.

152 **"Every lover of"** *Richmond Times*, November 5, 1898. *News and Observer*, November 8, 1898.

153 **On November 1** *Evening Star*, Washington, D.C., November 2, 1898.

154 **"We say now"** *Daily Record*, October 20, 1898, courtesy of a project to preserve copies of the *Daily Record*, John Jeremiah Sullivan and Joel Finsel, University of North Carolina, Wilmington, Cape Fear Museum, Williston Middle School, Friends School of Wilmington, cited in *Star-News*, Wilmington, N.C., July 21, 2017.

154 **"We have a"** *Indianapolis Freeman*, December 3, 1898.

155 **Others grumbled and** Prather, *We Have Taken a City*, 96. McDuffie, "Politics in Wilmington," 650. Riot Commission Report, 107.

155 **"if negroes do"** Riot Commission Report, 107.

156 **"The Sambos do"** *Wilmington Messenger*, September 21, 1898.

156 **But his capitulation** McDuffie, "Politics in Wilmington," 614. *Wilmington Messenger*, September 21, 1898.

156 **Wright suspended six** Contested Election Case, 375–378. McDuffie, "Politics in Wilmington," 614. *Wilmington Messenger*, September 21, 1898.

156 **"Listen to us!"** Rev. J. Allen Kirk, "A Statement of Facts Concerning the Bloody Riot in Wilmington, N.C. Of Interest to Every Citizen of the United States." Electronic Edition, *Documenting the American South*, University of North Carolina at Chapel Hill, 4.

157 **"We are further"** *News and Observer*, October 22, 1898.

158 **How the officers** *Wilmington Messenger*, November 6, 1898.

158 **The *Messenger* predicted** *Wilmington Messenger*, November 1, 1898.

158 **Some reporters accepted** Prather, *We Have Taken a City*, 150. B. F. Keith, *Memories* (Raleigh: Bynum Printing Company, 1922), 113.

158 ***Washington Post* correspondent** *Wilmington Messenger*, November 8, 1898.

159 **"It was this"** Henry Litchfield West, "The Race War in North Carolina," *Forum*, January 1899, 579–581.

159 **Even as white** Kirk, "A Statement of Facts," 2–3. McDuffie, "Politics in Wilmington," 654.

159 **In Washington, a** *Wilmington Messenger*, November 6, 1898.

160 **"There has never"** *Morning Post*, Raleigh, N.C., September 13, 1898.

160 **A committee of** *Evening Star*, Washington, D.C., November 2, 1898.

160 **The *Wilmington Messenger*** *Wilmington Messenger*, November 8, 1898.

160 **"the most remarkable"** *Evening Star*, Washington, D.C., November 8, 1898.

160 **"never look a"** *Wilmington Messenger*, November 8, 1898.

160 **For the city's** West, "The Race War in North Carolina," 581.

161 **They were drilled** *Evening Star*, Washington, D.C., November 8, 1898.

161 **"Shoot him down"** *Atlanta Constitution*, November 8, 1898. Prather, *We Have Taken a City*, 102.

161 **On board was** *Wilmington Messenger*, November 8, 1898.

161 **Inside, in the** Prather, *We Have Taken a City*, 105.

Twenty-Three: A Pitiful Condition

162 **"Proud Caucasians one"** *Wilmington Messenger*, November 8, 1898.

163 **Red Shirts paraded** Prather, *We Have Taken a City*, 102.

163 **"Pistols were held"** Kirk, "A Statement of Facts," 5.

163 **"There is no"** *Evening Star*, Washington, D.C., November 8, 1898.

163 **"frightened into"** Keith, *Memories*, 109.

163 **By the** *Washington Evening Star*, Washington, D.C., November 8, 1898.

164 **Fifty Red Shirts** *Union-Republican*, Winston-Salem, N.C., March 15, 1900.

165 **Finally convinced that** Hayden, *The Wilmington Rebellion*, 20. McDuffie, "Politics in Wilmington," 665–666. Umfleet, *A Day of Blood*, 218.

165 **"May God be"** Interview with Milo A. Manly by Professor Charles Hardy III, September 11, 1984.

165 **Strange was also** Susan Taylor Block, *Temple of Our Fathers: St. James Church 1729–2004* (Wilmington, N.C.: Artspeaks, 2004), 115, 118.

165 **According to Clawson** Clawson, "The Wilmington Race Riot in 1898," 7–8.

166 **"The outfit of"** *Wilmington Messenger*, November 10, 1898.

166 **The wagon lurched** Carrie Sadgwar Manly, letter to sons, January 14, 1954. Milo Manly interview by Charles Hardy III, September 11, 1984. (Manly family lore has offered several versions of Alex Manly's escape from Wilmington. I rely here on the accounts provided by Carrie Sadgwar Manly and by her son Milo A. Manly. Carrie Manly indicated in a series of letters to her sons in 1954 that her account came directly from her husband. It contained at least one contradiction: Carrie Manly wrote that Frank Manly had escaped the city with his brother. But Frank told a Washington newspaper that he was still at the *Daily Record* the morning of the riot and fled the city later that day. Milo Manly did not provide a source for the account he related during his 1984 interview with Professor Charles Hardy III. But he indicated that it had been passed down by family members, and he mentioned several conversations with his father on other matters. Milo Manly said the man who gave his father the password and money was a German grocer who had befriended Alex Manly, but he did not provide the grocer's name.)

Twenty-Four: Retribution in History

167 **The mayor had** McDuffie, "Politics in Wilmington," 664.

168 **This was in** Ibid., 667. Contested Election Case, 331–341. *Morning Star*, Wilmington, N.C., November 12, 1898. Hayden, *The Wilmington Rebellion*, 18.

169 **"they constantly carry"** Contested Election Case, 246.

169 **"I want to"** *Atlanta Constitution*, November 5, 8, 9, 1898.

170 **Lee wrote that** *Baltimore Sun* article, reprinted in *Wilmington Messenger*, November 18, 1898.

170 **"After being out"** Cronly, *Account of the Race Riot*, 6.

171 **The *Messenger*, which** *Wilmington Messenger*, November 9, 1898.

171 **The reporters assured** *Evening Star*, Washington, D.C., November 9, 1898.

171 **"The whites were"** *New York Times*, November 9, 1898.

172 **In fact, the** *News and Observer*, November 10, 1898.

172 **"The governor took"** *Wilmington Messenger*, November 10, 1898. *New Berne Journal*, November 10, 1898. Prather, "The Red Shirt Movement in North Carolina," 179.

172 **He looked ridiculous** Douglas Carl Abrams, "A Progressive-Conservative Duel: The 1920 Democratic Gubernatorial Primaries in North Carolina," *North Carolina Historical Review* 55, no. 4 (October 1978): 426–427.

172 **Some had been** *Wilmington Messenger*, November 10, 1898.

173 **"Bring him out!"** Prather, *We Have Taken a City*, 103–104.

173 **One drunken man** *Wilmington Messenger*, November 10, 1898.

173 **The next day** Ibid.

173 **The governor stormed** Crow and Durden, *Maverick Republican*, 134.

Twenty-Five: The Forbearance of All White Men

174 OUR STATE REDEEMED *Wilmington Messenger*, November 9, 1898.

174 OLD NORTH STATE *Atlanta Constitution*, November 9, 1898.

174 WHITE SUPREMACY RECEIVES *News and Observer*, November 9, 1898.

174 **In a matter of months** Wooley, "Race and Politics," 344.

175 **"And I am"** *News and Observer*, November 15, 1898.

175 **"The Game Is"** *News and Observer*, November 10, 1898.

175 **"the Little Giant"** Cash, "Jehovah of the Tar Heels," 313.

175 **Democrats now held** McDuffie, "Politics in Wilmington," 670.

175 **Roger Moore, the** *Wilmington Morning Star*, November 12, 1898.

176 **"A full attendance"** *Wilmington Messenger*, November 9, 1898.

176 **"I had never"** Rountree, "Memorandum of My Personal Recollection," 10.

176 **Inside, he encountered** Alfred Moore Waddell, "The Story of the Wilmington, N.C., Race Riot," *Collier's Weekly*, November 26, 1898. *Wilmington Messenger*, November 10, 1898.

177 **They were newspaper** *Wilmington Messenger*, November 10, 1898.

177 **Beside him, their** *Wilmington Morning Star*, November 10, 1898.

178 **But if the** *Wilmington Morning Star*, November 10, 1898. *Wilmington Messenger*, November 10, 1898. *Wilmington Evening Dispatch*, November 9, 1898. *News and Observer*, November 10, 1898.

178 **There were cries** Prather, *We Have Taken a City*, 109. *Wilmington Messenger*, November 10, 1898.

178 **"That ain't no"** *Wilmington Messenger*, November 10, 1898.

178 **They wanted Wilmington's** Prather, *We Have Taken a City*, 109.

178 **"Well, then, Wilmington"** Hayden, *The Wilmington Rebellion*, 23. *Wilmington Messenger*, November 10, 1898.

179 **"The pot needs"** *Wilmington Morning Star*, November 10, 1898. Hayden, *The Wilmington Rebellion*, 22.

179 **"It is the sense"** *Wilmington Messenger*, November 10, 1898. *Wilmington Morning Star*, November 10, 1898.

179 **The Colonel purposely** Rountree, "Memorandum of My Personal Recollection," 12.

179 **"Flushed with victory"** West, "Race War in North Carolina," 583.

180 **Armond W. Scott** Alfred M. Waddell Papers, Southern Historical Collection, University of North Carolina at Chapel Hill. *Wilmington Daily Star*, November 8 and 10, 1898.

180 **Waddell and others** Umfleet, *A Day of Blood*, 219.

181 **"The following named"** *Wilmington Messenger*, November 10, 1898. *Wilmington Morning Star*, November 10, 1898. Waddell Papers.

181 **The Red Shirts** *Indianapolis Freeman*, December 3, 1898.

181 **They arrived carrying** West, "Race War in North Carolina," 584.

182 **"Stern and determined"** *Wilmington Messenger*, November 19, 1898.

182 **He merely read** Prather, *We Have Taken a City*, 111. West, "Race War in North Carolina," 584.

182 **"We don't want"** McDuffie, "Politics in Wilmington," 683.

183 **Waddell ignored him** Prather, *We Have Taken a City*, 111.

183 **The next morning** *Wilmington Morning Star*, November 10, 1898.

184 **Armond had graduated** Riot Commission Report, 277.

184 **"disregard the first"** *Morning Star*, Wilmington, September 20, 1898.

184 **"We, the colored"** Waddell Papers.

185 **He deposited the** McDuffie, "Politics in Wilmington," 686.

185 **The gathering broke** Ibid., 687.

BOOK THREE: LINE OF FIRE

Twenty-Six: What Have We Done?

189 **Waddell had been** McDuffie, "Politics in Wilmington," 694.

189 **The next day's** *Wilmington Messenger*, November 11, 1898.

190 **"Every man brought"** Ibid.

190 **He had given** McDuffie, "Politics in Wilmington," 694.

191 **Colonel Taylor instructed** Minutes of the Organizational Meeting, Wilmington Light Infantry.

191 **He ordered them** Ibid. McDuffie, "Politics in Wilmington," 694–695.

192 **Many of the** *Wilmington Messenger*, November 11, 1898. Hayden, *The Wilmington Rebellion*, 22. McDuffie, "Politics in Wilmington," 695.

192   **They later made** *Evening Times*, Washington, D.C., November 22, 1898.

193   **"Situation here serious"** Colonel Walker Taylor, *Reports on the Riots at Wilmington*, Adjutant-General, State of North Carolina, November 22, 1898, document No. 9, 29.

193   **Some of the** Hayden, *The Wilmington Rebellion*, 26.

193   **With just a** Contested Election Case, 364.

194   **Broken furniture and** Prather, *We Have Taken a City*, 113.

194   **Other men ripped** Hayden, *The Wilmington Rebellion*, 26.

194   **Soon embers from** *Washington Evening Star*, November 10, 1898.

194   **Someone sounded an** Ibid., 27. *Wilmington Messenger*, November 11, 1898. *Washington Evening Star*, November 10, 1898.

195   **The bottom floor** Prather, *We Have Taken a City*, 113. Hayden, *The Wilmington Rebellion*, 27. *Wilmington Evening Dispatch*, November 10, 1898.

195   **"Now let us"** Waddell, "The Story," *Collier's Weekly*.

196   **The wives of** Rountree, "Memorandum of My Personal Recollection," 14. Prather, *We Have Taken a City*, 117. McDuffie, "Politics in Wilmington," 708.

196   **"They are going"** Prather, *We Have Taken a City*, 116.

198   **It was "a fool"** Rountree, "Memorandum of My Personal Recollection," 13–14.

198   **He warned that** James H. Cowan, "The Wilmington Race Riot," manuscript, New Hanover County Public Library, Wilmington, N.C. deRossett, *Pictorial and Historical New Hanover County*, 30. Hayden, *The Wilmington Rebellion*, 35.

199   **"It was little"** Minutes of the Organizational Meeting, Wilmington Light Infantry.

199   **The news seemed** Rountree, "Memorandum of My Personal Recollection," 15.

Twenty-Seven: Situation Serious

200   **Though Brooklyn was** Kirk, "A Statement of Facts," 9.

200   **From streetcar windows** Prather, *We Have Taken a City*, 122.

201   **Other men ran** Contested Election Case, 341–343. Prather, *We Have Taken a City*, 119. *Wilmington Evening Dispatch*, November 10, 1898. *Morning Star*, Wilmington, November 11, 1898. *Wilmington Messenger*, November 11, 1898. Hayden, *The Wilmington Rebellion*, 24–26.

201   **"Kill the niggers!"** Prather, *We Have Taken A City*, 171.

202   **"They're fighting over"** Hayden, *The Wilmington Rebellion*, 10. McDuffie, "Politics is Wilmington," 713.

202   **"Gunfire rattled all"** Clawson, "The Wilmington Race Riot in 1898," 6.

202 A correspondent for *Collier's Weekly* reported *Collier's Weekly*, November 26, 1898.

203 Fourteen bleeding men *Wilmington Messenger*, November 11, 1898.

203 The hospital was *Washington Post*, November 14, 1898.

203 "All except the" Dr. R. E. Zachary, "Gun-Shot Wounds—with Report of a Case of Gun-Shot Wound of Stomach," from *Transactions of the Medical Society of the State of North Carolina, Forty-Sixth Annual Meeting, Held at Asheville, N.C.* (Charlotte, N.C.: Observer Printing and Publishing House, 1899), 134.

203 "it appeared impossible" *Wilmington Messenger*, November 11, 1898. Clawson, "The Wilmington Race Riot in 1898," 5.

204 He toppled over Prather, *We Have Taken a City*, 120.

204 One of the *Wilmington Messenger*, November 11, 1898.

204 Armed guards were McDuffie, "Politics in Wilmington," 714.

204 Along the riverfront *Wilmington Messenger*, November 11, 1898.

204 "The governor directs" Report of the Commanding Officer, Public Documents, 28–32.

205 The governor's adjutant Ibid., 30.

205 The Maxton militia *Wilmington Messenger*, November 13, 1898.

205 "I need two" Report of the Commanding Officer, Public Documents, 30. *News and Observer*, November 11, 1898.

205 "Can bring fifty" *Wilmington Messenger*, November 12, 1898.

205 They grabbed their *Wilmington Messenger*, November 11, 1898.

205 But because of McDuffie, "Politics in Wilmington," 719. Contested Election Case, 344.

206 Before they left Clawson, "The Wilmington Race Riot in 1898," 7. Riot Commission Report, 146.

206 The naval commander Report of the Commanding Officer, Public Documents, 28.

206 The Naval Reserves Ibid., 29–32. Riot Commission Report, 137.

207 A correspondent for *Washington Evening Star*, November 10, 1898.

207 "Your action ordering" Report of the Commanding Officer, Public Documents, 31.

207 Between them, the McDuffie, "Politics in Wilmington," 718.

208 "So they said" Minutes of the Organizational Meeting, Wilmington Light Infantry, 10. Prather, *We Have Taken a City*, 118–119.

208 "As Captain MacRae's" Hayden, *The Wilmington Rebellion*, 34

208 The column stopped Minutes of the Organizational Meeting, Wilmington Light Infantry, 2.

208 "Boys I want" Ibid., 3.

208 **"several negroes lying"** Rountree, "Memorandum of My Personal Recollection," 16.

208 **By some accounts** Riot Commission Report, 145.

209 **White witnesses later** Edmonds, *The Negro and Fusion Politics*, 169. Prather, *We Have Taken a City*, 125.

209 **But another man** Prather, *We Have Taken a City*, 125–126.

209 **"They never saw"** *Wilmington Messenger*, November 11, 1898. Edmonds, *The Negro and Fusion Politics*, 169. Minutes of Organizational Meeting, Wilmington Light Infantry, 21.

210 **White housewives walked** Umfleet, *A Day of Blood*, 125–126. Hayden, *The Wilmington Rebellion*, 42.

211 **"The little white"** Kirk, "A Statement of Facts," 10–12.

211 **At Tenth and** Harry Hayden, "White Supremacy or Black Supremacy in The Wilmington Rebellion," typewritten manuscript, 1951, North Carolina Room, New Hanover County Public Library, Wilmington, N.C.

211 **When she offered** Minutes of Organizational Meeting Wilmington Light Infantry, 15. Hayden, *The Wilmington Rebellion*, 42.

211 **The Red Shirts** June Nash, "The Cost of Violence," *Journal of Black Studies*, 4, no. 2 (December 1973): 167.

211 **They finally set** Cronly, *Account of the Race Riot*, 4.

213 **On the fourth** *Wilmington Messenger*, May 29, 1904, reprinted from the *Charlotte Observer*. Prather, *We Have Taken a City*, 115, 131–132.

214 **"It was really"** Clawson, "The Wilmington Race Riot."

214 **As the flying** McDuffie, "Politics in Wilmington," 718.

214 **They found no** Ibid., 718. Minutes of Organizational Meeting, Wilmington Light Infantry, 6.

215 **"The mob took"** Kirk, "A Statement of Facts," 11–12.

215 **After waiting in** McDuffie, "Politics in Wilmington," 719.

215 **"When we tu'nd"** *Collier's Weekly*, November 26, 1898.

216 **"The poor creature"** Cronly, *Account of the Race Riot*, 4.

216 **But Maunder and** Minutes of the Organizational Meeting, Wilmington Light Infantry, 4.

216 **He was dead** Clawson, "The Wilmington Race Riot in 1898," 6. McDuffie, "Politics in Wilmington," 716. Report of the Commanding Officer, Public Documents, 29–30.

216 **James Sprunt and** *Morning Star*, Wilmington, November 13, 1898. *Wilmington Messenger*, November 13, 1898.

217 **Now, as he again** Cronly, *Account of the Race Riot*, 4.

217 **But Father Dennen** McDuffie, "Politics in Wilmington," 721.

217 **The soldiers responded** Cronly, *Account of the Race Riot*, 4.

218 **"For this was"** Ibid., 1.

218 **He had been** *Wilmington Messenger*, November 11, 1898. *Morning Star*, Wilmington, November 12, 1898.

218 **He died later** *Wilmington Messenger*, November 13, 1898.

218 **His body was** Hayden, *The Wilmington Rebellion*, 32. Umfleet, *A Day of Blood*, 119. Nash, "The Cost of Violence," 168.

218 **White witnesses said he had fired** *Wilmington Messenger*, November 14, 1898.

218 **White witnesses said he had pointed** *Wilmington Evening Dispatch*, November 11, 1898.

218 **Another was shot** Ibid.

218 **A black man was shot** *News and Observer*, November 12, 1898.

218 **A black man was killed** Ibid.

218 **A member of** McDuffie, "Politics in Wilmington," 738. Hayden, "White Supremacy or Black Supremacy."

219 **Another Red Shirt** McDuffie, "Politics in Wilmington," 738.

219 **A Red Shirt said** Hayden, "The Wilmington Rebellion," 32.

219 **The city's newspapers** Hayden, *The Wilmington Rebellion*, 31–32. Umfleet, *A Day of Blood*, 119.

Twenty-Eight: Strictly According to Law

220 **Black corpses were** Umfleet, *A Day of Blood*, 115. *Wilmington Messenger*, November 11, 1898.

221 **Reluctantly, he agreed** Hayden, *The Wilmington Rebellion*, 36.

221 **"a lot of"** Contested Election Case, 364.

222 **The two men** McDuffie, "Politics in Wilmington," 698.

222 **Eight white supremacists** *Wilmington Messenger*, November 11, 1898. Rountree, "Memorandum of My Personal Recollection," 17–18. McDuffie, "Politics in Wilmington," 699–700.

222 **There was no** *Messenger*, November 11, 1898. McDuffie, "Politics in Wilmington," 700.

222 **"Simply, the old"** Waddell, "The Story," *Collier's Weekly*.

223 **Waddell led the** Contested Election Case, 364.

223 **A boycott mounted** Keith, *Memories*, 97–111.

223 **Waddell ordered Mayor** Prather, *We Have Taken a City*, 138. McDuffie, "Politics in Wilmington," 700. Rountree, "Memorandum of My Personal Recollection," 18.

224 **"They resigned in"** *New York Times*, November 11, 1898.

224 **Finally, Struthers swore** Manuscript Minutes, Board of Aldermen, Wilmington, N.C., November 10, 1898. North Carolina Department of Archives and History, Raleigh.

224 **In a matter** Thorne, *Hanover*, 9.

225 **"They are utterly"** Waddell, "The Story," *Collier's Weekly*.

225 **"No people have"** McDuffie, "Politics in Wilmington," 748.

225 **He told Rountree** Contested Election Case, 364.

225 **Parmele was sworn** *Wilmington Messenger*, November 11, 1898.

225 **It was generous** Umfleet, *A Day of Blood*, 121. Prather, *We Have Taken a City*, 146.

226 **But in the** Manuscript Minutes, Board of Alderman, Wilmington, N.C.

226 **The aldermen again** *Wilmington Messenger*, November 11, 1898.

227 **"Nominees of citizens"** Rountree, "Memorandum of My Personal Recollection," 18. *New York Times*, November 11, 1898. *Charlotte Observer*, November 11, 1898.

227 **Several Red Shirts** *Wilmington Messenger*, November 11, 1898.

227 **"Further trouble of"** *New York Times*, November 11, 1898.

Twenty-Nine: Marching from Death

229 **"It was a"** Kirk, "A Statement of Facts," 9.

229 **"In the woods"** *Collier's Weekly*, November 26, 1898.

230 **"They were frightened"** Cronly, *Account of the Race Riot*, 6.

230 **It included the** Hayden, *The Wilmington Rebellion*, 39. *Atlanta Constitution*, November 12, 1898.

230 **They assigned a** Prather, *We Have Taken a City*, 139.

231 **It is more** Ibid., 126. *Wilmington Messenger*, November 11, 1898.

232 **"I would like"** *Wilmington Evening Dispatch*, November 11, 1898. Prather, *We Have Taken a City*, 143.

232 **He went to** Prather, *We Have Taken a City*, 143. Hayden, "White Supremacy or Black Supremacy."

233 **He climbed aboard** *News and Observer*, November 13, 1898. *New York Times*, November 12, 1898. *Atlanta Constitution*, November 12, 1898. Hayden, *The Wilmington Rebellion*, 40.

234 **He and French** McDuffie, "Politics in Wilmington," 723–724.

Thirty: Not the Sort of Man We Want Here

235 **"I feel it"** *Wilmington Evening Dispatch*, November 11, 1898.

236 **As Henderson thanked** *Indianapolis Freeman*, December 3, 1898.

236 **They were devoutly** Sally Bettie Henderson diary, courtesy of Lisa Adams.

238   **The man turned** *Indianapolis Freeman*, December 3, 1898.

238   **Some whites spread** Hayden, *The Wilmington Rebellion*, 20–39. Cody, "After the Storm," 39. Prather, *We Have Taken a City*, 24, 140

239   **He rode in** Hayden, "White Supremacy or Black Supremacy." Minutes of the Organizational Meeting, Wilmington Light Infantry.

239   DESERVING NEGROES WILL *Wilmington Evening Dispatch*, November 11, 1898.

239   **"There are not many Tom Millers"** *Wilmington Messenger*, November 30, 1898.

239   **"take his departure"** *Wilmington Evening Dispatch*, November 10, 1898.

242   **He reached Petersburg** Kirk, "A Statement of Facts," 12–15.

243   **The white men** Dancy, *Sand Against the Wind*, 70.

243   **On the same** *Wilmington Messenger*, November 12, 1898.

244   **The captives were** *Wilmington Messenger*, November 11, 1898.

244   **The News and** *News and Observer*, November 12, 1898. Umfleet, *A Day of Blood*, 188.

244   **"All we saw"** Minutes of the Organizational Meeting, Wilmington Light Infantry, 15. *News and Observer*, November 12, 1898. *Wilmington Messenger*, November 12, 1898. McDuffie, "Politics in Wilmington," 724.

244   **"They are all"** *Indianapolis Freeman*, December 3, 1898.

245   **"He was of"** *Wilmington Messenger*, November 11, 1898.

245   **The next day's** Ibid.

Thirty-One: Justice Is Satisfied, Vengeance Is Cruel

247   **His soldiers surrounded** *Wilmington Messenger*, November 11, 1898.

247   **Waddell no longer** Manuscript Minutes, Board of Alderman, Wilmington, N.C.

247   **The mayor explained** J. Allan Taylor addenda to Hayden, *The Wilmington Rebellion*.

247   **He wanted to** Cowan, "The Wilmington Race Riot."

248   **Waddell, Moore, and** *Morning Star*, Wilmington, November 11, 1898. *Wilmington Messenger*, November 11, 1898. *News and Observer*, November 11, 27, 1898. Thorne, *Hanover*, 3–4. McDuffie, "Politics in Wilmington," 726–727.

248   **"The undersigned upon"** *Wilmington Messenger*, November 11, 1898.

249   **Some whites on** Prather, *We Have Taken a City*, 142. *Atlanta Constitution*, November 12, 1898.

249   **Separately, J. Allan** J. Allan Taylor addenda to Hayden, *The Wilmington Rebellion*.

249   **Before the train** Waddell, "The Story," *Collier's Weekly*. *News and Observer*, November 12, 1898. *Wilmington Messenger*, November 12, 1898.

249   **"The negroes are"** *New York Times*, November 12, 1898.

249   **Josephus Daniels's** *News News and Observer*, November 13, 1898.

250 **A handwritten sign** Prather, *We Have Taken a City*, 140–141. *Fayetteville Observer*, November 11, 1898.

250 **The city was** Contested Election Case, 365.

251 **The *Morning Star*** *Morning Star*, Wilmington, November 12, 1898.

251 **"None of that!"** Contested Election Case, 366

251 **They later gave** J. Allan Taylor addenda to Hayden, *The Wilmington Rebellion.*

252 **"He could not"** Minutes of the Organizational Meeting, Wilmington Light Infantry.

252 **He felt humiliated** Contested Election Case, 360–387.

252 **The soldiers shoved** *Morning Star*, Wilmington, November 15, 1898.

252 **Bunting and Gilbert** *News and Observer*, November 12, 1898. *Morning Star*, Wilmington, November 12, 1898.

253 **"the double purpose"** *Atlanta Constitution*, November 12, 1898. *Morning Star*, Wilmington, November 12, 1898. Report of the Commanding Officer, Public Documents, 29–32.

253 **Nonetheless, Sprunt told** *Morning Star*, Wilmington, November 13, 1898.

254 **"self-appointed vigilantes"** *New York Times*, November 12, 1898. McDuffie, "Politics in Wilmington," 731.

254 **Waddell singled out** *Wilmington Messenger*, November 11, 1898.

254 **Their task now** *Morning Star*, Wilmington, November 13, 1898.

255 **Henderson pulled down** *Indianapolis Freeman*, December 3, 1898.

255 **"A worse scared"** *Wilmington Messenger*, November 15, 1898.

256 **The two exiles** *Indianapolis Freeman*, December 3, 1898. *News and Observer*, November 12, 1898.

256 **"If he had"** McDuffie, "Politics in Wilmington," 749.

256 **"The comparatively few"** *Morning Star*, Wilmington, November 12, 1898.

Thirty-Two: Persons Unknown

257 **Some of the** Prather, *We Have Taken a City*, 133. Umfleet, *A Day of Blood*, 115. *Wilmington Messenger*, November 11, 1898.

257 **Other bodies, concealed** Riot Commission Report, I, 177–180.

258 **"Some were found"** Kirk, "A Statement of Facts," 10.

258 **"On the bare"** *News and Observer*, November 13, 1898.

258 **The inquest was** *Morning Star*, Wilmington, November 12, 1898. *Wilmington Messenger*, November 12, 1898.

258 **"This fact, perhaps"** *Atlanta Constitution*, November 12, 1898.

259 **A coroner's jury** *Wilmington Messenger*, November 15, 1898.

259 **In a court** Contested Election Case, 342–343.

260 "The said deceased" *Wilmington Messenger*, November 11, 12, 15, 16, 1898. *Morning Star*, Wilmington, November 13, 1898. *Atlanta Constitution*, November 12, 1898. *Wilmington Evening Dispatch*, November 12, 1898.

260 Russell turned the *Wilmington Messenger*, November 13, 1898.

260 "I do not" *Morning Star*, Wilmington, November 15, 1898.

261 The infantrymen and Prather, *We Have Taken a City*, 149.

261 The board of McDuffie, "Politics in Wilmington," 737.

261 Black children ran *Wilmington Messenger*, November 13, 1898.

261 "I believe the" Waddell, "The Story," *Collier's Weekly*.

261 A group of *Wilmington Messenger*, November 15, 1898. *Charlotte Observer*, November 17, 1898.

262 One headline read *Wilmington Messenger*, November 12, 15, 1898.

262 But hundreds more *Wilmington Messenger*, November 13, 15, 1898.

262 The Reverend James McDuffie, "Politics in Wilmington," 735.

262 Another prominent white Ibid., 734. *News and Observer*, November 13, 1898. *Morning Star*, Wilmington, November 15, 1898.

263 "We will give" *News and Observer*, November 15, 1898.

263 "[W]ho can quietly" Ibid.

263 On November 10 McDuffie, "Politics in Wilmington," 721.

264 Parmele also instructed *Wilmington Messenger*, November 15, 1898. *Charlotte Observer*, November 17, 1898.

264 "Be still, be" *Baltimore Sun* article, reprinted in *News and Observer*, November 15, 1898.

Thrity-Three: Better Get a Gun

265 Kingsbury complained to McDuffie, "Politics in Wilmington," 755.

265 "Never more shall" *Wilmington Messenger*, November 12, 1898.

265 "It was not" *Morning Star*, Wilmington, November 15, 1898.

266 "In this Wilmington" *News and Observer*, November 13, 1898.

266 "'After the election'" Ibid.

266 "All of this" *Wilmington Messenger*, November 15, 1898.

266 "Some negroes were" *Richmond Times*, November 22, 1898, reprinted in *Richmond Planet*, November 26, 1898.

267 "It's the most" Waddell, "The Story," *Collier's Weekly*.

268 "There has been" *Washington Post* article, reprinted in *News and Observer*, November 13, 1898.

268 "This is a" *Philadelphia Record* editorial, reprinted in *News and Observer*, November 16, 1898.

268 **"The 10th was"** *New York Journal* article, reprinted in *Indianapolis Freeman*, December 3, 1898.

269 **"It was a"** *Richmond Planet*, November 26, 1898.

269 **"The Governor of"** *Washington Bee*, November 12, 1898.

269 **"The shotgun and"** *Indianapolis Freeman*, December 3, 1898.

269 **The National Anti** *New York Times*, June 16, 1897.

269 **"The treatment of"** Prather, *We Have Taken a City*, 158. McDuffie, "Politics in Wilmington," 750–751.

270 **In Brooklyn, a** *Morning Post*, Raleigh, November 15, 1898.

270 **"condemning the white"** McDuffie, "Politics in Wilmington," 751.

270 THE MOST REMARKABLE *News and Observer*, November 16, 1898.

272 **"We will do"** *News and Observer*, November 15, 16, 1898. *North Carolinian*, Raleigh, November 17, 1898.

Thirty-Four: The Meanest Animals

273 **Some children and** Charles S. Morris. "The Wilmington Massacre," in Phillip S. Foner and Robert James Branham, *Lift Every Voice: African American Oratory, 1787–1900* (Tuscaloosa: University of Alabama Press, 1998), 875–878. Cody, "After the Storm," 66.

273 **"were in a"** *New York Times*, November 13, 1898.

273 **Others waited** Reaves, *Strength Through Struggle*, 282.

273 **Some bought tickets** Prather, *We Have Taken a City*, 147.

274 **". . . last week 150"** Cody, "After the Storm," 85.

274 **The Atlanta Constitution** *Atlanta Constitution*, November 12, 1898.

274 **Dancy put the** Cody, "After the Storm," 85.

274 **White real estate** *Wilmington Messenger*, December 4, 1898.

274 **"They will be"** *Morning Star*, Wilmington, November 13, 1898. Gilmore, *Gender and Jim Crow*, 222.

275 **Of course, the** *Wilmington Messenger*, November 19, 1898.

275 **"If the occurrences"** *Wilmington Messenger*, December 18, 1898.

275 **"Under the policy"** *Wilmington Messenger*, April 18, 1899.

275 **"to give to"** *Wilmington Messenger*, November 12, 1898.

276 **The all-black** Prather, *We Have Taken a City*, 144.

276 **The city's ten** Riot Commission Report, 190.

276 **The new board** *Wilmington Messenger*, November 19, 1898.

276 **The black men's gear** Riot Commission Report, 191.

276 **The aldermen fired** Ibid., 190–191. Prather, *We Have Taken a City*, 145–146.

276 **He was fired** McDuffie, "Politics in Wilmington," 770.

277 **A White Laborer's** Riot Commission Report, 217. *Wilmington Messenger*, February 7, 1899.

277 **White farmhands drifted** Umfleet, *A Day of Blood*, 144.

277 **In the first** Prather, *We Have Taken a City*, 146.

277 **A White Labor** Riot Commission Report, 144. *Wilmington Messenger*, February 21, 1899. Prather, *We Have Taken a City*, 146.

278 **The wage cuts** *Wilmington Messenger*, November 24, 1898. Riot Commission Report, 191.

278 **"It is proposed"** *Wilmington Messenger*, November 19, 1898.

278 **Some white employers** Riot Commission Report, 192.

278 **"glad that 'dark town'"** Umfleet, *A Day of Blood*, 124.

278 **"Wilmington, N.C., is"** *Indianapolis Freeman*, November 3, 1898.

279 **Newspapers published purported** *Morning Post*, Raleigh, November 15, 1898.

279 **"He seemed to"** Daniels, *Editor in Politics*, 309.

279 **He was rescued** *Morning Star*, Wilmington, November 13, 1898.

279 **A headline caught** Nash, "The Cost of Violence," 159

279 **She did not** Carrie Sadgwar Manly, letter to sons, January 14, 1954.

280 **He had made** *Literary Digest* 17 (November 26, 1898): 625.

280 **Black ministers in** Ibid.

280 **The *Wilmington Morning*** *Morning Star*, Wilmington, November 17, 1898.

280 **They began providing bodyguards** *Wilmington Messenger*, November 19, 1898.

281 **It was of** *Baltimore Sun*, November 14, 1898. *Morning Star*, Wilmington, November 15, 1898. *Wilmington Messenger*, November 15, 1898.

281 **"When the negro"** *Literary Digest* 17 (November 26, 1898): 625. *News and Observer*, November 16, 1898.

281 **"Any utterance of"** *New York World* article, reprinted in *Wilmington Messenger*, November 19, 1898.

283 **Prior to Manly's** *New York Times*, November 21, 1898.

283 **"The manhood of"** Gilmore, *Gender and Jim Crow*, 230.

283 **"They are the"** McDuffie, "Politics in Wilmington," 752.

283 **But rather than** Gilmore, *Gender and Jim Crow*, 230.

284 **Down to his** *Afro-American*, Washington, D.C., January 26, 1957.

284 **"It has been stated"** *Morning Star*, Wilmington, November 15, 1898.

Thirty-Five: Old Scores

285 **Before the steamer** *Morning Star*, Wilmington, November 12, 1898. *News and Observer*, November 12, 1898.

285 **He was met** *Morning Star*, Wilmington, November 12, 1898; November 15, 1898.

286 They decided to *Wilmington Evening Dispatch*, December 28, 1898.

286 They demanded federal *Morning Star*, Wilmington, November 15, 1898.

286 With no attribution, *Morning Post*, Raleigh, November 15, 1898.

286 Some American troops *News and Observer*, November 12, 1898.

287 An American general Robert W. Merry, *William McKinley, Architect of the American Century* (New York: Simon and Schuster, 2017), 345.

287 Asked about the Prather, *We Have Taken a City*, 151. Umfleet, *A Day of Blood*, 130.

287 But Alger emphasized *Charlotte Observer*, November 11, 1898.

287 The *Star* reporter *Evening Star*, Washington, D.C., November 11, 1898.

287 Questioned by Southern *New York Times*, November 13, 1898. *Morning Star*, Wilmington, November 13, 1898.

288 Russell feared for Christensen, *The Paradox of Tar Heel Politics*, 21.

288 He wrote to a colleague Crow and Durden, *Maverick Republican*, 135. Riot Commission Report, 181.

288 "Mrs. Russell has" Riot Commission Report, 181.

288 He wrote to a friend Crow and Durden, *Maverick Republican*, 136.

289 "The President listened" *New York Times*, November 12, 1898.

289 "We the undersigned" Prather, *We Have Taken a City*, 155.

291 "The laws of" National Archives Materials Relating to the 1898 Wilmington Race Riot, RG 60, General Records of the Department of Justice, Box 117A "Year Files," 1887–1904. File 17743-1898, transcribed August 2002.

291 "Daughter, I understand" J. Allan Taylor addenda, Hayden, *The Wilmington Rebellion.*

291 "Men with white" *Wilmington Messenger*, November 12, 1898.

291 "Don't do it" National Archives Materials Relating to the 1898 Wilmington Race Riot, RG 60, General Records of the Department of Justice, Box 117A "Year Files," 1887–1904. File 17743-1898, transcribed August 2002.

292 "Caskets should be" Hayden, *The Wilmington Rebellion*, 36. Umfleet, *A Day of Blood*, 239.

292 He was the Merry, *William McKinley*, 17.

292 His final promotion Ibid., 20–34.

292 In 1879, he Karl Rove, *The Triumph of William McKinley: Why the Election of 1896 Still Matters* (New York: Simon and Schuster, 2015), 54.

292 At the 1888 Ibid., 70.

292 McKinley later championed Ibid., 81.

292 During his run Ibid., 114.

292 "We have but" Ibid., 336.

293 He did not Benjamin R. Justesen, *George Henry White: An Even Chance in the Race of Life* (Baton Rouge: Louisiana State University Press, 2001), 251–252.

293 **Blacks served in** *New York Times*, October 27, 1897; April 16, 1903.

293 **McKinley did not.** *News and Observer*, January 1, 1899.

294 **"Are not these"** Prather, *We Have Taken a City*, 153. Umfleet, *A Day of Blood*, 240.

294 **He told Bernard** McDuffie, "Politics in Wilmington," 756–757. Umfleet, *A Day of Blood*, 131.

295 **"I will thank"** McDuffie, "Politics in Wilmington," 758.

295 **Boyd was a** William S. Powell, *Dictionary of North Carolina Biography, Vol. A–C* (Chapel Hill: University of North Carolina Press, 1979–1996), 202.

295 **A few years** *Wilmington Messenger*, December 8, 1898.

295 **They departed for** Umfleet, *A Day of Blood*, 131.

296 **"We did not"** *Morning Post*, Raleigh, December 18, 1898.

296 **He dismissed French** *Wilmington Messenger*, December 20, 1898.

296 **But Bunting feared** *Morning Post*, Raleigh, December 18, 1898. *Wilmington Messenger*, December 8, 1898.

297 **"The opinion prevails"** *Morning Post*, Raleigh, December 18, 1898. McDuffie, "Politics in Wilmington," 758.

297 **On December 17,** *Morning Post*, Raleigh, December 18, 1898.

298 **Bernard suggested the** McDuffie, "Politics in Wilmington," 759.

298 **"This Department is"** Ibid., 759–760.

299 **He realized that** Ibid.

299 **"When he realized"** Prather, *We Have Taken a City*, 159, citing author interview with Milo Manly, May 25, 1977.

300 **"I said I"** *Providence Journal* article, reprinted in the *Wilmington Messenger*, January 10, 1899.

Thirty-Six: The Grandfather Clause

301 **To provide a** Daniels, *Editor in Politics*, 324.

302 **To help identify** McDuffie, "Politics in Wilmington," 775–776.

302 **He received a** Ibid., 782.

302 **The US Supreme** *Williams v. Mississippi*, 170 U.S. 213 (1898).

302 **But white politicians** Umfleet, *A Day of Blood*, 157.

303 **Rountree explained that** Crow and Durden, *Maverick Republican*, 142.

303 **Republicans held only** McDuffie, "Politics in Wilmington," 789.

303 **"Do that and stop"** Ibid., 782.

303 **He shortchanged North** McDuffie, "Politics in Wilmington," 781–782. Gilmore, *Gender and Jim Crow*, 122–123. Edmonds, *The Negro and Fusion Politics*, 229.

303 **He was ignored** McDuffie, "Politics in Wilmington," 781–782.

304 **"blunt our aspirations"** McDuffie, "Politics in Wilmington," 782.

304 **On February 21** Umfleet, *A Day of Blood*, 138.

304 Confident that Democrats Gilmore, *Gender and Jim Crow*, 246.

304 The two men Daniels, *Editor in Politics*, 374.

304 He did not Ibid., 380.

305 He described his *News and Observer*, May 18, 1900.

305 "It does not" Daniels, *Editor in Politics*, 375. *News and Observer*, May 9, 1900.

306 IT HAS ELIMINATED *News and Observer*, May 10, 1900.

306 IT IS AN *News and Observer*, May 12, 1900.

307 IT WORKS TO *News and Observer*, May 13, 1900.

308 "What the amendment" *News and Observer*, May 16, 1900.

308 "I. Eliminating the Negro" *News and Observer*, May 18, 1900.

308 "Why should not" *News and Observer*, May 13, 1900.

Thirty-Seven: Leave It to the Whites

309 Among those candidates *Morning Star*, Wilmington, March 24, 1899. *Wilmington Messenger*, March 24, 1899.

310 Waddell cruised to *Wilmington Messenger*, March 11, 1899. Prather, *We Have Taken a City*, 178. Umfleet, *A Day of Blood*, 243.

310 "there aren't enough" Gilmore, *Gender and Jim Crow* 251.

310 Young white boys Reaves, *Strength Through Struggle*, 34–37.

310 Blacks marked the *Wilmington Messenger*, January 3, 1899. Umfleet, *A Day of Blood*, 164.

311 In 1885, a C. Vann Woodward, *The Strange Career of Jim Crow* (New York: Oxford University Press, 1966), 39.

311 The bill was Edmonds, *The Negro and Fusion Politics*, 189.

311 A white legislator Ibid., 192.

311 "nine times out" Daniels, *Editor in Politics*, 336.

311 Jim Crow laws *Wilmington Star-News*, July 11, 2015.

312 The board argued *Wilmington Messenger*, June 2, 1899.

312 A white judge Reaves, *Strength Through Struggle*, 268.

312 Russell went to McDuffie, "Politics in Wilmington," 795.

313 "They are helpless" Crow and Durden, *Maverick Republican*, 154.

313 During the white Umfleet, *A Day of Blood*, 138–139.

313 On the campaign Christensen, *The Paradox of Tar Heel Politics*, 29.

313 The Red Shirt *Charlotte Observer*, July 20, 1900.

314 "Then we shall" *News and Observer*, April 12, 1900. *Charlotte Observer*, April 12, 1900.

314 "We have ruled" McDuffie, "Politics in Wilmington," 793.

314 "Question: Will the" William Alexander Mabry, *The Negro in North Carolina, Politics Since Reconstruction* (New York: AMS Press, 1940), 68.

315 **With each burst** *Wilmington Messenger*, August 3, 1900.

315 **The suffrage amendment** Hanes Walton Jr., Sherman C. Puckett, and Donald R. Deskins, *The African-American Electorate: A Statistical History, Vol. 1* (Los Angeles: Sage Publications, 2012), 351.

315 **It somehow passed** Ibid., 349–351.

315 **In another Black** Eric Anderson, *Race and Politics in North Carolina, 1872–1901: The Black Second* (Baton Rouge: Louisiana State University Press, 1981), 304.

315 **In many counties** Ibid., 307.

315 **Some registrars used** Mabry, *The Negro in North Carolina*, 71.

315 **In the Black** Justesen, *George Henry White*, 309.

315 **By 1900, the** Walton et al., *The African-American Electorate*, 360.

316 **Not a single** Justesen, *George Henry White*, 296, 303.

316 **Officials reported that** Gilmore, *Gender and Jim Crow*, 257. Umfleet, *A Day of Blood*, 139

316 **The *Messenger* claimed** *Wilmington Messenger*, August 3, 1900.

316 **Charles Aycock won** Our Campaigns website, N.C. Governor 1900, at https://www.ourcampaigns.com/RaceDetail.html?RaceID =133655.

316 **In Halifax County** Anderson, *The Black Second*, 306.

316 **Just four years** McDuffie, "Politics in Wilmington," 798–800.

316 **The following January** *New York Times*, January 23, 1901. *News and Observer*, January 23, 1901.

316 **"The stench is"** Christensen, *The Paradox of Tar Heel Politics*, 30.

317 **For many white** *Wilmington Messenger*, August 3, 1900.

317 **Inspired by the** Woodward, *The Strange Career of Jim Crow*, 85.

317 **"And the very"** Christensen, *The Paradox of Tar Heel Politics*, 30.

Thirty-Eight: I Cannot Live in North Carolina and Be Treated Like a Man

318 **Miller endured a** Prather, *We Have Taken a City*, 161.

318 **"I have been"** Umfleet, *A Day of Blood*, 230–231.

319 **His family was** Ibid., 186.

320 **He slowly built** *Ebony*, September 1958. *Baltimore Afro-American*, May 18, 1935; January 26, 1957.

320 **In 1935, President Franklin** *Afro*, July 26, 1955.

320 **He built a** *Ebony*, September 1958. *Baltimore Afro-American*, May 18, 1935; January 26, 1957.

320 **When he died** *Jet*, November 10, 1960.

320 **"Wilmington did you"** Dancy, *Sand Against the Wind*, 69–70.

320 **"Had it not"** *Afro*, July 26, 1955.

320 **Henderson defended them** *Indianapolis Recorder*, June 25, 1932.

320 **Indianapolis established segregated** Cody, "After the Storm," 37.

320 **"long recognized as"** *Indianapolis Recorder*, June 25, 1932.

321 **"while their parents"** *Indianapolis Freeman*, December 3, 1899.

321 **"walks cheerfully to"** Lisa Adams address, University of North Carolina Wilmington, November 1998.

322 **The** *News and* Justesen, *George Henry White*, 238–240.

322 **"White justifies assaults"** *News and Observer*, February 2, 1900.

322 **"But it ought"** Justesen, *George Henry White*, 282–283.

322 **It was buried** Ibid., 278.

322 **"But most people"** *News and Observer*, May 26, 1900.

323 **"I cannot live"** *New York Times*, August 26, 1900.

323 **"And from this"** *News and Observer*, March 5, 1901.

324 **The two men** *The Twentieth Century Union League Directory: A Historical, Biographical and Statistical Study of Colored Washington*, Union League, Washington, D.C., January 1901, courtesy of Robert Wooley.

324 **Alex continued to** Cody, "After the Storm," 30–31.

324 **The couple rented** Prather, *We Have Taken a City*, 159.

324 **"I'd rather be"** Baker, *Following the Color Line*, 161.

324 **It was taken** Prather, *We Have Taken a City*, 163.

325 **It was later** Reaves, *Strength Through Struggle*, 312.

325 **He never moved** Umfleet, *A Day of Blood*, 184.

327 **He did not** *Providence Journal* article, reprinted in *Wilmington Messenger*, January 10, 1899. (In his speech, Manly mistakenly referred to Josh Halsey as Caleb Halsey.)

327 **He started to** *New York World* article, reprinted in *Wilmington Semi-Weekly Messenger*, November 22, 1898.

Epilogue

329 **M. Hoke Smith,** John Dittmer, *Black Georgia in the Progressive Era, 1900–1920* (Urbana: University of Illinois Press, 1977), 100. Timothy B. Tyson, "The Ghosts of 1898 Wilmington's Race Riot and the Rise of White Supremacy," *News and Observer*, Raleigh, November 17, 2006.

330 **The United States** United States Supreme Court, 238 U.S. 347 (1915).

330 **The number of** Christensen, *The Paradox of Tar Heel Politics*, 39.

330 **After black carpenter** John L. Godwin, *Black Wilmington and the North Carolina Way: Portrait of a Community in the Era of Civil Rights Protest* (Lanham, Md.: University Press of America, 2000), 255.

330 **Ten years later** *Wilmington Star-News,* May 22, 2013.

330 **Before the 1898** Riot Commission Report, 33. Edmonds, *The Negro and Fusion Politics,* 125.

331 **The rate continued** United States Census reports. Reaves, *Strength Through Struggle,* 395. Godwin, *Black Wilmington,* 20.

331 **In 1972, North** *New York Times,* November 29, 2018.

332 **But in 2013** United States Supreme Court, *Shelby County v. Holder,* 570 U.S. 529 (2013).

332 **"Now we can"** *Washington Post,* September 1, 2016.

333 **"impose cures for"** United States Court of Appeals for the Fourth Circuit, No. 16-1468.

333 **In December 2018** *News and Observer,* December 19, 2018.

333 **Yet Republicans won** *New York Times,* March 11, 2016.

333 **"race was the"** United States District Court for Middle District of North Carolina, No. 1:13-CV-00949. *News and Observer,* February 5, 2016.

333 **"through the predominant"** United States District Court for the Middle District of North Carolina, No. 1:15-cv-399.

334 **"the spontaneous and"** Waddell, *Some Memories of My Life,* 243.

334 **"the slough of"** Alfred M. Waddell Papers, Southern Historical Collection, University of North Carolina at Chapel Hill.

334 **"the results of"** Sprunt, *Chronicles of the Cape Fear,* 554–555.

334 **He sold the** Hayden, *Wilmington Rebellion,* 1–2, 4.

335 **He boasted of** Ibid., J. Allan Taylor postscript.

335 **"Though Aycock was"** Alex Mathews Arnett and Walter Clinton Jackson, *The Story of North Carolina* (Chapel Hill: University of North Carolina Press, 1933), 406–408.

335 **"To put an"** Sarah William Ashe and Orina Kidd Garber, *North Carolina for Boys and Girls* (Raleigh, N.C.: Alfred Williams and Company, 1940), 321–322.

336 **"A number of"** Thomas C. Parramore, *Carolina Quest* (Englewood Cliffs, N.J.: Prentice-Hall, Inc., 1949), 324

336 **"The *News* and"** Edmonds, *The Negro and Fusion Politics,* 141.

336 **"was distinctly a"** Hossfeld, *Narrative, Political Unconscious and Racial Violence in Wilmington, North Carolina,* 75–78.

337 **Among the black** Melton A. McLaurin, "Commemorating Wilmington's Racial Violence of 1898: From Individual to Collective Memory," *Southern Cultures* 6, no. 4 (Winter 2000).

337 **One white man** Ibid., 47.

337 **First published as** Rhonda Bellamy, ed., *Moving Forward Together: A Community Remembers 1898* (Wilmington, N.C.: 1898 Memorial Foundation, 1998), 65. *Wilmington Journal* at http://wilmingtonjournal.com/about-us-page/. African American Heritage Museum of Wilmington at http://www.aahfwilmington .org/aahmw_virtualexhibits_placemaking_4daily.html.

338 **Even so, the** McLaurin, "Commemorating Wilmington's Racial Violence," 49.

338 **Organizers also settled** Ibid., 47. Bellamy, *Moving Forward Together*, 6.

338 **Then he emphasized** McLaurin, "Commemorating Wilmington's Racial Violence," 51.

340 **"I think people"** Author interview with George Rountree III, Wilmington, N.C., June 5, 2018.

340 **"declare openly their"** Bellamy, *Moving Forward Together*, 65.

340 **"We have taken"** McLaurin, "Commemorating Wilmington's Racial Violence," 53.

341 **Based on a** Cody, "After the Storm."

342 **In addition, the** Riot Commission Report, 359–367.

342 **"the ability of"** Ibid., Findings and Introduction.

342 **"Wilmington's 1898 racial"** Bellamy, *Moving Forward Together*, 16.

343 **In 1995, the** *News and Observer*, company history at https://www.newsobserver .com/advertise/market-data/article10350698.html.

343 **The *Charlotte Observer*** *Editor and Publisher*, November 20, 2006.

344 **"someone we continue"** *News and Observer*, November 17, 2006.

344 **"If the paper"** *News and Observer*, opinion page.

344 **"We were never"** Daniels, *Editor in Politics*, 295–296.

344 **"In the perspective"** Ibid., 145.

344 **"The *News and*"** Ibid., 147.

344 **He glorified Red** Ibid., 285, 288.

346 **"I never read"** Author interview with Frank Daniels Jr., Raleigh, N.C., June 8, 2018.

346 **After years of** *Daily Tar Heel*, September 18, 1898.

346 **In 2018, the** *News and Observer*, October 3, 2018.

347 **"a pleasing duty"** "Names in Brick and Stone: Histories from UNC's Built Landscape—The Most Generous White Supremacist, Julian Shakespeare Carr," History/American Studies 671: Introduction to Public History, University of North Carolina at Chapel Hill, at http://unchistory.web.unc.edu/ building-narratives/julian-shakespeare-carr-carr-building/.

347 **The toppled statue** *News and Observer*, August 20, 25, 2018.

348 **"Armed white mob"** *News and Observer*, December 29, 2017. *Wilmington Star-News*, January 3, 2018. Michael Hill, Research Supervisor, N.C. Office of Archives and History, N.C. Department of Natural and Cultural Resources, Raleigh.

349 **And that's why** Author telephone interview with Faye Chaplin, August 16, 2018.

349 **Chaplin's grandmother—her** United States Census, 1900, District 0053, Ward 02, Guilford County, North Carolina.

350 **He had told** Carrie Sadgwar Manly, letter to sons, January 14, 1954.

350 **Alex's wife, Carrie** Fairview Cemetery, Lot 176, Grave 1, Willow Grove, Pa.

351 **"I wonder who"** Caroline Sadgwar Manly letter to sons, January 14, 1954.

352 **"If there's a"** Author telephone interview with Lewin Manly Jr., June 7, 2018.

BIBLIOGRAPHY

Anderson, Eric. *The Black Second: Race and Politics in North Carolina 1872–1901*. Baton Rouge: Louisiana State University Press, 1981.

Aptheker, Herbert. *American Negro Slave Revolts*. New York: Columbia University Press, 1943.

Arnett, Alex Mathews, and Walter Clinton Jackson. *The Story of North Carolina*. Chapel Hill: University of North Carolina Press, 1933.

Ashe, Samuel A., Stephen B. Weeks, and Charles L. Van Noppen. *Biographical History of North Carolina, Vol. VIII*. Greensboro, NC: Charles Van Noppen, 1917.

Ashe, Sara William, and Orina Kidd Garber. *North Carolina for Boys and Girls*. Raleigh, NC: Alfred Williams & Company, 1940.

Atkinson, Val. *Southern Racial Politics & North Carolina's Black Vote*. Victoria, BC: Trafford Publishing, 2007.

Baker, Ray Stannard. *Following the Color Line: An Account of Negro Citizenship in the American Democracy*. Williamstown, MA: Corner House Publishers, 1973.

Beeby, James M. *Revolt of the Tar Heels: The North Carolina Populist Movement, 1890–1901*. Jackson: University Press of Mississippi, 2008.

Bellamy, John D. *Memoirs of an Octogenarian*. Charlotte: Observer Printing House, 1942.

Bellamy, Rhonda, ed. *Moving Forward Together: A Community Remembers 1898*. Wilmington: 1898 Memorial Foundation, 2008.

Blackmon, Douglas A. *Slavery by Another Name: The Re-Enslavement of Black People in America from the Civil War to World War II*. New York: Doubleday, 2008.

Block, Susan Taylor. *Temple of Our Fathers: St. James Church 1729–2004*. Wilmington: Artspeaks, 2004.

Browning, Judkin. *Shifting Loyalties: The Union Occupation of Eastern North Carolina*, Chapel Hill: University of North Carolina Press, 2011.

Cecelski, David S. *The Fire of Freedom: Abraham Galloway & the Slaves' Civil War*. Chapel Hill: University of North Carolina Press, 2012.

Cecelski, David S., and Timothy B. Tyson, eds. *Democracy Betrayed. The Wilmington Race Riot of 1898 and Its Legacy*. Chapel Hill: University of North Carolina Press, 1998.

Chestnutt, Charles W. *The Marrow of Tradition*. Boston: Houghton, Mifflin, 1901.

Christensen, Rob. *The Paradox of Tar Heel Politics: The Personalities, Elections, and Events That Shaped Modern North Carolina*. Chapel Hill: University of North Carolina Press, 2008.

Craig, Lee A. *Josephus Daniels: His Life & Times*. Chapel Hill: University of North Carolina Press, 2013.

Crow, Jeffrey J., and Robert E. Duren. *Maverick Republican in the Old North State: A Political Biography of Daniel L. Russell*. Baton Rouge: Louisiana State University Press, 1977.

Dancy, John C. *Sand Against the Wind: The Memoirs of John C. Dancy*. Detroit: Wayne State University Press, 1966.

Daniels, Josephus. *Editor in Politics*. Chapel Hill: University of North Carolina Press, 1941.

————. *Tar Heel Editor*. Chapel Hill: University of North Carolina Press, 1939.

Dawes, Charles G. *A Journal of the McKinley Years*. Chicago: Lakeside Press, R.R. Donnelley & Sons Company, 1950.

Dennett, John Richard. *The South as It Is*. Tuscaloosa: University of Alabama Press, 2010.

deRosset, William Lord. *Pictorial and Historical New Hanover County and Wilmington, North Carolina, 1723–1938*. Wilmington: Author, 1938.

Dixon, Thomas. *The Leopard's Spots: A Romance of the White Man's Burden, 1865–1900*. New York: Doubleday, Page & Co., 1902.

Downs, Gregory P. *After Appomattox: Military Occupation and the Ends of War*. Cambridge: Harvard University Press, 2015.

Du Bois, W. E. Burghardt. *Black Reconstruction: An Essay Toward a History of the Past Which Black Folk Played in the Attempt to Reconstruct Democracy in America, 1860–1880*. New York: Russell & Russell, 1935.

Evans, William McKee. *Ballots and Fence Rails: Reconstruction of the Lower Cape Fear*. Athens: University of Georgia Press, 1995.

Foner, Eric. *Reconstruction—America's Unfinished Revolution, 1863–1877*. New York: Harper & Row, 1988.

————. *A Short History of Reconstruction, 1863–1877*. New York: Harper & Row, 1990.

Foner, Philip S. *The Voice of Black America: Major Speeches by Negroes in the United States, 1797–1973, Volume 1: 1797–1900*. New York: Capricorn Books, 1975.

Foner, Philip S., and Robert James Branham, eds. *Lift Every Voice: African American Oratory, 1787–1900*. Tuscaloosa: University of Alabama Press, 1998.

Gerard, Philip. *Cape Fear Rising*. Durham, NC: John F. Blair, 1994.

Gilmore, Glenda Elizabeth. *Gender and Jim Crow: Women and the Politics of White Supremacy in North Carolina, 1896–1920*. Chapel Hill: University of North Carolina Press, 1996.

Godwin, John L. *Black Wilmington and the North Carolina Way: Portrait of a Community in the Era of Civil Rights Protest*. Lanham, MD: University Press of America, 2000.

Goldfield, David R. *Cotton Fields and Skyscrapers: Southern City and Region, 1607–1980*. Baton Rouge: Louisiana State University Press, 1982.

Gray, Thomas R. *The Confessions of Nat Turner, the Leader of the Late Insurrection in Southampton, Va., as Fully and Voluntarily Made to Thomas. R. Gray*. Baltimore: Lucas and Deaver, 1831.

Hahn, Steven, Steven F. Miller, Susan E. O'Donovan, John C. Rodrigue, and Leslie S. Rowland, eds. *Freedom: A Documentary History of Emancipation, 1861–1867. Series 3: Volume 1, Land and Labor, 1865*. Chapel Hill: University of North Carolina Press, 2008.

Hamilton, J. G. de Roulhac. *Reconstruction in North Carolina*. Gloucester, MA: Peter Smith, 1964.

Horn, Stanley F. *Invisible Empire—The Story of the Ku Klux Klan, 1866–1871*. Montclair, NJ: Patterson Smith, 1969.

Hossfeld, Leslie H. *Narrative, Political Unconscious and Racial Violence in Wilmington, North Carolina*. New York: Routledge, 2005.

Howell, Andrew J. *The Book of Wilmington*. Published privately, 1930.

Justesen, Benjamin R. *George Henry White—An Even Chance in the Race of Life*. Baton Rouge: Louisiana State University Press, 2001.

Keech, William R. *The Impact of Negro Voting: The Role of the Vote in the Quest for Equality*. Chicago: Rand McNally & Company, 1968.

Keith, Benjamin F. *Memories*. Raleigh: Bynum Printing Company, 1922.

Kantrowitz, Stephen. *Ben Tillman & the Reconstruction of White Supremacy*. Chapel Hill: University of North Carolina Press, 2000.

Kousser, J. Morgan. *The Shaping of Southern Politics: Suffrage Restriction and the Establishment of the One-Party South, 1880–1910*. New Haven: Yale University Press, 1974.

Larsen, Lawrence H. *The Rise of the Urban South*. Lexington: University Press of Kentucky, 1985.

———. *The Urban South: A History*. Lexington: University Press of Kentucky, 1990.

Lefler, Hugh Talmadge, and Albert Ray Newsome. *North Carolina: The History of a Southern State*. Chapel Hill: University of North Carolina Press, 1963.

Mabry, William Alexander. *The Negro in North Carolina, Politics Since Reconstruction*. New York: AMS Press, 1940.

Mann, Albert W. *History of the Forty-Fifth Regiment, Massachusetts Volunteer Militia.* Boston: Wallace Spooner, 1908.

Merry, Robert W. *President McKinley: Architect of the American Century.* New York: Simon & Schuster, 2017.

Morrison, Joseph L. *Josephus Daniels, the Small-d Democrat.* Chapel Hill: University of North Carolina Press, 1966.

Olmsted, Frederick Law. *A Journey in the Seaboard Slave States, with Remarks on Their Economy.* London: Sampson Low, Son, and Co., 1856.

Parker, Bowdoin S. *History of Edward W. Kinsley Post No. 113.* Norwood, MA: Norwood Press, 1913.

Parramore, Thomas C. *Carolina Quest.* Englewood Cliffs, NJ: Prentice-Hall, Inc., 1978.

Permen, Michael. *Struggle for Mastery: Disenfranchisement in the South, 1888–1908.* Chapel Hill: University of North Carolina Press, 2001.

Powell, William S. *Dictionary of North Carolina Biography.* Chapel Hill: University of North Carolina Press, 1979–1996.

———. *Encyclopedia of North Carolina.* Chapel Hill: University of North Carolina Press, 2006.

———. *North Carolina: The Story of a Special Kind of Place.* Chapel Hill: Algonquin Books, 1987.

Prather, H. Leon, Sr. *We Have Taken a City: Wilmington Racial Massacre and Coup of 1898.* Wilmington, NC: NU World Enterprises Inc., 1984.

Reaves, William M. *Strength Through Struggle: The Chronological and Historical Record of the African-American Community in Wilmington, North Carolina, 1865–1950,* ed. Beverly Tetterton. Wilmington: New Hanover County Public Library, 1998.

Rippy, James Fred. *F. M. Simmons: Statesman of the New South, Memoirs and Addresses.* Durham: Duke University Press, 1936.

Rove, Karl. *The Triumph of William McKinley: Why the Election of 1896 Still Matters.* New York: Simon & Schuster Paperbacks, 2015.

Simkins, Francis Butler. *Pitchfork Ben Tillman, South Carolinian.* Baton Rouge: Louisiana State University Press, 1944.

Singletary, Otis. *Negro Militia and Reconstruction.* Austin: University of Texas Press, 1957.

Smith, Jessie Carney, and Carrell Peterson Horton, eds. *Historical Statistics of Black America—Media to Vital Statistics.* New York: Gale Research, Inc., 1995.

Sprunt, James. *Chronicles of the Cape Fear River, 1660–1916.* Raleigh: Edwards and Broughton Printing Company, 1916.

Still, William. *Still's Underground Rail Road Records, with a Life of the Author. Narrating the Hardships, Hairbreadth Escapes and Death Struggles of the Slaves in Their Efforts for Freedom.*

Together with Sketches of Some of the Eminent Friends of Freedom, and Most Liberal Aiders and Advisers of the Road. Philadelphia: William Still, 1886.

Thorne, Jack. *Hanover: Or Persecution of the Lowly, Story of the Wilmington Massacre.* Published by M. C. L. Hill. Copy in the North Carolina Collection, University of North Carolina at Chapel Hill. [Jack Thorne is the pen name of David Bryant Fulton.]

Tocqueville, Alexis de. *Democracy in America*, trans. George Lawrence. New York: HarperCollins, 2006.

Umfleet, LeRae Sikes. *A Day of Blood: The 1898 Wilmington Race Riot.* Raleigh: North Carolina Office of Archives and History, 2009.

Waddell, Alfred Moore. *Some Memories of My Life.* Raleigh: Edwards & Broughton Printing Company, 1908.

Walton, Hanes, Jr., Sherman C. Puckett, and Donald R. Deskins Jr. *The African American Electorate: A Statistical History.* Thousand Oaks, CA: Sage Publications, Inc., 2012.

Watson, Alan D. *Wilmington, North Carolina, to 1861.* Jefferson, NC: McFarland & Company, Inc., 2003.

Woodward, C. Vann. *Origins of the New South, 1877–1913.* Baton Rouge: Louisiana State University Press, 1951.

———. *The Strange Career of Jim Crow.* New York: Oxford University Press, 1966.

UNPUBLISHED MEMOIRS/DIARIES

Ashley, Moses. Diary of Moses Ashley, September 1831. M. A. Curtis Papers, Southern Historical Collection, University of North Carolina at Chapel Hill.

Bellamy, Ellen Douglas. "Back with the Tide: Memoirs of Ellen Douglas Bellamy." North Carolina Room, New Hanover County Public Library.

Clawson, Thomas W. "The Wilmington Race Riot in 1898, Recollections and Memories." Louis T. Moore Collection, North Carolina Department of Archives and History, Raleigh.

Cowan, James H. "The Wilmington Race Riot." Louis T. Moore Collection, New Hanover County Public Library, Wilmington.

Cronly, Jane. "Account of the Race Riot." Cronly Family Papers, Duke University, Durham.

Hayden, Harry. "White Supremacy or Black Supremacy in the Wilmington Rebellion." New Hanover County Public Library, Wilmington, NC.

———. "The Wilmington Rebellion." New Hanover County Public Library, Wilmington, NC.

Henderson, Sally Bettie. Excerpts from Sally Bettie Henderson diary, courtesy of Lisa Adams.

Kinsley, Edward W. "A Little More About Mary Ann Starkey" and "Ordered to Newbern." Edward W. Kinsley Papers, University of Massachusetts Amherst Libraries.

————. "Raising the First North Carolina Colored Regiment," Edward W. Kinsley Papers, University of Massachusetts Amherst Libraries.

Rountree, George. "Memorandum of My Personal Recollections of Election of 1898." Henry G. Connor Papers, Southern Historical Collection, University of North Carolina at Chapel Hill.

ARTICLES

Abrams, Douglas Carl. "A Progressive-Conservative Duel: The 1920 Democratic Gubernatorial Primaries in North Carolina," *North Carolina Historical Review* 55, no. 4 (October 1978).

Bond, James E. "Ratification of the Fourteenth Amendment in North Carolina," *Wake Forest Law Review* 89 (1984).

Cash, W. J. "Jehovah of the Tar Heels," *American Mercury*, July 1929.

Gatewood, Willard B., Jr. "North Carolina's Negro Regiment in the Spanish-American War." *North Carolina Historical Review* 48, no. 4 (October 1971).

Gunter, Linda. "Abraham H. Galloway (First Black Elector)," *Quarterly of the North Carolina Afro-American Historical & Genealogical Society*, 5, no. 3 (Fall 1990).

Kirk, J. Allen, Rev. "A Statement of Facts Concerning the Bloody Riot in Wilmington, N.C. Of Interest to Every Citizen of the United States." Electronic Edition, *Documenting the American South*, University of North Carolina at Chapel Hill.

McLaurin, Melton Alonza. "Commemorating Wilmington's Racial Violence of 1898: From Individual to Collective Memory," *Southern Cultures* 6, no. 4 (Winter 2000).

Morris, Charles Edward. "Panic and Reprisal: Reaction in North Carolina to the Nat Turner Insurrection, 1831," *North Carolina Historical Review* 62, no. 1 (January 1985).

Nash, June. "The Cost of Violence," *Journal of Black Studies* 4, no. 2 (December 1973).

Olsen, Otto H. "The Ku Klux Klan: A Study in Reconstruction Politics and Propaganda," *North Carolina Historical Review* 39, no. 3 (July 1962).

Prather, H. Leon. "The Red Shirt Movement in North Carolina 1898–1900. *Journal of Negro History* 62, no. 2 (April 1977).

Reid, Richard. "Raising the African Brigade: Early Black Recruitment in Civil War North Carolina," *North Carolina Historical Review* 70, no. 3 (July 1963).

Rogoff, Leonard. "A Tale of Two Cities: Race, Riots, and Religion in New Bern and Wilmington, North Carolina, 1898," *Southern Jewish History* 14 (2011).

Steelman, Bennett L. "Black, White and Gray: The Wilmington Race Riot in Fact and Legend," *North Carolina Literary Review* 2, no. 1 (Spring 1994).

Tyson, Timothy B. "The Ghosts of 1898. Wilmington's Race Riot and the Rise of White Supremacy," *News and Observer*, Raleigh, November 17, 2006.

Watson, Richard L., Jr. "Furnifold Simmons: 'Jehovah of the Tar Heels?'" *North Carolina Historical Review* 44, no. 2 (April 1967).

Williams, Rachel Marie-Crane. "A War in Black and White: The Cartoons of Norman Ethre Jennett & the North Carolina Election of 1898," *Southern Cultures* 19, no. 2 (Summer 2013).

West, Henry Litchfield. "The Race War in North Carolina," *Forum*, January 1899.

Zachary, R. E., MD. "Gun-Shot Wounds—with Report of a Case of Gun-Shot Wound of Stomach," in *Transactions of the Medical Society of the State of North Carolina, Forty-Sixth Annual Meeting, Held at Asheville, NC* (Charlotte: Observer Printing and Publishing House, 1899).

THESES AND DISSERTATIONS

Appell, Stephen Maro. "The Fight for the Constitutional Convention: The Development of Political Parties in North Carolina During 1867." Master's thesis, University of North Carolina at Chapel Hill, 1969.

Cody, Sue Ann. "After the Storm: Racial Violence in Wilmington, North Carolina, and Its Consequences for African Americans, 1898–1905." Master's thesis, University of North Carolina at Wilmington, 2000.

Higuchi, Hayumi. "White Supremacy on the Cape Fear: The Wilmington Affair of 1898." Master's thesis, University of North Carolina at Chapel Hill, 1980.

Hodges, Alexander Weld. "Josephus Daniels, Precipitator of the Wilmington Race Riot of 1898." Honors essay, University of North Carolina at Chapel Hill, 1990.

McDuffie, Jerome A. "Politics in Wilmington and New Hanover County, North Carolina, 1865–1900: The Genesis of a Race Riot." Ph.D. dissertation, Kent State University, 1979.

Rivers, Patrick. "Unholy Minglings: Miscegenation and the 'White Revolution' in Wilmington, North Carolina, 1898–1900." Master's thesis, University of North Carolina at Chapel Hill, 1992.

Underwood, Evelyn. "The Struggle for White Supremacy in North Carolina." Master's thesis, University of North Carolina at Chapel Hill, 1943.

Wooley, Robert Howard. "Race and Politics: The Evolution of the White Supremacy Campaign of 1898 in North Carolina." Ph.D dissertation, University of North Carolina at Chapel Hill, 1977.

GOVERNMENT PUBLICATIONS
AND DOCUMENTS

1898 Wilmington Race Riot Report. 1898 Wilmington Race Riot Commission. LeRae Umfleet, Principal Researcher. Research Branch, Office of Archives and History, North Carolina Department of Cultural Resources. May 31, 2006.

Contested Election Case of Oliver H. Dockery v. John D. Bellamy from the Sixth Congressional District of the State of North Carolina. Washington, DC: Government Printing Office, 1899.

Manuscript minutes, Wilmington Board of Aldermen, November 10, 1898. North Carolina Department of Archives and History, Raleigh.

National Archives Materials Relating to the 1898 Wilmington Race Riot. RG 60, General Records of the Department of Justice, Box 1117A "Year Files," 1887–1904. File 17743-1898. Transcribed August 2000, North Carolina Department of Archives and History. New Hanover County Public Library.

Report of the Commanding Officer of Naval Battalion, Headquarters, N.C. Naval Battalion, Wilmington, NC, December 1, 1898, Reports on the Riot at Wilmington, November 22, 1898, North Carolina Public Documents, Document No. 9, North Carolina Collection, University of North Carolina at Chapel Hill.

Colonel Walker Taylor, *Reports on the Riots at Wilmington*, Adjutant-General, State of North Carolina, November 22, 1898, documents Nos. 9, 29.

Report of the Joint Committee on Reconstruction, at the First Session Thirty-Ninth Congress. Washington, DC: Government Printing Office, 1866.

Robert Dale Owen, James McKaye, and Samuel G. Howe, "Preliminary Report of the American Freedmen's Inquiry Commission," to E. M. Stanton, June 30, 1863, in US Adjutant General's Office, Negro in the Military Service, roll 2, vol. 3, pt. 1: Military Employment 1863.

Report of the Joint Select Committee to Inquire into the Condition of Affairs in the Late Insurrectionary States, Made to the Two Houses of Congress February 19, 1872. Washington, DC: Government Printing Office, 1872.

United States Congress and O. M. Enyart, *A Biographical Congressional Dictionary, 1774–1903*. Washington, DC: Government Printing Office, 1903.

The Democratic Hand Book, 1898. Prepared by the State Democratic Executive Committee of the North Carolina Democratic Party, State Executive Committee, Raleigh: Edwards and Broughton, 1898. North Carolina Collection, University of North Carolina at Chapel Hill.

NEWSPAPERS AND PERIODICALS

Afro Magazine
Afro-American, Washington, DC
American Mercury
Atlanta *Constitution*
Baltimore *Afro-American*
Baltimore *Sun*
Brooklyn *Daily Eagle*
Cape-Fear Recorder
Charleston *News and Courier*
Charlotte *Daily Observer*
Charlotte *Observer*
Chicago *Record*
Collier's Weekly
Daily Dispatch, Wilmington, NC
Daily Journal, Wilmington, NC
Daily Record, Wilmington, NC
Douglass' Monthly
Ebony
Editor & Publisher
Evening Dispatch, Wilmington, NC
Evening Star, Washington, DC
Evening Times, Washington, DC
Fayetteville *Observer*
The Freeman, Indianapolis
Indianapolis *Recorder*
Jet
Literary Digest
Morning Post, Raleigh, NC
Morning Star, Wilmington, NC

New Berne Daily Journal
New National Era
News and Observer, Raleigh, NC
New York *Journal*
New York *Times*
New York *World*
North Carolina Times
Philadelphia *Inquirer*
Philadelphia *Record*
Philadelphia *Times*
Providence *Journal*
Raleigh *Gazette*
Raleigh *Register*
Raleigh *Sentinel*
The Record, Wilmington, NC
Richmond *Times*
Semi-Weekly Messenger, Wilmington, NC
Union-Republican, Winston-Salem, NC
Washington *Bee*
Washington *Post*
Washington *Times*
Weekly Standard, Raleigh, NC
Wilmington *Daily Post*
Wilmington *Evening Dispatch*
Wilmington *Herald*
Wilmington *Messenger*
Wilmington *Post*
Wilmington *Star*
Wilmington *Star-News*

MISCELLANEOUS

Minutes of the Organizational Meeting of the Association of Members of the Wilmington Light Infantry, Lumina, Wrightsville Beach, December 14, 1905. North Carolina Collection, Wilson Library, University of North Carolina at Chapel Hill.

BIBLIOGRAPHY

"The 1898 Wilmington Racial Violence and Its Legacy: A Symposium." Video
recording. William Madison Randall Library, University of North Carolina
at Wilmington.
Carrie Sadgwar Manly, letters to sons Milo A. Manly and Lewin Manly, La Mott,
PA, November 10, 1953; November 19, 1953; December 3, 1953; January 14,
1954; February 19, 1954; May 18, 1955; November 19, 1955. Alex L. Manly
Papers, East Carolina University Manuscript Collection, Collection 0065.
Galloway Family Files, New Hanover County Public Library, Wilmington, NC.
Lisa Adams, great-granddaughter of William Everett Henderson, address to sym-
posium, University of North Carolina, Wilmington, November 1998.

INTERVIEWS

Milo Manly interview by H. Leon Prather Sr., May 25, 1977, Philadelphia, cited
in H. Leon Prather Sr., *We Have Taken a City, Wilmington Racial Massacre and Coup
of 1898*. Wilmington: Associated University Presses, NU World Enterprises
Inc., 1984.
Milo Manly interview by Charles Hardy III, September 11, 1984. Cited in Prather,
We Have Taken a City.
Transcript of interviews with Felice Sadgwar and Mabel Sadgwar Manly, by Beverly
Smalls, Wilmington, May 14, 1985. Cape Fear Museum, Wilmington.
Author telephone interview, Lisa Adams, January 12, 2016.
Author telephone interview, Faye Chaplin, August 16, 2018.
Author interview, Frank A. Daniels Jr., Raleigh, NC, June 8, 2018.
Author telephone interview, Lewin Manly, Jr., June 7, 2018.
Author interview, George Rountree III, Wilmington, June 5, 2018.

INDEX

"Address Delivered to the Colored People by Their Request, An" (Waddell), 13–16
African Americans. *See* black middle class of Wilmington; black soldiers; black working class of Wilmington; *individual names*
African Methodist Episcopal (AME) Zion Church, 58
Afro-American Council, 293
Afro-American Sentinel (Omaha), 283
Alabama, grandfather clause in, 317, 330
Aldridge, Bessie, 77–78
Aldridge, John, 77
Alger, Russell A., 287
American Baptist Publication Society, xvii
American Missionary Association, 47
American Tobacco Company, 288
Ames, John Worthington, 6–7
Anglo-African (New York), 31
artisans, black men as, 24–25, 37
Associated Press, 284
Atlanta Constitution
    on black exodus from Wilmington, 274
    on election day events, 169, 174
    fear about black men stoked by, 81
    Felton's letter to, 83–89
    on inquest, 258
Aycock, Charles
    Bernard and, 294
    as North Carolina governor, 301, 304, 313–314, 316–317, 335
    textbooks about, 335–336

Baltimore Sun
    on election day events, 169–170
    gun purchase attempt by black men and, 104

Manly's interview, 280–282
on return of blacks after November 10th, 264
banishment campaign, 246–256, 273–284
    attempt to return hiding families, 253–254
    Bunting and, 249–250, 251–252
    Dancy and, 242–243, 282–283
    French and, 231–233
    Gilbert and, 252
    Henderson and, 235–238, 255–256
    imprisonment of captives and lynching threats, 243–245, 246–249
    initial response by black middle class, 228–229
    Kirk and, 239–242
    Melton and, 250–252
    Miller and, 238–239
    Moore (William A.) and, 240–241
    North Carolina report on (2000), 342
    Peamon and, 230–231
    Scott and, 233–234, 284
    Wright and, 254–256
Basset, John Spencer, 256
Beadle, W. H. H., 7, 9
Bell, C. D., 259, 283
Bell, I. J., 245, 248–249
Bell, Salem J., 245, 248–249
Bellamy, John D., 105, 164, 169, 178, 321
Bernard, Claude M., xi, 294–299
"Big 6" ("Remember the 6") campaign, 114–120, 206, 221, 230–234, 296. *See also* Chadbourn, William H.; Foster, Flavel W.; French, George Z. "Gizzard"; Melton, John; Wright, Silas P.

Bizell (black man), 203
"Black Belt" region, defined, 66
Black Codes, 35–36
black middle class of Wilmington, 52–62. *See also* banishment campaign
   Committee of Colored Citizens, identification of, 180–185
   Dancy and, 57–59
   Emancipation Day and, 52–53, 310
   Henderson and, 55–57, 59
   intimidation of, by Light Infantry, 105–106
   Plessy v. Ferguson (1896) and, 53–54
   prior to riot of November 10, 1898, xvii–xviii
   on Spanish-American War, 111–113
   whites' fear of rebellion and, 49, 59–60
   Wilmington government overthrow of aldermen, 220–227
   Wilmington infrastructure (1898) and, 54–55
black newspapers. *See Raleigh Gazette*; *Record/Daily Record* (Wilmington); *Richmond Planet*; *Washington Bee*; *Wilmington Journal*
black soldiers
   pay disparity of white and black soldiers, 9, 28–29
   Russell's Black Battalion, 111–112
   in Spanish-American War, 321
   United States Colored Troops, 3–4, 9, 16, 27–30
Blackwell, Calvin S., 185
black working class of Wilmington
   after November 10th, 228–229, 275–278
   competition between Irish and, 149
   pay disparity of white and black brakemen and, 38
   population statistics, Wilmington after November 10th, 273–278
   return of, after November 10th events, 261–264
   Sprunt Cotton Compress, xix, 109, 191–199, 200, 211–213
   voting ultimatums by employers of, 128–131
   Wilmington population after November 10th, 273–278
board of aldermen
   black workers fired by, 276–278

election of August 1900, 309
overthrow of, 220–227
"Wilmington Declaration of Independence" and resignation demanded of, 178–185
Bourke, Charles Francis, 229
Boyd, James E., 295
Boylan, George, 244
Bragg, Braxton, 3, 4, 99, 124, 143, 150
Bray, Nicholas, 29–30
Brooklyn Baptist Church, 262–263
Brooklyn (Wilmington neighborhood), xviii–xxii, 195, 199. *See also* November 10, 1898, events
Brown, George W., 279
Bruce, John Edward, 283
Brunjes' Saloon, xix, xxi, 200
Bryant, Ari, 244–245, 248–249
Bunting, Robert H., xi, 249–250, 251–252, 285–286
Burkhimer, Buck, 217
Butler, Marion, 132

Cajuns, grandfather clause and, 306–308
"cake and wine" influence, 6
Cameron, Rebecca, 148
Cape Fear. *See also* Wilmington, North Carolina
   militia of, 121
   Piney Woods, 18–21, 116–117
   plantations of, 6
"Cape Fear carcasses" (Waddell's speech), 144–148, 160–161, 247
Cape-Fear Recorder, 61–62
Cape Fear Steam Fire Engine, 145, 194–195, 276
carpetbaggers, 39, 92, 115–116, 231, 263
Carr, Julian Shakespeare, 70, 291, 346–347
cartoons (Jennett)
   inception of, 76
   Red Shirt depiction by, 135
   of Russell, 81
   of Simmons on election day results, 175
Cash, W. J., 72, 175
Cassidey, Jesse J., 141
Central Baptist Church, 229, 239, 264
Chadbourn, William H., 114, 118, 197
Chadwick, N. B., 202
Chamber of Commerce (Wilmington), 277

Chaplin, Faye, 348–349
Charleston News and Courier, 266
Charleston Post and Courier, 258
Charlotte Observer
　apology issues by, 343
　fear about black men stoked by, 81
　on McKinley, 287
Chrysanthemum Committee, 271
citizenship. *See* Fourteenth Amendment
civil rights movement, Republican and Demo-
　cratic Parties on, 331
Civil War
　Fort Fisher, 3–4, 18, 110
　Forts Johnston and Caswell, 12
　Forty-First North Carolina Regiment, 100
　McKinley on, 292
　police abuse of blacks, 7–8
　prisoner of war camps (Confederate), 4
　Reconstruction following, 5, 13, 33–34,
　　38, 66–68
　Rountree family during, 339–340
　"Silent Sam" (monument), 346–347
　Unionists and secession opposition, 69–70
　Waddell's role during, 11–13
　Wilmington's losses during, xviii, 3–10
Clawson, Thomas. *See also Messenger*
　(Wilmington)
　during Brooklyn violence, 202, 203
　Hoe press sale to Manly by, 48, 50, 99, 165
　on November 10th events, 214
　overview, xi
　on Vigilance Committee plans, 99
　"Wilmington Declaration of Independence"
　　and, 177
Clayton, Eva, 330
Cleaves, Mary, 69
Cleveland, Grover, 56, 122–123
Clinton, Mildred, 259–260
Cody, Sue Ann, 341
Coleman, W. C., 49–50
Collier's Weekly
　on black exodus following November 10th
　　violence, 229
　on Brooklyn violence, 202, 216
　reaction to November 10th events,
　　266–267
　Waddell's account in, 195

colored troops. *See* United States Colored
　Troops
Committee of Colored Citizens'
　identification of, 180–185
　Jacobs as member of, 257
　misinformation about response of,
　　189–191
　Reardon as member of, 244
　response letter of, 197, 210, 235
　Scott's banishment, 233–234
Committee of Twenty-Five, 220–227,
　262–263
Company K, United States Volunteers of
　Wilmington Light Infantry, 107–108,
　110–113
Confederate Home Guards, 17–21
Conservative Party, 44, 66. *See also* Democratic
　Party
Constitutional Union Guards, 32–33. *See also*
　Ku Klux Klan
Convivial Cornet Band, 52
Cooper Union meeting, 270, 280
Cordill, C. C., 307
coup events (Wilmington), 220–227
Cronly, Jane, 100–101, 170, 216, 217–218,
　230
Cronly, Michael, 170
Crosby, John, 303
"crying nigger," 69
Cuba, Spanish-American War and, 107–108.
　See also Spanish-American War
Curtis, Moses Ashley, 60–61

D. C. Evans Funeral Home, 258
Daily Journal (Wilmington), 35–36, 39
Daily Record. See Record/Daily Record
　(Wilmington)
Dancy, Florence, 242–243
Dancy, John, Jr. (son), 58
Dancy, John C.
　banishment of, 242–243
　on black exodus from Wilmington, 274
　characterization of, 57–59
　excluded from Committee of Colored
　　Citizens, 180
　as federal customs collector, 57
　Harrison's appointment of, xvii

Dancy, John C. (*continued*)
late life of, 320
Manly confronted by, 94–95
in New York, 282–283
overview, xi
as port customs collector, 105
Russell's Black Battalion and, 112
on State Negro Council, 303–304
as "trimmer," 94
Daniels, Frank A., Jr. (grandson), 345–346
Daniels, Jonathan (son), 69
Daniels, Josephus. *See also News and Observer*
Aycock and, 294
biography and characterization, 69–72
on election results, 174
fear stoked about black rapists by, 77–82
grandfather clause and, 301–308
on gun purchase attempt by black men,
102–103
late life and legacy of, 341–346
on Manly's editorial, 92–93
on Manly's escape, 279
News and Observer financing, 291
North Carolinian, weekly paper of, 79
political career of, following 1900,
316–317
Pritchard and, 133
as public printer, 71
reaction to November 10th events and, 270
on *Record*, 85
on Red Shirt rally, 150
Russell and, 111
on Spanish-American War, 108
White and, 321–322
White Supremacy Campaign inception and,
65–69, 74–76
Daniels, Josephus "Jody" (father), 69–70
Daniels, Mary Cleaves (mother), 69
Dave (enslaved man), 60
Davis, George J., 203
Davis, W. J., 168
Democracy in America (Tocqueville), 59
Democratic Party. *See also* Red Shirts
characterization of, post-Civil War, 65–67
civil rights movement and changes in, 331
Conservative Party roots of, 44, 66
Democratic Party Hand Book (Simmons), 75–76

on grandfather clause, 304–308
Great White Man's Rally and Basket Picnic
in, 121–126
Red Shirts vigilante militia, 72
"Remember the 6" campaign of, 114–120,
206, 221, 230–234, 296
Taylor (Walker) and, 110
Vigilance Committee of, 97–101
White Government Unions of, 96–97
White Supremacy Campaign inception,
65–76
Dempsey, Frank, 276
Dennen, Christopher, 217
DeRosset family, 139–140
Douglass, Frederick, 22, 46
Dowling, Mike. *See also* Red Shirts
employment of, after November 10th, 276,
277–278
lynching plan of, 164–165
November 10th events and, 192
overview, xi
Red Shirt violence incited by, 149–150
Duke, Benjamin, 288
Dunston, A. S., 264

Easom, Inez, 338
Eden, Richard, 25–26
Edmonds, Helen, 336
education
Aycock as "Education Governor," 317
Galloway's demand for schools, 28, 29
literacy and, xviii, 22–23, 29, 54, 301–308
textbooks about November 10th events,
335–336
Waddell on segregated schools, 15
Washington on, 58
of white child laborers, 277
in Wilmington (1897), 54
Edwards, Elias, 18, 19
1898 Memorial Park, 342
election day events (November 8, 1898),
167–173
election results, 174–175
"fighting whiskey" and liquor ban, 150,
157–158, 164, 224
liquor ban, 164, 224
Manly's escape, 164–166

November 10th events (*See* November 10, 1898, events)
  rebellion fears and, 169–170
  Russell's voting on, 170–173
  stuffed ballot boxes, 167–168
  voting, 162–164
  "Wilmington Declaration of Independence," 175–185
Emancipation Proclamation
  civil liberties and, 5
  Emancipation Day, 52–53, 310
  Simmons on, 73
  voting rights and, 31
Emlen, John Thompson, 325
Evening Dispatch, 231, 239
Excelsior (French's plantation), 117

Fayetteville, Great White Man's Rally and Basket Picnic in, 121–126
federal investigation
  appeals to McKinley, 286–294, 299–300
  Bunting, Gilbert, and Melton in Washington, 286, 289
  Griggs on, 134, 286–287, 294–299
  Phoenix, South Carolina, events and, 288–289
  Spanish-American War as priority over, 286–287, 293, 300
Felton, Isaac K., 28, 30
Felton, Rebecca Latimer, 83–89, 280, 281–282
Felton, W. H., 83
Fifteenth Amendment
  congressional election (Wilmington) and, 46
  grandfather clause and, 302, 312
  ratification of, 38
  Redeemers and, 66
  Supreme Court on grandfather clauses, 330
Fifth Ward Cornet Band, 121, 122
First Baptist Church, 185
First North Carolina Colored Regiment of Volunteers, 27–30
First Presbyterian Church, 155, 263, 340
Fishblate, Silas, 107, 127, 176, 178–179, 192, 222
Fort Caswell, 12

Fort Fisher, 3–4, 18, 110
Fort Johnston, 12
Fortune, Junius, 174–175
Fortune, T. Thomas, 270
Forum magazine (New York), 158–159
Foster, Flavel W., 114, 296
Fourteenth Amendment
  gerrymandering and, 333
  grandfather clause and, 312
  ratification of, 35, 38
  Redeemers and, 66
Fowler, John J., 250, 309–310
freedmen
  "An Address Delivered to the Colored People by Their Request" (Waddell), 13–16
  Freedmen's Bureau (Wilmington), 6, 7, 9
  whites' fear of rebellion by, 49, 59–60, 98–101
  Wilmington at end of Civil War and, 5, 36–38
Freemasons, 45, 232–233
French, George Z. "Gizzard"
  banishment of, 231–233
  black deputies fired by, 156
  federal investigation and, 295–296
  French's Agricultural Lime, 117
  Naval Reserves and Brooklyn violence, 206
  November 10th events and, 198
  overview, xi
  "Remember the 6" campaign against, 114, 116–120, 206
Fulton, Abram, 168
Furlong, John, 230, 238, 243–245
Fusionists. *See also* banishment campaign
  banishment of, 230–234
  black vote encouraged by, 129, 156
  defined, 67
  election day (November 9) results, 174–175
  fired white workers, after November 10th, 276
  Pritchard and, 132–134
  "Remember the 6" ("Big 6") campaign, 114–120, 206, 221, 230, 296
  resignation demanded of aldermen, 197
  Wilmington government overthrow and, 220–227

Galloway, Abraham, 22–30, 31–40
  biographical information, 22–27
  death of, 45–46
  as delegate to North Carolina constitutional
    convention, 39–40
  elected to state senate, 44
  oratory skills of, 22–23, 32, 34–35
  overview, xi
  on suffrage, 31, 39
  United States Colored Troops raised by,
    27–30
  Wilmington election (1868) and, 42–43
  Wilmington KKK and, 32–34
Galloway, John Wesley, 24
George (black worker), 278
Georgia, grandfather clause in, 317, 330
Gilbert, Charles H., 252, 285–286, 289
Giles, I. N., 280
Goins, John, 180–185, 192
Graham, T. A., 130–131
grandfather clause, 301–308, 312–316,
    321–323, 330. See also voting and voter
    suppression
Grand United Order of Love and Charity, 193,
    261
Grant, Ulysses S., 295
Great White Man's Rally and Basket Picnic,
    121–126
Green, Elijah, 180–185
Gregory, John L., 218
Gregory, Sam, 203–204
Gregory Normal School (Wilmington), 85, 86
Griggs, John W., 134, 286–287, 294–299, 321
Grit, Bruce, 283
Group Six, 99, 103–104, 109

Halsey, Josh, 216, 217–218, 259–260, 327
Hamburg (South Carolina) Massacre (1876),
    123–124
Hamilton, Robert, 31
Hampton Normal and Agricultural Institute,
    47
Hankins, Hester, 24
Hankins, Marsden Milton, 24–25
Harris, Briscoe, 264
Harrison, Benjamin, xvii, 56, 57, 293
Harriss, William, 168

Hawley, Joseph, 6
Hayden, Harry, 334
Helms, Jesse, 331
Henderson, Sally Bettie (wife), 56, 236–237,
    255
Henderson, William E.
  banishment of, 235–238, 255–256
  characterization of, 55–57, 59
  as Committee of Colored Citizens member,
    180–185
  as deputy tax collector (Statesville, NC), 56
  on election threats, 154–155, 163
  late life of, 320–321
  overview, xi
  Russell's Black Battalion and, 112
Hilton Bridge, 215
Hoge, Peyton, 155, 262–263
Holden, William Woods, 13
Hose Reel Co. No. 3, 276
Huffman, Samuel E., 290
Humphrey, L. W., 73–74

Indianapolis Freeman
  on banishment campaign, 244
  on Manly, 279
  reaction to November 10th events and, 269
interracial marriage. See also sex and race
  Black Codes on, 35
  Dancy's comments and, 58
  Wilmington Journal on, 40
Invisible Empire of the Ku Klux Klan, 33
Ireland, Charles H., 102
Irish workers, black workers' competition with,
    149
Italian immigrants, grandfather clause and, 306

Jacobi, J. N., 127–128
Jacobs, David, 180–185, 257–258
James, Thomas C., xi, 191, 193, 208
Jennett, Norman E., 76, 81, 135, 175
Jervay, Robert S., 337
Jim Crow laws, 15, 311–318
Jim (enslaved man), 60
Johnson, Andrew, 5–6, 13
Jones, Frankye Manly, 337
Jones, Harry, 289–290
Jonkonnu (African holiday), 310

Justice Department
  Griggs and, 134, 286–287, 294–299, 321
  on voter ID laws, 332

Keith, Benjamin, 163, 223
Kenan, William Rand, Jr., 346
Kenan, William Rand, Sr., 57, 105–106, 346
Kingsbury, Theodore B., 265
Kinsley, Edward W., xi, 27–30
Kirk, J. Allen, xi, 163, 210, 215, 229,
    239–242, 258
Kitchin, Claude, 137
Kramer, James W., 262–263
Kruttschnitt, E. B., 305
Ku Klux Klan
  Boyd and, 295
  clandestine code of conduct of, 33–34, 130
  election intimidation by (1868), 41–44
  Holden and, 13
  names for, 32–33
  riot of November 10, 1898 and, xviii–xxii
  Saunders and, 10
  textbooks about, 335–336
  voting suppression by, 40
  Waddell and, 140–141

Lamb, Albert, 168
Lee, Guy Carleton, 169, 264
Lee, John Wesley, 103
Lee, John William, 102–106
Lee, Robert E., 295
Lee, W. H., 182
Lincoln, Abraham
  Emancipation Proclamation, 5, 31, 52–53,
    73, 310
  Galloway and, 31–32
  Kinsley and, 27
Lindsay, Charles, 201
Lindsay, Norman, xx
literacy. See also education
  Galloway on, 22–23
  grandfather clause and, 301–308
  North Carolina law and black schools, 29
  rates of, prior to November 10th events,
    xviii
  Wilmington education (1897) and, 54
Lockamy, Aaron, xx–xxii, 201, 259

Lockey, Caleb B., 114
Louisiana, grandfather clause in, 302–308
Love, Owen F., xvi
Love and Charity Hall, 193, 261
Lydia (enslaved woman, Manly's grandmother),
    46
"lying out," 18
lynchings
  banishment campaign and threats of,
    243–245, 246–249
  Dowling's plans for, 164–165
  Felton's letter on, 83–89, 280, 281–282
  National Anti Mob-and-Lynch Law Asso-
    ciation, 269–270
  rape accusations and, 50–51
  White on anti-lynching law, 321–323

Macfarlane, Sam, 218, 264
MacRae, Donald, xi, 164–165, 176, 198–199,
    207–208, 224
MacRae, Hugh
  as alderman, 261
  banishment campaign and, 230–234,
    243–245, 249–250, 251
  election of August 1900, 309
  Hugh MacRae Park, 312
  overview, xii
  Secret Nine planning and, 98, 99, 209, 210
  Wilmington government overthrow and,
    222
MacRae, Hugh, II (grandson), 337
MacRae, Walter, 247
Manly, Alexander Lightfoot. See also Record/Daily
    Record (Wilmington)
  accounts of November 10th events,
    326–327
  biographical information, 46–48
  black vote encouraged by, 153–154, 157
  Dancy and, 57
  death threats to, 125, 136, 153, 164–166
  as deputy registrar of deeds, 85, 119–120,
    175, 183
  descendants of, 337
  editorial about Felton's letter, 83–89,
    90–95, 129
  engagement to Sadgwar by, 85–86
  escape from Wilmington by, 178, 182, 235

Manly, Alexander Lightfoot (*continued*)
  Great White Man's Rally and Basket Picnic
    and, 125–126
  Henderson's friendship with, 57
  late life and legacy of, 323–327, 347–348,
    349–352
  middle class status of, 85
  in New Jersey, 278–283, 299–300
  overview, xii
  Record inception and, 48–51
  search for, 285
  on voting intimidation of blacks, 128
  "Wilmington Declaration of Independence"
    and, 177–180, 182–185
Manly, Carrie Sadgwar (wife), xii, 85–86, 279,
  324, 350–351
Manly, Charles (North Carolina governor,
  1849–1851), 46–47
Manly, Corrine/Corina (mother), 47
Manly, Frank (brother)
  brother's editorial and, 89, 95
  death threats to, 153
  escape of, 192, 235
  November 10th events and, 192
  Record inception and, 47–48
  in Washington, DC, 324
  "Wilmington Declaration of Independence"
    threats, 182–185
Manly, Henry (brother), 48
Manly, Lewin, Jr. (grandson), 350, 351–352
Manly, Lewin, Sr. (son), 350, 351
Manly, Lewin (brother), 48
Manly, Milo (son), 48, 299
Manly, Samuel Trimetitus Grimes "Trim"
  (father), 47
Manning, Pierre, 225
Mason, Robert, 128–129
Masons, 45, 232–233
Maunder, J. F., 211, 216
Mayo, William, 202, 209
McAllister, M. H., 102–106
McClatchy newspaper chain, 343
McFallon, Samuel, 202
McGill, Neill, 18–21
McKinley, William. *See also* federal investigation
  biography and characterization of, 292
  blacks in administration of, 293

Carr and, 346
election violence warnings and, 159–160
federal investigation appeals to, 286–294,
  299–300
grandfather clause and, 312
petitioning of, 284
Pritchard's letter to, 132–134
McLaurin, Kenneth, 330
McMillan, John, 19, 20–21
McQueen, Joseph, Jr., 330
Meares, Iredell, 103
Melton, Augusta, 115
Melton, John
  banishment of, 250–252, 285–286
  November 10th events and, 193, 198
  Record office protected by black men, 91–92
  "Remember the 6" campaign against, 114,
    115–116
  on voting intimidation of blacks, 128
  Waddell and, 142–143
  in Washington, DC, 286, 289, 295
  "Wilmington Declaration of Independence"
    and resignation demanded of, 178–185
  Wilmington government overthrow and,
    220–227
Memorial Day, early celebrations of, 52–53
Messenger (Wilmington). *See also* Clawson,
    Thomas
  on banishment campaign, 239, 243,
    244–245, 255
  on black exodus from Wilmington, 275
  black voter suppression and, 129
  Clawson and *Record* inception, 48, 50
  on election (1898), 171, 172, 173, 174
  on election (1898), violence fears, 160
  on election (August 1900), 314–315, 316
  fear about black men stoked by, 81
  gun purchase attempt by black men and,
    103, 104
  on Manly's editorial, 93
  on November 10th events, 209, 214,
    261–262
  reaction to November 10th events, 265, 266
  on Vigilance Committee plans, 99
  on Waddell's speech, 145, 148
  "White Men of Wilmington" meeting,
    175–176

on white-only labor policy, 278
"Wilmington Declaration of Independence"
and, 177, 182
Metropolitan Trust Company, 180
militias. *See also* weapons
Clinton and Maxton militias, 205
federal status of, 198–199, 207–208
formation of county militia companies, 7
MacRae (Donald) and, 198–199
Naval Reserves, xxii
Red Shirts, 72
Vigilance Committee and, 98–101
whites' fear of black rebellion and, 61–62,
98–101
in Williamston, 152
Wilmington Light Infantry, xxi–xxii
Miller, Lula, 349
Miller, Thomas C.
banishment of, 238–239, 245, 248–259
as Committee of Colored Citizens member,
180–185
late life and legacy of, 318–319, 348–349
overview, xii
wealth of, 55
Ministerial Union, 93–94
Mississippi
Black Codes and, 35–36
literacy test and poll tax of, 302
Moore, Alfred, 12
Moore, Bernice C., 201–202, 206, 259
Moore, James, 33
Moore, Louis T., 336
Moore, Roger ("King Roger"), 33
Moore, Roger (KKK leader)
election intimidation by (1868), 41–44
election to Board of Commissioners, 175
November 10th events and, 190–192,
197–199, 210
overview, xii, 33
Red Shirt rally and, 149
Spanish-American War and, 108–109
Vigilance Committee and, 100
"Wilmington Declaration of Independence"
and, 185
Moore, William A., 240–241
Morehouse, Henry Lyman, 48
Morning Post (Raleigh), 286, 297

Morning Star (Wilmington)
on banishment campaign, 251
Felton's speech in, 84, 87–88
on inquest, 260
on Manly, 280
reaction to November 10th events, 265
on voting intimidation of blacks, 129
on "Wilmington Declaration of Independence," 183
Morrison, Cameron, 172
Morro Castle (whorehouse), 211
Morton, George L., 206–207
Mouzon, William, 201
Mt. Zion Afro-American AME, 264
Murchison, J. W., xvi

N. Jacobi Hardware Co., 127–128
Nash, Francis, 12
National Afro-American Council, 283
National Anti Mob-and-Lynch Law Associa-
tion, 269–270
Native Americans, classified as "colored," 56
Naval Reserves
banishment campaign and, 248–249, 253,
254
demobilization of, 260–261
Spanish-American War and, 110, 113
weapons of and election violence expecta-
tions of, xxii, 161
naval store trades, 36–37
Navy (US), Fort Fisher capture by, 3–4. *See also*
Naval Reserves
"Needs of Farmers' Wives, The" (Felton),
84–85
"Negro and Fusion Politics, 1894–1901, The"
(Edmonds), 336
"Negro Rule/Domination"
"The Negro and Fusion Politics, 1894–
1901" (Edmonds) on, 336
overview, xvi
White Supremacy Campaign inception, 65–76
New Bern, North Carolina
black exiles turned away from, 274
black resistance before election, 152–153
Bunting, Gilbert, and Melton in, 285
as Daniels' and Simmons' power base,
65–66

New Bern, North Carolina (*continued*)
    freed slaves in, 22–30
    Simmons in, 285–286
New Hanover County, North Carolina
    election (1868), 44
    election day (1898) results, 175
    Historical Commission, 336
    Moore as commissioner of, 100
    "Remember the 6" campaign and, 119–120
New National Era (Washington, D.C.), 22, 46
News and Observer (Wilmington)
    apology issued by, 343
    on Bunting, 249
    Chronicle as competition to, 71
    continued/modern-day publishing of,
        343–346
    on election results, 174
    fear stoked about rape by black men, 66–72
    financing of, 291
    on grandfather clause, 304–308
    on gun purchase attempt by black men,
        102–103
    Jennett hired by, 76
    motto of, 344
    on November 10th events, 258
    reaction to November 10th events, 266,
        270–271
    Red Shirts and, 134, 135
    on Russell's Black Battalion, 111, 112
    on Spanish-American War, 107–108
    on White, 322
newspapers (white). *See also individual names of*
        newspapers
    "nigger," newspaper debate about term, 39
    November 10, 1898 events and reaction of,
        265–271
    "White Declaration of Independence," 165
    "Wilmington Declaration of Independence"
        and, 177
New York Age, 270, 327
New York Herald, 268
New York Journal, 268
New York Times
    on banishment campaign, 249
    on black exodus from Wilmington, 273
    on Dancy, 282
    on election day events, 171–172

on government overthrow, 224
White's interview, 323
New York World, 281
North Carolina. *See also* Cape Fear; militias;
        New Bern; Wilmington, North Carolina
    attorney general of (*See* Bernard, Claude M.)
    Aycock as governor of, 72, 294, 301, 304,
        313–314, 316–317, 335
    "Black Belt" region, defined, 66
    Black Codes and, 35
    black population of, post-Civil War, 37
    "Black Second" (Second District) of, 68,
        133, 330
    constitutional convention (1868), 38–40,
        43–44
    Fayetteville, Great White Man's Rally and
        Basket Picnic in, 121–126
    grandfather clauses and, 301–308,
        312–316, 321–323, 330
    legally mandated segregation in, 311–318
    Manly, Charles (governor, 1849–1851),
        46–47
    North Hanover County, black population
        statistics, 66
    North Hanover County, rape statistics
        (1896–1898), 80
    "The Old North State" (state song), 122
    Russell as governor of (*See* Russell, Daniel)
    state historical markers, 347–348
    State Office of Archives and History, 341
North Carolina Central University, 336
North Carolina Cotton Oil Company,
        128–129
North Carolina Naval Militia. *See* Naval Reserves
North Carolina State Militia (N.C.S.M.), 42
North Carolinian, 79
Norwood, Charles, 120
Norwood, John, 223, 330
November 10, 1898, events, 189–199. *See also*
        banishment campaign; November 10,
        1898, legacy; *Record/Daily Record* (Wilm-
        ington); Red Shirts; Russell, Daniel;
        Waddell, Colonel Alfred Moore
    black exodus from Wilmington following,
        228–229
    blacks' return to Wilmington following,
        261–264

in Brooklyn, 199, 200–212
calls for investigation of, 269–270
deaths of black men during, 201–204,
    208–210, 215–219, 257–258, 342
inquest, 257–260
Naval Reserves used during, 213–215
newspapers' reactions to, 265–271
property seizure claims, 341
at *Record* building, 191–195, 233
"situation serious telegram," 205–206
at Sprunt Cotton Compress, 191–199, 200,
    211–213
"Victory, White Supremacy and Good Gov-
    ernment" jubilee following, 270–271
Waddell's incitement of, 189–191
Wilmington government overthrow and,
    220–227
November 10, 1898, legacy
centennial anniversary of, 337–340
Daniels and, 341–346
Manly and, 347–348, 349–352
Miller and, 348–349
News and Observer, in later years, 343–344
North Carolina legislature report on
    (2000), 340–342, 346
University of North Carolina monuments
    and, 346–347
white supremacy and, 329–336
November 10th events. *See* November 10,
    1898, events

Odell Hardware Company, 102
Oklahoma, grandfather clause in, 317, 330
Olmsted, Frederick Law, 37
Opera House (Wilmington), 52
"Organization of Colored Ladies," 156–157

Parmele, Edgar G., 225, 250, 263–264
Peamon, Carter, 129, 230–231
Perkins (black policeman), 219
Philadelphia, Underground Railroad in, 26
Philadelphia Inquirer, 8
Philadelphia Record, 268
Philadelphia Times, 105
Phoenix (South Carolina), racial violence in,
    288–289
Pickens, Robert B., 245, 248–249

Pine Forest Cemetery, as hiding place, 228, 240
Piner, George, 202
Piney Woods, 18–21, 116–117
Plessy, Homre, 53–54
Plessy v. Ferguson (1896), 53–54
poll tax, 302
Populist Party (People's Party). *See also*
    Fusionists
election day (November 9) results,
    174–175
overview, 67
post-November 10th influence of, 303
White Supremacy Campaign inception and,
    67, 74, 76
Posse Comitatus Act (1878), 134
Pritchard, Jeter, 312

Quarterly Review (AME Zion Church), 58

race riot of 1898. *See* November 10, 1898,
    events
"Race War at the South" (Second Baptist
    Church, Washington, DC), 160
Raleigh Gazette, 49, 50–51
Raleigh Morning Post, 93
Randolph, John, Jr., 28, 30
rapists, fears/rhetoric about. *See* sex and race
Reardon, Robert, 244
rebellion fears (by whites)
about black women servants, 104, 170
election day rumors and, 162, 164,
    169–170
gun purchase attempt by black men,
    102–106
militias and, 61–62, 98–101
Record building protected by blacks and,
    91–92, 193
rumors of, during November 10th vio-
    lence, 191, 193–194, 196–197, 199,
    201–207, 209, 214–216
Turner's rebellion and, 59–60, 105
Reconstruction
end of, 66–68
Ku Klux Klan during, 33–34
Reconstruction Acts and postwar constitu-
    tions, 38
Wilmington at end of Civil War and, 5, 13

Record/*Daily Record* (Wilmington)
  advertising by white businesses, 50
  black vote encouraged by, 153–154, 157
  burning of, 191–195, 233, 261, 267, 281, 342
  as *Daily Record*, 50
  forced move to new building, 93
  inception of, 48–51
  Manly (Carrie) on, 351
  Manly's editorial in, 83–89, 90–95
  publication ceased by, 182
  on rape accusations against blacks, 51
  state historical marker of, 348
  on voting intimidation of blacks, 128
  Washington, DC edition of, 324
Redeemers, 66
Red Shirts, 132–138
  assaults on black citizens, before election, 129–131, 134–138, 149–151, 156
  banishment campaign and, 230–234, 240–245, 246–248, 250, 252–256
  election day behavior of, 163, 164–165, 169–170, 172–173
  end of mob violence, 260
  "fighting whiskey" and liquor ban, 150, 157–158, 164, 224
  at Great White Man's Rally and Basket Picnic, 125–126
  November 10th events and, 217
  Pritchard's letter to McKinley on, 132–134
  textbooks about, 335–336
  White Supremacist Campaign inception and, 72
  "Wilmington Declaration of Independence" demands, 181, 185
  Wilmington government overthrow and, 220, 222, 226, 227
religious leaders (black)
  arrests of, 245
  banishment of, 239–242, 245, 248–249
  on election threats, 153–154, 159
  Kirk on election day voting, 163
  November 10th events and, 210, 215
  return of blacks after November 10th, 263–264
religious leaders (white)
  banishment campaign and, 247, 248

  on November 10th events, 217
  return of blacks after November 10th, 262–263
  Strange and, 165
  on "Wilmington Declaration of Independence," 182, 185
"Remember the 6" ("Big 6") campaign, 114–120, 206, 221, 230–234, 296
Republican Party
  civil rights movement and changes in, 331
  election day (November 9) results, 174–175
  fired white workers, after November 10th, 276
  Fusionists, defined, 67
  post-November 10th influence of, 303
  "Remember the 6" campaign and, 118–120
  Republican Executive Committee, 103
"Revolution of 1898." *See* November 10, 1898, events
Richmond Planet, 268–269
Richmond Times
  gun purchase attempt by black men and, 104
  reaction to November 10th events, 266
  on Red Shirt rally, 150
"Rise Ye Sons of Carolina" (White Supremacy anthem), 162
Rivera, Thomas, 180–185
Robbins, Bill, 216
Roosevelt, Franklin D., 317, 320
Rountree, George
  biography and characterization of, 340
  election to state house, 175
  grandfather clause and, 302
  gun purchase attempt by black men and, 103
  November 10th events and, 197–199, 201, 208
  overview, xii
  "Remember the 6" campaign and, 118–120
  in state legislature, 301
  Vigilance Committee of, 97–101
  Waddell and, 143, 148
  "Wilmington Declaration of Independence" and, 176, 178–180
  Wilmington government overthrow and, 222, 225, 226–227

Rountree, George, III (grandson), 338–340
Rountree, Robert, 339
Rowan, Tom, 218
Russell, Daniel
  banishment campaign and, 253
  black policemen fired by, 156
  election deal imposed on, 155
  election of August 1900, 316
  federal troops, not requested, 287–288
  on grandfather clause, 312–313
  as last Republican North Carolina governor
    until 1972, 331
  Manly's editorial and, 92–93
  militia demobilization and, 260–261
  November 10th events and, 193
  overview, xii
  presiding at White Supremacy Campaign
    meeting, 81
  reaction to November 10th events and, 269,
    271
  Red Shirts and, 133–135
  "Remember the 6" campaign and, 118–120
  Russell's Black Battalion and, 111–112
  "situation serious" telegram and, 204–206
  voting by, and death threats against,
    170–173
  Waddell and, 142, 147
  Wilmington government overthrow and,
    226
  Wilmington Light Infantry commanded by,
    172, 191
Russell, Sarah, 288
Russell's Black Battalion, 111–113

Sadgwar, Carrie, xii, 85–86, 279, 324,
  350–351
Sadgwar, Felice, 350
Sadgwar, Frederick, Jr., 85–86, 180–185, 325
Sadgwar, Mabel, 350
Sasser, L. B., 164–165
Sasser's Drug Store, 164–165
Saunders, William L., xii, 10, 71, 140–141
Savage, W. T. "Tuck," 195
Schonwald, J. T., 259
Schurz, Carl, 5–6
Scott, Armond
  banishment of, 233–234, 310

  Committee of Colored Citizens, response
    by, 180–185, 189–191, 197, 210, 235
  late life of, 319–320
  overview, xii
  Russell's Black Battalion and, 112
  in Washington, DC, 284
Scott, Benjamin, 183–184
Second Baptist Church (Washington, DC),
  160
Second Regiment Band, 135
Secret Nine. See also MacRae, Hugh; Taylor, J.
    Allan
  banishment campaign by, 230–234,
    244–245, 249–250, 254, 256 (See also
    banishment campaign)
  Colt rapid-fire guns purchased by, 105
  November 10th events and, 209
  overview, 98–99
  "revolution" (November 10) planned by,
    137–138, 164–165
  Spanish-American War and, 109
  "Wilmington Declaration of Independence"
    and, 177, 178
segregation
  North Carolina's legally mandated segrega-
    tion, 311–318
  Waddell on segregated schools, 15
sex and race. See also interracial marriage
  "black beast rapist" narratives, 69, 76, 79,
    174, 334
  fear stoked about rape by black men,
    77–82
  Felton's letter/speech about purported
    rapes, 83–89
  Galloway on hypocrisy of, 23
  interracial marriage, 35, 40, 58
  interracial sex as illegal, 311
  Manly on Felton's letter/speech, 83–89,
    90–95
  Manly on white men's assaults on black
    women, 87–88, 321–322
  rape accusations against black men, 50–51
  rape statistics in eastern North Carolina
    (1897–1898), 80
  White Supremacist Campaign inception
    and, 69
Shelby County v. Holder (2013), 332–333

"Silent Sam" (Civil War monument), 346–347

Simmons, Furnifold
biography and characterization, 72–74
cartoon of, on election day results, 175
as collector of internal revenue, 74
Dowling and, 164
on election results, 174
fear stoked about black rapists, 79–82
grandfather clause and, 301–308
initial response to Manly's editorial by, 90
in New Bern, 285–286
overview, xii
political career of, following 1900, 316–317
reaction to November 10th events and, 271–272
Red Shirts and, 133, 135
US Senate election of, 301, 316
White Government Unions (white supremacy clubs), 96–97
White Supremacy Campaign inception and, 65–66, 74–76

Skelding, Mrs. A. B., 291

slavery
artisan work of slaves, 24–25
Black Codes and, 35–36
contrabands, 27
Emancipation Proclamation and, 5, 31, 52–53, 73, 310
Russell as slave owner, 92–93
Tillman family as slaveowners, 123
Underground Railroad, 26
Wilmington at end of Civil War, 5

Smith, James D., 211–213

South Carolina, Black Codes and, 35

Spanish-American War
black soldiers serving in, 321
events of, 108
Light Infantry procession following, 107–113
militia of MacRae (Donald) in, 199
as priority over Wilmington, 286–287, 293, 300
Russell's Black Battalion and, 111–112
weapons provided to private vessels during, 199

Wilmington Light Infantry and, xxi

spies
Galloway, 26
Sykes, 17–21

Sprunt, James
attempt to recover employees from hiding, 253
as British vice consul, 109, 217
on November 10th events, 334
November 10th events and, 196, 216–217
overview, xii
"Remember the 6" campaign and, 119–120
Spanish-American War and, 109

Sprunt Cotton Compress
November 10th events at, 191–199, 200, 211–213
overview, xix
Spanish-American War and, 109

St. James Episcopal Church, 165

St. Luke's AME Church, 194, 195, 264, 340

St. Matthew's Evangelical Lutheran Church, xxi

St. Paul's Episcopal Church, 46

St. Stephen AME Church, 338

Stanly, Edward (military governor, Union-controlled areas of NC), 29

Starkey, Mary Ann, 27–28, 30

Star of Zion (AME Zion Church), 58

State Chronicle (Raleigh), 70–76

State Negro Council, 303–304

Stedman, Frank, 232–233, 309–310

Stewartsville Township, Graham's abuse in, 130–131

Story of the Wilmington Rebellion, The (Hayden), 334

Strange, Robert, 165, 247, 248

Struthers, William, 224, 226

suffrage. See voting and voter suppression

Supreme Court (US)
on grandfather clauses, 330
Plessy v. Ferguson (1896), 53–54
Shelby County v. Holder (2013), 332–333
on voter ID laws, 331–333

Sykes, Catherine, 18, 20

Sykes, Matthew, 17–21

Sykes, Unity, 20, 21

Talented Tenth, 48
taxes, paid by blacks, 54
Taylor, J. Allan
    as alderman, 261
    banishment campaign and, 230–234,
        244–245, 249–250, 251–252
    election of August 1900, 309
    on November 10th events, 334
    overview, xii, 209, 210
    Wilmington government overthrow and,
        223, 224
Taylor, John, 180, 318
Taylor, Katharine, 337
Taylor, Walker
    militia demobilized by, 260–261
    November 10th events and, 204–207,
        213–216
    overview, xii
    on Red Shirts, 246
    Spanish-American War and, 110
    Wilmington Light Infantry command by,
        90, 110, 171, 191
Telfy, J. K., 264
Terry, Alfred Howe, 4, 129
Terry, S. Hill, 129
Thalian Hall
    "People's Declaration of Racial Inter-
        dependence" (1998), 340
    Waddell's "Cape Fear carcasses" speech at,
        144–148, 160–161, 247
Third North Carolina Cavalry, 11, 33
Thirteenth Amendment, Redeemers and, 66
Tillman, George, 123
Tillman, "Pitchfork" Ben, xii, 122–126,
    351
Tocqueville, Alexis de, 59
Tolbert, Robert "Red," 289
Tolbert, Thomas, 288–289
Toomer, F. P., 274–275
trains, Jim Crow laws, 311–312
Turner, Nat, 59–60, 100, 105
turpentine
    trade of, 3, 16, 36–37, 104, 145, 200
    as weapon against stowaway slaves,
        25–26
Tyson, Timothy, 343

Underground Railroad, 26
Union army. See also United States Colored
    Troops
    county militias allowed free rein by, 8–10
    Home Guards, 9
    Wilmington at end of Civil War and, 5
United States Colored Troops. See also black
    soldiers
    First North Carolina Colored Regiment of
        Volunteers, 27–30
    Fort Fisher captured by, 3–4
    Galloway and, 27–30
    pay of, 9, 28–29
    soldier's murder, 16
University of North Carolina, 336, 337,
    346–347

"Victory, White Supremacy and Good Govern-
    ment" jubilee, 270–271
Vigilance Committee
    banishment campaign and, 247
    financing of, 98
    inception of, 97–101
    Manly's escape and, 165–166
    "Wilmington Declaration of Independence"
        and, 185
vigilantes. See Red Shirts
Virginia, grandfather clause in, 317, 330
voting and voter suppression. See also Fifteenth
    Amendment; Red Shirts; White Govern-
    ment Unions (white supremacy clubs)
    ballot stuffing by white supremacists,
        160–161
    black vote, statistics, 305, 309, 315–316,
        330–331
    election day events, 162–164
    election threats, 152–160
    Galloway on, 23, 31, 39
    gerrymandering of black wards, 160, 163,
        167–168, 333
    grandfather clause, 301–308, 312–316,
        321–323, 330
    Holden on, 13
    by KKK, 40
    threats by white supremacists, 160–161
    voter ID laws, 331–332

voting and voter suppression (*continued*)
Voting Rights Act (1965), 330, 331
Waddell on, 15
white-capping, 127–131
White Supremacist Campaign inception
and, 69

Waddell, Colonel Alfred Moore
"An Address Delivered to the Colored
People by Their Request," 13–16
banishment campaign and, 233, 247,
248–249, 253–256
biography and characterization of, 139–143
on black exiles returning to Wilmington,
274–275
blacks' return to Wilmington and, 261
"Cape Fear carcasses" speech of, 144–148,
160–161, 247
Civil War role of, 11–13, 33
Confederate Home Guards and Sykes'
death, 17–21
election of August 1900, 309–310
election to Congress, 46
Manly's accounts of November 10th events,
326–327
as mayor, 247
November 10th events, incited by,
189–191
November 10th events, reaction to,
266–267, 269, 270
November 10th events, views of, 334
overview, xii
Spanish-American War and, 109
Vigilance Committee and, 97–98
white labor and, 277–278
White Supremacist Campaign inception
and, 72
"Wilmington Declaration of Independence"
and, 176–185
Wilmington government overthrow and,
223–224, 225–227
Waddell, Ellen Savage (second wife), 139
Waddell, Gabrielle DeRosset (third wife),
139–140
Waddell, Hugh (great-grandfather), 12
Waddell, Julia Savage (first wife), 139
Walker, W. A., xx–xxi, 201

Washington, Booker T., 58
Washington Bee, 110–111, 269
Washington Evening Star
on election day events, 163–164
on federal troops speculation, 287
on November 10th events, 207
reaction to November 10th events, 268
Washington Post
gun purchase attempt by black men and,
104
reaction to November 10th events, 268
Red Shirts and, 133, 158–159
on "Wilmington Declaration of Independence," 179
Watts, Alston, 323
weapons
black mens' attempted purchase of,
102–106
gun sales by Jacobi, 127–128
KKK ownership of guns, 42
Moore's drugstore and, 201–202, 206
of Naval Reserve, 213–214
for private vessels, during Spanish-American
War, 199
shortage of, 104
Spanish-American War and, 110
Weldon, Frank, 169
West, H. L. (Henry Litchfield), 148, 179,
181
White, Charles H., 106, 159–160
White, Cora Lena (wife), 322, 323
White, Della (daughter), 322
White, George Henry
grandfather clause and, 321–323
as last black congressman from North
Carolina until 1972, 330
as North Carolina congressman, 68, 293,
303, 311
overview, xii, 133
White Brotherhood, 32–33. *See also* Ku Klux
Klan
white-capping, 127–131
"White Declaration of Independence," 165
White Government Unions (white supremacy
clubs)
ballot stuffing and violence threatened by,
160–161, 167–168

black voting suppressed by, 96–97
Great White Man's Rally and Basket Picnic, 121–126
Spanish-American War and, 109–110
White Labor Bureau, 277
White Laborer's Union, 277–278
White Man's Convention, 135
White Supremacy Campaign
  fear stoked about rape by black men, 77–82
  financing of, 80–81
  Great White Man's Rally and Basket Picnic, 121–126
  inception, 65–76
  lasting impact of, 329–336
  naming of, 74–75
  "nigger," newspaper debate about term, 39
  rape accusations against blacks, 50–51
  revolution plans of, 137–138, 164–165, 183
  "Rise Ye Sons of Carolina" (anthem), 162
  Vigilance Committee, 97–101
  White Government Unions, 96–97
  Wilmington unrest at end of Civil War, 3–10
Williamston, militia in, 152
Wilmington, North Carolina. *See also* election
    day events (November 8, 1898); Manly,
    Alexander; November 10, 1898, events;
    November 10, 1898, legacy; Waddell,
    Colonel Alfred Moore; Wilmington
    Light Infantry; Wilmington police
    department
  black population statistics, 66, 68, 330–331
  Brooklyn neighborhood of, xviii–xxii, 195, 199
  Chamber of Commerce on white-labor campaign, 277
  1898 Memorial Park, 342
  election (1868), 41–44
  Galloway's move to, 32
  government overthrow, 220–227
  infrastructure (1898) of, 49, 54–55
  jobs in, post-Civil War, 36–38
  Melton and, 114, 115–116
  riot (November 10, 1898), xv–xxii

telegraph used in, 206–207
voting population statistics (1868), 40, 49
Wilmington Light Infantry, 90
Wilmington Cotton Mills Co., 98
Wilmington Daily Herald, 35–36
Wilmington Daily Journal, 35–36, 39
"Wilmington Declaration of Independence," 175–185
  Committee of Colored Citizens' response, 180–185, 189–191, 197, 210, 235
  "White Men of Wilmington" meeting (November 9, 1898), 175–180
Wilmington Gaslight Company, 107
Wilmington Herald, 4–5, 15
"Wilmington in Black and White" (lecture), 338
Wilmington Journal
  on election (1868), 42
  on French, 117
  history of, 337–338
  on interracial marriage, 40
  KKK on emerging alliance of whites, 10
Wilmington Light Infantry
  banishment campaign and, 238, 243–245, 246–247, 251, 253, 254, 255
  Brooklyn violence and, 202, 205–211, 214–215, 217–218
  demobilization of, 260–261
  mission of, 191
  post-election riots, 190–191, 198–199
  riot and, xxi–xxii
  Russell as commander of, 172, 191
  "situation serious" telegram and, 204–206
  Spanish-American War and, 107–108, 110–113
  Strange and, 165
  Taylor and, 171
  weapons and election violence expectations of, 161
  weapons of, xxii, 105
Wilmington Messenger. See Messenger (Wilmington)
Wilmington police department. *See also* Melton, John
  black employees fired by, 156
  overview, 91
  Perkins (black police officer) killed during November 10th events, 219

Wilmington police department (*continued*)
   police recruited for election day, 157–158,
     167
   preparedness of, for election, 158
   Wilmington government overthrow and,
     220–227
Wilmington Post
   on Galloway, 32
   Waddell and, 141–142
"Wilmington Rebellion." *See* November 10,
    1898, events
Wilmington Star. See also Morning Star (Wilmington)
   on election (1868), 43
   fear stoked about rape by black men, 79–80
   location of, 48
   on Manly's editorial, 93, 129
Wilmington Street Railway Company, 108
Wilmingtonton District Conference and Sunday
    School Convention of Methodists, 94
Wilson, Woodrow, 317
Winchester Repeating Arms Company,
    102–106
Worth, James S., 150, 278
Wright, Daniel, 209–210

Wright, Silas P.
   on alcohol restrictions before election,
    157–158
   banishment of, 254–256
   black policemen fired by, 156
   federal investigation and, 295–296
   Harriss and, 168
   Manly's editorial and, 92
   November 10th events and, 198, 216–217
   overview, xii
   police recruited for election day by,
    157–158, 167
   Red Shirts rally and, 149
   "Remember the 6" campaign against, 114,
    115
   resignation demanded of, 197
   "Wilmington Declaration of Independence"
    and resignation demanded of, 178–185
   Wilmington government overthrow and,
    220–224, 225–226

Young, James H., 111, 113, 133

Zachary, R. E., 203